The War on Error

The War on Error

Israel, Islam, and the Middle East

Martin Kramer

Transaction Publishers
New Brunswick (U.S.A.) and London (U.K.)

Library of Congress Catalog Number: 2016027265
ISBN: 978-1-4128-6433-6 (hardcover); 978-1-4128-6499-2 (paperback)
eBook: 978-1-4128-6448-0
Printed in the United States of America

Library of Congress Cataloging-in-Publication Data

Names: Kramer, Martin S., author.
Title: The war on error : Israel, Islam, and the Middle East / Martin Kramer.
Description: New Brunswick (U.S.A.) and London (U.K.) : Transaction Publishers, [2017] | Includes index.
Identifiers: LCCN 2016027265 (print) | LCCN 2016028138 (ebook) | ISBN 9781412864336 (hardcover) | ISBN 9781412864992 (pbk.) | ISBN 9781412864480 ()
Subjects: LCSH: Islam and politics. | Islam and politics--Islamic countries. | Middle East--History. | Arab-Israeli conflict--Influence.
Classification: LCC BP173.7 .K74 2017 (print) | LCC BP173.7 (ebook) | DDC 956.04--dc23
LC record available at https://lccn.loc.gov/2016027265

To Eden, Noy, Gefen, and Itamar,
lights of my life.

'Tis Ambition enough to be employed as an Under-Labourer in clearing Ground a little, and removing some of the Rubbish, that lies in the way to Knowledge.

—John Locke, *An Essay Concerning Human Understanding* (1689)

Contents

Acknowledgments

This book collects twenty-five of my articles, reviews, and lectures, framed by an introduction and epilogue. Some of the pieces are published here for the first time; all have been revised, some extensively. Many appeared originally at my weblog, *Sandbox,* now at www.martinkramer.org.

Chapter 1 was published in *Commentary* in 2007. Chapter 2 is a lecture I delivered to the graduate proseminar "Approaches to Middle Eastern Studies" at Harvard in 2007; this is its first publication. Chapter 3 originally appeared in *Asian and African Studies* in 1990; a new conclusion has been added to it. *Middle East Quarterly* published chapters 4 and 5 in 2003. Chapter 6 is a revision of a 2006 post to *Sandbox.* Chapter 7 appeared in *Middle East Quarterly* in 2002. Chapters 8, 9, and 10 originated as posts to *Sandbox* in 2010, 2013, and 2006, respectively. Chapter 11 was delivered as a speech to the Herzliya Conference in 2007, and appeared at *Sandbox.* Chapters 12, 14, and 16 all originated in speeches delivered (respectively) in 2007, 2004, and 2013; all three appeared at *Sandbox.* Chapter 13 appeared on the *Commentary* website in 2014. Chapter 15 is a lecture delivered in 2015, published here for the first time. Chapter 17 was posted at the blog of *The Weekly Standard* in 2013. *Mosaic Magazine,* an internet publication, ran chapters 18 and 20 in 2014 and 2015. Chapter 19 appeared at the *Commentary* blog in 2015. Chapter 21 was posted at *Sandbox* in 2011. Chapters 22 and 23 amalgamate a number of *Sandbox* posts from 2006, 2007, 2012, and 2013, and incorporate additions. *Mosaic Magazine* published chapter 24 in 2015. I delivered chapter 25 as a lecture for the Institute for the Study of Global Antisemitism in 2014; this is its first publication. I am grateful for permissions to reproduce previously published articles.

During the years when I wrote or revised these pieces, I had two primary affiliations. One was The Washington Institute for Near East Policy, where I served for over a decade as the Wexler-Fromer Fellow (named after four dear friends, Nina and Gary Wexler and Ann and

Robert Fromer). The director, Robert Satloff, offered me a home away from home, and indulged me when I strayed far from the policy preserve. The other was the Shalem Center, now Shalem College, where I began as a research associate, and where I am now president. This book would not have been possible without the friendship and patience of Daniel Polisar, founder and provost of Shalem College, who assumed countless administrative burdens that should have fallen on me. During this same time, I also benefited from three-year affiliations with the Middle East Forum, where I served as editor of *Middle East Quarterly* in partnership with Daniel Pipes; and the John M. Olin Institute for Strategic Studies at Harvard, where I founded and edited *Middle East Strategy at Harvard*, in partnership with Stephen Rosen. There could be no finer colleagues.

Three of the pieces here, including the longest, passed through the expert editorial hands of *Mosaic Magazine*'s Neal Kozodoy, who turns everything he touches into gold.

I am continually nurtured by the love of my parents, Al and Anita Kramer, and my wife, Sandy, who took my many absences in stride, and gave me moral encouragement whenever I got into scrapes. Finally, I am thankful for the confidence of Mary Curtis, Transaction's president and publisher, who sent me a contract less than twenty-four hours after receiving a one-paragraph proposal. It doesn't get better (or faster) than that.

Introduction

In these first decades of the twenty-first century, the Middle East has become the preoccupation of the world, and the most contested and conflicted region on the planet. It has replaced Europe as the prime arena for wars, insurgencies, revolutions, mass murder, and refugee flows. Much of the Middle East has failed or hovers on the brink of failure. In the world's capitals, the pressing question is this: can the Middle East be saved? Or, if it can't, can its noxious tide be stemmed?

Answering these questions is all the more difficult, because the Middle East is misunderstood. Despite the region's proximity to Europe and its history of continuous interaction with the West, it eludes the grasp of foreign publics, analysts, and policymakers. In the United States, half a globe away from the Middle East, the errors are endemic. This is a theme I developed in a 2001 book, *Ivory Towers on Sand: The Failure of Middle Eastern Studies in America*.[1] There I demonstrated how the academic field devoted to the study of the Middle East was itself the source of repeated errors of understanding.

This book is a kind of sequel to that one, and an expansion of its scope. It is a sequel in that the twenty-five chapters here were written or extensively revised post-9/11. The parade of error has continued straight through the terrorist attacks on New York and Washington, the wars in Afghanistan and Iraq, and the "Arab Spring" and the Islamic State (ISIS). It is an expansion of scope, in that the arena of investigation is not limited to academe but includes government, journalism, filmmaking, and punditry. In this book, I also deepen the perspective, to incorporate not only errors in the interpretation of the present, but serious flaws in the representation of the historical record. This is because misinterpretations of the past often have deleterious effects in the here-and-now, and present concerns can twist perceptions of the past.

What do I mean by error? For my purposes, an error is an unintentional lapse that leaves a gap between reality and its representation.

Such lapses may result from incomplete information. Parts of the Middle East long have been ruled by regimes that limit the free flow of information. When the evidence is thin, errors sometimes arise from the temptation to fill in a partial picture with theories and analogies. This is encouraged by the fact that the political and social categories of the Middle East may seem deceptively similar to those of the West. "Religion," "revolution," "political party," "democracy," "elections"—their use in the Middle East imparts a sense of familiarity, but they often mean something very different.

Then there is the bias that arises from wishful thinking. For those who see the Middle East as a series of "problems" to be "solved," the impulse to overlook contrary and discouraging evidence can be overwhelming. The conflicts of the Middle East may also provoke an eagerness to blame or exculpate one side or another, to the detriment of the truth. And those who set out to correct past errors occasionally overshoot their mark. In their zeal, they may end up substituting new myths for old.

The misinterpretations of the Middle East that arises from these causes may be described as "errors." No one is immune from them, because no one has complete information, and no one is entirely free of bias. Here the objective must be the accumulation of more information and correcting for bias. When people are collectively committed to the pursuit of truth, and agree on the rules for establishing it, knowledge advances through the discovery and presentation of evidence and logic-based debate over its interpretation.

But there are also deliberate misrepresentations, whose purveyors know perfectly well that the "facts" and "knowledge" they retail are either false or ripped out of context. The United States remains a formidable power in the Middle East; formal and informal lobbies work tirelessly to persuade it to act in one way or another. The truth is often deliberately distorted in such campaigns, which prey on the widespread ignorance of the Middle East that pervades both the wider public and those who make opinion and policies. These are not "errors" at all by the definition employed here, or they may be categorized as intentional errors. Not only do they beg to be corrected; their genesis must be traced, to determine the extent to which they are part of an intentional campaign of disinformation.

Do "errors" include predictions about the future that have missed the mark? It is difficult if not impossible to predict specific events, such as the 9/11 attacks or the toppling of a regime by a revolution. Not only do Western intelligence agencies regularly fail to make precise predictions on such a level. Middle Eastern regimes also fail to anticipate specific challenges, as the so-called Arab Spring amply demonstrated.

Predicted outcomes are little more than educated guesses, and given that scenarios always outnumber realities, most of them will turn out wrong in some respect, large or small. The nineteenth-century conservative statesman Lord Salisbury went so far as to assert that he bore no responsibility for the results of his decisions. In making an assessment "upon which peace or war may depend," he made his best judgment based "upon the materials for decision that are available." But since he could never possess full knowledge of the circumstances, or accurately account for the role of chance, "with the results I have nothing to do."[2]

Such an attitude is very much at odds with our own notion of "accountability," in which actions are judged not only by the (intended) process that produced them, but by their (unintended) consequences. Still, it should militate against viewing failed predictions as "errors," and I have tried to avoid doing so in these chapters. That said, the line between the present and the future is thin, and failed predictions may be symptoms of errors made in assessing the present or even the historical past. Responsibility for these is much more difficult to shed, for what we already know grows exponentially in scope as we go back in time. In this respect, the distortion of history is more grievous than a failed prediction, even though the consequences of the latter may be more far-reaching. (Here my perspective as a historian comes through clearly; a decision-maker may think otherwise.)

I do not pretend that I have reworked the chapters assembled here into a coherent narrative. But I have been highly selective in the cases I have included, to assure that they adhere to each other, at least within the five baskets in which they are organized.

Middle Eastern Studies

One inexhaustible source of error in understanding the Middle East is the academic field devoted to its study. Middle Eastern studies emerged in the mid-twentieth century from a longer European tradition known as Orientalism. Since the Enlightenment, scholars in Europe had worked to overcome medieval prejudice in order to take the true measure of Islam and the societies that professed it. Huge advances were made in retrieving and translating difficult texts, and in constructing an accurate account of the histories and cultures of Muslim peoples. Like all scientific knowledge, Orientalism was subject to constant revision in the light of empirical evidence, and it made dramatic progress over time.

Yes, England and France exploited and encouraged such study to facilitate their imperial expansion in the East. But this did not alter the fact that Orientalism was driven by an insatiable scientific curiosity, nor did it invalidate the accumulated knowledge of Orientalist scholarship. Orientalism constituted a prime example of Europe's capacity for exploring the entire span of humankind, in a spirit of empathy unprecedented in the history of civilization.

So it was viewed until the Palestinian-American critic Edward Said criminalized Orientalism and its American offshoot, Middle Eastern studies. Bestirred by a political grievance, Said published a book in 1978 casting Orientalism as a species of racism directed against Muslims in general, and Arabs and Palestinians in particular.[3] The indictment rode the surf of the fashionable postcolonialism that swamped the humanities and social sciences; by the century's end Said's notions constituted standard orthodoxy in Western academe. Under his influence, many practitioners of Middle Eastern studies abandoned the study of the Middle East, gravitating instead to identity politics and advocacy.

Four essays in this book amplify some of the themes I identified in *Ivory Towers on Sand,* my earlier critique of the field. In "Dangerous Orientalists" (chapter 1), a review of a landmark history of Orientalism, I revisit the Orientalism debate from a post-9/11 perspective, and ask whether the Saidian tide has been turned. In "The Shifting Sands of Academe" (chapter 2), I look back upon the actual writing of *Ivory Towers on Sand,* recall my intentions, identify what I see as the book's merits and shortcomings, and assess its reception. This lecture, originally offered to students at Harvard, ends upon a cautiously optimistic note, admittedly grounded more upon hope than any concrete evidence of change.

"Surveying the Middle East" (chapter 3) considers an overlooked sub-genre of scholarship, the contemporary survey of events, which enjoyed its heyday from the beginning of the twentieth century to its close. The contemporary survey exemplified the spirit of objective inquiry that informed Orientalism and pre-Saidian Middle Eastern studies at their best. I participated in such a project over many years (the *Middle East Contemporary Survey*), and came to appreciate both its virtues and limitations. Among the former, a belief in the value of bias-free scholarship stands out, even though the attempt to practice it usually left something to be desired.

In "Policy and the Academy" (chapter 4), I probe what happens when scholars devolve into political activists, and ask how the dilemma was addressed in the thought and career of a true iconoclast, the late Middle East scholar Elie Kedourie. While Kedourie took a firm and principled stand against the bleeding of activism into scholarship, he did not think scholars ceased being citizens, and he proposed an equally principled way to act politically without abusing the scholar's privilege. Alas, this kind of thoughtful distinction between scholarship and politics has died a thousand deaths in the academy, and Kedourie himself is too infrequently remembered for upholding it.

Middle Eastern studies have yet to recover from the blows delivered by Edward Said and the political activists who used his manifesto as a license to subvert the field. This is probably why the field is no longer identified with a genius of the caliber of the historian Bernard Lewis (Said's prime target). True genius flees from politicized fields that impose straightjackets and blinders. Still, there are some solid scholars in the field who could restore some of the prestige of Middle Eastern studies, if they would openly recognize the Saidian detour as an error and acknowledge what Orientalism (on its good days) got right. How that might happen, and when, are anybody's guess.

The Islamist Conundrum

Islam differs fundamentally from Christianity in the seamless amalgamation of religion and politics favored by its adherents. This gives rise to repeated misjudgments of the motives of Islamic political movements, which are erroneously translated into secular categories of Western political thought. These movements may not be inspired exclusively by religious conviction, but to write Islam out of their genesis and evolution is negligent malpractice.

It was Bernard Lewis who, in 1976, explained the West's inability to factor Islam into its understanding of the Middle East. The West had pushed religion out of its own public sphere, and so couldn't grasp the universality and centrality of Islam in the lives of Muslims. Lewis pointed to

> the present inability, political, journalistic, and scholarly alike, to recognize the importance of the factor of religion in the current affairs of the Muslim world and the consequent recourse to the language of left-wing and right-wing, progressive and conservative, and the rest of the Western terminology, the use of which in explaining Muslim political phenomena is about as accurate and as enlightening as an account of a cricket match by a baseball correspondent.[4]

Lewis also anticipated that Islam would become even more relevant to contemporary affairs. "The Return of Islam," the title of the 1976 article, preceded the Iranian revolution and the rise of all of today's familiar Islamic movements with the exception of the Muslim Brotherhood, which was then dormant. There he made this provocative claim:

> Islam is still the most effective form of consensus in Muslim countries, the basic group identity among the masses. This will be increasingly effective as the regimes become more genuinely popular. One can already see the contrast between the present regimes and those of the small, alienated, Western-educated elite which governed until a few decades ago. As regimes come closer to the populace, even if their verbiage is left-wing and ideological, they become more Islamic.[5]

Lewis was pilloried for having reached and retailed this conclusion. Said accused him of believing that "any political, historical, and scholarly account of Muslims must begin and end with the fact that Muslims are Muslims"—an absurd reading of Lewis's argument.[6] In retrospect, of course, Lewis has been vindicated by forty years of history, including Khomeini's revolution, the emergence of Hezbollah, Hamas and Al Qaeda, the 9/11 attacks, the triumph of political Islam in Turkey, the Muslim Brotherhood's surge after the "Arab Spring," the Islamic State, and the wave of Sunni-Shi'ite sectarianism. Islamism has diverted the trajectory of the Middle East, plunging it into an endemic civil war.

The chapter entitled "Fundamentalists or Islamists?" (chapter 5) explores the difficulty Western analysts have had in coming up with an agreed name to denote the renewed salience of Islam in politics. Each option has represented an alternative interpretation over whether Islam (the "religion") is or isn't contiguous with Islamism (the "political" movement). And in "'Islamic Fascism'" (chapter 6), a kind of footnote to the terminological debate, I look at one of the most controversial terms of all, and suggest that while it might mislead, it might also enlighten. Certainly some very distinguished minds thought it could.

"Islam for Viewers Like You" (chapter 7) considers the accuracy of *Islam: Empire of Faith,* a widely viewed documentary on Islamic history produced for PBS, America's public broadcasting corporation. The film systematically whitewashed the past to serve present purposes—a prime example of how current debates about the Middle East foster errors of historical interpretation. The U.S. government did something similar, by turning a nineteenth-century Iranian Muslim agitator into a symbol of Afghan unity, a lapse documented in "Afghani and America" (chapter 8).

"He Might Have Been Pope" (chapter 9) focuses precisely on the chasm that separates Islam and Christianity on the distinction between religion and politics. In 1976, one of the Vatican's most prominent and promising cardinals effectively placed a bet that he could persuade Libya's mercurial leader, Mu'ammar Qadhafi, to accept the distinction. The cardinal lost not only that bet, but his shot at the papacy; the chapter reconstructs what went wrong. "Hamas of the Intellectuals" (chapter 10) shows how secular Palestinian academics and writers placed a similar bet on Hamas—that its nationalist fervor would trump its Islamist loyalties. This was a point on which Edward Said had some clarity of thought: he distrusted Hamas (and the Palestinian Islamic Jihad). But many of his acolytes swooned to the Islamists once they took the lead in the "resistance" to Israel. The secularists lost their bet in Gaza, and they would have lost it in the West Bank, had Israel removed its finger from the scale.

"Know Thy Enemy" (chapter 11) is a short lecture that won an enthusiastic response when I first delivered it. I assumed the identity of an Islamist extremist, and asked a simple question of my Western audience: why do you refuse to acknowledge that I have a vision, and presume I am only a bundle of grievances? By this rhetorical device, I tried to cut to the very heart of the fundamental error in the Western estimate of Islamism. It is not some wayward expression of prosaic grievances, such as unemployment or political exclusion, although it may feed on them. It is a comprehensive view of world history, how it went wrong, and how it must be corrected. Any other interpretation is erroneous, condescending, and quite possibly dangerous.

Angry Arabs

It has been a long-standing Western desire to bring peace and democracy to the Arab world. It is a noble aspiration, and an outcome in which the West has a clear interest. But it is also the source of still more errors of interpretation, for it often discounts evidence of the obstacles that stand in the way of the desired objective.

As for peace, there are partial results, most notably the peace treaties between Israel and two of its Arab neighbors, Egypt and Jordan. It is often assumed that the key to widening the peace is reversing the consequences of the 1967 war, during which Israel came into possession of two territories it still holds, the West Bank and the Golan Heights. In

"1967 and Memory" (chapter 12) I caution that it is the Arab memory of the 1967 defeat—the pain of the humiliation and the stripping bare of the false pretenses of Arab nationalism—that underpins the existing peace. The key to preserving and expanding peace is not to make Arab publics forget 1967. It is to remind them of it constantly.

The most misunderstood of Arabs was Egyptian president Anwar Sadat. Israel and the United States dismissed him before the 1973 war. The Arab world underestimated him after it. He mastered the art of strategic surprise, and erected the most durable pillar of the status quo in the Middle East, the peace between Egypt and Israel. In "Sadat and Begin: The Peacemakers" (chapter 13), I question the conventional narrative that casts Sadat and Menachem Begin as two irreconcilable spirits, brought together only by the dogged determination of Jimmy Carter at Camp David. In fact, the career paths of both men bore striking similarities, as did their ideas about nation and territory. Perhaps no two leaders were more suited to making peace with one another.

While there has been progress toward peace, democracy remains as elusive as ever. True, the long-running dictatorships personified by Saddam Hussein and Qadhafi are mostly gone or fractured, blown away by war or revolution. But they have been replaced in many settings by militias waging turf battles and sectarian wars. One of the most consequential errors was the failure to recognize the narrow base of support in the Arab world for democracy. This began under the Bush administration, which thought Iraq could be democratized by force; and it continued under the Obama administration, which pressed for regime change in Libya, Egypt, and Syria. American neoconservatives and liberals united in demanding an end to authoritarian regimes, anticipating that budding democrats would rise to the occasion. Instead, Islamists of all sorts, nearly all of them hateful of America, rushed to fill the vacuum.

In three essays, I explore what went wrong. "When Minorities Rule" (chapter 14) explains perhaps the principal cause of Arab resistance to democracy: it threatens to deprive ruling minorities not only of power, but of their secure existence. And those who demand it are not themselves democrats, but simply seek to use elections to empower and enrich their sect, clan, tribe, or clique, all of which command far more loyalty than the state.

One claim is that the existing states cannot command the loyalty of citizens because of their flawed borders. This, it is asserted, is the fault of the West, particularly Sir Mark Sykes and Monsieur François

Georges-Picot, the British and French officials who authored the 1916 accord remembered to history as the Sykes-Picot agreement. They secretly drew up a map dividing the Arab provinces of the Ottoman Empire between Britain and France; Sykes and Picot, so the narrative goes, "carved up" Arab lands on arbitrary lines.

In "Syria and the Fertile Crescent" (chapter 15), I recall that another concept was born in 1916 alongside the Sykes-Picot accord: the Fertile Crescent, described as a zone of "age-long struggle" by the man who coined it, the American Egyptologist James Henry Breasted. That struggle, suspended under long Ottoman and colonial rule, is not the fault of the West, but represents a reversion to norm. "Arab Spring, Arab Crisis" (chapter 16) posits that the chaos also springs from a deeper failure of the hybrid civilization that the Arabs embraced at the start of the twentieth century. This is not a simple problem of borders, but of a mindset that has led the Arabs to fail the test of modernity.

One thing is certain: in the midst of this turmoil, the description of the Israeli-Palestinian conflict as "the Middle East conflict" is badly out of date. In a few corners, there are still believers in "linkage," the notion that an independent Palestine is just the balm needed to sooth the Arabs and put them back on track. Some claim to know this because Arab leaders have told them so. In "Listening to Arabs" (chapter 17), I offer a case study of one man, former U.S. senator and defense secretary Chuck Hagel, who claimed just that. Using diplomatic dispatches published by WikiLeaks, I demonstrate that he didn't listen carefully to his Arab interlocutors, who told him something very different.

Twisting Israel's History

In the 1980s, a group of self-described Israeli "new historians" set out to revise the then-dominant narrative of Israel's creation. They uncovered new material and drew new conclusions, undermining the heroic saga that had passed for history. The picture of 1948 that emerged was more nuanced and complex, but the effort overshot the mark, and created an insatiable market for new "revelations." When demand exceeds supply in history, it invites exaggeration and even fabrication.

Israel's history is not my primary field of research, but when I read Ari Shavit's 2013 bestseller *My Promised Land: The Triumph and Tragedy of Israel,* I sensed that something was amiss.[7] Shavit, in a chapter devoted to the Israeli conquest of the Palestinian Arab city of Lydda in July 1948, claimed it was the site of an Israeli massacre of Arab civilians—the largest of the 1948 war. This seemed to me highly improbable. "What

Happened in Lydda" (chapter 18) is my own meticulous reconstruction of an alternative scenario, based on the exact same range of oral testimony used by Shavit. His account of the massacre, I conclude, is indeed exaggerated, and in parts fabricated.

Shavit did not respond to my criticism. But Benny Morris, the foremost "new historian" who likewise maintains there was a massacre, did. My original piece and a two-round exchange between Morris and me are included in this book; I am grateful to Morris for permission to include his side of the debate. "Shabtai Teveth and the Whole Truth" (chapter 19), immediately following this exchange, is my personal tribute to Ben-Gurion's foremost biographer. Teveth, largely unknown to younger readers, may have been the first to challenge the excesses of the "new historians" (including Morris), and his work deserves to be rediscovered.

The next front of the "new history" is bound to be the 1967 Arab-Israeli "Six-Day" war, given the fact that it left Israel in occupation of the West Bank. Whatever one's view of today's political status quo, it originated in decisions made after the war, not during the war itself. But the temptation to distort the war's history, driven by present motives, proved irresistible to the young Israeli filmmaker who produced the 2015 documentary *Censored Voices*. The film drew upon audiotaped confessions by Israeli soldiers who claimed to have seen or committed war crimes. The film alleged that 70 percent of the materials in the tapes had been censored by the Israeli military. "Who Censored the Six-Day War?" (chapter 20) establishes that the tapes were never censored by the state, and argues that the film falls far short of minimal standards for vetting oral testimony.

All-Powerful Jews

One would think that world Jewry, and particularly American Jewish support for Israel, would be better understood than the intricacies, say, of Islamism. But fantasies of Jewish power and control continue to infect not only fringe antisemites but mainstream academics. This has resulted in grievous errors, often magnified by shoddy research, that effectively turn pro-Israel Jews into the puppet-masters of American politics and culture.

"The *Exodus* Conspiracy" (chapter 21) revolves around the claim, made by Palestinian-American historian Rashid Khalidi, that the famous 1958 novel *Exodus* by Leon Uris was set in motion by a scheming New York advertising man, and not by Uris himself. Through the testimony of people who were there, I show that this is untrue. Khalidi simply copied an error made by others, and then concocted an elaborate version of it. The purpose of this "error" was to allege the crucial role of a manipulative lobby, even in a work of creative art.

A similar spirit infused the effort to discredit a quote by Martin Luther King: "When people criticize Zionists, they mean Jews. You're talking anti-Semitism!" King was supposed to have said this at a dinner party in Cambridge, Massachusetts, shortly before his death. Palestinian-American critics claimed he couldn't have said it because he couldn't be placed in Cambridge at the time. They thus insinuated that the quote must have been invented—by no less a scholar than Harvard's Seymour Martin Lipset, who reported it. "In the Words of Martin Luther King" (chapter 22) relies on King's papers to establish a firm address, host, date, and time for the dinner. But while this evidence may gratify supporters of Israel, I also bring evidence (from FBI wiretaps) of King's profound ambivalence about Israel's 1967 victory. King supported Israel's right to exist, but he thought Israel would have to disgorge its military conquests—a position obscured by layers of pro-Israel polemic, and an Arab assumption that King sacrificed principle to appease his Jewish supporters.

In 2006, two professors of international relations, John Mearsheimer and Stephen Walt, advanced a full-blown thesis that the "Israel Lobby" had hijacked U.S. foreign policy. In particular, they insisted that this lobby had dragged the United States into war against Iraq, against America's own interests. In "Israel and the Iraq War" (chapter 23), I lay out the overwhelming evidence that contradicts this claim. In fact, Israel would have preferred that the United States focus on Iran and its nuclear project; it jumped on the Iraq war bandwagon only when it was given to believe that America would turn on Iran next. In the end, there was no Iran follow-up, so that the Iraq war, far from proving Israel's choke-hold over U.S. foreign policy, demonstrated the limits of Israel's influence. In short, Mearsheimer and Walt got it exactly wrong.

One believer in the Iraq war was the late Lebanese-born American scholar Fouad Ajami. Much maligned for his truth-telling about Arab political culture, Ajami became the *bête noire* of the Middle East studies establishment, and of Edward Said in particular. Some went so far as to call him "pro-Israel," even a "Likudnik." I knew Ajami from my student days, and often assisted him on his visits to Israel. "Fouad Ajami Goes to Israel" (chapter 24) sets the record straight on Israel in Ajami's worldview. Above all, he desired to see the Arabs exit the cul-de-sac to which their illusions had driven them. He believed that the refusal of the Arabs to acknowledge and learn from Israel had crippled them, and decided he wouldn't let it cripple him. Ajami thought he had a duty to tell Arabs the truth about Israel; they did not wish to hear it, so they cast him as a tool of the Jews. This wasn't an error; it was a lie.

Perhaps the most outlandish claim regarding world Jewish power nestles in the assertion that Israel acts as Nazi Germany did—what is known as "Holocaust inversion." For if a Nazi-like Israel can continue to enjoy a "special relationship" with the United States, this must be due to a massive cover-up, based upon a huge campaign of disinformation and abetted by secret influence. "'Gaza Is Auschwitz'" (chapter 25) delves into the history and deeper motives of Holocaust inversion. The bottom line: it isn't an error, it is a deliberate lie, not even believed by its purveyors. Its purpose is to shift the center of debate over Israel, and to intimidate Jews.

A War?

I have already discussed my definition of "error," a word used in the title of this book. What about that other word, "war"? Needless to say, the following chapters are not part of a military campaign. My usage alludes instead to those open-ended, never-ending struggles such as the "war on poverty," the "war on terror," the "war on drugs," the "culture wars." It is a metaphor, but its purpose is not simply to provoke. The Middle East today is a place of real wars, and some of them feed and grow upon errors in the West's understanding of the region. If errors can fuel real wars, then surely the struggle to correct them warrants the metaphor of war, if only to assure that it is taken seriously.

Of course, there is no end to error. Statesmen, officials, journalists, academics—all of them will continue to commit errors in assessing the past, present, and future of the Middle East. And there will certainly be no end to deception either. Is there nothing to be done? I offer some observations on this question in the epilogue. But before you go there, I invite you to sample these dispatches from the front lines of the "war on error," in any order you choose.

Notes

1. Martin Kramer, *Ivory Towers on Sand: The Failure of Middle Eastern Studies in America* (Washington, DC: The Washington Institute for Near East Policy, 2001).
2. Quoted by Robin Harris, *The Conservatives: A History* (London: Bantam, 2011), 209.

3. Edward Said, *Orientalism* (New York: Pantheon, 1978).
4. Bernard Lewis, "The Return of Islam," *Commentary* (January 1976), 40.
5. Ibid., 48.
6. Said, *Orientalism*, 318.
7. Ari Shavit, *My Promised Land: The Triumph and Tragedy of Israel* (New York: Random House, 2013).

Part I

The Middle East (Studies) Conflict

1

Dangerous Orientalists

The British historian Robert Irwin is the sort of scholar who, in times past, would have been proud to call himself an Orientalist.

The traditional Orientalist was someone who mastered difficult languages like Arabic and Persian and then spent years bent over manuscripts in heroic efforts of decipherment and interpretation. In *Dangerous Knowledge*, Irwin relates that the nineteenth-century English Arabist Edward William Lane, compiler of the great *Arabic-English Lexicon*, "used to complain that he had become so used to the cursive calligraphy of his Arabic manuscripts that he found Western print a great strain on his eyes."[1] Orientalism in its heyday was a branch of knowledge as demanding and rigorous as its near cousin, Egyptology. The first International Congress of Orientalists met in 1873; its name was not changed until a full century later.

But there are no self-declared Orientalists today. The reason is that the late Edward Said turned the word into a pejorative. In his 1978 book *Orientalism*, the Palestinian-born Said, a professor of comparative literature at Columbia University, claimed that an endemic Western prejudice against the East had congealed into a modern ideology of racist supremacy—a kind of antisemitism directed against Arabs and Muslims. Throughout Europe's history, announced Said, "every European, in what he could say about the Orient, was a racist, an imperialist, and almost totally ethnocentric."[2]

In a semantic sleight of hand, Said appropriated the term "Orientalism" as a label for the ideological prejudice he described, thereby neatly implicating the scholars who called themselves Orientalists. At best, charged Said, the work of these scholars was biased so as to confirm the inferiority of Islam. At worst, Orientalists had directly served European empires, showing proconsuls how best to conquer and control Muslims. To substantiate his indictment, Said cherry-picked evidence, ignored whatever contradicted his thesis, and filled the gaps with conspiracy theories.

Said's *Orientalism*, Irwin writes, "seems to me to be a work of malignant charlatanry in which it is hard to distinguish honest mistakes from willful misrepresentations." *Dangerous Knowledge* is its refutation. An Arabist by training, Irwin artfully weaves together brief profiles of great Orientalist scholars, generously spiced with telling anecdotes. From his narrative, Said's straw men emerge as complex individuals touched by genius, ambition, and no little sympathy for the subjects of their study.

Quirky Eccentrics

Some of the Orientalist pioneers were quintessential insiders. Thus, Silvestre de Sacy founded the great nineteenth-century school of Arabic studies in Paris; Bonaparte made him a baron, and he became a peer of France under the monarchy. Carl Heinrich Becker, who brought sociology into Islamic studies, served as a cabinet minister in the Weimar government. But it was marginal men who made the most astonishing advances. Ignaz Goldziher, a Hungarian Jew, revolutionized Islamic studies over a century ago by applying the methods of higher criticism to the Muslim oral tradition. Slaving away as the secretary of the reformist Neolog Jewish community in Budapest, Goldziher made his breakthroughs at the end of long workdays.

Some great scholars were quite mad. In the sixteenth century, Guillaume Postel, a prodigy who occupied the first chair of Arabic at the Collège de France, produced Europe's first grammar of classical Arabic. Irwin describes him as "a complete lunatic"—an enthusiast of all things esoteric and Eastern who believed himself to be possessed by a female divinity. Four centuries later, Louis Massignon, another French great at the Collège, claimed to have experienced a visitation by God and plunged into the cult of a Sufi mystic. When lucid, Massignon commanded a vast knowledge of Islam and Arabic, but he held an unshakable belief in unseen forces, including Jewish plots of world domination.

Above all, many Orientalists became fervent advocates for Arab and Islamic political causes, long before notions like third-worldism and postcolonialism entered the political lexicon. Goldziher backed the Urabi revolt against foreign control of Egypt. The Cambridge Iranologist Edward Granville Browne became a one-man lobby for Persian liberty during Iran's constitutional revolution in the early twentieth century. Prince Leone Caetani, an Italian Islamicist, opposed his country's occupation of Libya, for which he was denounced as a "Turk." And Massignon may have been the first Frenchman to take up the Palestinian Arab cause.

Two truths emerge from a stroll through Irwin's gallery. First, Orientalist scholars, far from mystifying Islam, freed Europe from medieval myths about it through their translations and studies of original Islamic texts. Second, most Orientalists, far from being agents of empire, were bookish dons and quirky eccentrics. When they did venture opinions on mundane matters, it was usually to criticize Western imperialism and defend something Islamic or Arab. In fact, it would be easy to write a contrary indictment of the Orientalists, showing them to be wooly-minded Islamophiles who suffered from what the late historian Elie Kedourie once called "the romantic belief that exquisite mosques and beautiful carpets are proof of political virtue."[3]

Pangs of Guilt

In other words, Edward Said got it exactly wrong. Other scholars said as much in the years after his book came out; Irwin's critique echoes those made by Jacques Berque, Malcolm Kerr, Bernard Lewis, and Maxime Rodinson. These doyens of Islamic and Arab studies came from radically different points on the political compass, but they all found the same flaws in Said's presentation. Even Albert Hourani, the Middle East historian closest to Said personally, thought that *Orientalism* had gone "too far" and regretted that its most lasting effect was to turn "a perfectly respected discipline" into "a dirty word."[4]

Yet the criticisms did not stick; what stuck was the dirt thrown by Said. Not only did *Orientalism* sweep the general humanities, where ignorance of the history of Orientalism was (and is) widespread; not only did it help to create the faux-academic discipline now known as postcolonialism; but the book's thesis also conquered the field of Middle Eastern studies itself, where scholars should have known better. No other discipline has ever surrendered so totally to an external critic.

As it happens, I witnessed a minute that perfectly compressed the results of this process. In 1998, to mark the twentieth anniversary of the publication of *Orientalism*, the Middle East Studies Association (MESA) invited Said to address a plenary panel at its annual conference. As Said ascended the dais, his admirers leaped to their feet in an enthusiastic ovation. Then, somewhat hesitantly at first, the rest of the audience stood and began to applaud. Fixed in my seat, I surveyed the ballroom, watching scholars whom I had heard privately damn *Orientalism* for its libel against their field now rising sheepishly and casting sideways glances to see who might behold their gesture of submission.

This may help us understand something in Irwin's account that might otherwise leave a reader bewildered. Why should Said have singled out for attack a group of scholars who had done so much to increase understanding of Islam, and who had tirelessly explained Muslim views to a self-absorbed West? The answer: for the same reason that radicals usually attack the moderates on their own side. They know they can browbeat them into doing much more.

By exposing and exaggerating a few of the field's insignificant lapses, *Orientalism* stunned Middle East academics into a paroxysm of shame. Exploiting those pangs of guilt, Said's radical followers demanded concession upon concession from the Orientalist establishment: academic appointments and promotions, directorships of Middle East centers and departments, and control of publishing decisions, grants, and honors. Within a startling brief period of time, a small island of liberal sympathy for the Arab and Muslim "other" was transformed into a subsidized, thousand-man lobby for Arab, Islamic, and Palestinian causes.

Sparks of Integrity

The revolution did not stop until Said was universally acclaimed as the savior of Middle Eastern studies and, in that ballroom where I sat in 1998, virtually the entire membership of MESA had been corralled into canonizing him. It did not stop until he was elected an honorary fellow of the association—that is, one of ten select scholars "who have made major contributions to Middle East studies." (No similar majority could be mustered to accord the same honor to Bernard Lewis.) It would not stop until it achieved the abject abasement of the true heirs of the Orientalist tradition.

This is the missing final chapter of *Dangerous Knowledge*. The established scholars in Middle Eastern studies never did deliver the crushing blow to *Orientalism* that it deserved. With the exception of Bernard Lewis, no one went on the warpath against the book (although, according to Irwin, the anthropologist Ernest Gellner was working on a "book-long attack" on *Orientalism* when he died in 1995). Going up against Said involved too much professional risk. He himself was famous for avenging every perceived slight, and his fiercely loyal followers denounced even the mildest criticism of their hero as evidence of "latent Orientalism"—or, worse yet, Zionism.

Still, the power of Said and his legions did begin to wane somewhat after the attacks of 9/11. Said had systematically soft-pedaled the threat of radical Islam. In a pre-9/11 revised edition of Said's *Covering Islam*, a book devoted to exposing the allegedly biased reporting of the Western press, he mocked "speculations about the latest conspiracy to blow up buildings, sabotage commercial airliners, and poison water supplies."[5] After the planes struck the towers, Said declined to answer his phone. Irwin writes that when, unrepentant, he finally responded, "he put the terrorists' case for them, just as he had put the case for Saddam Hussein." September 11 broke Said's spell. "Does this mean I'm throwing my copy of *Orientalism* out the window?" quipped Richard Bulliet, a professor of Islamic history at Columbia, in the week following the attacks. "Maybe it does."[6]

Since Said's death in 2003, more doubters have found the courage to speak out. Some of Columbia's own students did so in 2005, when they took on a number of Said's most extreme acolytes, whom he had helped to embed as instructors in the university's department of Middle East studies. Irwin's *Dangerous Knowledge* is a challenge to that minority of scholars in the field who still preserve a spark of integrity and some vestige of pride in the tradition of learning that Said defamed. They won't ever call themselves Orientalists again. But it is high time they denounced the Saidian cult for the fraud that it is, and began to unseat it. Irwin has told the truth; it is their responsibility to act on it.

Notes

1. Robert Irwin, *Dangerous Knowledge: Orientalism and its Discontents* (Woodstock, NY: Overlook Press, 2006), 165.
2. Edward Said, *Orientalism* (New York: Pantheon, 1978), 204.
3. Elie Kedourie, "Politics and the Academy," *Commentary* 94, no. 2 (August 1992): 53.
4. Interview with Albert Hourani in *Approaches to the History of the Middle East*, ed. Nancy Elizabeth Gallagher (London: Ithaca Press, 1994), 40–41.
5. Edward W. Said, *Covering Islam: How the Media and the Experts Determine How We See the Rest of the World* (rev. ed.; New York: Vintage, 1997), xi.
6. Quoted by Lionel Beehner, "SIPA Students, Faculty React to Terrorist Attacks," *The SIPA Communiqué*, September 4–19, 2001.

2

The Shifting Sands of Academe
(A lecture delivered to students at Harvard University)

Nothing is more stimulating, as a student, than living through a time of upheaval in one's field. Professors dislike upheaval—they are more interested in building and expansion, and in establishing their authority and reach. But perhaps once in thirty years, a field will experience a dramatic upheaval that changes its contours. In such times of trouble, there is much turbulence, and there are winners and losers. When the dust has settled, the field has a new configuration. I lived through just such a time as a student, over thirty years ago.

I began my study of the Middle East in 1972, which was the tail end of the long, massive expansion of Middle Eastern studies that had started twenty years earlier. Despite the growth, it was still a fairly small enterprise that hadn't quite found its place in the American university. It was rather heavily dependent on two things: the importation of scholars from abroad, especially from Europe and to a lesser extent the Middle East; and the influx of dollars from Washington, which floated the new Middle East centers and provided most of the fellowship money.

The mandarins of those days did everything possible to avoid identification with the political causes of the Middle East. Middle Eastern studies, it was thought at the time, would only prosper in the academy if their practitioners demonstrated a studied neutrality toward the conflicts they studied.

I had one professor who was meticulous to a tee in his wholly dispassionate and disinterested analysis of the Arab-Israeli conflict in his class. I asked him how he managed it. He asked me this question: what was Palestine in the year 600? I answered: a part of the Byzantine Empire. And what was it in 700? I answered: a part of the Arab Empire. And then he said: I simply analyze the transformations of the present at the same distance from which I analyze those of the seventh century. In other words, just imagine that you don't have a dog in the fight. He assumed that the whole point of scholarship was to act disinterested—not just to others, but to oneself.[1]

The Book and the Revolution

All this began to unravel in the 1970s, with dramatic events in the Middle East itself. After 1967, there was a great awakening among Jews and Arabs in America, and the rise of a new kind of identity politics. In the Middle East, Black September and terrorism, and the outbreak of civil war in formerly placid Lebanon, drew America into the region. Our teachers began to take sides; departmental brown bag lunches became less congenial.

And then, in my first years as a grad student, came a double crisis: publication of Edward Said's *Orientalism* and the Iranian revolution. Said's book landed like a bomb on Princeton, where I was a graduate student. I rushed down to the university book store to lay my hands on this incendiary work, and went straight to the index to look up all my teachers. The grad students had a meeting; the faculty were divided over whether to ignore the book or respond. Princeton's stars had been especially targeted by Said: the famous Bernard Lewis, the now-forgotten Morroe Berger, and others. The general inclination was to ignore the book, thinking it would fade away. It was so flawed, so lacking in rigor, so rife with egregious mistakes of fact and interpretation. Much of this was dutifully noted in various reviews.

What my teachers didn't understand was that the influence of the book would arise from a deeper need, as a manifesto for a group of younger political activists, who had decided that the academy was the perfect platform for politics and who wanted to break down its doors. They hoped to do so by delegitimizing the established scholars who approached the present like the seventh century, and by establishing their brand of advocacy as tantamount to scholarship. Said's book was the perfect manifesto for an insurgency.

The other event was the Iranian revolution. It cut entirely in the opposite direction. Why? The political activists misread it, the Orientalists got it right. While doing my thesis research in London, I ran down to Charing Cross Road to buy the first book on Iran's revolution, by one of the left insurgents. It predicted the imminent demise of the shah—and his replacement with a progressive government.[2] Back in Princeton, in February 1979, I attended an event hosted by Professor

Richard Falk, self-styled champion of the oppressed, who paraded before an audience of six hundred students an array of leftist Iranian revolutionaries. All of them had one message: pay no attention to the men in the turbans, they'll go back to the mosques when this is over, give the revolution your support. (I have returned to the *Daily Princetonian* to check my memory against the record. Quote from one of the speakers: "We are going to have a republic, a democracy. Every group in Iran is emphasizing the words 'democratic' and 'republic' as much as 'Islamic.'")[3] The speakers got a standing ovation.

But in the Near Eastern Studies department, someone had put his hands on Khomeini's treatise on Islamic government, in Arabic. No one in America had yet read it or translated it, but it had been in the bowels of Firestone Library, and photocopies began to circulate among us. If you could read Arabic, and knew something about reading an Islamic text, you got the message. Like *Orientalism*, Khomeini's book was also a manifesto, and it was about delegitimation and validation— yes, delegitimation of the shah, but validation of Islamic government, administered directly by the men in turbans. But you had to be an Orientalist to understand it.

So these were the two events that turned the world upside down in my graduate student days. Said's book had a profound influence, and largely achieved its intended effect. The insurgents rode the wave of the new left's academization, turning all their favorite causes, above all Palestine, into jobs, books, and tenure. But out there, in the real Middle East, the Iranian revolution set off the growth of Islamist movements that the new mandarins could never quite explain. They tried—and they still try—to squeeze them into convenient categories, to cast them—as Richard Falk did—as cousins to the revolutionary movements they did admire. But they couldn't (and, I would argue, still can't) get it right, which is why these movements consistently surprise them, and rarely surprise those who do the things Orientalists used to do—that is, take texts and ideas seriously.

Gestation of a Controversy

When I finished my studies, in 1981, the atmosphere had been poisoned against Bernard Lewis, my teacher. Having studied under him put a question mark by me. I have a rather vivid recollection of appearing before the Social Science Research Council grants committee in New York for an interview: I could have cut the animosity with a knife. So I didn't bother looking for a job in America. One was offered to me in

Israel (where I had spent two years as an undergraduate), and I took it. Over the years, I earned tenure at Tel Aviv University, I directed the Middle East center there, and I did what Middle East experts do. I focused on modern Arab history and Islamic movements. I had a reputation, in the United States too, as a thorough and solid scholar of these things.

But as the 1990s ensued, I saw a new trend in the field, and it troubled me. It was a certain approach to Islamist movements that abandoned the requisite scholarly distance, and cast them in an almost heroic light, as incorruptible, reform-minded, socially responsible, democratically inclined. Even Edward Said, who had never been a friend of Islamist movements, began not so much to praise them as to attack those who criticized them. It was a replay of what I had witnessed in the lead-up to Iran's revolution. So I began to write against this trend, still not naming names.[4] It was one thing for Middle Eastern studies to have elevated the Palestinians as exemplars of a new politics, a new hope—that was dubious enough. But to see the same glossy hyperbole heaped on the Muslim Brotherhood and Hamas, and the folks in Hezbollah whom I had studied in the 1980s—that was too much.

By the end of the 1990s, I was already on a collision course with some of my colleagues. But I think what resolved me to write a critique of Middle Eastern studies was an event that made clear to me how much I had missed while away from American academe. In 1998, the Middle East Studies Association (MESA) organized a panel to mark twenty years to the publication of *Orientalism*, and it featured Edward Said himself. Speaker after speaker declared the final and irreversible victory of Edward Said over the forces of reaction, and congratulated him on his triumph. His acolytes and disciples, now secure in their academic chairs and directorships, seemed to me even more smugly self-confident than the old mandarins they had dethroned and replaced. Their arrogance shocked me—it showed me just how little room remained for different approaches in the field. And so I decided to throw a rock through the window.

I should add that it wasn't a particularly pleasant task, because I had been on speaking terms with almost all the *dramatis personae*. But to have excluded people I knew and even liked would have been a kind of intellectual favoritism that would have diminished the credibility of the enterprise. Even as I wrote certain paragraphs, I suspected I would be burning bridges forever. It is not something I recommend to graduate students.

My book *Ivory Towers on Sand: The Failure of Middle Eastern Studies in America,* was published by The Washington Institute for Near East Policy in late 2001. I won't recap its arguments. But there are a few points worth noting. When you write a book, you imagine a certain reader standing over your shoulder, and you write it with that reader in mind. I did the writing, almost all of it, before 9/11, and my imaginary reader was someone within Middle Eastern studies. The book was intended to shift, however slightly, the balance within the field.

As it happened, though, *Ivory Towers on Sand* appeared just six weeks after 9/11, in the midst of a great debate over what it all meant, and this supercharged the book. It was the subject of an article in the *New York Times*, which brought me thousands of readers who had never cared a whit about Middle Eastern studies.[5] This included journalists, officials and concerned citizens, but it also included deans, provosts, and university presidents. Suddenly Middle Eastern studies became a flashpoint in the culture wars. It would have happened even without my book, but I suspect I accelerated the process.

I then poured oil on the fire: I wrote an op-ed in the *Wall Street Journal,* timed to coincide with MESA's first post-9/11 conference, calling on Congress not to put another penny into the field.[6] Franklin Foer, later editor of *The New Republic,* was prompted by my book to cover that conference (it was in San Francisco), and he reported that "there was one universally acknowledged villain at the conference—it just wasn't Osama bin Laden." It was Martin Kramer. Hissing followed mention of my name in a plenary session.[7] I resolved to take it as a compliment.

But the reaction within the field was not universally hostile. A little over a year after publication, I appeared in Washington with the then-president of MESA, Lisa Anderson, for a discussion of the state of Middle Eastern studies. She described my arguments as overstated, but also said that within the field, the book had been regarded as a useful intervention.[8] In 2005, I was invited (much to my astonishment) to speak at the thirtieth anniversary conference of the Center for Contemporary Arab Studies at Georgetown. I doubt that would have happened if my critique had been totally out of bounds. In my remarks there, I said something that perfectly summarized my limited aim vis-à-vis my colleagues: "My mission is very simple. It isn't to convince anyone in this room—that's beyond my power. It is to plant a seed of doubt. If you find yourself, against every impulse and instinct, agreeing with just one thing I say, I will regard this morning as well spent."[9]

13

The Critics Speak

My critics usually agreed with one or two things I said, but disagreed with much more of it. Just consult the review essays in *Foreign Affairs, International Affairs,* and the *Middle East Journal.* There weren't any surprises in the *International Journal of Middle East Studies* either. Some critiques were more interesting than others. The least interesting were the ones that attacked me for claiming that Middle Eastern studies should have predicted 9/11. That isn't the thrust of the book. I added only one page to the text after 9/11, at the last moment, and it was to show how some persons in the field had argued that a 9/11-type scenario was a scare tactic of the so-called terrorism industry.

But while I didn't argue that scholars could predict specific events, I do believe that it is hard to accept the validity of a paradigm if everything that occurs subsequent to its formulation seems to contradict it. In any case, it has always been the claim of Middle Eastern studies, in the pleas of its leaders for funding from Washington, that it somehow better equips the United States for anticipating trends in the Middle East. In fact, the motto of MESA might be: "If you'd only listened to us." And I haven't noticed any particular reticence among scholars about invoking their academic credentials when making predictions. So these critics, it seems to me, protest too much.

A more interesting criticism was that I had overestimated the influence of Said on the field. This came from several directions, most significantly from the left activist academics who got their start in something called MERIP. In my student days, these people had been developing their own critique of the establishment even before Said's book, which upstaged them. Now they were claiming that they, and not Said, had done more to revolutionize the field.[10]

But this raises the even more interesting question of why they turned Said into the icon of transformation in Middle Eastern studies. He was even made an honorary member of MESA, a rare distinction reserved for those who have made signal contributions to the field (and a distinction, by the way, withheld from Bernard Lewis). In almost every introductory course on methodology, *Orientalism* is required reading. It may be true that *Orientalism* has had less of an impact on Middle Eastern studies than on postcolonial studies. But in the only (ad hoc) survey to ask Middle East scholars to name the "best" books in the field, *Orientalism* emerged on top.[11] So the burden of proof rests on these critics, and they have yet to assume it.

The most valid criticism is that I committed the same sins as *Orientalism*—that is, I cherry-picked my evidence, and tied it up in a polemical package. I plead guilty to some of that, and I admit that I had *Orientalism* as one of my models in writing *Ivory Towers on Sand*. But I plead extenuating circumstances in these two respects. First, if this method is permitted to Said, why should it be denied to me? And second, at least I did my cherry-picking at the center of the orchard. I knew to distinguish between the center of Middle Eastern studies and the edges, and I took all my egregious examples from the heart of the field. Said's book is all over the orchard. You may accuse me of being selective; but you can't accuse me of citing marginal examples to indict the field as a whole.

Opening Space

What has been the long-term effect of my book? It has lived several lives. It has been taught in courses. It was invoked by organizations like Campus Watch as inspiration for their project. It was used by a university president to raise support for an alternative Middle East center. Lawrence Summers, when he was president of Harvard, took it with him to a meeting with the Middle East faculty, to ask if there was any truth to it. (He told me they weren't amused.) It was sent by various people to provosts and congressmen (and was cited in testimony before Congress). I can't keep track of all the purposes it has served, and I'm not responsible for them either.

My hope is that, ultimately, the book will be remembered as having opened some space in the academy for a wider range of views. Making more space is messy business in practice, because it is a zero-sum game. Some win, some lose, and at any one point in time, it's hard to tell the score. But I believe the field has become more diverse than it was a decade ago. This is mostly the result of larger changes in America's relationship to the Middle East, especially due to the wars in Afghanistan and Iraq. Since 9/11, perhaps two million Americans have come through the Middle East, and some have gone into academe. They have been influenced by harsh encounters with realities. But some small part of this change may be a legacy of *Ivory Towers on Sand,* and that gives me some satisfaction.

Today's students of the Middle East are fortunate, as I was, to witness a period of upheaval in the Middle East. Some months after I published *Ivory Towers,* I received a note from the head of a Middle East center, someone I wouldn't have thought sympathetic to my project.

"We don't know one another," he wrote, "but I wanted to let you know that I liked your book. And to thank you for leaving me out! I wish only that conditions were such that younger scholars-in-the-making were launching these polemics."

He had a point. People ask me sometimes whether I intend to write another book on Middle Eastern studies. My answer is no—the next book should be written by people who are thirty years younger than I am. It should be written by young scholars like you.

Notes

1. I leave it to Don Peretz to reveal this professor's identity: "There are quite a few academicians and writers who seem to have dealt with the Middle East in a fashion that does not betray their ethnic, class, or religious roots. I believe that J. C. Hurewitz sought to attain this 'objectivity' in his work and attempted to instill it in his students. Of course this irritated, even exasperated, some of his students and readers who complained that they never could find out where he stood on sensitive issues such as the Arab-Israel dispute." Don Peretz, "Vignettes—Bits and Pieces," in *Paths to the Middle East: Ten Scholars Look Back*, ed. Thomas Naff (Albany: State University of New York Press, 1993), 255.

2. This was Fred Halliday. He opined that "the ayatollahs and mullahs on their own can probably not sustain or channel the popular upsurge," but he felt certain others might, and the book ended on this optimistic note: "It is quite possible that before too long the Iranian people will chase the Pahlavi dictator and his associates from power, will surmount the obstacles in its way, and build a prosperous and socialist Iran." Fred Halliday, *Iran: Dictatorship and Development* (Harmondsworth: Penguin, 1979), 299, 309.

3. Douglas Schwartz, "Falk Discusses Iranians, Khomeini," *Daily Princetonian*, February 9, 1979. Only one week later, Falk published his most memorable op-ed, where he wrote this: "The depiction of [Khomeini] as fanatical, reactionary and the bearer of crude prejudices seems certainly and happily false. . . . Having created a new model of popular revolution based, for the most part, on nonviolent tactics, Iran may yet provide us with a desperately needed model of humane governance for a third-world country." Richard Falk, "Trusting Khomeini," *New York Times*, February 16, 1979.

4. Most notably, "Islam vs. Democracy," *Commentary* 95, no. 1 (January 1993): 35–42.

5. Richard Bernstein, "Experts on Islam Pointing Fingers at One Another," *New York Times*, November 3, 2001.

6. Martin Kramer, "Terrorism? What Terrorism?!," *Wall Street Journal*, November 15, 2001. This prompted a letter of response from Edward Said, which appeared on December 4, 2001.

7. Franklin Foer, "San Francisco Dispatch: Disoriented," *The New Republic*, December 3, 2001.

8. Martin Kramer and Lisa Anderson, "Middle Eastern Studies: What Went Wrong?," Washington Institute for Near East Policy, *Policywatch* no. 691 (December 16, 2002).

9. Martin Kramer, "Arab Studies: My Critical Review," *Sandbox* blog, April 1, 2005, archived at http://web.archive.org/web/20101226223436/http://www.martinkramer.org/sandbox/2005/04/arab-studies-my-critical-review/.

10. Most notably, Fred Halliday, "9/11 and Middle Eastern Studies, Past and Future: Revisiting Ivory Towers on Sand," *International Affairs* 80, no. 5 (October 2004): 953–62; and Zachary Lockman, *Contending Visions of the Middle East: The History and Politics of Orientalism* (Cambridge: Cambridge University Press, 2004), 257–65. Lockman allowed that my critique "may seem to resonate with those set forth in this book," an interesting convergence.

11. Garth Hall, "The 21 'Best' Books in Middle East Studies," *MESC Newsletter* 2, no. 2 (November 2005), archived at https://web.archive.org/web/20060209102204/http://www.aucegypt.edu/academic/mesc/PDF/MESC%20November%202005%20Issue.pdf.

3

Surveying the Middle East

There can be no history (or critique) of the modern Western study of the Middle East without an appreciation of survey writing. Such surveys, compiled annually or periodically, met the demand for a record of contemporary affairs before the internet put the world's databases in every pocket. Throughout the twentieth-century heyday of survey writing, it contributed systematically to the ways different Western publics understood the living Middle East, and it figured in careers of great distinction.

Yet in the histories of Middle Eastern studies, all of these projects are ignored. They are regarded as ancillary to scholarship—something akin to the compilation of bibliographies or the collation of manuscripts. The following essay is intended to provoke a reassessment, and propose that survey writing played a significant role in the formation of the field now known as Middle Eastern studies.

Reading the Press

Up until the end of the nineteenth century, the interpretation of the contemporary Middle East was the province of diplomats, colonial administrators, soldiers, travelers, traders, and missionaries—persons who boasted the credential of extended residence in the region. Contemporary affairs were the business of men (and a few women) of affairs, whose analyses often served political, commercial, or clerical interests.

The "news from Turkey" had no proper place in the universities of Europe, where Orientalists concerned themselves almost exclusively with the classical languages and literatures of Arabic and Persian, and the theology and early history of Islam. The scholarly conventions of nineteenth-century Orientalism, fixed as they were upon the study of Oriental languages and classical periods of Oriental history, discouraged inquiry into contemporary affairs. So long as such inquiry remained outside formal disciplines, the interpretation of contemporary Islam in the West lacked the authority claimed by scholars for their interpretations of historical Islam.

But as the nineteenth century closed, a growing number of academic Orientalists turned their attention to the contemporary march of events in Muslim lands. The rise of an indigenous Middle Eastern press made this possible, especially after constitutional revolutions in Turkey and Persia. The study of contemporary affairs no longer required continuous residence in the Middle East, but could be done in a disciplined manner through the systematic reading of newspapers in Turkish, Persian, and Arabic. Orientalists, armed with evidence provided by the press, could speak with authority on contemporary affairs without leaving their studies.

Again and again, the pattern was repeated across Europe. Once enough scholars shared an interest in contemporary events, they organized themselves for the acquisition of the press, its systematic translation and analysis, and finally the production of contemporary surveys. Such projects were necessarily the work of highly organized research teams, commanding resources on a scale most readily achieved in countries that had political, economic, or imperial interests in the Middle East.

Seen from Paris

The initial breakthrough occurred in Paris in 1906, with the first publication of the *Revue du monde musulman*. Its founding editor, the dynamic Alfred Le Chatelier, was a veteran of the Algerian Bureaux Arabes, who in 1902 emerged from a series of political maneuvers as the incumbent of a new chair of "Muslim sociology and sociography" at the Collège de France.[1] The preoccupation of France with pan-Islamic "intrigue" before the First World War had spread the conviction that ideas generated in one corner of the Muslim world affected French interests in another. Le Chatelier played upon this idea to build official support for a journal that would provide comprehensive coverage of trends of opinion throughout the Muslim world.

In sixty-four issues published between 1906 and 1926, the *Revue du monde musulman* provided readers with a sensitive, informed, and fundamentally sympathetic account of the crisis then confronting Islam. Le Chatelier pledged that the journal would steer clear of politics; it would deal objectively with "the history and present state of the social organization of the Muslim world," "the contemporary movement of deeds and ideas," and future "tendencies and orientation."[2] The *Revue du monde musulman* carried regular articles, but its most innovative features were the notes and documents, a survey of the Muslim press, and a section entitled "around the Muslim world."

The contributors to the *Revue du monde musulman* succeeded in registering remote tremors of Muslim opinion, and the review quickly acquired a singular voice of authority.[3] At the heart of Le Chatelier's small team was Lucien Bouvat, a master of Oriental languages who specialized in Turkish. He was so painfully timid and self-effacing that he could not teach. But he was industrious, a trait as essential to the success of the project as Le Chatelier's personal dynamism. Still more promising scholars were not above performing the routine work of the review: Louis Massignon, who would become France's preeminent interpreter of Islam, wrote nearly two hundred pages of the review's Arabic press summary immediately before and after the First World War.

In its time, the *Revue du monde musulman* represented a great stride forward in the technique of gathering, organizing, and disseminating knowledge about current affairs. A well-connected leader-scholar mobilized the financial resources and political support essential to the project. Once he secured these, he founded a research institute to house the project, and that institute employed a diverse research team to handle the materials in the relevant languages. Affiliation with respected academic auspices enhanced the authority of the finished product. The resulting work obviously filled a pressing need, for the press run of the *Revue du monde musulman* reached 1,200 during its first year, a figure as impressive now as it was then.

A preoccupation with pan-Islam ran through the pages of Le Chatelier's journal. The *Revue du monde musulman* appeared at a time of great French apprehension lest the contagion of militant Islam spread to French North Africa via the network of religious orders and the pilgrimage. Le Chatelier was not an alarmist, and he discounted pan-Islam as a force for political disruption. But he did believe in what he called "social pan-Islam," and the *Revue du monde musulman* devoted many pages to the trek of ideas and opinions across the Muslim world. It did this so effectively that the journal developed a substantial readership among Muslim intellectuals who wished to follow currents of opinion elsewhere in the Muslim world.

Yet for all its success, the *Revue du monde musulman* left much to be desired. The journal did not present a systematic narrative of change, but rather a series of glimpses into the elusive spirit of contemporary Islam. From an editorial point of view, the journal's arrangement often bordered on the chaotic. The *Revue du monde musulman* dealt principally with intellectual expression on social questions, and its selection and presentation of this material often seemed capricious. Coverage of the press was uneven and highly erratic. Names of persons and places were transliterated inconsistently, adding to the confusion. The *Revue du monde musulman* often had the character of a grab bag; its contents are retrievable only because the editors published a comprehensive index as the journal's last act. (Massignon solemnly reported that the card manuscript of the index "weighs 17.930 kilograms, and measures 1.64 meters long in a compacted and compressed state.")[4]

The review appeared regularly for two decades, but began to falter after 1919, when Massignon became director. The war had damaged the scholarly credibility of the review, for it had been briefly enlisted as an instrument of French propaganda among Muslims. One wartime issue, entitled "Le Salut au Drapeau," was filled with African Muslim professions of allegiance to France. In an editorial written in 1919, Massignon promised that the journal would return to "precise, methodic, and independent documentation," presented in a "manageable" fashion; the journal would be "strictly objective, benevolent, courteous, and impartial."[5]

But it was too late to redeem the journal's tarnished reputation, and the presentation became no more manageable than before. On a deeper level, a fundamental assumption of the review's approach—that Muslim lands had the coherence of a world unto itself, that the events in one part of that world were bound to affect another—had been undermined by the failure of pan-Islam during the war. By the war's end, the idea of Islam as the point of departure for all interpretation of the region had lost its persuasive power. It had yielded to the growing conviction that there was no "Muslim world" but a vast expanse in the Middle East and North Africa inhabited by peoples of different nationalities, each charting its separate course.

Massignon saw the new national movements as so many departures from the bonds of spiritual solidarity and the universalism of Islam.[6] As the Muslim world drew away from its spiritual vocation, so Massignon drew away from the documentation of its changing political moods. In 1927, Massignon—newly ensconced in Le Chatelier's chair—refashioned the review into a journal of articles, the *Revue des études islamiques*, which dropped the press summaries and gradually distanced itself from the interpretation of contemporary affairs.[7]

The Founder

The demise of the French initiative did not leave a vacuum. In March 1921, a group of Italian academics and officials came together to establish the Istituto per l'Oriente in Rome. In May, the new institute published the first issue of a monthly journal, *Oriente Moderno*. The editors explained that the war had created new opportunities for Italy in the Middle East. Yet the Italian public remained ill-informed about the region's recent past and present. Italian public opinion needed "disinterested" information drawn from genuine sources on the various problems of the Middle East.

The journal would be concerned with political, administrative, and military events as they happened; the trends and ideas behind them; and the social, economic, and cultural circumstances in which they were formed. All these would be assessed on the basis of indigenous press sources, supplemented by explanatory notes. *Oriente Moderno* planned to shun "colonial questions"—matters of Italian policy best left to policy journals. "*Oriente Moderno* does not intend to propose particular solutions to the different problems raised in political debates, but to furnish such elements and such information as would permit makers of policy and men of affairs to know the truth about the Orient."[8]

Oriente Moderno won immediate international recognition as the preeminent source for information on the emerging nationalist movements of the contemporary Middle East. Extensive press coverage, systematic presentation, and rigorous editorial control combined to set new standards for the documentation of contemporary affairs. *Oriente Moderno* applied the uncompromising Orientalist respect for texts to the daily Arabic, Turkish, and Persian press, for it was under the "scientific direction" of an exacting master: Carlo Alfonso Nallino, professor of Muslim history and institutions at the University of Rome and Italy's preeminent Orientalist.

Nallino had been schooled in the traditional disciplines of history and philology. But during the previous decade he had placed his knowledge of Muslim institutions at the service of his government, issuing advice on the reform of Muslim education in Libya and the question of the caliphate. He had also taught in Egypt. Nallino soon acquired a standing in Rome as an authority on contemporary Muslim affairs, and drew upon his prestige to win the support of leading parliamentarians for the creation of the Istituto per l'Oriente.

Oriente Moderno published documents, chronologies, articles, book reviews, and a section of scholarly news. But its unique standing derived from the "various notices" culled from the press. The staff of the institute selected items from newspapers in Middle Eastern and European languages, and meticulously translated and summarized their

contents according to precise rules established by Nallino and his closest associate, Ettore Rossi. Nallino did not visit the institute often, but
all material was brought to him at his home, and his critical eye assured
the highest standards of selection, translation, and transliteration.

Oriente Moderno interpreted events through selection, and its
attributions of significance were made with careful consideration.
The Middle East that emerged from its pages teemed with nationalist
activity, mostly against Britain and France: *Oriente Moderno* constituted
the most systematic account of indigenous protest against the policies
of the powers, and won a very select and influential readership. While
its circulation never exceeded eight hundred, many subscribers relied
upon it heavily for their information on Arab opinion, including such
otherwise well-informed quarters as the British Foreign Office.

The fact that *Oriente Moderno* gained an international reputation
for accuracy and objectivity was a remarkable achievement, given that
it was compiled and published during the Fascist era. Its meticulous
documentation of Arab nationalist activity in Syria, Palestine, and Iraq
gave Italy a political advantage, and Italian representatives often cited
the journal in challenging British and French reports to the Permanent
Mandates Commission of the League of Nations in Geneva. The Istituto per l'Oriente also received modest subventions from the Foreign
and Colonial Ministries, and served as an informal press service by
providing advance copies of its press summaries to the government.[9]

But Nallino proved incapable of propagandizing, because he refused
simplification. His Middle East, and that of *Oriente Moderno,* was a
vast, complex, and ever-changing canvass.[10] Politically, Nallino was a
liberal, and he did not spare Italian readers of *Oriente Moderno* the
Arab criticism leveled against Italy over General Graziani's ruthless
crushing of Muslim resistance in Cyrenaica in 1930—notices which
the censorship did not touch, lest their absence damage the journal's
international reputation for comprehensiveness.[11] Nallino's immense
prestige assured the inviolability of *Oriente Moderno;* his death in 1938
did not bode well for the journal's continued independence.

There were many reasons why *Oriente Moderno* should have folded
after the Second World War. Not only was the leader-scholar gone,
but Italy had been defeated and deprived of all imperial possessions.
But the end of Italian empire actually worked to the advantage of the
Istituto per l'Oriente, for its work suited Italy's campaign to win the
friendship of the new states of the Middle East. The official subsidies
continued to flow.

More to the point, Nallino's collaborators were worshipful disciples who could not bear to abandon the project launched by "the Founder." What one collaborator described as the "heroic era" had passed, but *Oriente Moderno* geared up again under Rossi's directorship, and reappeared in its original format. The volumes dealing with the postwar world of independent Middle Eastern states were rarely as thick as the prewar volumes, and as other publications appeared, fewer foreigners with an interest in contemporary Middle Eastern affairs were prepared to read about them in Italian. Yet only in 1979 did financial troubles brought on by rampant inflation compel the Istituto per l'Oriente to abandon its venerated format. *Oriente Moderno* became a conventional academic journal composed of disparate articles.[12]

Moral Judgment

Readers who found the presentation of Middle Eastern events in *Oriente Moderno* too austere for their tastes could turn to the *Survey of International Affairs* of the Royal Institute of International Affairs—Chatham House—in London. Edited and largely written by the historian Arnold Toynbee, the *Survey* was conceived as an annual narrative of world events. The volumes were to be "confined to facts," wrote the secretary of the Institute in his preface to the first volume: "The primary object of these publications is to enable speakers and writers to gather in the time available for their task the factual material, carefully checked, upon which to base the advice which they offer to the public."[13] The first volumes of the *Survey* did not include the Middle East, but in 1927 Toynbee published a large tome under the title *The Islamic World since the Peace Settlement*, and the Middle East subsequently figured in most of the annual volumes of the *Survey*.

While Toynbee was schooled in classical history, he had dealt with the contemporary Middle East in an earlier study of the Turkish-Greek conflict, and so regarded himself as particularly qualified to provide coverage of the region. He had the writing discipline of a journalist, an imaginative grasp of history, and an intuitive sense of how to season the interpretation of contemporary events for the British palate. The prestigious auspices of the *Survey*, its interpretative flourish, and Toynbee's own dynamism assured that its treatment of Middle Eastern affairs would gain a more influential readership than any comparable publication before or since.

But the *Survey* covered the world, and the Middle East could not command the undivided attention of Toynbee or his collaborators.

It was crisis-driven, and the Middle East warranted attention only when it threatened trouble. The region did not receive equal coverage in every volume, for in certain years it had to compete with the Italian invasion of Abyssinia or the Spanish Civil War.[14] The *Survey*, in the words of the British historian Elie Kedourie, "was chained to the chariot of current affairs, endeavouring breathlessly to keep up with them. But this was a vain endeavour since history cannot be written from newspaper cuttings. The attempt to do so only meant that partiality to fashionable political rhetoric was not checked, but rather reinforced by the uncritical assertions of restless 'newsmen' avidly questing for 'stories.'"[15]

The reliance on "newsmen" was particularly acute because the *Survey* was not based on indigenous press sources. It relied heavily upon Western press reports and (until the mid-1930s) upon *Oriente Moderno*, which Toynbee acknowledged as "by far the best existing periodical dealing with current Islamic affairs which is published in either Europe or America in any Western language."[16]

In covering the Middle East, the *Survey* confined its purview to the international affairs of the region. Toynbee did not seek to cover Egypt or Arabia or Turkey per se, but emphasized their relations with the European powers and the outside world (although he included internal Westernization in his scope). In particular, his emphases skewed toward the relationship of the Middle East with Britain; the Middle East figured in the *Survey* principally as a problem of British policy. The *Survey* paid detailed attention to relations and treaties between Middle Eastern states and the European powers, and the border disputes between Middle Eastern states themselves. But it had little to say on the nature of the newly emerging regimes of the region.

These lacunae arose from the ambitiously comprehensive scope of the *Survey*. But British historian Albert Hourani struck upon a more substantial defect of the *Survey*, in a review of the *Survey* volume on the Middle East during the Second World War. The *Survey*'s coverage of the Middle East, wrote Hourani, had always been "marked by respect for the Muslim world as an entity with its own standards and forms of development, and by sensitiveness to all the implications, in time and eternity, of the relations between Islam and Christendom." But a tendency to moralize clouded the *Survey*'s presentation of contemporary events:

> What makes me uneasy is the element of moral judgment which has entered so prominently into the *Survey* since the nineteen-thirties. In this volume there is perhaps too much of it. The Zionist leaders are

guilty of "intrigue, deceit, flattery, and corruption"; the Iraqi officers were filled with "a desire to hurt and avenge"; Rashid Ali and his group were victims of "ignorance and egoism," and so on . . . . A foreigner reading this book might well be bewildered by the contrast between its studiously objective, detached, and impersonal manner and the intensely subjective feelings and convictions it expresses.[17]

In his response to this criticism of the *Survey's* moralizing, Toynbee argued that there was an "inescapable necessity of making moral judgments," particularly on those contemporary issues that might constitute matters of life or death for author and reader alike. There was also "an inescapable moral obligation to judge as justly as human nature can," and to do so in "parliamentary language."[18] As the years passed, it was Britain that bore the brunt of his moral judgment, especially for its policy in the Middle East. The Middle Eastern sections of the *Survey* revolved around the confrontation of Middle Eastern nationalism and Western imperialism, portrayed as a moral rather than political contest.

When that contest ended, the *Survey* became unmanageable. The postwar multiplicity of loyalties and states, in the Middle East and elsewhere, made the continuation of the *Survey* along previous lines an impossible task. When "international relations" meant the relationship of a small number of European powers to one another and the rest of the world, they could be covered from a few accessible sources in one annual volume. But in the 1950s and 1960s, the Survey was overwhelmed by the emergence of dozens of new states and a flood of material generated by and about them. The discussion of the Middle East in the postwar volumes was freed from Toynbeean strictures once the editorship passed to other hands. But the region received less attention in the diminished volumes of the postwar years. By the time the *Survey* wound down—a victim, like *Oriente Moderno,* of the diminished standing in the world of the host country, and a drying up of resources—it had ceased to command the attention of students of the Middle East. The last volume covered 1963.

To Promote Understanding

The Second World War accelerated the processes of decolonization and independence in the Middle East, making Paris the center of another major initiative. The war had dealt a sharp blow to the standing of France in the Middle East, and the Free French under General de Gaulle sought a systematic understanding of the changes wrought by the war in the region. To fill the gap in knowledge, the Free French turned to Évariste Lévi-Provençal.

A professor at the University of Algiers before the war, Lévi-Provençal had devoted his scholarly career to the study of Muslim Spain and Morocco. The Orientalist scholar was wrenched from his pursuits when he lost his chair following the implementation of racial laws by the Vichy regime. Lévi-Provençal then joined the Free French in 1942, setting aside his historical research to interpret contemporary Middle Eastern affairs. In December 1943, in liberated Algiers, the Free French decreed the establishment of the Institut d'études de l'Orient contemporain and entrusted its development to Lévi-Provençal.

Its purpose was "to proceed, by direct observation and by acquisition of printed documentation, to the scientific study of the problems posed by the political, social, economic, and cultural evolution of the peoples of the Orient (Muslim Asia and Africa)." Following the Liberation, Lévi-Provençal came to Paris, and in April 1945 he was appointed to a professorship created for him at the Sorbonne. The Institut d'études de l'Orient contemporain moved to Paris that same year, and set up shop in a hotel suite; Lévi-Provençal lived in one of the back rooms. That year, the new institute published the first issue of the *Cahiers de l'Orient contemporain*.[19]

In launching this new initiative, Lévi-Provençal noted the great French contribution to the development of Orientalist scholarship.

> All the same, one might observe that too often, in this highly merito-rious labor, the present is sacrificed to the past. For several decades, other European countries have had official bodies charged with the mission of exploring the modern Orient, while France still lacks a scientific institution expressly devoted to guiding and coordinating the efforts of all those who, under various auspices, are interested in aspects of Islam today.[20]

Lévi-Provençal, too, had the Istituto per l'Oriente in mind, and drew his inspiration from *Oriente Moderno*. His new journal claimed to be "exclusively documentary, conceived and compiled according to a strictly objective plan." Its sponsoring institute disclaimed any political bias. As with *Oriente Moderno*, the *Cahiers* defined the Orient as the Middle East, and its structure also resembled that of the Italian journal. Each issue included an overview of the period under review, documents in translation, and a "synthèse chronologique" on foreign involvement, inter-Arab relations and political developments in each surveyed country—all based on a systematic reading of the indigenous press. This synthesis constituted the core of the journal, and its high editorial standards matched those of *Oriente Moderno.*

Lévi-Provençal was a scholar of profoundly liberal spirit, who envisioned the new institute as a means to promote French understanding of the new Middle East of independent states. One of the declared purposes of his institute was "to promote, on scientific grounds, cooperation and mutual understanding between French and Oriental elites." Once in Paris, Lévi-Provençal became a critic of attempts to reestablish France's damaged standing in Muslim lands by force; he was later an active member of the Comité France-Maghreb, alongside many other leading French Orientalists. French readers could find a surfeit of evidence for Middle Eastern outrage against French policy in North Africa on the pages of the *Cahiers.*

The *Cahiers* covered twenty-six years of the contemporary Middle East. It drew strength from the presence in Paris of eminent institutions of Islamic studies, which provided a succession of leaders and the battery of researchers who scoured the Middle Eastern press. But the combination of state support and scholarly resources began to come apart in the mid-1960s, and the *Cahiers* finally fell casualty to the turmoil that swept the Sorbonne in 1968. The last issue of the *Cahiers* appeared in 1969, and nothing succeeded it as a French survey of the contemporary Middle East.

Information Revolution

All of the great press-based projects—*Oriente Moderno,* the *Survey of International Affairs,* and the *Cahiers de l'Orient contemporain*—eventually collapsed because they could no longer sustain the commitment of official and scholarly communities. By their nature, they were expensive initiatives that involved the acquisition of masses of material, its processing by highly skilled teams, and rapid publication of the results. The withdrawal of Europe from the Middle East made it difficult to justify these projects in terms of national interest.

But another cause for the decline of the great press-based projects was a revolution in the dissemination of information from Middle Eastern sources. The European powers had used radio transmissions in Middle Eastern languages as means of propaganda during the war; after the war, the airwaves of the Middle East were filled by the radio transmissions of newly independent Middle Eastern states.

The British began the systematic monitoring of these transmissions, and the Americans soon followed. The British and Americans also published the transcripts of these transmissions on a daily basis, eliminating the need for press summaries.

Projects with a core element of press summary, like *Oriente Moderno* and the *Cahiers de l'Orient contemporain,* were gradually overwhelmed by this information revolution. For a time, the monitoring bulletins of the British Broadcasting Corporation enjoyed preeminence, but they could not keep pace with the American appetite for information. The daily report on broadcasts from the Middle East prepared by the Washington-based Foreign Broadcast Information Service, and the parallel press translations of the Joint Publications Research Service, constituted an investment of time and talents on a scale that only the government of a superpower could afford.

These publications, which gradually revolutionized the way academics researched contemporary events in the Middle East, were not produced under academic auspices. No academic institution could meet the demanding needs of governments, which now required information not on a quarterly or monthly basis, but from day to day and hour to hour. But while no scholarly enterprise could satisfy this kind of urgency, scholars did aspire to give order to this mass of information. From comprehensive and systematic documentation, the academic emphasis shifted to comprehensive and systematic interpretation.

The first strides perhaps should have been made in the universities of the United States, the seats of the fastest-growing interest in the contemporary Middle East. But nothing emerged in the United States to succeed the large contemporary surveys that had flourished in Europe. The style of American academic expertise created many obstacles to such a project. The ethos of individualism in American academe, reinforced by requirements of promotion, channeled the American study of contemporary affairs into books and journals. Other obstacles might best be described as structural. These included the geographic dispersal of Middle Eastern studies in many centers, and the distance of leading academic centers from the fulcrum of political power in Washington. The individualism and geographic decentralization of American Middle Eastern studies drove American universities to vie with one another in the recruitment of the best European scholars. But the European approach of collective scholarship failed to take root in the expanses of America.

Sober Fact

This was not the case in the new state of Israel, where prevailing conditions made for a successful graft of this branch of the European tradition of scholarship. Israel not only inherited the most exacting philological methods, imported by Jewish émigré scholars from Central Europe. Israel also encouraged the study of the contemporary Middle East, which occupied a high rung on the ladder of national priorities. And this study tended to be concentrated in a few select institutions.

In 1959, the Israel Oriental Society in Jerusalem gained official support for the establishment of the Reuven Shiloah Research Center. The Shiloah Center began much like its European predecessors, as an independent research institution operating under academic auspices with official support. The research council of the new center included noted academics and analysts, but the lead figure was Yitzhak Oron, a veteran of the research branch of Israeli military intelligence. It was Oron who had the idea of launching an annual survey, which would distinguish itself by its straightforward and disinterested presentation of the facts. Oron, born in what had been East Prussia (which he had escaped as a teenager in 1939), embodied the tradition of German Jewish precision. He assembled a research staff for the production of the new annual publication, entitled the *Middle East Record*. The first volume, covering 1960, appeared in 1962.

An avowed positivism informed the *Middle East Record*. "The student of Middle East politics has at his disposal a wealth of analysis, comment and judgment," announced the preface to the first volume, "but singularly little sober fact is readily available by which to check them." This made it difficult for the historian or analyst to proceed to interpretative studies. The *Middle East Record* proposed to establish the irreducible core of facts from which all other work could proceed:

> The aim of this work is to present the facts in full detail and from the widest possible variety of sources. Where the facts are disputed—and that happens frequently enough in the Middle East—all available versions are quoted, precedence being given to official statements. When it is a matter of underlying motives and causes, or the significance and consequences of events, both official statements and unofficial comment are treated as facts to be recorded.[21]

The *Middle East Record* shunned explicit interpretation, preferring a straightforward and dry narrative of events. But an appetite for "facts" was the great merit of the *Middle East Record*: nearly everything brought up in the research net was deemed suitable for presentation, and the *Middle East Record* immediately became a formidable source of information, both useful and arcane. The contributors drew upon radio monitoring reports and a collection of Middle Eastern newspapers unrivaled in the world (much of it supplied by agencies of the state). The research staff scoured the newspapers and established a disciplined regimen for the processing of their findings into a highly organized final product. The *Middle East Record* covered the Middle East's relations with the wider world, the relations between countries of the region, and the internal political affairs and international relations of the individual countries. The first volume ran to six hundred pages, each comprised of two solemn columns of small print. The table of contents alone filled fifteen pages.

Did the *Middle East Record* achieve its aim of neutral objectivity? The answer depended on the beholder. An Arab reviewer found it "highly unreliable—not so much for what it says, but for what it does not say. At best, it is a self-image and a portrayal of how the Israelis regard their neighbors and the world; and at worst, a piece of Israeli propaganda with sugar coating."[22] But the British Arabist S. H. Longrigg, after describing himself as "a life-long non-Zionist," marveled at "the patent impartiality with which both sides of all questions, however bitterly controversial, are treated. Although it is wholly an Israeli production, the Arab side, whether of events or claims or opinions, is given as fully and unemotionally as that of Israel . . . . Can one of the Arab universities produce something equivalent to this volume? It could be very interesting."[23]

But in one instance, the *Middle East Record* was forced to omit "the facts." In the first volume, the chapter on Israel included forty-five pages on domestic politics, including the Lavon Affair—a political scandal of personal concern to then-prime minister and defense minister David Ben-Gurion. A prerelease copy of the completed book was submitted to his office, which informed Oron that the volume could not appear if it included this chapter. Oron protested in a letter: "1960 was a stormy year in Israel, and we could not record it as anything but stormy . . . . The world will respect us if we demonstrate objectivity about ourselves . . . Otherwise, we will be regarded as propagandists."[24] To no avail: the chapter would have to go, or the book would be banned. The offending chapter was removed, causing a publication delay of two and a half months. The second volume also omitted Israeli domestic affairs. They finally received their due in the third volume, devoted to the crucial year of 1967, by which time Ben-Gurion had left politics (and Oron had left for the Mossad).[25]

The *Middle East Record* constituted an achievement that could not be matched—and one that the Shiloah Center could not sustain. The retrievable "facts" of politics were simply too numerous. The gap between the year of record and the year of publication widened with the second volume—an unmistakable sign that the concept of the project exceeded its resource base. Nor was the Shiloah Center in a position to appreciably expand that base. Its product was the first of its kind addressed primarily to an audience outside the country where it was produced. For this reason, the *Middle East Record* did not secure the consistent state support needed by the Shiloah Institute to survive.

The Shiloah Center was saved through incorporation in Tel Aviv University in 1966, but it did not have the resources to sustain the overly ambitious plan of the *Middle East Record*. All told, the *Record* covered six years of the decade between 1961 and 1970; the last volume, published in 1977, lagged seven years behind the events it surveyed.

At that point, the Shiloah Center regrouped, to produce a more compact annual publication, the *Middle East Contemporary Survey (MECS)*. The first volume, covering 1976–77, appeared in 1978. In some respects, the new venture was but a scaled-down version of the *Middle East Record*. But the downsizing also required a different approach. Contributors were no longer charged with harvesting masses of "facts" for a narrative. Instead they were to produce analytical essays incorporating only that factual material deemed significant to the individual contributor's own interpretation of events. *MECS* declared itself an "annual record and analysis of political, economic, military, and international developments in the Middle East," implicitly confessing the obvious truth that even the selection of "sober fact" rested upon analytic judgment. *MECS* incorporated a large amount of factual material, drawn from a wide array of press sources and radio monitoring reports. But contributors, for the most part historians of the Middle East, were expected to place this material not only in chronological and thematic order, but in analytical frameworks of their own choice. Ultimately, twenty-four volumes appeared, the last covering the year 2000.

MECS became a standard reference work, appearing in a more timely manner than the *Middle East Record* and employing both Israeli and foreign contributors. It became the distinctive flagship publication of the Dayan Center (which replaced the Shiloah Center), and an entire generation of its researchers produced chapter after chapter, year after year. Many of the contributors took the material assembled for *MECS* and recycled it for the production of scholarly books. Yet when the Dayan Center finally discontinued *MECS*, it was because younger scholars saw survey writing as drudgery, and preferred to invest in forms of scholarly publication held in higher esteem by the academy. In any event, *MECS* could not have continued into the twenty-first century without transitioning (like other reference works) to an online platform—a move that would have been costly and complicated.

Lasting Legacy?

Two questions are posed by a retrospective consideration of these twentieth-century surveys. First, would it be most useful to view them as state-sponsored, quasi-official intelligence operations? Virtually all of them enjoyed the support of their governments at some point in their development, and they flourished usually in tandem with the growth of official interest in the Middle East. Is it Edward Said's condemnatory approach that should inform how we understand and judge these projects?

If it is, then we are liable to succumb to the same ahistorical distortion that is the hallmark of the broader Saidian critique of Orientalism. Yes, the rise and decline of the surveys broadly followed the rise and decline of official interest in the Middle East. These were complex and costly projects, and without some form of external support, they would have been impossible to sustain over decades.

Yet it would be myopic to overlook the tension between the scholars, motivated by the pursuit of truth, and state sponsors, with their mixed agenda of collecting some truths and suppressing others. This tension manifested itself in the financial history of every survey project. In virtually every instance, survey projects had to scramble for resources, for which some more practical project always had a superior claim. In this ongoing negotiation, sometimes the scholars prevailed, sometimes the state did. Usually, compromise relieved the tension and allowed the surveys to go forward. Like any human endeavor, the surveys have to be set in a political, economic, and social context. But it would be a gross error to cast them only as complicit and dependent, when in many respects they were subversive and independent.

The second question is whether humankind today is poorer for the absence of such surveys. The chain has been broken: nowhere today is there a successor to these twentieth-century projects, which once engaged the talents of scholars at the very center of their disciplines. If there even exist modern equivalents of Massignon, Nallino, or Lévi-Provençal, it seems doubtful they would submit to the grinding routine of writing or editing annual surveys. The contemporary Middle East has become a hot topic. Far more glamorous work now attracts specialists, whether it is writing for general audiences, or spinning out social science theories that testify to a scholar's originality and ingenuity—that is, until reality interrupts theory.

Agenda-driven think tanks are not likely to renew the survey tradition either. Think tanks are policy-oriented or harnessed to causes. Some put out annual reports about the Middle East, on subjects as diverse as terrorism, human rights, press freedom, and military affairs. But none of these reports pretends to be comprehensive, or to offer a narrative of events for the record. Instead they are designed and written to inspire some action, usually by agencies of government, and they include and omit information in accord with the policies they advocate.

Finally, it may be that the immediacy of the internet has rendered the survey, annual or otherwise, superfluous. One obvious need met by the surveys was the quick checking of a fact. One (unfriendly) reviewer of *MECS*, writing in the late 1980s just before the internet, still allowed that "it is easier (and more convenient) to look through this volume than to go through newspaper microfilms to reconstruct events."[26] But why should one consult a costly reference work, produced at some delay in time, when one can find an up-to-date answer that is "good enough" in a Wikipedia entry? The powerful search engines constructed by Google put a range of authoritative sources within easy reach, and it is possible to access the Arabic, Persian, Hebrew, and Turkish press from anywhere in the world, at the click of a mouse. With a password to a few major databases, any scholar or student can quickly reconstruct the events of a given year, month, week, or day. This revolution is profound, and it will only gather momentum with the passage of time.

Yet when one revisits the work on the contemporary Middle East written in real time right through the twentieth century, does anything hold up as well as the surveys? Most of the books and articles that excited readers in their time are period pieces, relics of long-forgotten debates of scant interest today. In contrast, the contemporary surveys still repay reading, because they document and describe the Middle East in an almost timeless narrative style. There is lasting value in the scrupulous accounting of deeds and misdeeds, of the choices made by states, leaders, and peoples even as they made them. Will anything in the running commentary on the Middle East in this twenty-first century prove as enduring?

Notes

1. Henry Laurens, "Le Chatelier, Massignon, Montagne: Politique musulmane et orientalisme," in *Istanbul et les Langues orientales = Varia Turcica* 31 (1997): 497–529; Edmund Burke, III, *The Ethnographic State: France and the Invention of Moroccan Islam* (Berkeley: University of California Press, 2014).

2. A. Le Chatelier. "A un maitre d'école de Médinet el-Fayoum," *Revue du monde musulman* 1/1 (November 1906): 1–5. The *Revue* is available online at http://gallica.bnf.fr/ark:/12148/cb328592223/date.r=revue+du+monde+musulman.langFR.

3. *The Revue du monde musulman* is set in its contemporary context by Edmund Burke, III, "The First Crisis of Orientalism, 1890–1914," in *Connaissances du Maghreb: Sciences sociales et colonisation*, ed. Jean-Claude Vatin (Paris: CNRS, 1984), 220–22.

4. *Revue du monde musulman* 65–66 (3rd and 4th trimesters 1926), vi (footnote).

5. "Ce que doit être une documentation périodique sur les problèmes politiques et sociaux du Monde musulman," *Revue du monde musulman* 36 (1918–19): 1–9.

6. For Massignon's ambivalence toward Arab nationalism, see Giuseppe Contu, "Il mondo arabo contemporaneo nell'opera di Louis Massignon," in *Atti del Convegno sul centenario della nascita di Louis Massignon*, ed. Carmela Baffioni (Napoli: Istituto Universitario Orientale, 1985), 71–82.

7. In 1924, Massignon published the first edition of the *Annuaire du Monde musulman*; subsequent editions appeared in 1926, 1929, and 1955. Massignon wrote that the *Annuaire* was inspired by the *Handbooks* produced by the British of the Cairo Arab Bureau during the First World War. Massignon's *Annuaire* was a yearbook of facts and figures, not an annual survey of events, and it enjoyed neither the reputation nor the longevity of the *Revue du monde musulman*.

8. "Il nostro programma," *Oriente Moderno* o.s. 1 (1921): 1–2. *Oriente Moderno*, with the exception of its first year, is available at JSTOR, http://www.jstor.org/journal/orientemoderno.

9. Virginia Vacca, "Nallino e l'Istituto per l'Oriente," *Levante* (Rome) 20/1 (March 1973), 60–66.

10. The judgment of G. Levi Della Vida, "Carlo Alfonso Nallino," *Oriente Moderno* o.s. 18 (1938): 475.

11. Vincenzo Strika, "C.A. Nallino e l'impres libica," *Quaderni di Studi Arabi* (Venice) 2 (1984): 9–20, and Federico Cresti, "Il professore e il generale: La polemica tra Carlo Alfonso Nallino e Rodolfo Graziani sulla Senussia e su altre questioni libiche," *Studi Storici* 45 (2004): 1113–49.

12. A brief personal history of *Oriente Moderno*'s production is provided by Francesco Gabrieli, "I vecchi tempi dell'Istituto per l'Oriente," *Oriente Moderno* n.s. 3 (1984): 51–55.

13. Preface to Arnold J. Toynbee, *Survey of International Affairs, 1920–23* (London: Royal Institute of International Affairs, 1925), vi.
14. Coverage of the Middle East may be found in the *Survey* for 1925, 1928, 1930, 1934, 1936, 1937 and 1938; in the volumes by George Kirk entitled *The Middle East in the War, 1939–1946* and *The Middle East, 1945–1950*; and in all subsequent volumes of the *Survey* beginning in 1951.
15. Elie Kedourie, *The Chatham House Version and other Middle-Eastern Studies* (London: Weidenfeld and Nicolson, 1970), 382.
16. Arnold J. Toynbee, *Survey of International Affairs, 1925*, vol. 1: *The Islamic World since the Peace Settlement* (London: Royal Institute of International Affairs, 1927), vii.
17. *International Affairs* 24 (1953): 204–5.
18. Arnold J. Toynbee, "The Writing of Contemporary History for Chatham House," *International Affairs* 29 (1953): 138–9.
19. Emilio Garcia Gomez, "E. Lévi-Provençal," *Al-Andalus* 21 (1956): xi–xvi.
20. "L'Institut d'études de l'Orient contemporain," *Cahiers de l'orient contemporain* 1 (1945): 1.
21. *Middle East Record* 1 (1960): vii.
22. Review by: Fahim I. Qubain, *Middle East Journal* 17 (Autumn 1963): 454.
23. Review by Stephen H. Longrigg, *International Affairs* 48 (January 1972): 141.
24. Yitzhak Sokolovsky Oron, *Le-Toldotav shel ha-Merkaz le-Mehkar al-shem Reuven Shiloah, 1958–1965* (Tel Aviv: The Moshe Dayan Center for Middle Eastern and African Studies, 2006), 43.
25. Obituary of Oron by Ofer Aderet, *Ha'aretz*, July 31, 2014.
26. Review by Madeleine Tress, *Middle East Studies Association Bulletin* 22, no. 2 (December 1988): 233.

This article is republished with the generous permission of the Jewish-Arab Center at the University of Haifa.

4

Policy and the Academy

One of the issues that is much discussed since 9/11 is the proper relationship between policy and the academy. For a host of reasons, a very wide gap exists between the two.

In part, this has to do with the political predilections of the academy. Much of the academy is left of center, distrusts anything that smacks of national security, thinks of itself in opposition to power, and imagines that the slightest contact with agencies of policy might infect and corrupt the agencies of thought represented by the academy. But the gap also arises from the highly overspecialized state of academe—its domination by theories, methodologies, and jargons that are inaccessible to anyone beyond the campus gates (and to many people inside the campus gates as well).

Since 9/11, some have made bold to ask whether something should be done to close the gap, especially when it comes to the knowledge needed to formulate foreign policy. In the United States, government has made a sweeping gesture: since 9/11, it has showered the academy with new funds to promote the study of foreign languages and cultures, especially of Muslim countries. And a few voices have been raised, especially among political scientists, arguing that the academy has been shirking its duty, and that it should render service if it expects to remain relevant.[1] Some in academe are beginning to appreciate a point made by the Orientalist Gustave von Grunebaum back in 1965:

> No group, society, or civilization, so history allows us to postulate, will consistently support an intellectual endeavor unless it believes this effort to be serviceable either to its practical or to its existential needs—and one may do well to remind oneself that it is, in the last analysis, the existential need that determines what is to be recognized as socially useful and thus as a practical need.[2]

Von Grunebaum's law is as demonstrable as gravity, as every academic empire-builder is bound to discover sooner or later.

But there is a fly in this ointment, in the form of an essay by Elie Kedourie. It is entitled "Foreign Policy: A Practical Pursuit," and it was originally published in 1961, in *The Princetonian*.[3] In it, the author repudiates the idea that academics have any business urging foreign policies on their governments. It is an argument that few would make today. Yet can the argument be lightly dismissed? Who was Elie Kedourie, and why should his essay of half a century ago detain us now?

Dissident Conservative

Elie Kedourie (1926–92), professor of politics at the London School of Economics (LSE), was the most formidable practitioner of a dissident historiography of the Middle East.

In detailed studies of British diplomatic history, Kedourie attributed the failure of British imperial will in the Middle East to romantic illusions about the Arab-Muslim world. In his studies of Middle Eastern politics, he documented the importation of radical nationalism that ultimately transformed the Middle East into what he called "a wilderness of tigers." A deep conservatism, born of a disbelief in the redemptive power of ideological politics, suffused all of Kedourie's writings. Armed with a potent and lucid style, he waged a determined defense against the siege of Middle Eastern history by leftist theory, the social sciences, and fashionable third worldism. Kedourie's iconoclastic work forms the foundation of that diffuse school that views the modern history of the Middle East not as an "awakening" but as a resurgence of its own despotic tradition, exacerbated by the West's dissemination of the doctrine of self-determination.

In Kedourie's later years, he became a well-known public intellectual in the United States, warning Americans against the same flagging of will that had diminished Britain. While his influence among conservative American intellectuals grew, he became disillusioned by the declining standards of British universities, including his own. He retired from the LSE in 1990, and was about to take up a new chair in modern Middle Eastern history at Brandeis University when he died suddenly at the age of sixty-six. In an essay, the historian Efraim Karsh described Kedourie as a "forgotten iconoclast."[4] Yet his work remains an inspiration for the small but influential group of scholars who continue to challenge the orthodoxies of Middle Eastern studies.

Had Kedourie been an economic or social historian, his ideas on foreign policy and the academy might be brushed aside. But he was first and foremost a diplomatic historian. No one outside the British

Foreign Office understood the mechanisms of British policymaking better than he did, and no one knew the archival record of Britain's choices in the Middle East as well as he did. For all these reasons, the essay entitled "Foreign Policy: A Practical Pursuit," deserves—and repays—close reading.

Learned Fools

Kedourie begins his essay by stating the obvious: foreign policy is a practical pursuit. It is not speculation; its purpose is "the attainment of advantage or the prevention of mischief." At which point, Kedourie asks this question: "Is the academic fitted by his bent, his training, his usual and wonted preoccupations, to take or recommend action of the kind which generals and statesmen are daily compelled to recommend or take?"[5]

Some would say yes, adds Kedourie; after all, academics have "a highly trained intelligence, they are long familiar with the traffic of ideas, and long accustomed scrupulously to weigh evidence, to make subtle distinctions, and to render dispassionate verdicts." But Kedourie begs to differ:

> If the academic is to recommend action here and now—and in foreign policy action must be here and now—should he not have exact and prompt knowledge of situations and their changes? Is it then proposed that foreign ministries should every morning circulate to historians and "social scientists" the reports of their agents and the dispatches of their diplomats? Failing this knowledge, the academic advising or exhorting action will most likely appear the learned fool, babbling of he knows not what.[6]

Kedourie then immediately anticipates the riposte:

> It may be objected that this is not what is meant at all; we do not, it may be said, want the academic to concern himself with immediate issues or the *minutiae* of policies; we want his guidance on long-term trends and prospects; and here, surely, his knowledge of the past, his erudition, his reflectiveness will open to him vistas unknown to the active politician, or unregarded by him. And should not this larger view, this wider horizon be his special contribution to his country's policies and to its welfare?[7]

Yet this, too, Kedourie rejects. "This appeal to patriotism, this subtle flattery, needs must be resisted," he writes. Why? "The long view, the balanced view, the judicious view, can positively unfit a man for action, and for giving advice on action." To make policy, writes Kedourie, is to leap into the unknown.

> Shall academics presume to instruct a man how he shall leap? Presumption is the pride of fools, and it ought to be the scholar's pride not to presume. It is pursuit of knowledge and increase in learning which gives scholars renown and a good name. How then should they, clothed as they are in the mantle of scholarship, yet imitate this lobby or that pressure group, and recommend this action or that, all the time knowing full well that in politics one is always acting in a fog, that no action is wholly to the good, and that every action in benefiting one particular interest will most likely be to another's detriment.[8]

Contra Toynbee

From these passages, one might conclude that there was no equivocation in Kedourie's position. In fact, we shall see that Kedourie did allow for a seemingly narrow exception to his rule. But before we explore it, some aspects of the essay are worth noting.

Kedourie published it during a stint as a visiting professor at Princeton, and at a time when he must have been largely unknown in America. But it would have been especially apt for an American readership.

Remember that in 1961, Harvard professors were flooding Washington, invited down from Cambridge by John F. Kennedy. It was as close to an academic takeover of Washington as there ever would be. That year, McGeorge Bundy, dean of arts and sciences at Harvard, left the university to become Kennedy's special assistant for national security. In 1961 another Harvard professor, John Kenneth Galbraith, left the university to serve as U.S. ambassador to India. Again in 1961 a Harvard history professor, Arthur Schlesinger, Jr., left the university to serve as Kennedy's adviser and speechwriter. No American reader could have read through Kedourie's piece without thinking of the so-called best and brightest from the academy who had assumed key policy positions. (Interestingly, *The Princetonian* elected to publish Kedourie's piece. It is difficult to imagine that all the to-do about Harvard in the new Kennedy administration did not grate on the Princetonians.)[9]

But Kedourie himself may not have had these Harvard professors in mind when he wrote his 1961 essay. The best evidence is that the essay gives only one specific example of an academic's folly, and it relates to none other than Arnold Toynbee, the celebrity historian against whom Kedourie would serve his most famous indictment, his 1970 essay "The Chatham House Version."

As it happened, the reference to Toynbee in this article touched not on the Middle East, but on China. It will be recalled that the Republican regime in China had made Nanjing its capital between the world wars, and that Toynbee had adduced this as more evidence for one of his laws, about the migration of power from the interior of countries to their coastal marches. In 1949, the Chinese communists broke Toynbee's law, by restoring Beijing as China's capital.

Kedourie chose this instance as the prime exhibit of academic obtuseness in his essay, in these memorable words: "The famed academic, Dr. Toynbee, writing his *Study of History* in 1935 came to the conclusion, on the weightiest and most erudite of grounds, that there was no likelihood of Peking ever again in the future becoming the capital of China! Should he not have remembered the sad and moving confession of Ibn Khaldun—a writer he much admired—that his minute knowledge of prosody unfitted him for the writing of poetry?"[10] It appears to have been Kedourie's first shot at "the famed academic, Dr. Toynbee," and he would repeat this very same Chinese example in a footnote to "The Chatham House Version."[11]

It is impossible to separate Kedourie's hard-line position on policy and the academy from his contempt for the policy interventions of Toynbee—a contempt that reached a crescendo in the 1960s. Indeed, a careful reading of "The Chatham House Version" reveals that at various points, Kedourie finds the very root of Toynbee's errors in his harnessing of history to policy and advocacy. As Kedourie put it: "The belief that there is a tight connection between the study of policy and the making of it, the assumption of the unity of theory and practice, has deeply marked the character and activities of Chatham House."[12] Toynbee himself, wrote Kedourie, "believed in the practical uses of history and had no compunction in exhorting and advising."[13] All of which not only had a deleterious effect on policy, but on the writing of history: "The desire to prescribe and prophesy was clearly one main reason why the Chatham House Version, as has been shown, also failed as history."[14]

The academic left justifies its rejection of an advisory role by arguing that proximity to power corrupts—that the mere interaction of the academy with policymakers could easily corrupt the professors and so should be abjured. Kedourie believed that the greater danger was that the professors would corrupt the policymakers—that they would infect them with dangerous theories. A consistent theme in Kedourie's work is the destructiveness of half-baked academic theories planted in the minds of decision-makers, whether democrats or despots. It was not only in the interest of academe, of its freedom and self-regulation, that it should refrain from advising. It was in the interest of society and the polity that the hazardous speculations of scholars be contained within the academy, lest they mutate into doctrinaire policies. Certainly this is what had happened at Chatham House, which Toynbee made into a transmission belt for English radicalism into British foreign policy.

Making Exception

So much for Kedourie's principled position. But Kedourie allowed for an exception to his rule, both in the 1961 piece and later. In 1961, he put it this way:

> Scholars, of course, are also citizens, and as such jealous for the welfare and honor of their country. Equally with other citizens they can recommend and exhort, but they should take care that a scholarly reputation does not illicitly give spurious authority to some civic or political stance.[15]

And again, in his posthumous essay on politics and the academy:

> The notion of freedom from political commitment does not imply that an author floats in some colorless empyrean, removed from all sublunar judgments and references. Such a being is simply unthinkable. Freedom from political commitment signifies what it says—namely, that *in his work*, the writer is not concerned to defend or attack some political cause in order to ensure either its victory or its defeat.[16]

As a particular example of a scholar who had failed to distinguish between his academic responsibilities and his politics, Kedourie offered Sir Hamilton Gibb. Gibb, Britain's preeminent Orientalist, had disapproved of Kedourie's Oxford thesis, on what Kedourie regarded as purely political grounds. Kedourie withdrew his dissertation and never received his degree. "Gibb was politically committed," Kedourie wrote years later. "He had strong sympathies and equally strong views about the right policies for the Middle East. In itself, this was not objectionable, but the political commitment fatally spilled over into, and encouraged, academic tendentiousness."[17]

Here we come closer to the heart of the issue. It is legitimate to have strong views about policies, writes Kedourie, but not to allow them to spill over into one's academic work, one's professional realm. One may advise, admonish, exhort, demonstrate—but not bring such commitments into the work area. Here was Kedourie's first concession to the fact that an academic is also a man (or a woman), and that man is a political animal. But Kedourie also insisted that the academic not be a political animal everywhere and always—not in his dominant role among students (as Gibb had been), and not in his university study.

Having written a book decrying what Kedourie called "academic tendentiousness"—the way in which political commitment has penetrated scholarly writing—I find myself in strong agreement with Kedourie on this point. Yes, academics are entitled to their views like anyone else, and they are entitled to demonstrate for them in the streets, hobnob with policymakers to express them, or even take a leave of absence to work as practitioners. What they are not entitled to do is inflict them on either their students or the readers of their academic work.

But how does one translate Kedourie's principle of virtuous scholarly conduct into practice? Consider his exhortation that scholars "should take care that a scholarly reputation does not illicitly give spurious authority to some civic or political stance." It is a fine principle, easiest to implement for scholars with very small reputations. But scholars do not control their scholarly reputations; it would be a very different world if they did. When those reputations grow large, scholars' names become inseparable from their scholarly accomplishments.

If a scholar takes a political position as a citizen, how can he possibly neutralize the effect of his scholarly reputation on the reception of that political position? How would one expect a Noam Chomsky, or an Edward Said, or a Bernard Lewis, or an Elie Kedourie to actually *do* this? Would it suffice if Professor Noam Chomsky, MIT, signed his diatribes on Palestine as Mr. Noam Chomsky, Lexington, Massachusetts? It probably would be a good thing if scholars could agree never to sign a political petition with their academic titles and affiliations, never to speak at a political gathering as professor of this or that. But it is obvious that such an attempt to separate the person from the persona is destined to fail.

More intriguing is Kedourie's admonition that a scholar, *in his work*, should not defend or attack some political cause in order to ensure either its victory or its defeat. Elsewhere, Kedourie gives examples of "work" that might serve as models: Edward Gibbon's *Decline and Fall*, von Grunebaum on medieval Islam, Jakob Burckhardt on the Italian Renaissance, Fustel de Coulanges on the ancient city, S. D. Goitein's *A Mediterranean Society*. Of these works, Kedourie writes, "by no conceivable stretch of the imagination can they be said to work in favor of a political cause or against it."[18] Kedourie is most probably right, although it is telling that he does not cite a work of modern history among these examples (or, for that matter, von Grunebaum's work on modern Islam).

But where does "work" end in contemporary academe? The classroom should not be a forum for political advocacy by professors. But once an academic has taught his hours, supervised his theses, and written for peer review and promotion, there is occasion for other pursuits, other lecturing, and other books.

For example, professors Chomsky and Said are committed to the Palestinian cause. In Professor Chomsky's book *Syntactic Structures*, Palestine is not mentioned. Nor is it mentioned in Edward Said's *Beginnings: Intention and Method*. Both gentlemen did their "work" in their respective fields, linguistics and literature. Is Chomsky's subsequent authorship of *Fateful Triangle*, or Said's later writing of *The Question of Palestine*, a transgression of Kedourie's principle? If so, how? Kedourie takes Edward Granville Browne to task for his 1911 book, *The Persian Revolution*, a volume that Kedourie rightly calls a "failure" as history.[19] But Browne did not purport to be a historian. He was a philologist and incumbent of a chair of Arabic, whose principal "work" was his four-volume *Literary History of Persia*. When it came to contemporary politics, Browne was a naked partisan, but it could well be argued that *The Persian Revolution* was not his "work," only his pleasure.

In sum, even Kedourie allows sufficient exception to his own principle as to make it nearly unworkable. In no realm of endeavor does the notion of "company time" have less meaning than in academe. And in no realm of endeavor is the notion of "work" more elastic. Kedourie was always a staunch defender of the academy's privilege of self-regulation—he was an LSE adherent of the Oxbridge ideal. But what is the mechanism of academic self-regulation, if not peer review? And has not peer review defined what once would have been considered blatant political advocacy as "work"? It is peer review that determines what is "work" and what is not, so that we stand today in astonishment at what university presses publish, which books appear in syllabi, which publications confer tenure.

So while Kedourie may have restated the problem, he didn't solve it. And his exceptions to his rule—a scholar might act politically as a citizen, outside his "work"—opened precisely those loopholes that have made the academy so political a place. In any case, arguing that advocacy is inappropriate—that it is a betrayal of a professional code—is something akin to confronting a stampede of cattle with a stop sign. The more practical question, then, is this one: what does a scholar do, once surrounded by other scholars who advocate foolish or dangerous policies? This was the actual situation in which Kedourie found himself, time and again, to which he found an interesting answer.

Discreet Consultant

The answer is that Kedourie began to take advantage of that very exception he himself had allowed. As his reputation grew, more people from the media and government called upon him for his advice on foreign policy. He gave it. By the 1980s, Kedourie's views on matters of policy were very much in demand, and his writing also became more contemporary. It was never straightforward policy writing, which is a distinct art, but Kedourie led his reader ineluctably to a policy conclusion—even if he did so only by way of a question.

Here is but one example. In 1978, Kedourie published an article in *Encounter* entitled "How to (and How Not to) Seek Peace in the Middle East." In it, he analyzed the weaknesses of a now-forgotten policy report on the Middle East prepared by the Brookings Institution in the mid-1970s. The report had determined that the security and future development of Arabs and Israelis would remain in jeopardy "until a durable settlement is concluded." This sort of banality is so ubiquitous that we no longer notice it. Yet listen to Kedourie interrogate it:

> Is it not conceivable that the very search for a "durable" settlement between Arabs and Israelis will so exacerbate matters, and arouse among various parties such fears for their security and interests, that tensions in the area will be *increased* rather than lessened? Again, may it not be the case that a "durable settlement" will do nothing to provide "security and future development"? This is simply because the political and social problems of the Middle East are such as to preclude stability in any conceivable future. The Arab world today is the prey of an ideological and activist style of politics that is not compatible with stability.[20]

Without having stated a policy preference, Kedourie effectively expressed one. Had he only been in America in the 1990s to argue for it, perhaps his cautionary questions would have dampened the giddy euphoria for a "durable settlement" that has produced the present impasse.

Kedourie did more than write on policy. He also advised. Yet he gave advice with an exquisite discretion that reflected his determination to maintain something of that sacrosanct distinction between the academic cloister and the political arena. Peter Roberts, in his contribution to Kedourie's memorial volume, has an interesting passage on Kedourie and policymakers that strikes just the right tone:

> Those directly concerned with government also had a high regard for his [Kedourie's] knowledge of, and insight into, the contemporary world. He was discreet and modest about his relations with leading politicians and never discussed them with me. The interviewer in Canada asked him about his influence on Pierre Trudeau. Elie made clear the former prime minister was never his student. When pressed about acknowledgement in Trudeau's books, Elie conceded that "there were some references." The open record of consultations made by political leaders is slight. It is, however, difficult to ignore it altogether. . . . It may be enough to say that the teacher of "government" had opportunities to observe those who governed. His observations perhaps reinforced his view that the tasks of the academic and even the journalist are different from the craft of making foreign policy.[21]

More could be said here, and some more was said in some of Kedourie's obituaries, especially about his occasional advice to Lady Thatcher during her premiership.

Scholar's Skepticism

Kedourie was a principled scholar but not a doctrinaire man. His position on policy and the academy might best be summarized in this manner: in an ideal world, the two should not meet, and to the extent feasible, the two should be separated; but in this less-than-ideal world, where the radical part of academe has so intruded itself in policy, the conservative part has a license to neutralize it by doing the same. Kedourie did not stand entirely above the fray. But at least he knew it was a fray and never confused it with academic "work"—"work" that he continued to pursue to his dying day, in his research on conservatism and Hegel. Kedourie had something to say on policy, and he said it; but he never professed to speak as a policy expert.

But there is one mischievous passage where Kedourie suggests that policymakers might have something to learn from professors after all. It perfectly summarizes where he came to rest on the question, and where perhaps all of us should come to rest. It is the last paragraph in his essay on "How to (and How Not to) Seek Peace in the Middle East."

> It is usually (and rightly) said that the academic's virtues—his critical turn of mind, and his willingness to follow the argument wherever it leads—become defects in the man of action, who must accustom

himself to make quick decisions on the basis of hunches and imperfect information. But in a region like the Middle East, where yesterday's friend can become today's opponent, where alliances and allegiances shimmer and dissolve like the *fata morgana*, the academic's skepticism, his readiness to scrutinize far-fetched theories and unlikely suppositions, are perhaps qualities that even busy men of action should cultivate.[22]

And perhaps, one might add by extension, busy men of action should cultivate academics who possess these qualities, and those academics should allow themselves to be cultivated. Why? Kedourie makes the ultimate exception to his own rule, and it is this: We are dealing, after all, with the Middle East.

Notes

1. Bruce W. Jentleson, "The Need for Praxis: Bringing Policy Relevance Back In," *International Security* 26, no. 4 (Spring 2002): 169–83; Larry Diamond, "What Political Science Owes the World," *PS: Online*, March 2002.
2. Gustave E. von Grunebaum, "Specialization," in *Arabic and Islamic Studies in Honor of Hamilton A. R. Gibb*, ed. George Makdisi (Cambridge, MA: Harvard University Press, 1965), 285.
3. Elie Kedourie, "Foreign Policy: A Practical Pursuit," *The Princetonian*, January 4, 1961, reproduced in Kedourie, *The Crossman Confessions and other Essays in Politics, History, and Religion* (London: Mansell, 1984), 133–6.
4. Efraim Karsh, "Elie Kedourie: The Forgotten Iconoclast," *International History Review* 21 (1999): 704–13.
5. Kedourie, "Foreign Policy," 133.
6. Ibid.
7. Ibid., 134.
8. Ibid., 135.
9. Kedourie later held up one of these Kennedy professors as an example of the dangers of the academic's intervention. He did so in his essay, "The Apprentice Sorcerers," where he reviewed Miles Copeland's *Game of Nations*. Kennedy had sent one of his economics professors, Edward Mason, to meet Nasser and report on the regime. As Copeland related, Professor Mason reported back to Kennedy that "he could not conscientiously find fault with any of Nasser's major actions"—including nationalizations, press censorship, arrests of dissidents, and propaganda assaults on Arab leaders friendly to the West. They were "actions which Nasser could logically be expected to take given his circumstances." As Kedourie wryly noted, it was "doubtful whether Nasser and his fellow-conspirators had any need to call on the resources of American political science for such lessons in tyranny." Elie Kedourie, *Arabic Political Memoirs and Other Studies* (London: Frank Cass, 1974), 174–5.
10. Kedourie, "Foreign Policy," 134.
11. Elie Kedourie, *The Chatham House Version and other Middle-Eastern Studies*, new ed. (Hanover, NH: University Press of New England for Brandeis University Press, 1984), 459, n. 51.

12. Ibid., 353.
13. Ibid., 392.
14. Ibid., 394. When Toynbee, in a rejoinder, claimed that the "key" to "The Chatham House Version" was "the tragic fate of the Jewish community in Baghdad," Kedourie shot back: "Has it not occurred to Professor Toynbee that the wish to rescue history from prescription and prophecy could actually be the key to my book?" Elie Kedourie, "Was Britain's Abdication Folly? I: A Reply to Arnold Toynbee," *The Round Table* (July 1970): 358.
15. Kedourie, "Foreign Policy," 135.
16. Elie Kedourie, "Politics and the Academy," *Commentary* (August 1992): 55.
17. Elie Kedourie, *England and the Middle East* (rev. ed.; London: Mansell, 1987), 8b.
18. Kedourie, "Politics and the Academy," 55.
19. Ibid., 53.
20. Elie Kedourie, *Islam in the Modern World and Other Studies* (New York: Holt, Reinhart, and Winston, 1980), 244.
21. Peter Roberts, "A Personal Memoir," in *Elie Kedourie CBE, FBA, 1926–1992: History, Philosophy, Politics,* ed. Sylvia Kedourie (London: Frank Cass, 1998), 82.
22. Kedourie, *Islam in the Modern World*, 248.

Part II

Missing Islam

5

Fundamentalists or Islamists?

No one who reads or writes about events in the Muslim world can avoid the question of how to label those Muslims who invoke Islam as the source of authority for all political and social action. Should they be labeled Islamic (or Muslim) fundamentalists? Or are they better described as Islamists?

The issue has been the subject of a heated debate for several decades. For a while, both general and scholarly usage in America accepted fundamentalism. Islamism emerged in the late 1980s in French academe and then crossed into English, where it eventually displaced Islamic fundamentalism in specialized contexts. More recently, the term Islamism has gained even wider currency, and since 9/11, it may even have established itself as the preferred American usage. Still newer terminology may lie over the horizon.

Behind the battle over usage lies another struggle, over the nature of the phenomenon itself. In fact, the two contests, over English usage and analytical understanding, are inseparable. Nor are they free of associations left by past usages. Here follows a short history of changing usage—itself a history of changing Western perceptions of Muslim reality.

The Debut of Islamism

The term Islamism first appeared in French in the mid-eighteenth century. But it did not refer to the modern ideological use of Islam, which had not yet come into being. Rather, it was a synonym for the religion of the Muslims, which was then known in French as *mahométisme,* the religion professed and taught by the Prophet Muhammad.

This usage dated to the early seventeenth century. It reflected a new willingness, born of the Renaissance, to recognize Islam as a religious system with a founder, like Christianity. But it rested upon the erroneous presumption that Muhammad stood in relation to Islam as Christ stood in relation to Christianity.[1] Nevertheless, the usage became pervasive across Europe. In 1734, George Sale, whose English translation of the Qur'an set a new standard, wrote: "It is certainly one of the most convincing proofs that Mohammedism was no other than a human invention, that it owed its progress and establishment almost entirely to the sword."[2] Even a century later, when attitudes to Islam had changed dramatically, it was still common to call the faith after the Prophet. In 1833, the French poet Alphonse de Lamartine demonstrated the change in European attitudes, even as he employed the old usage: "*Mahométisme* could effortlessly and painlessly accommodate a system based on religious and civil liberty . . . by nature, it is moral, forbearing, uncomplaining, charitable and tolerant."[3]

In the eighteenth century, the Western study of Islam made enormous strides, and polemical denigration no longer informed every Western pronouncement. The thinkers of the Enlightenment knew perfectly well that Muslims called their faith Islam. They searched for a way to reflect that understanding through usage and thus classify Islam as a religion appreciated in its own terms.

It was the French philosopher Voltaire who found the solution, when he coined the term *islamisme*. Voltaire had an abiding interest in Islam, and wrote extensively about it, comparing it to other faiths, sometimes favorably. He also understood the role of Muhammad in Islam, leading him to correct his readers: "This religion," he wrote, "is called *islamisme*."[4] Not only did his usage depart from Sale's, but so did his conclusion: "It was not by force of arms that *islamisme* established itself over more than half of our hemisphere. It was by enthusiasm and persuasion." The great nineteenth-century French dictionary by Littré quoted just this passage from Voltaire's *Essai sur les mœurs* when it defined *islamisme* as "the religion of Mahomet."

In the course of the nineteenth century, this usage gained ground throughout Europe. Alexis de Tocqueville, writing in 1838, found the "root of *islamisme* in Judaism."[5] In 1883, Ernest Renan, pioneer of philology, published an influential essay entitled *L'Islamisme et la science*. As a French historian has noted, Renan's use of *islamisme* "did not have the present-day sense of the political utilization of Islam."[6] Rather, he meant Islam. It is in this sense, too, that Islamism appeared in the *New English Dictionary* (now known as the *Oxford English Dictionary*) in a fascicle published in 1900. It defined Islamism as "the religious system of the Moslems; Mohammedanism." Even the word Islamist appeared there, defined as "an orthodox Mohammedan," and the entry included this example from a magazine article published in 1895: "Judgment should not be pronounced against Islam and Islamists on rancorous and partisan statements."

There are two points worth noting about the use of Islamism and *islamisme* in the nineteenth century. First, while it reflected a more accurate understanding of Islam's doctrine, it did not exclude critical interpretations of Islam's character. In a dispatch of 1873, a British consul wrote of "the inherent characteristics of Islamism," which he called "deficient in vitality," "aggressive," and "carrying in its bosom the seeds of decay."[7] The French Orientalist Baron Bernard Carra de Vaux wrote in 1901: "*Islamisme* is a spent religion."[8] In both cases the reference is to the religion of Islam per se, and in both cases it is clearly derogatory.

The second point is that Islamism and *islamisme* did not completely displace Mohammedanism and *mahométisme*, even in scholarship. In 1890, Ignaz Goldziher, the Hungarian Orientalist regarded as the founder of modern Islamic studies, published his two-volume study of the Muslim oral tradition (*hadith*) under the title *Muhammedanische Studien*. Other notable instances of its continued use in book titles include D. S. Margoliouth's *Mohammedanism* (1911), A. A. Fyzee's *Outlines of Muhammadan Law* (1949), and Joseph Schacht's *Origins of Muhammadan Jurisprudence* (1950).

Only at mid-century did this usage expire, primarily because Western writers realized that they also had Muslim readers who resented it. In 1946, the British Orientalist H. A. R. Gibb wrote an introduction to Islam in the same series that had included Margoliouth's *Mohammedanism* thirty-five years earlier. The publisher wished to keep the same title. Gibb assented, but he was quick to disavow it on the very first page: "Modern Muslims dislike the terms Mohammedan and Mohammedanism, which seem to them to carry the implication of worship of Mohammed, as Christian and Christianity imply the worship of Christ."[9] In the text that followed, Gibb referred to the believers as Muslims and to the faith as Islam.

But Islamism also began to disappear from the lexicon from about the turn of the twentieth century. Many scholars simply preferred the shorter and purely Arabic term, Islam. In 1913, Orientalists from many countries joined together to produce the *Encyclopaedia of Islam*. By the date of its completion in 1938, Islamism had all but disappeared from usage, replaced simply by Islam.

In summation, the term Islamism enjoyed its first run, lasting from Voltaire to the First World War, as a synonym for Islam. Enlightened scholars and writers generally preferred it to Mohammedanism. Eventually both terms yielded to Islam, the Arabic name of the faith, and a word free of either pejorative or comparative associations. There was no need for any other term, until the rise of an ideological and political interpretation of Islam challenged scholars and commentators to come up with an alternative, to distinguish Islam as a modern ideology from Islam as a faith.

Fundamentalism and Islam

The term fundamentalism originated in America in the 1920s. As the pace of social change accelerated, Protestant Christians felt threatened by the higher criticism of the Bible and the spread of philosophical skepticism. They sought to reaffirm their belief in the literal text of the Bible and the "fundamentals" of Christian belief, including creationism. These Christians called themselves fundamentalists, a term that gained wide currency at the time of the Scopes ("Monkey") trial in 1925. At the time, it acquired a strongly pejorative association in the minds of liberals and modernists.

In the subsequent few decades, odd references to Islamic fundamentalism appeared in print, but they were rare and inconsistent in their meanings. "If you looked in the right places," wrote the British historian Arnold Toynbee in 1929, "you could doubtless find some old fashioned Islamic fundamentalists still lingering on. You would also find that their influence was negligible."[10] From the context, it is obvious that by fundamentalists, Toynbee meant Muslim traditionalists and not the new activists who, the year before, founded the Society of the Muslim Brethren in Egypt.

Only fifty years later did Islamic fundamentalism come into widespread usage, thanks in large measure to media coverage of Iran's revolution. Journalists, ever on the lookout for a shorthand way to reference things new and unfamiliar, gravitated toward the term fundamentalism. It was American English, it was already in *Webster's Dictionary*, and it evoked the antimodernism that Ayatollah Khomeini seemed to personify. The use of fundamentalism in connection with Islam spread rapidly—so much so that by 1990, the *Concise Oxford English Dictionary* defined it not only as "the strict maintenance of traditional Protestant beliefs," but also as "the strict maintenance of ancient or fundamental doctrines of any religion, especially Islam."[11] By sheer dint of usage, Islamic fundamentalism had become *the* most cited fundamentalism of all.

Yet the more popular Islamic fundamentalism became in the media, the more scholars of Islam recoiled from it. The reasons varied. Some thought that the term fundamentalism failed to capture the methodology and style of Iran's revolution and comparable Muslim movements. Bernard Lewis, preeminent historian of Islam, made this case against it:

> The use of this term is established and must be accepted, but it remains unfortunate and can be misleading. "Fundamentalist" is a Christian term. It seems to have come into use in the early years of this century, and denotes certain Protestant churches and organizations, more particularly those that maintain the literal divine origin and inerrancy of the Bible. In this they oppose the liberal and modernist theologians, who tend to a more critical, historical view of Scripture. Among Muslim theologians there is as yet no such liberal or modernist approach to the Qur'an, and all Muslims, in their attitude to the text of the Qur'an, are in principle at least fundamentalists. Where the so-called Muslim fundamentalists differ from other Muslims and indeed from Christian fundamentalists is in their scholasticism and their legalism. They base themselves not only on the Qur'an, but also on the Traditions of the Prophet, and on the corpus of transmitted theological and legal learning.[12]

Other scholars, particularly those who sympathized with the new Muslim movements, protested that the label of fundamentalist unfairly stigmatized forward-thinking Muslims. John Esposito, America's foremost apologist for Islam-driven movements, made this argument against using fundamentalism in an Islamic context:

> For many liberal or mainline Christians, "fundamentalist" is pejorative or derogatory, being applied rather indiscriminately to all those who advocate a literalist biblical position and thus are regarded as static, retrogressive, and extremist. As a result, fundamentalism often has been regarded popularly as referring to those who are literalists and wish to return to and replicate the past. In fact, few individuals or organizations in the Middle East fit such a stereotype. Indeed, many fundamentalist leaders have had the best education, enjoy responsible positions in society, and are adept at harnessing the latest technology to propagate their views and create viable modern institutions such as schools, hospitals, and social service agencies.[13]

Esposito added that fundamentalism "is often equated with political activism, extremism, fanaticism, terrorism, and anti-Americanism," a prejudgment by label. Unlike Lewis, who was prepared to make a concession to widespread usage (it "must be accepted"), Esposito balked: "I prefer to speak of Islamic revivalism and Islamic activism rather than of Islamic fundamentalism."[14]

Edward Said, defender of Palestine and critic of Western representations of Islam, also weighed in. He did not so much object to the term (if it were properly defined) as to the way it had come to be employed *against* Islam:

> Instead of scholarship, we often find only journalists making extravagant statements, which are instantly picked up and further dramatized by the media. Looming over their work is the slippery concept, to which they constantly allude, of *"fundamentalism,"* a word that has come to be associated almost automatically with Islam, although it has a flourishing, usually elided relationship with Christianity, Judaism, and Hinduism. The deliberately created associations between Islam and fundamentalism ensure that the average reader comes to see Islam and fundamentalism as essentially the same thing.

In this usage, claimed Said, "fundamentalism equals Islam equals everything-we-must-now-fight-against, as we did with communism during the Cold War."[15]

The term fundamentalism did have a few academic defenders. In 1988, the University of Chicago, backed by the American Academy of Arts and Sciences, launched the Fundamentalism Project, devoted to comparing trends in Christianity, Islam, Judaism, Hinduism, Buddhism, and Confucianism. The project began with the hypothesis that the acceleration of modernity was forcing the faithful of all religions into a reactive (and sometimes violent) mode. Its organizers defined fundamentalism as "a strategy, or set of strategies, by which beleaguered believers attempt to preserve their distinctive identity as a people or group . . . by a selective retrieval of doctrines, beliefs, and practices from a sacred past."[16] Some 150 experts on diverse religious traditions contributed to the project, and their papers appeared in five hefty volumes, bearing titles like *Fundamentalisms Observed* and *Fundamentalisms and the State*. The Fundamentalism Project was the most sustained effort to legitimize the term as a tool of comparison across religions. Yet its impact remained limited, perhaps because it never generated a single powerful statement of its case. Quite often, the organizers and participants hedged their own use of the term with a thicket of reservations and disclaimers.

Sadik J. al-Azm, the Syrian philosopher, provided perhaps the strongest intellectual defense of the use of fundamentalism in an Islamic context. Al-Azm, an iconoclast famous for his past clashes with religious authorities, surveyed the doctrines of the new Islamic movements, and found them to consist of "an immediate return to Islamic 'basics' and 'fundamentals.'" Arab Muslims themselves, he added, had resorted to the Arabic neologism *usuli* (from *usul*, the "fundamentals"), as a calque for fundamentalism.[17] "It seems to me quite reasonable," he concluded, "that calling these Islamic movements 'Fundamentalist' (and in the strong sense of the term) is adequate, accurate, and correct."[18] The Egyptian philosopher Hasan Hanafi performed the same analysis and reached the same conclusion: "It is difficult to find a more appropriate term than the one recently used in the West, 'fundamentalism,' to cover the meaning of what we name Islamic awakening or revival."[19]

The Dutch Islamicist J. J. G. Jansen reinforced this argument with a practical one. The term was convenient. "In a way the discussion of the word 'fundamentalism' echoes the discussion once caused by the invention of the telephone," he wrote. "Would not the term 'telephone' be much too simplistic? Would it do justice to the beauty and the many possibilities of the device? How about 'speaking telegraph' or 'electrical speaking telephone'?" Jansen spoofed those who proposed elaborate alternatives like "revolutionary extremist neotraditionalist ultra-Islamic radicalism." The definitions of these far-fetched creations usually were not much different from what people meant by fundamentalism.[20]

But the strongest argument for fundamentalism was its sheer ubiquity. In an entry entitled "Fundamentalism," published in the *Oxford Encyclopedia of the Modern Islamic World* in 1995, historian John Voll enumerated the most common objections to the term and made a list of alternatives. These included Islamism, integrism, neo-normative Islam, neo-traditional Islam, Islamic revivalism, and Islamic nativism. "However," he added with a hint of resignation, "'fundamentalism' remains the most commonly utilized identification of the various revivalist impulses among Muslims. More technically accurate terms and neologisms have not gained wide acceptance."[21]

As it turned out, Voll underestimated the potential of Islamism.

The Islamist Alternative

The resurrection and redefinition of Islamism, like its birth, took place in France.

In the late 1970s, the French grappled with the problem of how to describe the new Islamic movements that had moved to the fore. *Islamisme* appealed to French scholars for two reasons. First, it had a venerable French pedigree going back to Voltaire. *Fondamentalisme*, the loan word from American English, had none. Second, there was a certain reluctance to deploy the only French alternative, *intégrisme*, because it remained too embedded in its original Catholic context and too implicated in ongoing debates about authority in the church. *Islamisme* in any case had been retired from daily use as a synonym for Islam. Why not impart new meaning to the term? Soon *islamisme* was cropping up in the titles of articles and books.

The retrieval of *islamisme* and its deployment to describe the new movements did not pass without criticism, most notably by Maxime Rodinson, the greatest living French historian of Islam. "In the dictionary, *islamisme* is given as a synonym for Islam," Rodinson reminded his colleagues. "If one chooses this term, the reader may become confused between an excited extremist who wishes to kill everyone and a reasonable person who believes in God in the Muslim manner, something perfectly respectable."[22] For this reason, Rodinson preferred *intégrisme*, which he found perfectly serviceable provided it was carefully defined. But his objections did not persuade younger French scholars, who did not feel bound by entries in old dictionaries. By the mid-1980s, *islamisme* was no longer simply, or even primarily, a synonym for the religion of Islam in contemporary French usage. Increasingly, it was understood to mean only one thing: Islam as a modern ideology and a political program.

It is possible to date almost precisely when the term made the crossing from French to English. In 1983, it had not yet arrived. That year, Georgetown University's Center for Contemporary Arab Studies organized its annual conference on "New Perspectives on Islam and Politics in the Middle East." Bruce Lawrence, a professor of religious studies, opened with an exhaustive survey of the pros and cons of the term Islamic fundamentalism, as well as its alternatives, but made no mention of Islamism.[23] Neither did any other conference participant. A year later, in 1984, the French sociologist of Islam, Gilles Kepel, published an influential book with the subtitle *Les mouvements islamistes dans l'Egypte contemporaine*.[24] In 1985, it appeared in English translation as *Muslim Extremism in Egypt*. The English translator had difficulty with Kepel's extensive use of *islamiste* and translated it as "Islamicist." A footnote in the translation made this apology: "The term 'Islamicist' is used throughout to render the French 'islamiste'. The loan word 'Islamist' did not gain currency until after this translation had been completed."[25] By about 1985, then, the French seed had been planted in English (though not much before that).

Initially, the term encountered some principled resistance. The American anthropologist Henry Munson, Jr., in a book published in 1988, listed the disadvantages of fundamentalism, but decided to retain it anyway: "I cannot think of an adequate alternative term to characterize those Muslims who advocate a strictly Islamic policy. The term *Islamist* strikes me as a clumsy neologism."[26] Clumsy or not, however, Islamism began to displace fundamentalism in specialized usage. It particularly appealed to scholars who disliked the supposedly pejorative associations of fundamentalism.

Graham Fuller, a RAND analyst and enthusiast for the new Islamic movements, made an early statement in its favor. Fundamentalism, he determined in 1991, "is an unsatisfactory term, suggesting as it does a strict reversion to the institutions of a medieval or even early Islamic state. This more recent phenomenon is better termed *Islamism*, suggesting not so much theology as an ideology whose implications are not at all old-fashioned, but thoroughly modern."[27] In 1993, the political scientist Louis Cantori likewise argued that fundamentalism

> conveys a sense of extremism and dismissal. In reference to Islam, in the world of scholarship, and now internally within U.S. agencies, it is being abandoned as being prejudicial and polemical. Instead, the term Islamism is used increasingly to denote the political manifestation of the religion of Islam. "Islamism" permits one to more dispassionately make distinctions between extremist and mainstream Islam.[28]

Cantori still noted that Islamism had not carried the day in the media: "Unfortunately, journalists especially still use the term fundamentalism and, in the process, fail to recognize and appreciate the moderation of the Islamic revival's mainstream."[29] But Cantori left no doubt that the term Islamism was gaining ground in academe and in Washington. In this early stage, the use of Islamism was also a marker for scholars more likely to sympathize with the new Islamic movements.

In Washington, Islamism did gain at the expense of fundamentalism. The term made a few cameo appearances in policy statements, and then received an official definition from Robert Pelletreau, Jr., assistant secretary of state for Near Eastern affairs, in remarks made in 1994. Pelletreau warned that "Islamic fundamentalism" had to be used "with requisite caution," and only to refer to the broad revival of Islam. Within that broad revival, there were subdivisions:

> In the foreign affairs community, we often use the term "Political Islam" to refer to the movements and groups within the broader fundamentalist revival with a specific political agenda. "Islamists" are Muslims with political goals. We view these terms as analytical, not normative. They do not refer to phenomena that are necessarily sinister: there are many legitimate, socially responsible Muslim groups with political goals. However, there are also Islamists who operate outside the law. Groups or individuals who operate outside the law—who espouse violence to achieve their aims—are properly called extremists.[30]

Here, then, was a three-tiered division: there were fundamentalists; some of these were Islamists; and some of these were extremists. Only the last constituted a threat. This statement was pregnant with its own analytical contradictions. For example, did a decision by a Middle Eastern government to put a movement outside the law automatically render it extremist? Or did only espousal of violence do so? What about movements that employed both bullets and ballots simultaneously?

But despite the statement's logical lacunae, it established Islamism in the official lexicon as a synonym for politicized and ideological Islam. By 1996, Pelletreau had devised a full-blown definition of Islamism, firmly establishing the term's privileged status:

> We normally use the term "Islamist" to refer to Muslims who draw upon the belief, symbols, and language of Islam to inspire, shape, and animate political activity. We do not automatically seek to exclude moderate, tolerant, peaceful Islamists who seek to apply their religious values to domestic political problems and foreign policy. We do, however, object strongly to Islamists who preach intolerance and espouse violence in the domestic and international arenas.[31]

The shift in preferences could be measured by running terms against one another on Internet search engines. In a Google search early in 2003,[32] the exact phrases "Muslim fundamentalists" and "Islamic fundamentalists" together returned 45,300 results; "Islamists" returned 82,100. The exact phrases "Islamic fundamentalism" and "Muslim fundamentalism" still returned more results than "Islamism," 58,280 compared to 23,900. But it was apparent that the growth lay in the use of the term Islamism. The clear preference for "Islamists," and the strong showing of "Islamism," were especially remarkable given that the major print media outlet in the United States, the *New York Times*, used neither Islamism nor Islamists.[33]

But the very success of these neologisms undermined the intent of those who had imported them from France. They had hoped that the term Islamist, used in place of fundamentalist, would dispel prejudice. But militant Muslims continued, as before, to commit or justify highly publicized acts of violence. As Islamism gained currency, it too became associated with benighted extremism, from the Taliban to the Algerian Armed Islamic Group, culminating in the mega-terror of Osama bin Laden. Critics of Islamism found it easy to add Islamism to the list of dangerous twentieth-century "isms" that had defied the liberal West and gone down to defeat.

"Islamism Is Fascism"—thus ran the headline of an interview with analyst Daniel Pipes.[34] "Islamism Is the New Bolshevism"—thus went the headline of an op-ed column by former British prime minister Margaret Thatcher.[35] The entry of Islamism into common English usage had not improved the image of these movements and paradoxically made it easier to categorize them as threats of the first order. As fundamentalists, these Muslims might have claimed some affinity to Christian and Jewish fundamentalists, who were generally tolerated. As the Muslim equivalent of fascists or Bolsheviks, they were clearly marked as the enemies of democracy and freedom.

Ultimately, of course, the problem of these movements was not what they were called. It was what they did. And as long as these movements continued to spawn, nurture, or tolerate the most violent forces in contemporary Islam, they would bring stigma to whatever term was applied to them.

Muslim Responses

On the whole, the debate over usage in the West bore little relationship to the parallel debate in the Muslim world over what to call the new Islamic movements. The arguments on behalf of various Arabic, Persian, and Urdu terms deserve their own treatment, based on other sources. But from time to time, Muslims expressed opinions over what terms Westerners should use.

Leaders of the new movements generally followed the lead of their Western sympathizers in rejecting the use of "fundamentalism." Rashid al-Ghannushi, the then-exiled leader of Tunisia's Nahda party, gave a speech in London in 1992 in which he "emphatically" rejected the term fundamentalism "insofar as it reflects the negative connotations implied by Western usage."[36] The same year, the head of the National Islamic Front in Sudan, Hasan Turabi, told a U.S. congressional committee that fundamentalism was "a misleading term in the sense that it describes a phenomenon which is very liberal, very progressive, and forward-looking, rather than a movement which is dogmatic, conservative, if not reactionary."[37]

If fundamentalism was unacceptable, then what term did these Muslims recommend to Westerners? In 1988, the French academic François Burgat published *L'Islamisme au Maghreb*, a landmark book very sympathetic to the new movements. Nonetheless, Abbassi Madani, the leader of the Algerian Islamic Salvation Front (FIS), reprimanded him: "In your book, you must first of all change the title! Why 'Islamism'? It is Islam that is at work in Algeria, nothing but Islam. We are Muslims!"[38] From Madani's point of view, any label but Muslim was pejorative by definition.

Ayatollah Muhammad Hussein Fadlallah, the spiritual mentor of Hezbollah, was asked by an English-language periodical in 1992 whether he thought fundamentalist or Islamist was more appropriate. Like Ghannushi and Turabi, Fadlallah rejected fundamentalist because of its "violent" associations. But like Madani, he also found Islamist unacceptable. It was a term "used by outsiders to denote a strand of activity which they think justifies their misconception of Islam as something rigid and immobile, a mere tribal affiliation." And his conclusion was identical to Madani's: "Having thought a good deal about this matter, I am satisfied to use the word 'Muslim,' which includes all the activities carried on within the scope and fold of Islam."[39]

Fadlallah later revised his position, apparently when he learned that Western sympathizers with movements like Hezbollah were promoting the term Islamist. "I object to the word 'fundamentalism,'" he told the same English-language periodical six months later, "a term which has overtones of exclusivism. I prefer the term 'Islamist movement,' which indicates a willingness to interact and live harmoniously with other trends of opinion, rather than to exclude them. In the Western perspective, 'fundamentalism' has implications of violence, and the Islamists have never chosen violence. Rather, violence has been forced upon them."[40] Fadlallah had taken his cue from foreign friends. But like other so-called Islamists, he was ambivalent about being called one—and with good reason. If Islamism came to be presented by its critics as a deviation from Islam itself, it too could appear pejorative.

New Permutations

To all intents and purposes, Islamic fundamentalism and Islamism have become synonyms in contemporary American usage. An author's choice can no longer be regarded automatically as a substantive statement about the subject itself. The preference for one term or another has been reduced to a matter of editorial style.

Yet the Muslims whom these terms purport to describe are in constant motion, and their actions are sure to have an impact upon Western perceptions and the categories created in the West to explain them. The pressures will come from two directions.

The first will be the theory mills of France, which twice invented Islamism, in the eighteenth and twentieth centuries. The wheels are turning again. The same French scholars who defined *islamisme* twenty years ago have now determined that it is *passé*, since it never succeeded in seizing power. Where there was once *islamisme*, there is now only *postislamisme*, also sometimes labeled *néofondamentalisme*. Its adherents are supposedly more interested in Islamizing society than pursuing power.

This purported discovery has prompted a debate in France over whether Islamism ever existed in the first place.[41] Alain Roussillon, an authority on Egypt, claims that it didn't. The concepts of *islamisme* and *postislamisme*, he argues, are impositions of ethnocentric Western sociology. Orientalist in effect, they make Muslims into exceptions and postulate one "truth of Islam" that supposedly defines Muslims from one end of the Islamic world to the other. And the inevitable confusion between Islam and *islamisme* "reduces the analysis of contemporary Muslim societies to the discourse and practices of their most radical and marginal components."[42] Not so, responds Oliver Roy, one of the chief interpreters of the new movements (and father of the term *postislamisme*). *Islamisme* may be a construct, he admits, but Muslims themselves constructed it. If it appears to be Western in origin, this is because thinkers like Ayatollah Khomeini were deeply influenced by radical Western thought.[43]

Arcane as this debate may sound, it touches on the question of whether Western scholars have a license to represent "the other" in categories they themselves label and define. At some point, the debate is sure to cross the Atlantic, and it is not impossible that scholars who once embraced the term Islamism as nonprejudicial may yet repudiate it.

The second source of pressure will come from the ascent of other terms that have gained in popularity since 9/11. "It was called 'Muslim

Fundamentalism' in the beginning. Now the term 'Jihadism' is in vogue."
So wrote a columnist in Pakistan's leading English-language daily in
2000.[44] At that time, the use of jihadism was largely confined to the
Indian and Pakistani media. But the terror attacks in the United States,
the war in Afghanistan, and the battle against Al Qaeda, facilitated the
term's migration to the West. At present, jihadism is used to refer to the
most violent persons and movements in contemporary Islam, including
Al Qaeda.[45] But the widespread Muslim reaffirmation of the duty of
jihad, coupled with expressions of Muslim sympathy for Al Qaeda and
suicide bombings, could transform jihadism into a household word in
the West. Since 9/11, it has figured in the titles of several university-press
bestsellers dealing with Islamism or Islamic fundamentalism as a whole,
such that the transformation may already be underway.[46]

Some media outlets have adopted the phrases militant Islam and
militant Muslims. The dictionary definition of a militant is someone
prepared to do battle; in American English, its clearest association is
with the violent fringes of the antiwar and civil rights movements of
the 1960s. The implication of militant Islam is that the new Muslim
movements have a propensity toward violence.[47] In contrast, sympathizers of these movements have shown some preference for the phrase
political Islam. This choice suggests that the defining characteristic
of the new movements is not their inclination to do battle, but their
willingness to engage in the give-and-take of politics.[48] Political Islam
may well be a redundancy, since nowhere in the Muslim world have
politics been separated from religion. But political Islam, like militant
Islam, is immediately intelligible to the English reader, and one or both
phrases might overtake Islamism in the future.

Western Desires

The actions of Muslims will affect the Western choice of terms. But
Western perceptions, hopes, and prejudices will play an equal or greater
role. Debate over terminology has always surrounded the West's relations with Islam, and its outcome has been as much a barometer of the
West's needs as a description of the actual state of Islam.

At the turn of the seventeenth century, the traveler Sir Thomas
Shirley complained about fellow Englishmen who called the "Great
Turke" (the Ottoman sultan) the "king of the Muslims" (*Musselmanni*).
Why? "Musselman" meant believer, and any Christian who acknowl-
edged "a Mahometan to be a faithful believer doth confess himself to
be an infidel."[49] At various times, Westerners have needed Muslims to

be infidels or believers, threatening or peaceable, foreign or familiar. It is impossible to predict which terms will prevail in the West's own struggle to come to terms with change in contemporary Islam. It will depend on what Muslims do, and on what the West desires.

Notes

1. This was, however, an improvement over terms like Saracen, Moor, and Turk. Bernard Lewis points to a European "reluctance to call the Muslims by any name with a religious connotation, preferring rather to call them by ethnic names, the obvious purpose of which was to diminish their stature and significance and to reduce them to something local or even tribal." But as Dominique Carnoy points out, "*mahométisme* perhaps had the name of a religion, but it was limited to rituals that lacked the essence of belief: the presence of the True God." Bernard Lewis, *Islam and the West* (New York: Oxford University Press, 1993), 7; Dominique Carnoy, *Représentations de l'Islam dans la France du XVIIe siècle* (Paris: Harmattan, 1998), 312.

2. Quoted by Norman Daniel, *Islam and the West* (Edinburgh: Edinburgh University Press, 1960), 300.

3. Quoted by Claudine Grossir, *L'Islam des Romantiques, 1811–1840* (Paris: Maisonneuve et Larose, 1984), 157.

4. Quoted in André Versaille, *Dictionnaire de la pensée de Voltaire par lui-même* (Brussels: Complexe, 1994), 829.

5. Alexis de Tocqueville, *Oeuvres complètes*, ed. J. P. Mayer (Paris: Gallimard, 1961–77), 3:155.

6. Henry Laurens, *La royaume impossible: La France et la genèse du monde arabe* (Paris: Armand Colin, 1990), 202, n. 23.

7. Quoted by Marwan R. Buheiry, "Islam and the Foreign Office: An Investigation of Religious and Political Revival in 1873," in his *Formation and Perception of the Modern Arab World* (Princeton, NJ: Darwin Press, 1989), 72.

8. *Questions diplomatiques et coloniales* (May 15, 1901), 582.

9. H. A. R. Gibb, *Mohammedanism* (London: Home University Library, 1949), 1.

10. Arnold Toynbee, *A Journey to China* (London: Constable, 1931), 117.

11. *Concise Oxford Dictionary of Current English* (8th rev. ed.; Oxford: Clarendon Press, 1990), 477, 628.

12. Bernard Lewis, *The Political Language of Islam* (Chicago, IL: University of Chicago Press, 1988), 117, n. 3.

13. John L. Esposito, *The Islamic Threat: Myth or Reality?* (NewYork: Oxford University Press, 1992), 7.

14. Ibid., 8. The term revivalism, although it had some currency in the 1970s, lacked a clear political dimension. It has fallen into disuse.

15. Edward W. Said, *Covering Islam: How the Media and the Experts Determine How We See the Rest of the World* (rev. ed.; New York: Vintage, 1997), xvi, xix.

16. Martin E. Marty and R. Scott Appleby, "Introduction," in *Fundamentalisms and the State*, eds. Marty and Appleby (Chicago, IL: University of Chicago Press, 1993), 3.

17. *Usuliyyun*, wrote the political scientist Nazih Ayubi, "is a term, less than a decade old, that represents a direct translation of the English word 'fundamentalists'. It is not a bad translation, as there is actually a branch of Islamic studies known as *usul al-din* (fundamentals of the religion)." Nazih Ayubi, *Political Islam: Religion and Politics in the Arab World* (London: Routledge, 1991), 256.

18. Sadik J. al-Azm, "Islamic Fundamentalism Reconsidered: A Critical Outline of Problems, Ideas and Approaches," *South Asia Bulletin, Comparative Studies of South Asia, Africa and the Middle East*, 1 and 2 (1993): 95–7.

19. Quoted by Bassam Tibi, "The Worldview of Sunni Arab Fundamentalists: Attitudes toward Modern Science and Technology," in *Fundamentalisms and Society*, eds. Martin E. Marty and R. Scott Appleby (Chicago, IL: University of Chicago Press, 1993), 85.

20. Johannes J. G. Jansen, *The Dual Nature of Islamic Fundamentalism* (London: Hurst, 1997), 14–5.

21. *Oxford Encyclopedia of the Modern Islamic World*, s.v. "Fundamentalism."

22. Quoted by François Burgat, *L'islamisme au Maghreb* (Paris: Karthala, 1988), 14.

23. Bruce B. Lawrence, "Muslim Fundamentalist Movements: Reflections toward a New Approach," in *The Islamic Impulse*, ed. Barbara Freyer Stowasser (Washington, DC: Center for Contemporary Arab Studies, 1987), 15–36.

24. Gilles Kepel, *Le prophéte et pharaon: Les mouvements islamistes dans l'Egypte contemporaine* (Paris: La Découverte, 1984). According to Rodinson, it was Kepel who popularized the term: "Recently I reproached Gilles Kepel, who had briefly been my student, for giving currency to the term *'islamisme'* to designate present-day Muslim political *intégrisme*." Interview with Gérard D. Khoury (1996 or 1997), in Maxime Rodinson, *Entre Islam et Occident* (Paris: Les Belles Lettres, 1998), 249.

25. Gilles Kepel, *Muslim Extremism in Egypt: The Prophet and the Pharoah* (Berkeley: University of California Press, 1985), 22, n. 1. "Islamicist" is the term most often used to describe Western students of Islam (on the model of physicist).

26. Henry Munson, Jr., *Islam and Revolution in the Middle East* (New Haven, CT: Yale University Press, 1988), 4.

27. Graham E. Fuller, *Islamic Fundamentalism in the Northern Tier Countries: An Integrative View* (Santa Monica, CA: RAND, 1991), 2. Nevertheless, he used fundamentalism in the title of this paper, suggesting that had he used Islamism, its meaning would not yet have been widely understood.

28. Interview with Louis J. Cantori, *Middle East Affairs Journal* (Spring-Summer 1993): 57.

29. Ibid.

30. Remarks by Robert H. Pelletreau, Jr., Middle East Policy Council, May 26, 1994, "Symposium: Resurgent Islam in the Middle East," *Middle East Policy* (Fall 1994): 2.

31. Speech by Robert H. Pelletreau, Jr., Council on Foreign Relations, May 8, 1996, archived at http://web.archive.org/web/20011110123203/http://dosfan.lib.uic.edu/ERC/bureaus/nea/960508PelletreauMuslim.html.

32. Google search conducted by the author on January 26, 2003.

33. In the author's search of the newspaper's electronic archive on January 25, 2003, "fundamentalism" and "fundamentalists" appeared in connection with

Islam in over 9,000 articles published since 1996. "Islamism" and "Islamists" appeared in less than 300 articles.

34. Eric Boehlert, "Islamism Is Fascism: An Interview with Daniel Pipes," *Salon.com*, November 9, 2001, archived at http://web.archive.org/web/20090208012243/http://www.danielpipes.org/81/islamism-is-fascism. Pipes: "Islamism is a totalitarian ideology. An Islamist is a danger in the same way a fascist is a danger."

35. Margaret Thatcher, "Islamism Is the New Bolshevism," *The Guardian* (London), February 12, 2002. In the body of the article, Thatcher did not use the term "Islamism." "Islamic extremism today, like bolshevism in the past, is an armed doctrine," she wrote. "It is an aggressive ideology promoted by fanatical, well-armed devotees. And, like Communism, it requires an all-embracing long-term strategy to defeat it."

36. Rachid Ghannouchi, "Islam and the West: Realities and Potentialities," in *The Politics of Islamic Resurgence: Through Western Eyes*, eds. Ahmed Bin Yousef and Ahmad Abul Jobain (Springfield: United Association for Studies and Research, 1992), 48. This was a speech delivered in London on October 6, 1992.

37. Hearing testimony of Hasan Turabi, May 20, 1992, Committee on Foreign Affairs, House of Representatives, *Islamic Fundamentalism in Africa and Implications for U.S. Policy* (Washington, DC: Government Printing Office, 1993), 8.

38. Quoted by François Burgat and William Dowell, *The Islamic Movement in North Africa* (Austin, TX: Center for Middle Eastern Studies, 1993), 9–10, n. 3.

39. Interview with Fadlallah, *Monday Morning* (Beirut), August 10, 1992.

40. Interview with Fadlallah, *Monday Morning*, February 1, 1993.

41. *L'Esprit* (August–September 2001) published contributions to the debate, which was also summarized in *Le Monde*, October 8, 2001.

42. Alain Roussillon, "Les islamologues dans l'impasse," *L'Esprit* (August–September 2001): 93–115

43. Olivier Roy, "Les islamologues ont-ils inventé l'islamisme?," *L'Esprit* (August–September 2001): 116–38.

44. Jafar Wafa, "Recalling Islamic Millennium," *Dawn* (Karachi), February 4, 2000.

45. French academics have put the term into academic circulation as "jihadist-Salafism." The qualifier of Salafism—an historical reference to the precursor of these movements—will inevitably be stripped away in popular usage. "Jihadist-Salafism" is defined by Gilles Kepel, *Jihad: The Trail of Political Islam* (Harvard: Harvard University Press, 2002), 219–22; and Guilain Deneoux, "The Forgotten Swamp: Navigating Political Islam," *Middle East Policy* (June 2002), 69–71.

46. Two prime examples: Kepel, *Jihad*; and Ahmed Rashid, *Jihad: The Rise of Militant Islam in Central Asia* (New Haven, CT: Yale University Press, 2002).

47. Daniel Pipes used the term in the title of his book *Militant Islam Reaches America* (New York: Norton, 2002).

48. Fawaz Gerges and François Burgat used political Islam in book titles: Gerges, *America and Political Islam* (Cambridge: Cambridge University Press, 1999); Burgat, *Face to Face with Political Islam* (London: Tauris, 2002). Burgat's

book is a translation from a French original, entitled *L'Islamisme en face.* The author or the publisher decided against using "Islamism" in the English book title—perhaps evidence of doubt about the term's status in English.

49. Quoted by Nabil Mattar, *Islam in Britain, 1558–1685* (Cambridge: Cambridge University Press, 1998), 30.

6

"Islamic Fascism"

In August 2006, President George W. Bush described America's adversary in the Middle East in these words: "It's Islamo-fascism. It comes in different forms. They share the same tactics, which is to destroy people and things in order to create chaos in the hopes that their vision of the world becomes predominant in the Middle East."[1]

About a month later, Senator Russ Feingold (D-Wisconsin) issued this rejoinder:

> I call on the President to stop using the phrase "Islamic Fascists," a label that doesn't make any sense, and certainly doesn't help our effort to fight terrorism. Fascist ideology doesn't have anything to do with the way global terrorist networks think or operate, and it doesn't have anything to do with the overwhelming majority of Muslims around the world who practice the peaceful teachings of Islam.[2]

At the White House press briefing the day after Feingold's challenge, spokesperson Tony Snow came to the defense of President Bush. A journalist read him a dictionary definition of fascism, adding: "It doesn't quite seem to fit what we're talking about." Snow's reply: "Well, it actually does fit."[3]

I prefer the terms Islamism and jihadism, depending on the context. But I cannot rise up against the use of Islamic fascism with the righteous indignation mustered by, say, University of Michigan professor Juan Cole, who denounced the "lazy conflation of Muslim fundamentalist movements with fascism."[4] The reason is that this conflation, or comparison, has had some rigorous champions within Middle Eastern studies. It didn't originate in the Bush White House; it has a long pedigree, including some pioneering social scientists. These scholars, who knew rather more than Senator Feingold about both Islamism and fascism, did think the comparison had merit.

71

Experts on Fascism

Any student of my generation first would have encountered it in the work of the late Manfred Halpern, who spent nearly forty years as a politics professor at Princeton. Halpern grew up with fascism: born in Germany in 1924, he and his parents fled the Nazis in 1937 for America. He joined the war against the Nazis as a battalion scout in the 28th Infantry Division, and saw action in the Battle of the Bulge and elsewhere. After Germany's surrender, he worked in U.S. Counterintelligence, tracking down former Nazis. In 1948 he joined the State Department, where he worked on the Middle East, and in 1958 he came to Princeton, where he did the same.

In 1963, Princeton University Press published his *Politics of Social Change in the Middle East and North Africa*. For years, this book was the basic text in the field, and it included the only academic treatment of Islamism, which no one much cared about at the time. Halpern labeled it "neo-Islamic totalitarianism," and this is how he described it:

> The neo-Islamic totalitarian movements are essentially fascist movements. They concentrate on mobilizing passion and violence to enlarge the power of their charismatic leader and the solidarity of the movement. They view material progress primarily as a means for accumulating strength for political expansion, and entirely deny individual and social freedom. They champion the values and emotions of a heroic past, but repress all free critical analysis of either past roots or present problems.

Halpern, citing examples from the Muslim Brotherhood, continued:

> Like fascism, neo-Islamic totalitarianism represents the institutionalization of struggle, tension, and violence. Unable to solve the basic public issues of modern life—intellectual and technological progress, the reconciliation of freedom and security, and peaceful relations among rival sovereignties—the movement is forced by its own logic and dynamics to pursue its vision through nihilistic terror, cunning, and passion. An efficient state administration is seen only as an additional powerful tool for controlling the community. The locus of power and the focus of devotion rest in the movement itself. Like fascist movements elsewhere, the movement is so organized as to make neo-Islamic totalitarianism the whole life of its members.[5]

At the time, Halpern was a central figure in Middle Eastern studies, and his book—reprinted six times—appeared in every syllabus for the next fifteen years. His critical analysis of Islamism very much cut against the grain, at a time when Cold War strategists ardently wooed Islamists as allies against Communism. In the 1970s, Halpern walked away from the field, and his reputation within it slipped. (He died in 2001.) But his rigorous treatment of Islamism stands up well, and his equating it with fascism was a serious proposition, made by someone who had seen fascism up close.

The comparison of Islamism with fascism also made sense to Maxime Rodinson, the preeminent French scholar of Islam, who pioneered the application of sociological method to the Middle East. As a French Jew born in 1915, Rodinson also learned about fascism from direct experience. He escaped to Syria in 1940, but the Vichy regime deported his parents to Auschwitz, where they perished. Rodinson was a man of the left—in his early years, militantly so—but he took his thinking from no one.

In 1978, during Iran's revolution, enthusiasm for Islamism began to spread among his colleagues on the French left, who romanticized it as the vibrant, new anti-West. The French philosopher Michel Foucault became famously enamored of Ayatollah Khomeini.[6] Rodinson decided to set things straight, in a long front-page article in *Le Monde*, targeted at those who "come fresh to the problem in an idealistic frame of mind." Rodinson admitted that trends in Islamic movements such as the Muslim Brotherhood were "hard to ascertain."

> But the dominant trend is a certain type of archaic fascism (*type de fascisme archaïque*). By this I mean a wish to establish an authoritarian and totalitarian state whose political police would brutally enforce the moral and social order. It would at the same time impose conformity to religious tradition as interpreted in the most conservative light.[7]

By "archaic," Rodinson referred to the religious component of the ideology, largely absent from European fascism.

By making this statement on the front page of *Le Monde*, Rodinson accused his colleagues on the left of celebrating a form of fascism, from his perch at the pinnacle of Islamic scholarship. This especially sharp critic of Eurocentric distortions of Islam didn't shy from the comparison of Islamism with fascism, at a moment just as politically charged as the present one. (Rodinson died in 2004.)

In 1984, Said Amir Arjomand, a prominent Iranian-American sociologist at SUNY-Stony Brook, picked up the comparison and ran with it. With a nod to Halpern, Arjomand pointed to "some striking sociological similarities between the contemporary Islamic movements and the European fascism and the American radical right.... It is above all the strength of the monistic impulse and the pronounced political moralism of the Islamic traditionalist and fundamentalist movements which makes them akin to fascism and the radical right alike."[8]

In 1986, he took the comparison even further, in an influential article for the journal *World Politics* entitled "Iran's Islamic Revolution in Comparative Perspective." Arjomand entertained a number of comparisons, but in the end settled on fascism as the best of them. Islamism (he called it "revolutionary traditionalism") and fascism "share a number of essential features," including "an identical transposition of the theme of exploitation" and a "distinct constitutive core."

> Like fascism, the Islamic revolutionary movement has offered a new synthesis of the political creeds it has violently attacked. And, like the fascists, the Islamic militants are against democracy because they consider liberal democracy a foreign model that provides avenues for free expression of alien influences and ideas. (Also like the fascists, however, the Islamic militants would not necessarily accept the label of "antidemocratic.")

Arjomand's conclusion: "The emergence of an Islamic revolutionary ideology has been in the cards since the fascist era."[9] (He later repeated the argument almost verbatim in his 1989 book *The Turban for the Crown*.)[10]

Lazy Comparisons?

Within a few weeks of President Bush's remark, it was reported that the State Department had persuaded the White House to stop talking about "Islamic fascism." In March 2008, the National Counterterrorism Center, via its "Extremist Messaging Branch," explained why the phrase should be banned from U.S. government usage: "We are communicating with, not confronting, our audiences. Don't insult or confuse them with pejorative terms such as 'Islamo-fascism,' which are considered offensive by many Muslims."[11]

This may make some sense for government, driven as it is by the need to formulate effective propaganda in the midst of a war. But academics should continue to revisit the comparison as a serious analytical tool. No one learns anything from simple analogies ("Islamism is fascism"). But comparing two phenomena to identify both similarities and differences is the essence of the scholarly endeavor. For example, my retrieval of the statements of Rodinson and Halpern inspired Walter Laqueur, author of an authoritative book on fascism, to revisit the comparison constructively. His bottom line: the differences outweigh the "striking similarities."[12] Laqueur may be right, but the subsequent rise of the Islamic State (ISIS) invites a reevaluation, based on an instance in which the *prima facie* similarities appear to outweigh the differences.

This comparative exercise also serves a corrective purpose within the academy, because self-styled campus progressives are repeating Foucault's error. It started in earnest in 2006, when Noam Chomsky made a pilgrimage to the lair of Hezbollah's maximum leader, Sayyid Hasan Nasrallah, and came out praising him for defying America.[13] Some months later, Hamid Dabashi, professor and a keeper of Edward Said's flame at Columbia, offered this: "Both Hamas and Hezbollah, becoming even more integral to the Palestinian and Lebanese national liberation movements, will one day succeed in helping establish a free, democratic, and cosmopolitan republic in their respective countries."[14] He was followed by celebrity philosopher and queer theorist Judith Butler, who told a Berkeley audience that Hamas and Hezbollah are "social movements that are part of the global left."[15]

It is this conflation that is truly "lazy." In contrast, the Islamism-fascism comparison has distinguished and rigorous academic precedents. Younger scholars and students should seize the opportunity to explore it further, with intellectual rigor and without fear.

Notes

1. President Bush's news conference with Condoleezza Rice, Crawford, Texas, August 7, 2006, *Public Papers of the Presidents of the United States: George Bush, 2006* (Washington, DC: Government Press Office, 2010), 2:1501.
2. Remarks of U.S. Senator Russ Feingold at the Arab American Institute's 2006 Leadership Conference, September 12, 2006, archived at https://web.archive.org/web/20061022091141/http://www.feingold.senate.gov/~feingold/statements/06/09/20060912.htm.
3. White House press briefing by Tony Snow, September 13, 2006, archived at https://web.archive.org/web/20060920044542/http://www.whitehouse.gov/news/releases/2006/09/20060913-3.html
4. Juan Cole, "Bush, Islamic Fascism and the Christians of Jounieh," *Informed Comment* (blog), August 8, 2006, archived at http://web.archive.org/web/20151031064248/http://www.juancole.com/2006/08/bush-islamic-fascism-and-christians-of.html.
5. Manfred Halpern, *Politics of Social Change in the Middle East and North Africa* (Princeton, NJ: Princeton University Press, 1963), 135–36, 140–41.
6. See Janet Afary and Kevin B. Anderson, *Foucault and the Iranian Revolution: Gender and the Seductions of Islamism* (Chicago, IL: University of Chicago Press, 2010).

7. *Le Monde*, December 6, 1978; Afary and Anderson, *Foucault and the Iranian Revolution*, 233.
8. Said Amir Arjomand, *From Nationalism to Revolutionary Islam* (Binghamton, NY: SUNY Press, 1984), 21, 24.
9. Said Amir Arjomand, "Iran's Islamic Revolution in Comparative Perspective," *World Politics* 38 (1986): 405.
10. Said Amir Arjomand, *The Turban for the Crown: The Islamic Revolution in Iran* (New York: Oxford University Press, 1988), 204.
11. "Words that Work and Words that Don't: A Guide for Counterterrorism Communication," *Counterterrorism Communication Center*, March 14, 2008, archived at http://documents.scribd.com/docs/q0jdlrtjgl9jegyxhyp.pdf.
12. Walter Laqueur, "The Origins of Fascism: Islamic Fascism, Islamophobia, Antisemitism," *OUPblog*, October 25, 2006, archived at http://web.archive.org/web/20070630165331/http://blog.oup.com/2006/10/the_origins_of_2/.
13. Noam Chomsky and A. J. Khoury, *Inside Lebanon: Journey to a Shattered Land with Noam and Carol Chomsky* (New York: Monthly Review Press, 2007).
14. Hamid Dabashi, "How Do We Sleep while Beirut Is Burning?," *Al-Ahram Weekly*, August 3–9, 2006.
15. Berkeley Teach-In Against the War, September 7, 2006, http://www.shiatv.net/video/a7d8c2c43d504b2babd8 at minute 17:50, accessed March 3, 2016.

7

Islam for Viewers Like You

It hardly needs saying that the United States and the Muslim world are locked in an embrace. There are more than a billion Muslims in the world, and there are millions of Americans who are Muslim. American relations with the believers in Islam run the entire gamut, from mutual cooperation to violent confrontation.

Since 9/11, Americans have been preoccupied with current events in the Muslim world and the present struggles within Islam. They have no choice. But it behooves the citizenry of this great power to know something of the history and legacy of the Islamic world—knowledge that goes beyond daily headlines. And there is no more effective way to inform a wide public, especially on subjects that are foreign, than the medium of film.

No doubt this was the motive of PBS, America's public television network, when it commissioned Robert Gardner to produce and direct a documentary on the history and civilization of Islam. *Islam: Empire of Faith* is the result: a three-part, 150-minute sweep through the first thousand years of Islamic history, from the appearance of the Prophet Muhammad in seventh-century Arabia to the reign of Süleyman the Magnificent in the sixteenth century.[1] PBS broadcast the film in May 2001 and made it available immediately as home video. In the aftermath of 9/11, PBS broadcast it again. It seems safe to say that, for the foreseeable future, most Americans will encounter the civilization of Islam through *Islam: Empire of Faith*. That is not altogether a good thing.

$1.54 Million

The first point worth noting about Gardner's creation is that it breaks the usual barrier between documentary and cinematic film.

Most films on Islamic history have a predictable format: lots of architecture, images from illustrated manuscripts, and a parade of "experts." The camera pans across the arcaded façade of the Great Mosque in

Damascus and lingers on the fountain in the Court of the Lions in the Alhambra. The usual illustrations are dusted off to depict court life, early astronomy, medical knowledge, and siege warfare. Familiar talking heads offer familiar assessments.

Islam: Empire of Faith dishes up plenty of shots of the best-known mosques, palaces, and manuscripts. And of course it has its "experts." But it offers something more: a few landmark events in Islamic history, reenacted by meticulously costumed actors on big sets. Such reenactments are one of Gardner's specialties. His bio relates that his earlier award-winning series on Near Eastern antiquity featured reenactments of the discoveries of the Rosetta Stone, Tutankhamen's tomb, the Dead Sea Scrolls, and an Assyrian tomb "complete with live rats."[2] Clearly we are in the hands of an artist.

For the Islam venture, PBS provided Gardner with $1.54 million in funding from "viewers like you." He took this money to Iran, home to a sophisticated film industry, and there shot all of the reenactments. Many of these are stock scenes, right out of *Lawrence of Arabia*: bazaars, caravans, and camel charges. But a few of the reenactments are quite evocative and are arguably worth the price of admission. Most notably, Gardner built a four-story reproduction of the Ka'ba, the pre-Islamic shrine in Mecca that the Prophet Muhammad purified and that all Muslims face in prayer. The (entirely speculative) reenactment of pre-Islamic totem worship in this *faux*-Ka'ba is memorable.

Watching part one, "The Messenger," I was reminded of the passage in Richard Grenier's wicked novel, *The Marrakesh One-Two*, where the American protagonist contemplates his assignment of making a film about Muhammad in a Muslim country:

> We're doing *The Mohammed Story*, you understand, but Mohammed's got to go. Too holy to be portrayed. We've got to "shoot around" Mohammed. But also all his immediate family has to go: This wealthy widow he married who gave him his start in life. All his ten or so other wives. His children, all the daughters. His famous sons-in-law. Ali goes. Omar goes. The four first caliphs go. Mohammed's mother and father go. The ten Companions of Mohammed go. That's the ten apostles right there. Talk of Hamlet without the prince. This was Hamlet without the prince, king, queen, Ophelia, Polonius, Horatio, Laertes, Rosencrantz, and Guildenstern. It was going to be Hamlet with the gravediggers and Fortinbras.[3]

In his reenactments, Gardner too "shoots around" all of the *dramatis personae*—less of a disadvantage in a documentary film, but an indication to the viewer that the producer is determined or resigned to work within limits set by Muslim sensibilities.

And Gardner left no room for guesswork in his effort to stay within Muslim bounds. Just before the release, he took the added precaution of screening the film to representatives of American Muslim organizations. The film passed muster with only one minor change. (Viewers might have gotten a glimpse of Muhammad in a shot of an illustrated fourteenth-century manuscript of Rashid al-Din's *Tavarikh*. Out went that frame.)[4] But if Gardner's fare is *halal*, this is because he made all of the necessary compromises well in advance. The result is a film that viewers will rightly regard as a compliment to the high civilization of Islam. But a compliment is not a history, and it is as history that the film ultimately runs aground.

Empire of Swords

The history of a great empire is a messy thing. "Sword-blades are foundations that never settle," wrote the historian Arnold Toynbee, mocking the labors of "happy empire builders" who would delude themselves that their achievements might endure.[5]

Toynbee denied the obvious: that great empires, for all their faults, have been history's most civilizing force. Certainly the sword-blades under Islam's empires settled well enough to allow the erection of magnificent edifices on their foundations. But Toynbee (who also thought that Islam had been "militant from first to last") was right to point out the indispensable role of the sword. The depiction of Islamic empire as an "empire of faith" is already a limiting one, since Islam was spread by fear as well as faith, by conquest as well as commerce. Anyone who has taken an elementary course in Islamic history will know this. Anyone who has only watched this film will not.

The problem is evident from the very beginning in the representation of the Prophet Muhammad. Through the mists of time and obfuscation, the historical Muhammad is beyond retrieval. All that remains are the canonical accounts preserved by the believers themselves. But even these present Muhammad as a man of battle as much as a man of faith. Gardner has no problem presenting Muhammad as a believer—dark desert mountains evoke a man wrestling with his soul and God's revelation—but how is he to present Muhammad as warrior?

Answer: cast him as the forgiving conqueror. This is achieved in Gardner's dramatic reenactment of Muhammad's conquest of Mecca. We are told that in seventh-century Arabia, the usual treatment meted out to conquered enemies was grim: men were slain, women and children were sold into slavery. But in Mecca, Muhammad refused to exact bloody revenge. He did violence only against the idols in the Ka'ba. "Within the very founding of the religion," intones Michael Sells of Haverford College, "one finds episodes of great generosity, often extraordinary acts of kindness and mercy." And that's that: Muhammad as MacArthur.

This is true as far as it goes, but there were also episodes of ordinary retribution and revenge. "The Messenger of God ordered that every adult male of Banu Qurayza be killed," relates Ibn Hisham, the ninth-century compiler of Muhammad's biography, "and then he divided the property, wives, and children of Banu Qurayza among the Muslims."[6] (The Banu Qurayza were a Jewish tribe that surrendered to the Muslims; the men, between six hundred and nine hundred, were beheaded.) The notion retailed in this film, that Muhammad put a complete end to vengeance, cannot be squared with the historical record preserved by Muslims themselves. Of course, it would be absurd to judge Muhammad's warfare by the Geneva Convention, but it is no less absurd to suggest that Muslims conducted their early battles within its limits. They didn't.

Their early politics get the same laundering. The film emphasizes the unity and solidarity of the early Muslim community as the prime explanation for its lightning conquests. But there is no mention of the fact that three of the first four caliphs were assassinated. More important, we are not told that a Muslim army massacred the grandson of the Prophet, Hussein, and his entire retinue on a baked plain in Iraq, creating a permanent fissure in Islam. Gardner would not even have had to provide costumes and actors for a reenactment of Hussein's martyrdom. In Iran, Shi'ites reenact it on their own, in passion plays held every year. Mock-ups of severed heads are the main props.

One can understand why Gardner would choose to omit Shi'ite references from a film shot in Iran. There are plenty of Sunni viewers who would take offense. But this is a bit like making a documentary on Henry VIII without Sir Thomas More. The dramatic expansion of Islam is remarkable precisely because it occurred despite very deep divisions among Muslims. Cutting out all references to the vengeful rivalries of early Islam makes it impossible to understand the early breakup of the empire and the process of dissent and rebellion that created new Muslim empires. By all means, let us admire the Dome of the Rock in all its perfection. But there are other symbols dating to these earliest years, soaked in blood, which live in Muslim hearts to this day. In Gardner's film, they are swept under a very ornate oriental carpet.

By the standards of the time, the Muslim conquerors dealt with conquered peoples in a relatively enlightened way. But here, too, there is a risk of mythologizing, a temptation strengthened by the contemporary demand for greater Muslim-Christian "understanding." Take, for example, the fate of the Church of St. John the Baptist in Damascus, a city conquered by the Muslims in 636. Should we believe the film? "Side by side, the two faiths shared the same building—in peace." Or should we trust the *Encyclopaedia of Islam?* "A legend which tells of the division of the Church of St. John between Christians and Muslims springs from an error in translation." Should we follow the film? "As the Muslim community grew, they bought the old church from the Christian congregation." Or should we follow the *Encyclopaedia?* "In spite of previous agreements, the Caliph al-Walid confiscated the Church of St. John the Baptist from the Christians."[7] Yes, Islamic rule tolerated the practice of Christianity (and Judaism), but Gardner resorts to legend to suggest that it placed all religions on one moral plane. Islamic rule did nothing of the sort.

By the time Gardner gets to the apex of Islamic civilization, he has done a very thorough job of burying all the blades. The admiring portrayal of the renaissance of Islam, centered on Baghdad, renders a genuine service to the average American viewer, who may be unaware of the extent of medieval Muslim achievement in commerce, art, philosophy, and science. Scholars will debate whether Muslims really made this or that breakthrough, or whether they made it alone. Gardner certainly gives them the benefit of any doubt. But who among us, if suddenly compelled to live a thousand years ago, would not choose Baghdad? Gardner has done an evocative reenactment of the busy intellectual activity in Baghdad's famous House of Wisdom (*bayt al-hikma*), and it is arguably the high point in the film. The filmmaker's problem, of course, is that the old glories of Baghdad are long gone, and when his film premiered, Saddam's own palaces were off-limits and far too gaudy. Alas for the Iraqis, their House of Wisdom gets reenacted in a ruined nineteenth-century mansion—in Iran.

Crusade and Jihad

Like Islamic civilization itself, Gardner's film goes into decline thereafter. For if the film until this point has been devoted to idealizing Islam, it now turns to an indictment of the West, in the form of the Crusades.

A proper historical understanding of the Crusades is not easy to achieve, and it certainly cannot be reached without taking into account the Muslim view. The problem is that many of today's Muslims have turned the Crusades into something like a holocaust, better to extract confessions of culpability from the West. (Churches have been especially vulnerable to this moral extortion.) The Crusaders waged a cruel war even by medieval standards, and there is nothing easier than to moralize over it. Gardner does, with the academic sanction of British historian Carol Hillenbrand, who calls the Crusader massacres in Jerusalem "a blot on the name of Christendom in the Muslim view, and justifiably so."

Perhaps, but then one would expect some consistency. In part three, Gardner devotes eight minutes to the fall of Constantinople, capital of Byzantium, to the armies of Mehmet the Conqueror in 1453. The importance of the city, its formidable walls, the Ottoman strategy, the siege tactics—all aspects are covered in painstaking detail. When we enter the city, we proceed triumphantly with Mehmet into the Hagia Sophia church, destined to become a mosque. Yet not one word or frame is spent on the treatment meted out by Mehmet to the people of the city. Because the city had not surrendered, Islamic law allowed the conquerors three days of unlimited killing, rape, and plunder. The destruction of the vanquished was certainly a blot on the name of Islam in the Christian view—"and justifiably so," a moralizing historian might add. Alas, the poor Byzantines have no modern lobbyists whose job is to turn medieval atrocities into political capital for some present purpose.

The imbalance caused by this omission is particularly unfortunate now that *Islam: Empire of Faith* has been trotted out to do service as an antidote to 9/11. Gardner made a deliberate and legitimate choice not to bring the film up to the present. But the decision by PBS to rebroadcast it after the attacks effectively revoked that choice. If the film has some relevant message, it is the one made by a raft of "experts" who claim that violence is not a part of Islam and that jihad was never anything more than peaceful persuasion. But it's not true. Wars of conquest expanded Islam's frontiers, and every one of them was conducted under the banner of jihad. And if anyone doubts the Islamic legitimacy of slaughtering innocents in the assault on an enemy city, they have only to look to the fall of Constantinople. They just won't be able to find it in this film.

Race and Sex

It is not exactly true that none of the Prophet's Companions is portrayed. There is one exception: Bilal bin Rabah, the manumitted Ethiopian slave and early convert to Islam, who issued the call to prayer when it was first instituted by Muhammad in Medina. He is shown in part one, ascending the roof of a building, cupping his hand to his mouth, and issuing a sonorous *Allahu akbar*. The exceptional depiction of Bilal is a clear mark that this is an American film. For Bilal was black. He personifies the indifference to race that presumably characterizes Islam—a virtue crucial to Islam's acceptance in contemporary America.

In part two, this subtle portrayal of Islam as enlightened in matters of race produces an instance of crude censorship. The screen fills with an image from an illustrated manuscript showing two turbaned merchants facing one another over a set of scales. In the voice-over, art historian Sheila Blair of Boston College explains the importance of credit in the development of long-distance trade within the Islamic world.

But what were the merchants trading? If you want to know that, you have to refer back to the complete illustration, from a thirteenth-century manuscript of Hariri's *Maqamat* in the Bibliothèque Nationale in Paris.[8] And here, just below the scales, we find the objects of trade: black slaves. This is a well-known illustration of a slave market in Yemen, a major way station on the slave route into the Arab lands. Apparently the filmmaker decided that his American audience should be spared the knowledge that black slaves were major commodities in the heyday of Arab commerce.

Race and slavery in Islam are issues too complicated to sort out in a documentary film of this length and emphasis. Yet Gardner chooses to make a subtle statement in favor of Islam by giving us the black believer and withholding from us the black slaves. Islamic empires, we are led to assume, escaped the usual imperial practices of enslavement and racial prejudice.

This borders on deliberate deception. Islam's "empire of faith," like all great empires before it, sanctioned slavery. Islam's very expansion and its great material wealth created a constant demand for slaves—a demand met in large measure from black Africa. One would think that a PBS film would suggest that the actual record of Islamic civilization on this point was a mixed one. Instead, the past is whitewashed—partly, no doubt, because so many American Muslims are black.

Race is one issue that is finessed for a liberal American audience; sex is another. Islam at its pinnacle, like Greece and Rome, had sexual mores vastly different than those of twenty-first century America. One would think that we are now mature enough to discuss them dispassionately and learn whatever they can teach us about the variety of the human experience. Gardner's film instead obliterates them, so as to make these long-dead people of another time and place seem just like the neighbors next door. The film's treatment of these issues tells us nothing about historical Islam, and everything about contemporary America.

For example, we learn at length about Khadija, Muhammad's first wife and a widow older than he. She is portrayed as an entrepreneur (no glass ceilings in seventh-century Arabia!), and Muhammad becomes her partner, then husband. Who in suburban America doesn't know an affable couple like this? But A'isha, Muhammad's favorite wife, gets no mention at all in the film—probably because she was married to him at around the age of ten. When she moved into his home, relate the Muslim sources, she brought along her toys. The omission says more about contemporary American sensitivities than it does about Muhammad, who married completely within the mores and conventions of his time.

In part three, Gardner spends several reenactments on the relationship between Süleyman the Magnificent and his slave, confidant, and grand vizier, Ibrahim Pasha. Because, one assumes, this film is also destined for the schools, it demurs over the sexual aspect of their bond. The elision is not an insignificant one: Gardner's "experts" are adamant that the Ottoman Empire, like America, was a pure meritocracy, even though some historians now believe that homosexual nepotism often compromised the palace system.[9] Watch the distinguished University of Chicago Ottomanist, Cornell Fleischer, squirm: "The two were very close in age and, apparently, very close in other ways."

It is a purely American constraint that the issue cannot be raised, even in a discussion of the Ottoman Empire in the sixteenth century. (Or maybe Fleischer was the wrong person to ask: his university chair, half-funded by the Turkish government, is named after Süleyman.) But it is just as smart of Gardner to build up Süleyman's relations with Ibrahim via so many reenactments and "expert" commentaries. The whole episode is "apparently" a discreet nod to gay viewers. Gardner tosses in the Roxelana story, Süleyman's "straight" romance and a favorite of cheap novels, and he has covered pretty much the range of accepted sexual preferences, each with precisely the amount of discretion that "viewers like you" expect.

So there is something for everyone—the guiding principle of the blockbuster movie. The real genius of Gardner's film is not its cinematography, and certainly not its accuracy. It is Gardner's uncanny ability to appeal to so wide a range of traditional viewers of public television, and the increasingly affluent American Muslim minority. This is Islamic history as PBS needs it, wants it, and now has to have it. It is a quintessentially American artifact, and a pointer to the kind of Islam many Americans hope (against hope) will emerge from the present turmoil.

Expert Overreach

Finally, there are the experts. They are a photogenic lot, competent in their specializations—mostly, art history. The problem is that several of them are called upon to comment on areas well beyond their competence. If you ask a historian of Ottoman art to characterize the relationship between Muhammad and Khadija, don't be surprised to get a line like this one: "It was a wonderful partnership, and I'm sure he learned a lot from her."

And not all of the experts sound like experts. What was the significance of the Dome of the Rock in Jerusalem? "Imagine, if you will, these new guys coming in and taking over this piece of prime real estate. . . . This is not a fly-by-night, this is something big and important. Islam has come to stay." How did the Muslims view the Mongol invaders? "To the cultured, urban Muslims, these guys were a bunch of savages." When narrator Ben Kingsley sounds more academic than the academics, something has gone wrong in the script. (Kingsley, though, completely mangles the Arabic word for the conquests, *futuh*, and also botches the word *kanuni*, lawgiver, applied to Süleyman the Magnificent.) The inclusion of one or two of the surviving doyens of Islamic historical studies might have added some *gravitas* to the proceedings. As it stands, the overall (and largely erroneous) impression is that American expertise in this area is fairly thin, stuck somewhere at a stage of uncritical acceptance of the Muslim sources.

In sum, *Islam: Empire of Faith* is a compliment to Islamic civilization, but it is no compliment to the intelligent and inquisitive viewer. "There were a lot of areas we just didn't have the money to go to," Gardner has been quoted as saying. "Television always involves a lot of compromise."[10] True enough. But the same can be said of art, literature, and scholarship. The problem arises when compromises become consistent, even to the point of deliberate misrepresentation. And there is too much of a pattern in this film to assume Gardner's naïveté.

Gardner's peculiar approach to his medium also makes this film a particularly potent form of propaganda. He set out, in his words, "to borrow from the visual vocabulary of feature films and even music videos to create an authentic and truly evocative portal through which the audience can experience the deep past."[11] This is not the documentary art. Opening "portals" to "experience the deep past" is the art of the Florida theme park and the Vegas theme hotel. And by emulating them, Gardner has driven his subject closer to the center of American culture. Let us admit it: no amount of scholarship could ever achieve that.

But why draw lines? Why not share the "experience" with those who don't watch public television? Perhaps an "Islam experience" is really the ideal medium by which to introduce Americans to the grandeur of Islam. Imagine Gardner's reenactments before us on a giant screen; from behind our 3D glasses, the idols of the Ka'ba seem to crash down around us. Imagine the call to prayer from Cairo's thousand mosques in surround-sound. Surely there is enough money in Arabia and the Muslim dispersion to bring this off, especially after the recent drubbing of Islam's image. Islam, camera, action.

Notes

1. Gardner Films in association with PBS and Devillier Donegan Enterprises, 2000. Website at http://www.pbs.org/empires/islam/.
2. Archived at https://web.archive.org/web/20010419234445/http://realscreensummit.com/speakers/gardner.html.
3. Richard Grenier, *The Marrakesh One-Two* (Boston, MA: Houghton Mifflin, 1983), 3.
4. John Maynard, "After Request, PBS Edits 'Islam,'" *Washington Post*, May 8, 2001.
5. A. J. Toynbee, *A Study of History*, vol. 6 (London: Oxford University Press, 1939), 196.
6. Ibn Hisham, *Life of the Prophet*, quoted in *Encyclopaedia of Islam*, 2 ed., s.v. "Muhammad."
7. *Encyclopaedia of Islam*, 2nd ed., s.v. "Dimashk."
8. Available, most readily, on the cover of Bernard Lewis, *Race and Slavery in the Middle East: An Historical Inquiry* (New York: Oxford University Press, 1990).
9. Stephen O. Murray, "Homosexuality among Slave Elites in Ottoman Turkey," in *Islamic Homosexualities*, eds. Stephen O. Murray and Will Roscoe (New York: New York University Press, 1997), 174–86.
10. Quoted by Elizabeth Jensen, "'Islam: Empire of Faith' Keeps Eye on Culture, Not Religion," *Los Angeles Times*, May 27, 2001.
11. "About the Producer," archived at http://web.archive.org/web/20011215135726/http://www.pbs.org/empires/islam/filmproducer.html.

8

Afghani and America

In 2010, the U.S. State Department released a photograph of Ambassador Frank Ricciardone, number two at the U.S. embassy in Kabul, paying his respects at the mausoleum of Sayyid Jamal al-Din al-Afghani on the campus of Kabul University. Afghani (1838–97) is revered in Afghanistan as a native son who inspired the modern revival of Islam, and who championed both internal reform and resistance to Western imperialism. Reformists and Islamists around the Muslim world equally claim him as their precursor. In the course of his peripatetic career, he preached in Iran, Egypt, the Ottoman Empire, India, Russia, and Europe. His famous Paris-based newspaper, *al-Urwa al-wuthqa*, spread his ideas far and wide.[1]

This was not the first time the United States had paid tribute to the memory of Afghani. In 2002, then-U.S. ambassador Robert Finn came to the dilapidated mausoleum and pledged $25,000 from his government to restore it. Finn said this about Afghani:

> This is, in a sense, a double tribute by my country. In doing so we honor the memory of an Afghan and Muslim intellectual giant of the nineteenth century: a scholar, journalist, political thinker, advisor to kings and a revolutionary who inspired Muslims from Egypt to India.
>
> This was a man steeped in the learning of the Qur'an who called for freedom, reason and scientific inquiry. He was a learned man, a skilled writer and debater, he had the moral courage of strong convictions, criticizing the West for its materialism but not shying away from criticizing the Muslim rulers of the day and what he saw as self-destructive tendencies in his own religion.

Finn concluded: "This donation is also a recognition that the day will come when Afghanistan will again produce great leaders and thinkers that will shake the world and inspire hope and reform."[2]

No doubt it made diplomatic sense for the United States to help restore this Afghan national monument, and for its ambassador to praise Afghanistan's national hero. At the same time, it is ironic in more ways than one can count.

Our Kind of Muslim?

First, Jamal al-Din al-Afghani is not exactly the sort of Muslim role model the United States usually promotes. He was what used to be called an agitator, someone who hated the great Western power of the era (Britain) not just for its materialism but for its imperialism, and who didn't just criticize Muslim rulers but actively plotted against them. On both counts, Osama bin Laden could just as readily claim Afghani's mantle.

In particular, Afghani believed that the rulers of the day had to be removed, if necessary by the bullet. A disciple once found him pacing back and forth, shouting, "There is no deliverance except in killing, there is no safety except in killing."[3] These were not idle words. In 1896, he inspired a disciple to assassinate Nasir al-Din Shah, ruler of Iran. Afghani said this about the assassination:

> Surely it was a good deed to kill this bloodthirsty tyrant, this Nero on the Persian throne . . . who nonetheless knew how to throw sand in the eyes of civilized Europe so that it did not recognize his deeds. It was well done then to kill him, for it may be a warning to others. This is the first time that a Shah has found his death not in a palace revolution but at the hand of an ordinary man, and thus for a tyrant to receive just recompense for his deeds.[4]

It is no accident, then, that Afghani is regularly honored by the Islamic Republic of Iran, where his name graces a public square in the capital and his image appears on a postage stamp.

So Afghani is not exactly an exemplar of someone who tried to "shake the world" peacefully, and one cannot help but imagine that were he alive today, he would be on some agency's no-fly list. He also died a wanted man. At the time of the shah's assassination, Afghani resided in the Ottoman capital, Istanbul, and Iran sought his extradition. The Ottoman authorities refused, but they put Afghani under house arrest. He died there less than a year later, and the Ottoman authorities buried him without ceremony in an unmarked grave, the fate reserved for subversives.

But that is not the only irony. Afghani wasn't an Afghan. He called himself Afghani in his travels around the Muslim world, but he was born and raised in a small town near Hamadan in Iran. As a young man, he spent some years in the Shi'ite academies in Iraq. In his travels to Sunni lands, his origins would have been held against him, so he took to calling himself "Afghani," leaving Muslim listeners to presume him to be a Sunni. The documentary record on this point is clear, and the irrefutable evidence is marshaled in an appendix to the definitive biography of Afghani by the historian Nikki Keddie.[5]

Afghani's Iranian nationality was well known to intelligence agencies and Orientalists in his own day. The State Department later established it as well. In 1936, J. Rives Childs, an American diplomat then stationed in Cairo, visited Tehran, and in an official dispatch laid out the evidence, which included the presence in Iran of Afghani's family. The historian Elie Kedourie described Childs as "probably the first Westerner conclusively to establish Afghani's Shi'ite and Iranian origin."[6] Afghans obviously believe otherwise, but it is still odd that a U.S. ambassador, even to Afghanistan, should take a position in favor of the Afghan claim, which the State Department disproved even before scholars debunked it.

I have referred to Afghani's putative remains, and for good reason. There is no certainty that Afghani is buried in Afghani's tomb. This is due to yet another American, the wealthy philanthropist and Islamophile Charles Crane. In 1924, Crane set out to find Afghani's grave in Istanbul, to satisfy his penchant for "visiting the graves of men who have made a deep impression on humanity." He explored several cemeteries but had no luck until "a fine old green-turbaned sheikh appeared," showed him an "absolutely flat and unmarked" spot, and proclaimed it to be Afghani's grave. In 1926, Crane erected a tombstone and iron balustrade on the plot. As Afghani's reputation grew, Muslims began to make pilgrimages to the grave marked by Crane. This was also the grave from which, in 1944, remains were removed for transfer to Kabul, via Iraq and India. Elie Kedourie later put it succinctly: "Whether what was moved from Istanbul to Kabul was Jamal al-Din's body, or whether the monument at Kabul, in seeking to do honour to someone who, in any case, was not an Afghan, was merely sheltering the remains of some unknown Muslim, God alone knows."[7]

The final irony in this story of America and Afghani may be found in the account of the British ambassador to Afghanistan who, in 1944, witnessed what he called the "pious fraud" of Afghani's reburial in Kabul. In his report on the event, the British diplomat described how the U.S. ambassador to Afghanistan, Cornelius Van H. Engert, succumbed to the chaos that accompanied the historic occasion: "My American colleague who was sitting on a chair somewhat in the background was completely overwhelmed by the mob. He had borne the previous delay and the lack of organization with scant patience, but this was the last straw, and he left the proceedings in disgust." So Americans have twice refurbished Afghani's tomb, but didn't have the patience to stay through his funeral.

The United States had nothing to do with Afghani while he lived, but it has become his present-day patron out of necessity, given the dearth of neutral symbols on which to build an Afghan identity. Afghani is serviceable precisely because he wasn't an Afghan at all. But if a moral lurks in this story, perhaps it is that in Afghanistan, where the truth is a rare commodity, be especially careful not to deceive yourself.

Two Documents

Below are two of the documents quoted above, neither published before.

- *Charles Crane's unpublished memoirs.*[8] *Crane begins by noting that while in Istanbul, in December 1924, he met "a splendid young Afghan by the name of Abdul Rahman."*

For a long time I had been searching the world for a really great Moslem but without much success. Everywhere, however, I kept hearing the remark, "Oh, you ought to have been here a generation earlier when Jemal Al din el Afghani was alive."

I like to visit the graves of men who have made a deep impression on humanity, so I decided to search for the grave of Jemal Al din el Afghani. Abdul Rahman was greatly touched that I showed appreciation of his fellow-countryman and said that he, too, would like to search for the grave and would try to find out where Jemal Al din el Afghani was buried.

In the previous year at San Remo I had seen the last of the Sultans of Turkey, who is living there in exile, and he had told me that el Afghani had been his tutor; he knew he had died in Chislis, a suburb of Constantinople, and was buried in that vicinity. Abdul Rahman volunteered to find the place for me and we visited the larger cemeteries in Chislis, and searched them from end to end without result. None of the old men who worked around the cemeteries had ever heard of el Afghani.

One day a fine old green-turbaned sheikh appeared and said, "They tell me you're looking for the grave of el Afghani."

"Yes," I said, "I've been hunting a long time for it and am rather surprised that a man of so much distinction could have lived here in the capital of the Caliphs without anyone knowing where he was buried."

"My father," he said, "was his sheikh in Balkh and later when el Afghan came to Constantinople from Cairo, he became my sheikh, and I was very close to him all the time he was here. When he died I, unhappily, was in a hospital and he was carried to his grave by only the porters of the cemetery. The cemetery is in Chislis and if you would like me to take you there I would be glad to do so."

As we went to the cemetery the old sheikh said, "There is no mark on the grave of el Afghani but I know its place by the line from two trees which I noted when I first found it."

We found the two trees and on taking our bearings came to the little plot of ground, absolutely flat and unmarked, where this man, one of the most distinguished Moslems that ever lived, was buried.

• *Despatch by Giles Frederick Squire, British minister to Afghanistan.*[9]

British Legation, Kabul.
6th January 1944 [read: 1945]

Sir,

1. For the past fortnight the attention of the Afghan Government has been largely devoted to the ceremonies connected with the arrival from Turkey and reinterment at Kabul of the coffin of Sayyid Jamaluddin Afghani. The whole procedure had been planned with a view to promoting Afghan solidarity and stimulating Afghan nationalism by laying emphasis on the example of one of their own countrymen who was also one of the protagonists of Islam in the 19th century and who undoubtedly passed several years of his early manhood in Afghanistan. It is of course unfortunate that, although in India and Afghanistan he appears to be accepted without question as having been a native of Afghanistan, Persian historians state categorically that he was in fact a Persian by birth, having been born near Hamadan.

2. I am told that ever since the time of Amir Habibullah Khan the Afghans have made periodical attempts to have the remains brought back to Afghanistan, but it is only with the recent decision on the part of the Turkish Government to remove the original tomb in Istanbul to make room for a road improvement scheme that they have been successful.

3. Preliminary arrangements were made by the Afghan Ambassador at Ankara in consultation with his Government with some secrecy in order if possible to avoid arousing the opposition of the Persians in time for them to sabotage the project. This object appears to be achieved but by a somewhat narrow margin. The coffin, accompanied by the Afghan Minister in Iraq, was brought first to Baghdad, and thence by air to Karachi. From there it was brought by train successively to Lahore, Peshawar, Jalalabad and finally to Kabul. After being met at Dakkar [read: Dakka] by a deputation specially sent from Kabul for the purpose, the coffin was brought to Jalalabad where the Prime Minister, who is in residence there, took the leading part in its reception. The last stage of the journey to Kabul was made on December 30th. The cortege was met at Bagrami some 6 miles out of town by Cabinet Ministers, important civil and military officials, members of [the] National Assembly and other notables, and escorted in state to the Assembly Hall of the Faculty of Law which is temporarily housed in Habibiya College where the coffin remained for the night guarded by students. The streets were lined by police and military and the population of Kabul and the surrounding villages were turned out by order to view the procession.

4. The final scene was enacted on December 31st when the coffin was interred in state in a plot of open ground in the suburb of Aliabad, some 3 miles out of the town. The grave was covered for the occasion by a temporary awning but presumably a suitable building will in due course be erected over it. I understand that it will eventually be the central feature of a public garden. Although the most elaborate official program for these two days was drawn up, the Afghans felt somewhat diffident in inviting the diplomatic corps officially to take part in the ceremonies as, except in the case of the Persian Embassy of whose hostility they were assured, they were by no means certain of the reception that might be accorded to their invitation. They therefore merely informed the Legations by telephone some two or three days in advance that the coffin was expected shortly in Kabul, that the interment would take place at 10.30 AM on the morning after its arrival, and that if members of the diplomatic corps would like to attend they would be welcome. Subsequently messages were sent to the effect that we were not expected to go in morning coats but that if we wished to take wreaths for the grave, the Protocol Department would be happy to provide them! In the event the Turkish Ambassador and Egyptian Charge d'Affaires both met the cortege at Bagrami and accompanied it on the following morning from the Habibiya College to Aliabad. The

Axis Legations were content to be represented only at Aliabad by the German Chancellier, Schmidt (the only person to wear a top hat for the occasion) and by two secretaries from the Japanese Legation. All the heads of missions of Allied nations, with the notable exception of the Persian Embassy, attended, accompanied by one or more members of their staff, the Russian Embassy in particular turning out in force.

5. I have never yet seen a funeral ceremony in the East carried out with order and dignity and this was no exception. We were told that the interment would take place at 10.30 AM and were on the ground at the appointed time. It transpired however that the procession was not even due to leave Kabul until 10.15, and as it was to be accompanied by a mounted police escort and an infantry guard of honour it was hardly to be expected that it would cover the three miles to Aliabad in a quarter of an hour. It was in fact not until 11.30 that the head of the procession made its appearance in the distance. Fortunately it was a sunny day without much wind and the snow that had recently fallen had melted so that the hour's wait was no great hardship.

6. When the cortege at last arrived the coffin was taken from the hearse and carried to the grave by members of the Cabinet, the procession being headed by the Minister of Court and Minister of Education. The Minister of Defence, in the absence of the Prime Minister, was expected to be the principal personage at the ceremony and his absence has since excited some comment. Immediately the coffin reached the graveside the crowd of spectators, which had hitherto been kept at a respectful distance by a rope barrier, surged forward and crowded round to get a closer view of the proceedings. Fortunately those of us who were standing fairly close to the grave were not seriously incommoded but my American colleague who was sitting on a chair somewhat in the background was completely overwhelmed by the mob. He had borne the previous delay and the lack of organization with scant patience, but this was the last straw, and he left the proceedings in disgust. Eventually some policemen were found to restore some sort of order and the proceedings continued with a recital from the Koran, a sermon in Persian, a lengthy oration by M. Najibullah Khan and finally a poem by Khalili, the Afghan poet laureate. The great services of the deceased Sayyid to Islam were eulogized in glowing terms and stress was laid on his abiding affection for his native country and his longing to return to it, a desire which had now at last been fulfilled. Afghanistan was congratulated in having received back one of her most distinguished sons into her bosom. To those of us who were by no

means convinced that the Saint's native country was not in reality Persia the proceedings could not but seem somewhat farcical. Wreaths were then brought forward and deposited on the grave, the German Chancellier accompanying his with a fine Nazi salute, and the proceedings ended with an undignified scramble for our waiting cars which, without any attempt at any police control, were left to make their way as best they could through the crowd. On the following day January 1st His Majesty the King visited the grave and placed a wreath on it.

7. It is not easy yet to gauge the political effect of the action taken by the Afghan Government in this case. The bitter opposition aroused in Persia and especially in the Persian press, has been carefully concealed from the public who are quite unaware that there is any doubt as to the Sayyid's real origin. And in fairness to Afghanistan it must be admitted that, since their failure to secure the extradition and execution of his living person, the Persians have never shown the least interest in their countryman during all the years that his remains have been reposing in Turkey, nor do they appear hitherto to have insisted that "The Afghan" was in fact a Persian. The Afghans, on the other hand, have always taken it for granted that he was an Afghan and as such have venerated his tomb. The wide publicity which has recently been given to his life and political activities in the Afghan press appears to have had considerable effect and all classes seem to be highly satisfied at the arrival of his remains in their country, and to give their Government full credit for what they have done. From this point of view therefore the policy of the Government seems to have been vindicated.

8. I admit having been myself at one time doubtful of the wisdom of assisting the Afghan Government too openly in what may be held to be their pious fraud, but from the point of view of our political relations with Afghanistan the provision of facilities for bringing the coffin by air from Baghdad to Karachi and the attention paid to it during its passage through India have been amply rewarded. The Afghans are highly gratified and I have received the most cordial letter from the Minister for Foreign Affairs expressing the appreciation of his Government for all the assistance afforded by the Government of India and for the respect paid to the coffin in India. They were particularly touched by the fact that the Premier of the North West Frontier Province with his Finance Minister accompanied it to the Indian border. The Afghan Minister to Baghdad has made repeated reference in public speeches to the courtesies offered by the Indian Government and the Indian public and the press has freely echoed these sentiments. The whole affair has in fact

done a great deal to bring all classes of Afghans in the Eastern Province and in Kabul itself to a realization of the genuine friendliness with which "our Indian brothers" are now regarded by their Government.

9. I am sending copies of this despatch to the Secretary of State for India, the Government of India and to His Majesty's Ambassador in Tehran.

I have the honor to be,
with the highest respect, Sir,
Your most humble obedient servant,
G.F. Squire
HIS MAJESTY'S MINISTER, KABUL.

Notes

1. See the definitive biography by Nikki R. Keddie, *Sayyid Jamal ad-Din "al-Afghani": A Political Biography* (Berkeley: University of California Press, 1972).
2. "Remarks of Ambassador Robert P. Finn on the Occasion of the Ceremony Commemorating a Grant from the U.S. Government for the Reconstruction of the Tomb and Monument of Sayed Jamaludin al-Afghani," October 9, 2002, archived at https://web.archive.org/web/20090519013357/http://www.america.gov/st/washfile-english/2002/October/20021009162600s-domowit@pd.state.gov0.9141504.html.
3. Quoted by Sylvia G. Haim, *Arab Nationalism: An Anthology* (Berkeley: University of California Press, 1962), 8.
4. Quoted by Keddie, *Sayyid Jamal ad-Din "al-Afghani,"* 412.
5. Ibid., 427–33.
6. E. K. [Elie Kedourie], review of J. Rives Childs's memoirs, *Middle Eastern Studies* 9 (1973): 374.
7. Elie Kedourie, *Afghani and 'Abduh: An Essay on Religious Unbelief and Political Activism in Modern Islam* (London: Frank Cass, 1966), 63.
8. Institute of Current World Affairs Records, Columbia University Library, Subseries I.2: Charles Richard Crane Memoirs, box 71, 288–89.
9. The British National Archives, Public Record Office, London, FO371/45210.

9

He Might Have Been Pope

The election of the Argentine Cardinal Jorge Mario Bergoglio as Pope Francis in March 2013 took seasoned Vatican observers by surprise. The media had profiled other candidates, leaving the impression that a long-shot took the title. Pundits began to invoke the so-called Pignedoli Principle, named (by George Weigel, Vatican analyst) for Cardinal Sergio Pignedoli, a media favorite who was passed over after the death of Pope Paul VI in 1978. The principle? "A man's chances of becoming pope decrease in proportion to the number of times he's described as *papabile* [a possible pope] in the press."

The affable Pignedoli (pronounced *Peen-yeh-doly*) had been very much in the race in August 1978. He was said to be Paul VI's preferred successor, and the Italian news magazines sang his praises. The London bookmaking firm Ladbroke's pegged him as a 5-2 favorite. As the media predictions piled up, Pignedoli reportedly prepared for victory by going on a crash diet so that he could fit into the white cassock of a new pope. (In another version, he had a cassock specially tailored.) Weigel described what happened next: "When the cardinals assembled in the Sistine Chapel to choose a successor to Pope Paul in August 1978, Cardinal Pignedoli—according to reliable accounts—was left so far behind that you'd have needed a telescope to find him at the end of the second ballot. He died a few years later, forgotten by those who had once confidently declared him *papabile*."[1]

So Pignedoli, if he is remembered at all, is remembered as an also-ran. But the story is more interesting than that. When he died in June 1980, he was still important enough to warrant an obituary in the *New York Times*. The item mentioned his failed run for the papacy in August 1978, and added that he was again regarded as *papabile* when John Paul I, Paul VI's successor, died in September 1978 after only thirty-four days in office. (In the resulting conclave, the cardinals passed him over again and surprised the world by electing a Polish pope.) The obituary then added this: "The Cardinal was also remembered, to his regret, for having signed a statement at an Islamic-Christian conference in Tripoli in 1976 condemning Zionism. He said afterward that he was a victim of an incomplete if not mistaken translation."[2]

Therein lies a story, and it puts Pignedoli in an additional category: not just of papal also-rans, but also of Westerners used by Libya's late dictator Mu'ammar Qadhafi to enhance his rule.[3] According to some experts, the episode may even have cost Pignedoli his shot at the papacy. Regime change in Tripoli and personnel change in Rome constitute a reasonable pretext for revisiting the subject. And since it is one more cautionary tale about the risks of appeasement, especially in the Middle East, the lesson may well be timeless.

"The Pope's Kissinger"

The Italian-born Pignedoli started off as a naval chaplain in the Second World War (a direct hit on his cruiser famously sent him flying into the sea), and he later built a reputation over many years as a roving Vatican emissary. He served in various capacities in South America, Africa, and Canada, reputedly spoke a dozen languages, visited well over a hundred countries, and had a rolodex of ten thousand contacts around the globe. (It was once written of him that "he has a preposterous number of friends.")[4] In 1967, as apostolic delegate to Canada, he drove 7,300 miles across the country and back in thirty-three days, visiting mission outposts. Paul VI created him cardinal in 1973, and immediately named him president of what was then called the Secretariat for Non-Christians. ("Non-Christians" for that purpose excluded the Jews, a sensitive issue handled by a separate commission.) For someone reputed to be "the Pope's Kissinger," treating with the wider world seemed like the perfect assignment.

The energetic and gregarious Pignedoli quickly concluded that he should launch a campaign to improve Vatican relations with the world of Islam. The Catholic Church had its ear to the ground in Muslim lands, and had picked up the rumbling of the coming Islamic resurgence. The new cardinal thought that the Vatican could diminish Muslim-Christian tensions (and protect its interests in Muslim lands) by engaging a reputable Muslim partner in a conciliatory religious dialogue.

Ah, but who? Where was the equivalent of the Catholic Church? Who was the Muslim pope? The impossibility of answering these questions immediately highlights one of the key distinctions between Christianity and Islam. Bernard Lewis has put it succinctly:

> There is no church in Islam. There is no priesthood in the sense of an ordination and a sacred office. There is no Vatican, no pope, no cardinals, no bishops, no church councils; there is no hierarchy such as exists in Christendom.[5]

For non-Muslims, it is often tempting to see Saudi Arabia, seat of Islam's holiest places, as some sort of "center" of the Islamic faith. So did Pignedoli, setting out in April 1974 to visit the kingdom, armed with a letter from the Pope. King Faisal gave him an audience—and an earful. The Saudi king had only one thing on his mind: the Jews. They had no holy places in Jerusalem, he insisted; only Muslims and Christians had incontestable rights to holy places in the city. At one point, King Faisal raised his voice to declare (erroneously) that under Islam, "Jews had never been allowed in Palestine and particularly in Jerusalem."[6] The Saudi king's purpose was plain: to line up the Catholic Church behind the demand for Muslim sovereignty over the holy city.

This was not the sort of exchange Pignedoli had in mind, so he looked elsewhere. He next visited Egypt, in September 1974, hoping to open a channel to Al-Azhar, the famed university and another "center" of Islam. But the Sheikh al-Azhar didn't express any interest in a religious dialogue. Instead, he loaded his guest with books on Palestine and the historic role of Al-Azhar in resisting foreign aggression. Pignedoli began to see a pattern. Muslims did not make a distinction between the spiritual and the temporal. As he (later) concluded, "one of the greatest hindrances to dialogue is political intervention in religion. Some people do not make the Gospel's distinction between what is Caesar's and what is God's, and people's minds are, moreover, troubled by local tensions or fear of losing their freedom."[7]

At this moment of impasse, the Vatican received an unexpected overture. In May 1975, a confidant of Mu'ammar Qadhafi, ruler of Libya, arrived in Rome bearing a message. Libya was eager to host an official religious dialogue with the Vatican, for which it would assemble a delegation of influential Muslims from around the world. The dialogue, the Libyan promised, would be limited to theology and religion. A breakthrough! Negotiations commenced, a date was set for a meeting in Tripoli in February 1976, and the Libyans accommodated every request from the Vatican side.[8]

What explained the Libyan initiative? Libya is not a "center" of Islam on par with Saudi Arabia or Egypt—far from it. As important as it is to the world oil market, it has been marginal to the evolution of the faith. Yet Qadhafi thought otherwise—if not about Libya, then certainly about himself. Early in his rule (he seized power in 1969), Qadhafi styled himself as a final authority on Islam, which he depicted as the embodiment of true socialism. True, few Muslims outside Libya took him seriously. But what better way to boost his claim than to demonstrate that Christians took him seriously—and not just any Christians, but the Catholic Church?

"Caught Napping"

The appointed day finally arrived. Pignedoli's fourteen-man contingent landed in Tripoli, expecting a discreet gathering with an equal number of Muslim delegates, and an audience of no more than twenty experts and journalists. But the Libyan organizers had a completely different plan. They had invited over five hundred activists, journalists, and hangers-on (including an American, Kwame Turé, formerly the Black Panther Stokely Carmichael). "Every conceivable revolutionary and conspiratorial movement sent representatives to Tripoli," wrote the journalist Peter Scholl-Latour (who devoted a searing chapter to the episode in his book *Adventures in the East*).[9]

The crowd filled the seaside congress hall where the seminar met, and the proceedings quickly took on a circus atmosphere. The Libyans had failed to honor a promise to name their delegates and provide the texts of their speeches in advance. The reason soon became clear: the Muslim delegates were political operatives, not men of religion. Their speeches would later be described (by the secretary of the Vatican delegation) as "aggressive and recriminatory."[10] They attacked the Church for falsifying scripture, launching the Crusades, and proselytizing among Muslims. This was punctuated by repeated and vehement attacks against Israel, Zionism, and the Jews. In the face of this assault, "the delegates from the Vatican cut a poor figure," wrote Scholl-Latour. "Cardinal Pignedoli, naturally short of stature, seemed to shrink even more; he had adopted a strategy of permanent apology."[11]

The highlight came with the arrival of Qadhafi himself. Scholl-Latour:

> He did not bother to go as far as the stage; with exaggerated modesty he sat down among the spectators. And immediately the Cardinal, his stance expressing servility, sped toward the Libyan head of state, took his hand—he came close to kissing it—and led the Libyan, who

was going through the motions of protesting, to the dais. Tumultuous applause broke out; the Moslems in the audience had caught sight of God's elect. In fact Qaddafi appeared like a beaming movie star. He radiated an attractive youthfulness. . . . His clothes were chosen with the utmost simplicity: black trousers and a black turtleneck sweater. He moved with the grace of a cat. Alongside this desert warrior the overzealous Roman prelate with his red skullcap, the red sash across his cassock, the red socks in pumps, seemed a comedian.[12]

Another journalist thought he detected an awkward moment in the encounter between the colonel and the cardinal:

A path was made for Cardinal Pignedoli who came down from his place on the rostrum to greet the Libyan leader. It was an interesting moment, with one revealing result which probably no one in the entire building was aware of except those, like myself, who happened to be a few feet away. The Cardinal made a gesture to indicate that he would like to sit down next to "Brother Colonel." Gaddafi was taken aback and clearly did not want to share the inverted limelight. Visibly thinking quickly, he made a flourishing gesture indicating that the Cardinal's rightful place was one of honor on the platform. It was nevertheless a snub, as I could clearly see from the Cardinal's disappointed expression, though it cast a shadow over his face for only a split second.[13]

Qadhafi later mounted the stage, producing what appeared to one journalist "like a medieval tableau of the Sultan and the wise men."[14] In fact, it was more like a medieval disputation. In a later address to the conference, Qadhafi said that there was no great gap between Christianity and Islam. All that was needed to close it was for Christians to correct the falsifications in their Gospels and recognize the Prophet Muhammad as the bearer of the divine revelation. Pignedoli's delegation (according to Scholl-Latour) was "overcome by obvious confusion and consternation."

So how was the gap to be bridged? Away from the congress hall, Libyan and Vatican secretaries worked behind the scenes to formulate a joint communiqué—for how could such a meeting end without one?

What happened next astonished everyone. At the close of the conference, as Pignedoli and Qadhafi left the congress hall together, the Libyans announced the text (in Arabic) of a joint communiqué. It included two paragraphs devoted to Palestine. Paragraph 20 denounced Zionism as "an aggressive racialist movement, extraneous to Palestine and the whole region of the East." Paragraph 21 affirmed "the Arab character of Jerusalem" and rejected "plans to Judaize, partition or internationalize" the city. Both "parties" affirmed "the national rights of the Palestinian people and their right to return to their lands" and demanded "the liberation of all the occupied territories."[15] A bombshell! The assembled media rushed out the doors to report a dramatic shift in Vatican policy toward Israel and the Palestinians.

Except that there was no shift. According to Pignedoli, the final communiqué was shown to him only "at the very last minute," and he signed off on it unaware that it included the offending paragraphs. It may have been a literal case of *tradurre è tradire*: according to one source, "the Vatican's representatives in the drafting committee were Arab Christians who did not fully explain the text" to Pignedoli.[16] The cardinal made a desperate attempt to convene a press conference and issue a "clarification," but his Libyan hosts blocked the move, citing "technical reasons." By then, it was too late anyway: he had been "caught napping" (the words of a journalist), the Libyans had taken advantage, and the media had a story. A wire service report set the tone: "Whoever suggested the Vatican send delegates to Libya for a great religious meeting with Moslem leaders may be in deep trouble. The widely publicized Islamic-Christian symposium in Tripoli this week is one of the biggest fiascoes of recent Vatican diplomacy."[17]

The Roman Curia—the Vatican's government—went into damage control mode, formally disavowing the two offending paragraphs, as "their content does not correspond, in its essential points, to the well-known position of the Holy See."[18] Vatican sources informed a Jewish press agency that the Vatican delegation to Tripoli "was not empowered to reach political decisions," and should not have done so.[19] A "highly informed" Vatican source reported that the Holy See was "mortified" by the episode, but "understandably wants to avoid charging bad faith on the part of the Muslim participants or admitting incompetence or naiveté on its own part."[20] Of course, those were precisely the ingredients that produced the debacle.

The "Pignedoli Principle"

Had Pignedoli's ambitions been limited, the Tripoli fiasco would not have mattered much. But he aspired to be pope, and this was no secret when the vacancy opened in 1978. One journalist noted that while the Holy See hadn't reprimanded the cardinal, "memories in the Curia are long, and Vatican watchers believe that Pignedoli's prospects of becoming pope have declined seriously."[21] Another assessment, while describing Pignedoli as "the current papal frontrunner," reported that the Tripoli conference "has once again become an item for controversy, resuscitated by factional opposition to Pignedoli's candidacy to succeed Paul as Pope. It has been claimed by such diverse publications as the *London Times, Corriere della Sera, Le Monde,* and others that Pignedoli's management of the Vatican-Islamic conference will weigh heavily against his election as Paul VI's successor."[22]

When Pignedoli lost out, another Vatican expert estimated that his chances had been "badly damaged" by the episode, which "was widely regarded as a gaffe and as an indication of his unsuitability for the Papacy."[23] According to Vaticanologist Peter Hebblethwaite, the Tripoli debacle gave Pignedoli's opponents a lever to use against him: "I was present on that occasion [in Tripoli], and thought the mistake forgivable. But this incident was exploited by Pignedoli's enemies who resented his approachableness and popularity."[24]

Of course, it is easy to come up with other reasons for Pignedoli's falling short in the Sistine Chapel.[25] Perhaps it really was the "Pignedoli Principle"—an excess of media attention. But some experts claim it isn't a principle at all, since there are plenty of examples of frontrunners taking the papal title.[26] If so, then the "Pignedoli Principle" may be up for redefinition, lest the man be forgotten completely. A good alternative might be this: the closer you dance with a dictator, the more likely your toes are to be crushed.

Notes

1. George Weigel, "The Pignedoli Principle," in his syndicated column *The Catholic Difference,* May 3, 2001, archived at https://web.archive.org/web/20151031122412/http://eppc.org/publications/the-pignedoli-principle/.
2. "Cardinal Pignedoli Dies in Italy at 70: Diplomat Was a Leading Contender in the Last 2 Papal Elections," *New York Times,* June 16, 1980.
3. Paul M. Barrett, "The Professors and Qaddafi's Extreme Makeover," *BusinessWeek,* April 6, 2011.
4. Alexander Chancellor, "Notebook," *The Spectator* (London), August 19, 1978.
5. Bernard Lewis, "Islamic Revolution," *New York Review of Books,* January 21, 1988.
6. *Proche-Orient chrétien* 24 (1974), 203–4.
7. *Secretariatus pro non Christianis Bulletin* 36 (1977), 95.
8. The fullest account of the Tripoli "dialogue," with bibliography, is by Maurice Borrmans, "Le seminaire du dialogue islamo-chrétien de Tripoli (Libye)," *Islamochristiana* 2 (1976): 135–70 (with Arabic text of final declaration). See also the official "Report," *Secretariatus pro non Christianis Bulletin* 31 (1976): 5–21.

9. Peter Scholl-Latour, *Adventures in the East: Travels in the Land of Islam*, trans. Ruth Hein (New York: Bantam Books, 1988), 18–29.

10. Piero Rossano, "Terzo periodo romano: Segretario del Segretariato per i non cristiani (1973–1980)," archived at https://web.archive.org/web/20130429082557/http://www.pierorossano.net/sez1104916681/sez1105293273/pag1105352545.

11. Scholl-Latour, *Adventures in the East*, 19.

12. Ibid., 21.

13. Gerard Noel, "I foresaw problems right from the start," *Catholic Herald* (London), February 13, 1976.

14. Desmond O'Grady, "Gaddafi's Vatican weirdness," *Eureka Street*, June 17, 2009, archived at https://web.archive.org/web/20110218211411/http://www.eurekastreet.com.au/article.aspx?aeid=14487.

15. *Osservatore Romano*, February 12, 1976; Arabic text in Borrmans, "Le seminaire du dialogue islamo-chrétien de Tripoli," 169.

16. *Africa Confidential* 17 (1976), 18.

17. United Press International, February 9, 1976.

18. Associated Press, "Vatican Rejects Attack on Zionism," *New York Times*, February 12, 1976.

19. "Vatican Says Its Mideast Position Has Not Changed in Any Way," Jewish Telegraphic Agency, February 10, 1976, archived at https://web.archive.org/web/20130427040740/http://archive.jta.org/article/1976/02/11/2974142/vatican-says-its-mideast-position-has-not-changed-in-any-way.

20. Religion News Service, "Vatican-Moslem Dialogue Ends in Dispute," *Courier-Journal*, February 18, 1976, archived at http://web.archive.org/web/20160303203128/http://lib.catholiccourier.com/1976-courier-journal/courier-journal-1976%20-%200129.pdf.

21. Gary MacEóin and the Committee for the Responsible Election of the Pope, *The Inner Elite: Dossiers of Papal Candidates* (Kansas City, KS: S. Andrews and McMeel, 1978), 222.

22. "The Scientific Ecumenicism of Paul VI," *Executive Intelligence Review* 5, no. 12 (August 22–28, 1978), 35.

23. Vincent Browne, "The Making of a Pope," *Politico*, September 1, 1978, archived at https://web.archive.org/web/20151031202438/http://politico.ie/archive/making-pope.

24. Peter Hebblethwaite, *In The Vatican* (Bethesda, MD: Adler & Adler, 1986), 163.

25. A breezy account of the proceedings appears in Gordon Thomas and Max Morgan-Witts, *Pontiff* (New York: Doubleday, 1983).

26. David Leonhardt, "In Papal Elections, Are Long Shots the Rule?," *FiveThirtyEight* blog, *New York Times*, March 13, 2013, archived at http://web.archive.org/web/20130314180318/http://fivethirtyeight.blogs.nytimes.com/2013/03/13/in-papal-elections-are-long-shots-the-rule/.

10

Hamas of the Intellectuals

*The fundamentalists do not make me angry, for they are
believers in their own way. But I am angered by their secular
supporters and by their atheist supporters who believe but in one
religion—their own pictures on television.*
—Mahmud Darwish, Palestinian poet[1]

They were, those people, a kind of solution.
—Constantine Cavafy, *Waiting for the Barbarians*

The late Edward Said, the Palestinian-American icon, described the
role of the intellectual as "speaking truth to power." In that spirit, many
Palestinian academics and thinkers followed Said in breaking with
Yasser Arafat and Fatah in the decade after the Oslo Accords, accusing
the Palestinian regime of corruption and compromise. Then in 2006,
the Islamist movement Hamas surprised the world by winning free
Palestinian elections, ushering in a new era of rivalry and division in
Palestinian politics. Hamas in power similarly accused the nationalist
old guard of corruption and compromise, but from a different point
of departure.

By that time, Edward Said was gone (he died in 2003), so no one
could know for certain how he would have interpreted the power
shift. But during his last decade, he made occasional references to
Hamas (and the Palestinian Islamic Jihad). When these references are
assembled, as they are below, they convey a consistent message. In
the immediate aftermath of the Hamas victory, Palestinian academics
seemed to have ignored it, as they rushed headlong to embrace an
Islamist regime.

A Devil's Pact

Said made his first reference to Hamas in 1993, after two visits to the
West Bank. At the time, Hamas hadn't yet become a household word

in the West. Nor had it perfected the method of the suicide attack. Said was underwhelmed by the encounter:

> In 1992 when I was there, I briefly met a few of the student leaders who represent Hamas: I was impressed by their sense of political commitment but not at all by their ideas. In 1993 I arranged to spend some more hours with them and with their rivals for political sway, Islamic Jihad. I found them quite moderate when it came to accepting the truths of modern science, for instance (interestingly the four young men I spoke to were students with outstanding records: all of them were scientists or engineers); hopelessly reductive in their views of the West; and irrefragably opposed to the existence of Israel. "The Jews have to leave," one of them said categorically, "except for the ones who were here before 1948." . . . In the main, their ideas are protests against Israeli occupation, their leaders neither especially visible nor impressive, their writings rehashes of old nationalist tracts, now couched in an "Islamic" idiom.[2]

In 1994, Said was interviewed for the BBC, and he repeated his opinion that Hamas had no ideas on offer:

> In my opinion, their ideas about an Islamic state are completely inchoate, unconvincing to anybody who lives there. Nobody takes that aspect of their programme seriously. When you question them, as I have, both on the West Bank and elsewhere: "What are your economic policies? What are your ideas about power stations, or housing?", they reply: "Oh, we're thinking about that." There is no social programme that could be labelled "Islamic." I see them as creatures of the moment, for whom Islam is an opportunity to protest against the current stalemate, the mediocrity and bankruptcy of the ruling party.[3]

That same year, 1994, Said sharpened his critique of Hamas, even as the movement gained momentum as an oppositional force:

> As to Hamas and its actions in the Occupied Territories, I know that the organization is one of the only ones expressing resistance. . . . Yet for any secular intellectual to make a devil's pact with a religious movement is, I think, to substitute convenience for principle. It is simply the other side of the pact we made during the past several decades with dictatorship and nationalism, for example, supporting Saddam Hussein when he went to war with "the Persians."[4]

By placing Hamas in the same box as Saddam, and by equating Islamism with dictatorship, Said left little room for doubt as to the responsibility of the secular critic.

In 1996, the year Hamas gained international notoriety with a series of devastating suicide bombings, Said found still more disparaging adjectives for the growing movement of "Islamic resistance":

> Unfortunately, it is not to my taste, it is not secular resistance. Look at some of the Islamic movements, Hamas on the West Bank, the Islamic Jihad, etc. They are violent and primitive forms of resistance. You know, what Hobsbawn calls pre-capital, trying to get back to communal forms, to regulate personal conduct with simpler and simpler reductive ideas.[5]

In 2000, Said again returned to the poverty of ideas in Hamas:

> They don't have a message about the future. You can't simply say Islam is the only solution. You have to deal with problems of electricity, water, the environment, transportation. Those can't be Islamic. So they've failed on that level.[6]

In 2002, in the midst of the second intifada, Said made his last and most devastating critique of the Islamists, chiding Arafat for allowing them to wreak havoc with the cause:

> He [Arafat] never really reined in Hamas and Islamic Jihad, which suited Israel perfectly so that it would have a ready-made excuse to use the so-called martyr's (mindless) suicide bombings to further diminish and punish the whole people. If there is one thing that has done us more harm as a cause than Arafat's ruinous regime, it is this calamitous policy of killing Israeli civilians, which further proves to the world that we are indeed terrorists and an immoral movement. For what gain, no one has been able to say.[7]

So from an early date, Said discovered that Hamas hadn't a clue as to how to govern. He described it as gripped by "hopelessly reductive" ideas. He dismissed its violent resistance as "primitive" and "mindless," and deplored that violence for doing more harm to the Palestinian cause than the harm done by Arafat. Above all, he warned secular intellectuals against concluding a "devil's pact" with Hamas that would sacrifice principle to convenience. Said would not compromise his secularism. In 1999, he succinctly explained why he could not ally himself with Islamists, even in the shared cause Palestine: "First, I am secular; second, I do not trust religious movements; and third, I disagree with these movements' methods, means, analyses, values, and visions."[8]

Reasonable Hamas

Given Said's standing as the guiding light of Palestinian intellectuals, it is remarkable that not a single one of them echoed his critique of Hamas after the Palestinian elections. To the contrary: several of them rushed to enter that "devil's pact" against which he had warned.

For example, there was Said's own nephew, Saree Makdisi, a professor of literature at UCLA, who kept a weblog, "Speaking Truth to Power." (The title suggested he had anointed himself to keep Said's flame alive.) Makdisi seemed to have forgotten his uncle's dismissal of Hamas rhetoric as "rehashes of old nationalist tracts," when he wrote these fawning words in praise of an article by Hamas politburo chief Khalid Meshaal.

> Meshaal revives the language of genuine struggle rather than that of hopelessness and defeat; he relies on the unapologetic rhetoric of national liberation, rather than the tired cliches and bureaucratic language ("performance," "interim status") borrowed from Israeli and American planners. . . . What was refreshing about Meshaal's piece was his use of a defiant language of struggle.[9]

Similarly, George Basharat, a University of California law professor and activist, wrote an op-ed praising the Palestinians for doing exactly what Said said he could never do on principle: trust a religious movement.

> The Palestinians have gained a government with spine—one they trust will be far less yielding of their fundamental rights. It is to the shame of the secular nationalist Palestinian movement that it was not the one to offer this alternative. One day, Palestinians will have to wrestle with questions of what kind of polity they truly want, Islamic or other. For now, they have entrusted their future to Hamas, and the world will have to grapple with their democratic choice.[10]

Issa Khalaf, Palestinian-American author of a book on Palestinian politics and holder of an Oxford PhD, shared nothing of Said's view of Hamas policy as a danger to the Palestinian cause. To the contrary: he hailed the Hamas "strategy" as "eminently sound, including its principled defense of the Palestinians' core interests, its efforts to create a national consensus and a countervailing balance to the one-sided American-Israeli alliance." He also added his expert assurance that Hamas "will recognize Israel in its pre-1967 lines," and that "its Islamist militancy will be dramatically curtailed upon assumption of the perquisites and symbols of state power." ("There is no question in my mind," he insisted.)[11]

After the elections, Rami Khouri, a Palestinian-Jordanian columnist affiliated with Harvard, met a few Hamas members in the Palestinian refugee camp of Burj al-Barajneh in Beirut. Unlike Said, he came away glowing from his encounter (which lasted all of two-and-a-half hours). In an article entitled "Talking to the Guys from Hamas," he reported his epiphany:

> What does one learn from such encounters? The two most significant themes that emerge from discussions with Hamas officials, and from their many statements, are a commitment to national principles and a clear dose of political pragmatism. . . . Hamas will surely continue its three-year-old slow shift towards more pragmatism and realism, because it is now politically accountable to the entire Palestinian population, and to world public opinion. Incumbency means responsibility and accountability, which inevitably nurture practicality and reasonable compromises.[12]

The following year, Hamas seized power in Gaza by violent force, ignoring Khouri's promise of its "inevitable" transformation. Of course, that was a promise Hamas itself never made; it was made instead by Palestinian intellectuals and their Western academic allies. In making it, they hurriedly jettisoned their own secular principles. "I do not trust religious movements," said Edward Said. After the election of Hamas, not a single Palestinian intellectual dared to repeat that sentence. Instead, an entire raft of them (the sample above is comprised entirely of nominal Christians) insisted that those whom Hamas openly reviled should trust the "Islamic Resistance," and conclude just the sort of "devil's pact" that would strengthen its grip on the Palestinian cause.

In the West Bank, there were some secular Palestinian intellectuals who did criticize Hamas, especially after its bloody seizure of power in Gaza in 2007. But they received little support from their academic peers in the West. In 2009, one of Edward Said's most loyal acolytes, Joseph Massad at Columbia University (another nominal Christian), lashed out viciously against them. From his perch on Morningside Heights, he claimed that they opposed Hamas because it might take away their Johnny Walker Black Label:

> West Bank-based Palestinian intellectuals, like their liberal counterparts across the Arab world, have been active in the last several years in demonizing Hamas as the force of darkness in the region. These

intellectuals (among whom liberal secular Christians, sometimes referred to derisively in Ramallah circles as "the Christian Democratic Party," are disproportionately represented) are mostly horrified that if Hamas came to power, it would ban alcohol. Assuming Hamas would enact such a regulation on the entire population were it to rule a liberated Palestine in some undetermined future, these intellectuals are the kind of intellectuals who prefer an assured collaborating dictatorship with a glass of scotch to a potentially resisting democracy without.[13]

This wasn't tongue-in-cheek. It was the sum of Massad's political analysis of why, in Ramallah, there was no desire to fall into the grip of Hamas and its "resisting democracy." And if booze did not motivate them, it was cash. Massad once claimed that Palestinian poet Mahmud Darwish's criticism of Gaza's secession "can be explained by the monthly checks Darwish receives from the Fatah-controlled Palestinian Authority."[14]

Academic Parasites

There is no more dangerous enterprise in the Middle East, and not only in Gaza, than speaking truth to (and about) Islamist power. If anyone can do so without running a serious risk, it is the secular and secure pro-Palestinian academy in the West. But at crucial moments, these comfortable academics failed to emulate Edward Said, even as they pretended to venerate him. Perhaps this is because the privileges and preferences accorded to these academics depend on the endless conflict Hamas foments. Since 2006, they have existed in a parasitical symbiosis with Hamas, which provides the war-without-end flare-ups that fill teach-ins and classrooms, justifying the constant expansion of the Palestine industry in academe—its appointments, research centers, and grants.

Of course, living in gilded exile, these academics need not contend with the realities of Islamist rule. In particular, they can continue to enjoy *their* booze. When the *New York Times* visited Joseph Massad at home in Manhattan to profile the armchair resister, it reported that *The World Atlas of Wine* rested on his coffee table. "His elaborate freestanding Egyptian water pipe is stoked with apple-flavored tobacco as a weekend indulgence, accompanied by Cognac, after dinner parties."[15]

Notes

1. "Leading Palestinian Poet Mahmoud Darwish on the Events in Gaza," *MEMRI Special Dispatch* no. 1639, June 29, 2007, archived at http://web.archive.org/web/20160303205344/http://www.memri.org/report/en/0/0/0/0/0/0/0/2272.htm.

2. Edward W. Said, *The Politics of Dispossession: The Struggle for Palestinian Self-Determination: 1969–1994* (New York: Vintage Books, 1995), 403–5.
3. Tariq Ali, "Remembering Edward Said, 1935–2003," *New Left Review* 24 (November–December 2003): 64.
4. Edward W. Said, *Peace and Its Discontents: Essays on Palestine in the Middle East Peace Process* (New York: Vintage, 1996), 111.
5. Edward W. Said, *Power, Politics, and Culture* (New York: Vintage, 2007), 416.
6. Edward W. Said and David Barsamian, *Culture and Resistance: Conversations with Edward W. Said* (Cambridge, MA: South End Press, 2003), 62.
7. Edward W. Said, *From Oslo to Iraq and the Road Map: Essays* (New York: Vintage, 2005), 185.
8. Said, *Power, Politics, and Culture,* 437.
9. Saree Makdisi, "Politics, Language and the Palestinians," *The Electronic Intifada*, February 3, 2006, archived at http://web.archive.org/web/20121127014014/http://electronicintifada.net/content/politics-language-and-palestinians/5861. The article in question: Khalid Mish'al, "We will not sell our people or principles for foreign aid," *Guardian*, January 31, 2006.
10. George Basharat, "The Palestinians Have Spoken," *Occupation Magazine*, February 3, 2006, archived at http://web.archive.org/web/20060221002420/http://www.kibush.co.il/show_file.asp?num=11890.
11. Issa Khalaf, "What Options Left for Palestine?," *Palestine Chronicle*, March 17, 2006, archived at http://web.archive.org/web/20060515042339/http://www.imemc.org/content/view/17405/79/.
12. Rami Khouri, "Talking with the guys from Hamas," *The Daily Star* (Beirut), February 11, 2006.
13. Joseph Massad, "Israel and the Politics of Friendship," *Electronic Intifada*, February 3, 2009, archived at http://web.archive.org/web/20110629051527/http://electronicintifada.net/content/israel-and-politics-friendship/8039.
14. Joseph Massad, "Subverting democracy," *Electronic Intifada*, July 4, 2007, archived at http://web.archive.org/web/20110629053220/http://electronicintifada.net/content/subverting-democracy/7043.
15. Robin Finn, "At the Center of an Academic Storm, a Lesson in Calm," *New York Times,* April 8, 2005.

11

Know Thy Enemy

(Speech delivered to the Herzliya Conference)

My role here this morning is to serve as a proxy for "the enemy." Now it might have been more interesting to invite "the enemy" and have him speak for himself. But Israel has so many enemies that one wouldn't know quite where to start. And once one goes beyond "enemy" to include "regional adversaries," as our panel title does, the list grows long. Then if I define these adversaries from a dual perspective, American and Israeli, the list becomes a who's who. It includes states like Iran and Syria, an array of Islamist movements, Sunni and Shi'ite, and insurgents and terrorists of all stripes. As someone once said, friends come and go, but enemies accumulate.

In a mere ten minutes, then, all I can do is give you a flavor of how Israel and the United States might look to a composite enemy, someone you couldn't invite because he doesn't exist. And to get you in the proper mood, I'll do it in first person. I know it is hard, but imagine me as some sort of composite of Ahmadinejad, Nasrallah, Osama bin Laden, Bashar Assad, Muqtada Sadr, and Khalid Meshaal. You'll admit it's a good disguise; good enough to get me through the security cordon outside this hall.

Bismillah ar-Rahman ar-Rahim

In the name of God, the Compassionate, the Merciful. I'm flattered that you wish to know me better. As it happens, the phrase "know thy enemy" isn't in our Holy Qur'an, but it comes from the ancient Chinese general Sun Tzu. The full quote goes like this: "Know thy enemy and know yourself; in a hundred battles, you will never be defeated. When you are ignorant of the enemy but know yourself, your chances of winning or losing are equal. If ignorant both of your enemy and of yourself, you are sure to be defeated in every battle."

Now it is true that your societies are self-critical. The purpose of your famous conference is to look hard at yourselves. We follow it most closely, for what it tells us of your strengths and weaknesses. This self-knowledge works in your favor. But fortunately for us, your knowledge of us is deeply flawed. That is the prime reason why you've been losing every other battle.

It's not that you don't understand our decision-making processes. Your intelligence agencies probably have a good idea of who answers to whom in Damascus and Tehran, and among our brothers in Hamas, Hezbollah, the Sunni *mujahidin* in Iraq, and Al Qaeda. What you don't begin to understand is how we see the world.

To summarize your problem in a sentence: you don't give us credit for having what you have, which is vision. In America and Israel, you keep your greatest thinkers in tanks, where they come up with grand visions and strategies. These minds produce fresh ideas of how to engineer a "new Middle East" to your liking. Then you give these ideas imposing names: the peace process, globalization, democratization. Your ideas usually fail, but you keep generating them, because you have a sense of destiny. And your destiny, so you think, is to remake the world in your image.

Too often, you aren't prepared to give us credit for having visions of our own. And when you overhear snippets of our own big ideas—a map without Israel, a resurrected caliphate, and so on—you say: oh, that's not really serious. No, you assure yourselves, all that the Muslims want is that we address some of their grievances and accommodate a few of their interests. A gesture by you here, a concession by you there, and before you know it, you think you've turned us into your servants.

We find it amusing how you persuade yourselves that just one more gesture, just one more concession, is all that's needed to impose your will.

Here are some examples we've collected from your press (mostly from *Ha'aretz*). If only Israel would give up the Shebaa Farms, our brethren in Hezbollah would surrender their weapons. If only our imprisoned fighters were released by Israel, we would allow your "peace process" to be renewed. If only the United States would wink at Syria over the Golan, our brother Assad would ditch Iran. If only Iran were given economic incentives, it would ditch its nuclear program. If only Hamas were recognized, it would recognize Israel in return. If only Israel acknowledged responsibility for the plight of the refugees, the Palestinians would shelve the "right of return."

And on and on. There's even someone at Harvard who claims that Al Qaeda "is likely to bring an end to the war it declared in return for some degree of satisfaction regarding its grievances."[1] Our brothers in Al Qaeda felt insulted: just what do they have to do to be regarded as visionaries, and not as angry Arabs with so-called grievances?

A Grand Vision

Not a single one of these "if-thens" is true; time and again, we've told you so. Yet still you're disappointed when your "generous offers" are spurned. The offers are generous, so you think; but to us, such "generosity" is a mark of weakness, a signpost reassuring us that we are on the road to realizing our grand vision.

And we do have a grand vision. It is as deeply rooted in our hearts as the idea of liberty and freedom is rooted in yours. Our leaders, thinkers, intellectuals, and clerics have spread it to millions of people. Untold numbers are prepared to fight for it. It exists in several versions— Islamist, Arabist, nationalist. But in the end, all of these versions revolve around the same idea, and it's this:

We Arabs and Muslims can and must seize control of our destiny. This means wresting the Middle East away from America and its extension, Israel. Every move we make thus has the ultimate purpose of pushing you back, out, and away. We have no interest whatsoever in "final settlements" or a "new Middle East" that would fortify the status quo. We are out to defeat you—and to replace your vision with our own.

You may think this is impossible. We admit it: the Arab and Muslim world isn't a seat of great technological achievement. It struggles with poverty, illiteracy, and ignorance on a daunting scale. But our cadres have taken Sun Tzu to heart. We know ourselves, and we have made a careful study of you, from Bint Jbeil to Baghdad. We demand of our followers sacrifice, but we promise them victory, and we prepare for it. Of course we make mistakes; we are human too. But on balance, we have played a weak hand with skill, while you have played a strong hand ineptly.

Now you may enjoy a brief respite from us, because Sunnis and Shi'ites are regrettably at each other's throats. Your diplomats whisper to you that this is an opportunity. Don't rejoice. If Sunnis and Shi'ites can demonize and massacre one another—fellow Muslims who profess the same faith, speak the same language, share the same culture—what does this portend for you? The Sunni-Shi'ite strife is a warning to you: our visions, our history don't ever go away, they always come back.

Let's set aside the Chinese general, and end with a quote from our own Osama bin Laden: "When people see a strong horse and a weak horse, by nature, they will like the strong horse." He is right. We sense, not that you're weak, but that you are weakening. We see America's "wise men" produce an alternative plan for Iraq comprised of gestures to us, disguised under the thin euphemism of a "new diplomatic offensive."[2] We hear America's best-placed foreign policy analyst declare that "the American era in the Middle East has ended."[3] And Israel, defeated in Lebanon in the summer of 2006, now debates concessions and initiatives toward us, all of which suggest that Israel is anxious to forestall further defeats.

We know you will launch more offensives, to reverse your decline, or at least create the illusion of its reversal. We expect many "surges." We can't defeat you yet in a straight confrontation. But you are already defeating yourselves, in your think tanks, in your universities, in your editorial boardrooms, in the conclaves of your "wise men."

Finally, you ask us about the place of Iran's nuclear program in our vision. It's an excellent question. Unfortunately for you, Martin Kramer's time is up. We return him to you—unharmed.

Notes

1. Mohammad-Mahmoud Ould Mohamedou, "Time to talk to Al Qaeda?," *Boston Globe,* September 14, 2005.
2. James A. Baker, III and Lee H. Hamilton, co-chairs, *The Iraq Study Group Report: The Way Forward—A New Approach* (New York: Vintage Books, 2006), 6.
3. Richard N. Haass, "The New Middle East," *Foreign Affairs* 85, no. 6 (November–December 2006): 2–11.

Part III

Misunderstood Arabs

12

1967 and Memory

How did the outcome of the June 1967 Six-Day War change the way Arabs think about themselves and the world? It was the late Malcolm Kerr, one of America's leading Arabists at the time, who perfectly summarized the consensus. (Kerr was a UCLA professor, later president of the American University of Beirut, who was killed there in 1984.) He put it thus, in a famous passage written only about four years after the 1967 war:

> Since June 1967 Arab politics have ceased to be fun. In the good old days most Arabs refused to take themselves very seriously, and this made it easier to take a relaxed view of the few who possessed intimations of some immortal mission. It was like watching Princeton play Columbia in football on a muddy afternoon. The June War was like a disastrous game against Notre Dame which Princeton impulsively added to its schedule, leaving several players crippled for life and the others so embittered that they took to fighting viciously among themselves instead of scrimmaging happily as before.[1]

I leave aside the identification of the Arabs with Princeton. Kerr was a Princetonian, but so am I, and I would have preferred to identify the Arabs with Columbia, for all sorts of reasons. But it is the way Kerr contrasts pre-1967 with post-1967 Arab politics that is striking—and misleading. Even in 1967, Arab politics hadn't been "fun" in a very long time. As early as the 1940s, they had become a serious and deadly game of costly wars and bloody coups. True, Kerr was writing in the aftermath of Black September in Jordan, a time when Arab politics seemed to have come completely unhinged. But the idea that 1967 put an end to the "good old days" of Arabs "scrimmaging happily" was a pure piece of nostalgic romance in the grand Arabist tradition.

Unfortunately, such nostalgia is seductive. For years, it has been at the root of a notion that persists even today: if we could somehow undo the 1967 war—if we could undo the injury inflicted in those six days—we could put the Middle East back to where it was in the "good old days." In this view, the Arabs and the world could have "fun" again if only we could erase the Arab memory of that war—by erasing its every consequence.

But the "good old days" analysis is entirely false, and not only in its distortion of Arab politics prior to 1967. It is false because it overlooks how the 1967 trauma trimmed the ideological excess of the prewar period, and opened the way to pragmatic Arab acceptance of Israel.

That ideological excess, known as pan-Arabism or Nasserism, rested upon a prior sense of injury, in which 1948 played the major part. In that earlier war, Israel succeeded in defeating or holding off an array of Arab armies, and three-quarters of a million Palestinian Arab refugees ended up in camps. The injury of 1948 was so deep that, over the following twenty years—Kerr's "good old days"—there was no peace process. The Arabs nursed their wounds and dreamed only of another round.

1948 also had a profoundly destabilizing effect on Arab politics. Three coups took place in Syria in 1949, and often thereafter; Jordan's King Abdullah was assassinated (by Palestinians) in 1951; Free Officers toppled the monarchy in Egypt in 1952. Everywhere, the 1948 regimes were faulted for their failure to strangle Israel at birth. Military strongmen seized power in the name of revolution, and promised to do better in the next round. Those "good old days" were in fact very bad days, during which Arab politics became militarized in the certainty and even desirability of another war with Israel.

In 1967, the other war came, and these regimes suffered a far more devastating defeat, delivered in a mere six days. Unlike 1948, when they had lost much of Palestine, in 1967 they lost their own sovereign territory. The shock wave, it is generally assumed, was even greater.

Yet what is telling is that the regimes didn't fall. Nasser offered his resignation, but the crowds filled the streets and demanded that he stay on—and he did. The defense minister and air force commander of Syria, Hafez Assad, held on and ousted his rivals two years later, establishing himself as sole ruler. King Hussein of Jordan, who had lost half his kingdom, also survived, as did the Jordanian monarchy. The only regime that failed to withstand the shock waves of 1967 was Lebanon's, and Lebanon hadn't even joined the war. Kerr wrote that 1967 had left the Arab players "crippled for life." In the three Arab states that lost the war, the regimes survived, the leaders ruled on, and two would be succeeded by their sons.

Fear of Repetition

What explains the fact that 1967 didn't destabilize the Arab system as 1948 did? It is true that even before 1967, these regimes had started to harden themselves. The evolution of the Arab state as a "republic of fear" dates from the decade before 1967, and this probably helped regimes weather the storm. Unlike in 1948, there weren't many refugees either—the Arab states lost territory, but the war was quick, and most of the inhabitants of the lost territory stayed in their homes.

But I believe the reason 1967 didn't destabilize the Arab order is this: Arab regimes and peoples drew together in the fear that Israel could repeat 1967 if it had to, and that it might show up one day on the outskirts of Cairo or Damascus (as it threatened to do in 1973), or come right into an Arab capital (as it did in Beirut in 1982).

The memory of 1967 thus became the basis of an implicit understanding between the regimes and the peoples: the regimes will avert war, and in return the people will stay loyal, even docile. The regimes have upheld their end, by gradually coming to terms with Israel, and by leaving the Palestinians to fight their own fight. Pan-Arabism—which largely meant sacrificing for the Palestinians—faded away because no Arabs were prepared to risk losing a war for them. The skill of rulers in averting war has helped to secure and entrench them.

I call this understanding implicit—it doesn't have an ideological underpinning. Pragmatism rarely does. But the evidence for it is that no Arab state has entered or stumbled into war with Israel in over forty years. The memory of the 1967 trauma has been translated into a deep-seated aversion to war, which underpins such peace and stability as the region has enjoyed. 1967 thus marks the beginning of the end of the Arab-Israeli conflict—the conflict between Israel and Arabs states, which had produced a major war every decade. 1973 marks the end of the end, in which two Arab states stole back some honor and territory, precisely so they could lean back and leave Israelis and Palestinians to thrash out their own differences. This narrower Israeli-Palestinian conflict has been a sore, but its costs have been limited compared to a state-to-state war.

It is important to note that pan-Arabism did survive elsewhere in the Arab world, where its illusions continued to exact a very high cost. I refer to Ba'thist Iraq, which wasn't defeated in 1967, and where pan-Arabism continued to constitute one of the ideological pillars of the regime vis-à-vis Iran and the West. There it also led to miscalculation, war, and defeat on a truly massive scale. The Iraq wars—they have persisted now for some four decades—provide a striking contrast to the relative stability in Israel's corner of the Middle East—a stability which rests, I suggest, on the Arab memory of 1967, which restructured Arab thinking in the states surrounding Israel, away from eager anticipation of war and toward anxiously averting it.

So in regard to Arab politics, I have offered a possible revision of the usual view of 1967: perhaps its memory, far from making the Arabs angry and volatile, underpins the stability of the Arab order and regional peace. If so, then perhaps we should recall it as a year of net benefit all around—as compared, say, to 1979, the year of Iran's revolution, or 2003, the year of the U.S. invasion of Iraq. The impact of 1967 was to create a new balance, and push ideology to the margins of politics. The impact of 1979 and 2003 has been to unbalance the region and strengthen radical ideologies. 1967 ultimately produced a process that led to the finalizing of borders between states. The combined impact of 1979 and 2003 threatens to erase borders from the map.

The risk today, nearly fifty years later, is not that the consequences of 1967 are still with us. It is that memory of 1967 is starting to fade, and its legacy is being eroded. I am struck by the subtitles of the two leading books on 1967. Michael Oren's is *June 1967 and the Making of the Modern Middle East.*[2] Tom Segev's goes even further: *Israel, the War, and the Year that Transformed the Middle East.*[3] If only it were so. The problem is that the Middle East continues to be remade and transformed by subsequent events, whose legacy is much more damaging than the legacy of 1967.

What then happens when the Arab world is dominated by generations that no longer remember 1967 or, more importantly, no longer think Israel capable of reenacting it? What memories are replacing the memory of 1967? The 2006 summer war in Lebanon? (To rework Kerr's analogy, that was like Columbia playing Notre Dame to a draw.) Without the memory of that defeat of almost fifty years ago, the ranks of the Islamists could swell with people who imagine victory. Without the fear of war, peoples could turn away from those rulers who have made peace—away from the implicit understanding that underpins order. Will it be possible to build stability and peace on other memories, or other promises?

Notes

1. Malcolm Kerr, *The Arab Cold War: Gamal 'Abd al-Nasir and His Rivals, 1958–1970*, 3rd ed. (London: Oxford University Press, 1971), v.
2. Michael Oren, *Six Days of War: June 1967 and the Making of the Modern Middle East* (New York: Oxford University Press, 2002).
3. Tom Segev, *1967: Israel, the War, and the Year that Transformed the Middle East* (New York: Metropolitan Books, 2007).

13

Sadat and Begin: The Peacemakers

It is now more than thirty-five years since the signing of the Israeli-Egyptian peace treaty, most famously evoked by the three-way handshake on the White House lawn that changed the Middle East. Israeli prime minister Menachem Begin and Egyptian president Anwar Sadat put war behind Israel and Egypt, and in so doing, ended the Israeli-Arab conflict. The Israeli-Palestinian conflict continues, and so too does the Israeli-Iranian struggle. But Israeli-Egyptian peace put an end to the destructive battlefield wars between Israel and Arab states, of the kind that erupted in 1948, 1956, 1967, and 1973. Since the famous handshake among Begin, Sadat, and Jimmy Carter, there has been no battlefield war between Israel and a conventional Arab army. And Egypt and Israel now have been at peace longer than they were at war.

It has often been said of Begin and Sadat that the two men were like oil and water. "The two men were totally incompatible," recalled Jimmy Carter, describing the Camp David negotiations that produced the treaty. "There was intense perturbation between them, shouting, banging on the tables, stalking out of the rooms. So for the next seven days, they never saw each other. And so we negotiated with them isolated from one another."[1]

Yet in a briefing paper prepared for the U.S. team prior to Camp David, these sentences appear: "Both Begin and Sadat have evidenced similar personal and national objectives throughout their familiar transformation from underground fighter to political leader. Despite their often vituperative comments, each should be able to recognize the other as a politician basically capable of change, compromise, and commitment."[2] The idea that the similarities between Begin and Sadat made peace possible has been scanted in that interpretation of the negotiations that casts Jimmy Carter as hero.[3]

This is no surprise. No two leaders could have seemed more different, and it is almost too easy to enumerate the contrasts. For starters,
Anwar Sadat came from a poor village in the Nile Delta, a place of
almost immemorial permanence. Begin came from the crumbling
world of East European Jewry, later erased from the earth. Sadat was
an Axis sympathizer during the Second World War. Begin's parents and
brother were murdered by the Nazis. Sadat made a career of the military, and even died in a military uniform. Begin was a civilian through
and through. Americans found Sadat to be alluring and easy-going,
a gregarious man in a leisure suit. They regarded Begin as rigid and
ideological; one American official remarked that, even at Camp David,
Begin was always dressed "as though he were about to go to a funeral."[4]
Sadat was an authoritarian dictator who sent his opponents to prison.
Begin was a classic liberal with a firm commitment to democracy and
the rule of law.

But the similarities between the two are just as striking—perhaps
even more so—and it may be precisely the personal parallels that
brought them together at the crucial moment, and made the achievement of peace possible.

Marginal Men

One obvious similarity is the one to which the U.S. briefing paper
alluded, in describing both as "underground fighters." In fact, both
entered politics through the back door, as conspirators who planned
political violence and who were steeled by long stints in political prison.

Sadat, as a young revolutionary, immersed himself in conspiratorial
plots, both against the British (who then controlled Egypt), as well as
against Egyptian leaders he regarded as collaborators. As a result, he
found himself in and out of prison. In 1945, the twenty-seven-year-old
Sadat and his friends decided to assassinate the on-and-off prime minister of Egypt, Nahhas Pasha. The group staked out Nahhas's motorcade;
one of the members threw a grenade, but it missed his car. The group
was disappointed; eager to assassinate someone, they decided to kill
the former finance minister, Amin Osman Pasha. This succeeded, and
while Sadat was not the triggerman, he was tried as part of the conspiracy and was acquitted only after a lengthy trial.

Menachem Begin had the more famous "underground" career. He
was first sent off to prison during the Second World War by the Soviet
secret police, the NKVD—an eight-month travail he recounted in his
memoir *White Nights*. By then, he too had been initiated into a life of

clandestine conspiracy—methods of operation he would bring with him to Palestine in the last days of the British mandate. There, at the age of thirty-one, he would rise to leadership of an underground organization, the Irgun. This group was responsible for the 1946 bombing of the King David Hotel in Jerusalem, which killed ninety-one persons. (Begin would always claim that a telephone call had been placed to warn that the bombs had been planted.) In 1947, Begin ordered the retaliatory hanging of two kidnapped British sergeants. Begin managed to stay underground throughout this campaign; the British never caught up with him.

Clandestine nationalist "underground" activity, involving violence against the British Empire and its collaborators, represented a clear parallel in the careers of Sadat and Begin. So, too, was their eclipse during their middle years, as the British Empire retreated from the Middle East, and Egypt and Israel gained full independence. Both men spent many years on the political margins, overshadowed by domineering leaders who had a stronger grip on the imaginations of their peoples.

Sadat was a member of the Free Officers conspiracy in 1952, and was part of the cabal of young officers who overthrew the monarchy. But after Nasser emerged decisively as the leader, Sadat came to be regarded as the most colorless man in the ruling clique. He was socially conservative, rather more religious than his colleagues, and seemingly a bit less sophisticated because of his rural origins. He spent eighteen years in the shadow of Nasser, and became his number two only in the year before Nasser's death. No one could have guessed, during Nasser's long-running high-wire act, that Sadat would succeed him. (Sadat's deferential posture may have spared him being purged by Nasser, who never considered him a threat.) When Sadat became president, he was fifty-two years old—the same age as Nasser on his death.

Begin languished even longer on the margins. The Zionist revolution was credited to David Ben-Gurion, the man associated most directly with Israel's war of independence and institution-building. The Revisionists led by Begin would always claim to have played a crucial role in Israel's struggle for independence, by their acts of resistance—some would call them terror—against the British and the Arabs. But this was a disputed narrative—one put forward by Begin in his book *The Revolt*—and one that failed to persuade the great majority of Israelis. The evidence for this was the weak performance of Begin's political party in Israeli elections. It left Begin a perpetual denizen of the opposition benches in the Israeli parliament. In a political landscape dominated by the Labor party, he spent decade after decade delivering speeches and doing little else.

His opening only came after the 1973 war, launched by Sadat, which finally precipitated a crisis of confidence in the Labor Party leadership, and opened the door for Begin. (Here was a paradox: it was a decision of Sadat that cleared the way for Begin.) When Begin became prime minister in 1977, after leading his own party to defeat in eight election cycles, the world was astonished. He was sixty-four years old when he assumed the premiership.

Sadat and Begin thus spent decades in the shadow of men who effectively issued the declarations of independence of their countries. (Ben-Gurion actually declared Israel's independence in 1948, and Nasser effectively declared Egypt's independence by nationalizing the Suez Canal in 1956.) But neither of these giants had managed to bring peace to their peoples. Nasser drove Egypt to defeat in 1967, while Ben-Gurion, despite leading Israel to victories in 1948 and 1956, had been unable to translate military prowess into peace. This was true of his Labor Party successors as well. They left unfinished legacies, which provided the openings for Sadat and Begin.

Who Dwell Alone

Begin and Sadat also shared a strongly pro-Western, anti-Soviet orientation. Begin had been thrown in prison by the Soviets. Although it was the struggle against the Nazis that formed him, his animosity toward the Soviet Union, while less in degree, was similar in kind. A champion of Jewish peoplehood first and foremost, he saw the Soviet Union as an oppressive regime of antisemitic evil—in contrast to many on the Israeli left at the time, who remembered the Soviet Union as the great ally of the Second World War, and who persisted in admiring its (supposedly) socialist values.

Sadat shared this aversion to the Soviets. During Nasser's years, Egypt aligned itself squarely with the Soviet Union, which became Egypt's major arms supplier, financier of the Aswan dam, and principal source of diplomatic backing. But Sadat never trusted the Soviets. He was certain they represented another form of colonialism, and that their policies were meant to keep Egypt subservient. He came to power as president in 1970, and already by 1972 he had expelled thousands of Soviet advisers, whom he regarded as agents of a foreign empire, no different than the British of an earlier era. It would be his desire to align Egypt with the West—and particularly the United States—which would set the stage for his decision to visit Jerusalem.

Both men also relied heavily on the technique of the strategic surprise. Sadat had attempted, through his first few years in power, to achieve the return of the Sinai peninsula to Egypt through back-channel diplomacy. He ultimately concluded that what had been taken by force could only be restored by force. That led him to the bold decision to launch war against Israel in October 1973, in cooperation with Syria. His war goals were limited: to compel Israel to come to the table and force the United States to take Egypt seriously as its potential Arab partner. The war produced just enough military success to be portrayed to the Egyptian people as a victory, so that Sadat could claim to have achieved the battlefield triumph that had eluded Nasser. But to translate his (limited) military achievement into something more, there had to be a political move of comparable audacity. This would come in the form of his surprise decision to violate all the norms of Arab political conduct, and pay a visit to Israel. There he appeared in the Knesset, Israel's parliament, and made a famous speech of reconciliation.

Begin also was given to the audacious act. Three of them marked his premiership. First, there was the decision to withdraw from all of Sinai, involving the demolition of Yamit, a large Jewish settlement there. It was the first time Israel had ever dismantled a settlement, and it came as a shock, especially to Begin's admirers. Second, there was his decision in 1981 to bomb Iraq's nuclear reactor—a complete surprise to the world, driven by an inner conviction that he was acting to save Israel. This was followed by his decision to invade Lebanon—a move intended by Begin to complement the peace with Egypt, in remaking Israel's strategic environment. Begin, like Sadat, could also surprise both friends and adversaries with bold moves.

Both men were also driven by an almost isolationist nationalism. Nasser had placed Egypt squarely in the Arab circle: Egypt was to lead the Arab world, and the Egyptians were first and foremost Arabs. In 1958, he even briefly subsumed Egypt in something called the United Arab Republic, which joined Egypt and Syria in a single polity. Sadat, in contrast, extricated Egypt from its Arab commitments. He regarded it as a civilization unto itself, so weighty that it could stand aloof and alone. Yes, it would engage in alliances and relationships with other Arab states, but Sadat was determined to put Egypt first, even if other Arabs might shun it.

Begin proceeded from a similar set of assumptions. The Jews were alone in the world, they were a people unto themselves, and they had been repudiated by East and West, even in those lands where they had been first emancipated. Begin did not regard this as tragedy, but as destiny. The Jews were destined to dwell alone, and he accepted the fact with equanimity. Here too there would be alliances and relationships, but Israel did not belong to any larger club, and ultimately it could rely only upon itself. This set the stage for the bilateral agreement between two leaders seeking to isolate their peoples from the threats around them. (It also meant that the peace itself, as much as it was intended to reconcile Egypt and Israel, was also bound to isolate them from one another.)

The two men also had a shared concept of the territorial limits of peoplehood. For Sadat, Egyptian territory was sacred, and the Sinai was part of Egyptian territory. The commitment to the Palestinians, in contrast, was vague—diminished, in no small measure, by Egypt's overall withdrawal from the Arab world. For Begin, the West Bank was sacred—not occupied territory, but Judea and Samaria, Israel's patrimony. Yet the Sinai was foreign land. Had Begin been driven only by security considerations, he might have resisted withdrawal from the valuable strategic buffer represented by the Sinai. (Some of his advisers thought he should.) But his precise sense of where the Jewish homeland began and ended made possible an agreement based on a total Israeli withdrawal from the peninsula.

Triumph and Tragedy

The saga of Camp David and the Israeli-Egyptian peace has been told many times. That Jimmy Carter faced a formidable challenge in bringing Sadat and Begin to an agreement is indisputable. Begin himself, in remarks that immediately followed negotiations, said that the Camp David conference "should be renamed the Jimmy Carter conference."[5]

But the parallels in the lives of Sadat and Begin may have worked, in ways subtle but strong, in favor of an agreement. Here were two men forged by prison and violence into believers in their own destiny, but who had been written off politically for decades. By the time they came to power, they were in a hurry to achieve something that would transcend the legacies of their celebrated predecessors. Here were two men who believed that their peoples were fated to struggle alone, but who were prepared to go to extraordinary lengths to cement relations with the United States, in the interests of their peoples but also in order to shut the Soviet Union out of the Middle East. Here were two men who did not shy from the bold gamble, and who actually saw a greater risk in inaction. And above all, here were two men possessed not only by a strong sense of peoplehood, but of its geography, which they conceived in ways that left no overlapping territorial claims.

There is one more parallel. Both men finished their lives tragically. Sadat was assassinated in 1981 on the reviewing stand during the annual celebration of Egypt's October 6, 1973 military offensive. While world leaders attended his funeral, the Egyptian crowds stayed home, and so too did Arab leaders. He died in splendid (personal) isolation, mirroring that which he brought upon Egypt. Begin also died in isolation—one he had imposed on himself after he resigned the premiership in 1983, in the wake of the Lebanon war. In the decade between his resignation and his death, in 1992, he went into seclusion. He was buried, as he wished to be, not among Israel's leaders on Mount Herzl, but on the Mount of Olives, and not in a state funeral, but in a simple Jewish ceremony.

For many Egyptians, Sadat's achievement in war was tainted by an ill-conceived peace. For many Israelis, Begin's achievement in peace was tainted by an ill-conceived war. The two men who, with Jimmy Carter, shared the world's stage on March 26, 1979 to thundering accolades departed this earth to mixed reviews.

But the peace treaty has turned out to be the most durable feature of the Middle Eastern landscape, and the bedrock on which the stability of the region rests. Two "incompatible" men forged it—perhaps because, ultimately, they were so much alike.

Notes

1. *Camp David 25th Anniversary Forum* (Atlanta, GA: The Carter Center, January 2004), 7.
2. "Study Papers for the Camp David Talks," Tab 4, "Considerations for Conducting the Summit Meetings: I. Approaching the Political Personalities," archived at http://web.archive.org/web/20031229222701/http://www. cartercenter.org/documents/nondatabase/campdavidstudy.pdf.
3. See, for example, the riveting blow-by-blow account of Camp David by Lawrence Wright, *Thirteen Days in September: Carter, Begin, and Sadat at Camp David* (New York: Knopf, 2014).
4. Zbigniew Brzezinski's interview in David Ash and Dai Richards, dirs., *The 50 Years War: Israel and the Arabs* ([Virginia]: PBS DVD Video, 2000).
5. Begin remarks at conclusion of the Camp David meeting, September 17, 1978, in *Public Papers of the Presidents of the United States: Jimmy Carter, 1978, Book II* (Washington, DC: Government Press Office, 1979), 1521.

14

When Minorities Rule

When we hear the phrase "minority rule," the first inclination is to think that it is something abhorrent. It is precisely the phrase that was used to categorize South Africa under apartheid: white minority rule. We assume that such rule is illegitimate by definition. The European ideal of the nation, as it formed in the nineteenth century, is predicated on the nation as a numerical majority, formed by people who share some fundamental attribute of culture, be it language, ethnicity, religion, or shared descent. The numerically smaller groups within the polity that do not share this attribute are described as minorities, and as such should be entitled to various protections even as they are offered avenues of assimilation. What is insufferable is minority rule—an inversion of the natural order.

Historical Legacy

But this is a very modern and very European idea. Minority rule has long been the norm in the Middle East. The traditional Muslim polity was not concerned with establishing the numerical superiority of Muslims. Indeed, in the most dynamic Muslim empires, Muslim minorities ruled over non-Muslim majorities. We do not have hard figures, but the evidence suggests that in the great Arab empires, Muslims did not form the majority of the population until the early Middle Ages. In the Ottoman Empire, for most of its existence, and while it encompassed the Balkans, Muslims were in the minority. In the Moghul Empire in South Asia, the Muslims formed a thin ruling crust resting upon a predominantly Hindu society.

Muslims did not agonize over their status as numerical minorities in these situations. The natural order since time immemorial had been imperial rule by elites who embraced a different culture, language, and religion than those of the populations over which they ruled. And since sovereignty belonged to God, and through him to the divine-right ruler, the question of who was in the majority or the minority had no relevance. Legitimacy had other sources, in Islamic law, and in the ideal of just rule.

Muslim empires generally ruled according to the precept that "there is no coercion in religion." And because non-Muslims were subject to extra taxation, it actually served the rulers to remain in a minority. The result was that the Middle East, even after the Islamic conquests and the gradual conversions to Islam, remained home to a plethora of religious and other minorities, which enjoyed considerable autonomy.

This gave rise to the mosaic that we see today, comprised of enclaves of different religions, sects, and ethnic groups. This is a consequence of the kind of social contract that prevailed across the Islamic Middle East for centuries: authority tolerated the autonomy of varied groups in society, and society accepted rule by an elite minority.

Now there are debates about the nature of this system, and the tradeoffs it involved. There is the harsh view of Bat Ye'or, who believes that the traditional system of state relations with non-Muslim minorities constituted a kind of thousand-year apartheid, systematically discriminating against non-Muslims, leaving them in an endemic state of insecurity. She has named this sort of apartheid dhimmitude, after the word *dhimmi*, which means a Christian or Jew living as a subordinate protected person under Islamic rule.[1]

There is the rather more nuanced view of Bernard Lewis, who argues that the cases of actual persecution of minorities were few, certainly as compared to Europe, and that they occurred as a consequence of general societal crises. Lewis holds that in most places and times, minorities did thrive in their own autonomous space. He has been keen to stress that such tolerance was not equality, which would have been a dereliction of Islamic law, but his is a generally favorable assessment.[2]

Finally, there is a view best articulated by the late Elie Kedourie, who believed that the Islamic system in its last, Ottoman phase had achieved a nearly perfect equilibrium among social groups. He regarded European nationalist ideas as a virus that brought disease. Europe's destruction of the Ottoman Empire in the First World War was an act of hubris, one that unleashed the very worst forces, and substituted a "wilderness of tigers" for an ordered world in which everyone had a defined place.[3]

Whatever one thinks of these approaches, it is clear that the Middle East since the end of the Ottoman Empire, if not also in its last years, has been a dangerous place for many minorities. The list is long: the

Armenian genocide; the depredations against Assyrians upon Iraq's independence; the persecution of ancient Jewish communities across the Arabic-speaking lands; the enslavement and massacre of non-Muslim blacks in Sudan; and the list goes on. As a result, parts of the Middle East have become much less diverse than they were two generations ago. Just visit Alexandria, which was once a Mediterranean melting pot, and which has become a bleak and monolithic city with its back to the sea. Just visit Bethlehem, now largely emptied of its Christian population. There are many such cities and towns and villages across the Middle East, where monotone has replace mosaic.

That change was the result of coercive nationalism, which declared that you must either shed all your particular beliefs and traditions, in order to join the Arab (or Egyptian or Syrian) nation; or you will be regarded as a foreigner and fifth-columnist of imperialism, and be gradually dispossessed and driven out. It is true that both Britain and France used minorities as allies in their efforts to find economical ways to exert imperial control. They recruited from minorities, as a counter-balance to the very same Arab nationalism they had once promoted. But the Arab nationalists then took this as a license to suppress and dispossess those very same minorities.

The predominant effect of half a century of Arab nationalism has been this: those who would not or could not conform, had to submit or leave. Christians submitted or left. Kurds and Shi'ites in Iraq faced a similar choice. Jews left or reassembled in Israel, a kind of redoubt for a minority that made a programmatic plan to become a majority in one place, and so chart its own course.

Now the interesting thing about Arab nationalism is that, while it purports to represent the identity of the majority of Middle Easterners, many of its prime promoters have been members of minorities. Many of its early ideologues were Christians, who saw in Arab identity a way to escape their own subordinate status in an Islamic state. The Hashemites, who were installed in Transjordan, Iraq, and briefly before that in Syria, were outsiders—a small ruling clique imported from Arabia. In Syria, it was minority groups, such as Alawis, Druze, and Ismailis, who seized the mantle of Arabism from the old Sunni elite, and used it to make Syria into a pan-Arab champion. And in Iraq, when the minority regime of the Hashemites fell, it was eventually replaced by minority regimes of Sunni Muslims who concocted a notion of Arab-Iraqi identity, precisely to deflect the charge that they were ruling on behalf of a minority sect. Jordan is a case of minority rule twice over: by the imported Hashemites, and by the native East Bankers in preference to the imported Palestinians, who form a majority.

So even in the era of nationalism, the Middle East, east of Suez at least, continued to be ruled by minorities. This applied not only to Sunni-ruled Iraq, Alawi-ruled Syria, and Hashemite-ruled Jordan. It has also come to apply to the Arab Gulf states, in which the number of foreigners now wildly exceeds the number of natives. This is one of the paradoxes of Arabism: it was used by regimes to give themselves a veneer of populism, when in fact these regimes had their bases in minority groups.

Democracy versus Social Order

Outsiders, especially Westerners, look at this and say to themselves: this is not legitimate and it cannot last. Each person should be allotted one equal vote. If that means that power will shift from the Sunnis to the Shi'ites in Iraq, so be it; if that means it will shift from the Alawis to the Sunnis in Syria, so be it; if that means it will make the Shi'ites into Lebanon's power-brokers, so be it; and if that means dominance will shift from the Hashemites and the East Bankers to the Palestinians in Jordan, then so be it. Minority rule is a vestige of the past; let it be phased out, through the implementation of real democracy.

This is the reason democracy promotion is so feared in the Middle East. We see democratization as a noble enterprise to erode authoritarian rule. They see it as a foreign demand for a fundamental shift of power among sectarian and ethnic groups. In a homogenous place like Egypt, and in other parts of North Africa where the rulers come from the majority social or ethnic group, democracy does not have that same association. But across the Fertile Crescent, to empower "the majority" means to take power away from a long-empowered sectarian or ethnic or kinship group that happens to be smaller, and vest it in one that happens to be larger.

The problem with this is that minority rule can sometimes be more respectful of difference, more tolerant, and more open than majority rule. That certainly was the case in the Ottoman Empire for much of its history. It has arguably been the case in places like the progressive Gulf states and Jordan. In Iraq, of course, minority rule was a disaster. In other words, minority rule may be good, or it may be bad; it may be enlightened or it may be despotic; it depends on the circumstances.

The same goes for majority rule. The principal effect of the removal of Saddam Hussein has been to bring the Shi'ites to the fore of politics in the Arab world. The United States, willy-nilly, has allied itself to Shi'ite power, by dint of its democratizing message. But it is by no means certain that Shi'ite power will be tolerant of the pluralistic values that democracy is supposed to nurture and protect. Indeed, in Iraq, the prospects for such an outcome would seem to rest on the shoulders of one elderly man, Ayatollah Sistani. In Lebanon, too, it is not at all clear that an enhancement of Shi'ite power would make the country more open and tolerant of differences, be they political, cultural, or religious. And would we really want Palestinians, with their historic long-running grievances, to set the course of Jordan?

The democracy agenda tampers with much more than the political order. It tampers with the social order, in a number of places where that order functions passably. These are conservative societies; they fear disorder; and if democracy means overturning ethnic and sectarian balances, and opening the door to possible conflict, they are bound to suspect it.

In fact, the unseating of such minorities already has a reputation for serving as a precursor to civil strife. It could well be argued that Lebanon would not be Lebanon without the Maronites; in the same measure, Iraq would not be Iraq without the Sunnis. These minorities founded both states, and they legitimized their separate existence. In Lebanon, the decline of the Maronite minority has left a vacuum that persists to this day, and that makes it uncertain even now whether the country can be restored to sovereignty. The same holds true of Iraq: the displacement of the Sunnis, who have always been the hinge of Iraq, has unhinged the country. One does not have to be a follower of the Phalanges or the Ba'th party to realize that these two communities have cultural roles in both countries beyond their numbers, and that their marginalization might be as fateful for pluralism as the earlier marginalization of Jews, Greeks, and the other groups that leavened Middle Eastern society.

America's inadvertent overturning of the group hierarchy is one of the reasons why "they hate us." The people who really hate America think that it will do everywhere what it has done in Iraq: shift power to the benighted Shi'ites, in the name of democracy. The empowerment of the Jews via the creation of Israel overturned one traditional order, but empowering Shi'ites is an escalation that reaches into the very essence of Islam. That is what fuels the insurgency in Iraq, and that is what keeps new recruits coming to Al Qaeda. All one has to do to find evidence is look at the jihadist websites to see what they say about Shi'ites. We are tampering with a 1,400-year-old hierarchy, the product of untold generations of struggle within Islam.

Self-Determination First

If democracy contains within it the seed of disorder, what is the alternative? The problem in the Arab world is not a lack of democracy. It is a lack of self-determination. Here I do not mean national self-determination; I mean latitude for ethnic, religious, and kinship groups to exercise the maximum autonomous control over their collective lives. This is what has been eroded by the cancerous growth of the state over the past fifty years, exemplified by Iraq. The problem is the overbearing state, which has achieved efficiency in one thing only: depriving the Middle Easterner of the freedom he most cherishes, which is to be left alone to practice his faith, speak his language, and enjoy the traditions of his subnational community.

This community does not always value democracy. In Iraq's Sunni triangle, they like their tribes and they might want a tough-minded sheikh to keep order among them; in the Shi'ite south, they might wish to venerate a white-bearded recluse in a turban, and have him resolve all their disputes; and so on. What they crave is not democracy, but subnational self-determination, for both majorities and minorities. More important to them than one-man one-vote, are guarantees for social, religious and linguistic freedom, implied by the retreat of the state.

To what point should it retreat? Ideally, to the distance at which the Ottomans stood. We have much more to learn from the Ottoman way of empire in the Middle East than from the British or the French. The European imperial powers also overturned hierarchies, which is why they constantly had to put down the kinds of insurgencies that the United States came to face in Iraq. The Ottomans obviously had certain advantages over Europeans: first, they were Muslims, and second, the peoples of the Middle East were not at a heightened level of political consciousness until the Empire's last days. But the Ottomans ruled for as long as they did because they did not threaten their subjects with an all-intrusive state, and did not seek to turn the social order on its head.

An interviewer once asked the late Elie Kedourie whether he was nostalgic for the Ottoman and Hapsburg Empires. Kedourie replied:

> Nostalgia is not a very profitable sentiment nor is there any sense in regretting something that cannot be revived. All one can say, is that these political systems and institutions, contraptions, or call them whatever you will, worked while they were there. They functioned; and

considering the societies which Ottomans and Austro-Hungarians ruled, they did not do a bad job of it. What one can also say, is that the successor states have failed lamentably.

He went on to praise the Ottomans for their "very sensible attitude to the problems raised by large groups of people who were under their control. When it came to insurrection, the Ottomans were quite ruthless. But apart from that they tried very hard to maneuver, to meander, to try and conciliate."[4]

The United States cannot revive the Ottoman Empire, but it might take a lesson from its legacy: that empire is most effective when it is invisible, that there are things worse than minority rule, that there is no greater evil in the Middle East than an intrusive state, that people who do not rebel deserve to be left alone to run their affairs as they see fit, and that it is wisest not to overturn existing hierarchies, but to maneuver and meander within them. Pursue the idea of majority rule, come what may, and we may eventually find the majority of the Middle East agreed on one thing: that America is an evil empire. That kind of consensus is bound to undermine American interests, and would be the worst outcome of the best intentions.

Notes

1. Bat Ye'or, *The Dhimmi: Jews and Christians under Islam* (Rutherford, NJ: Fairleigh Dickinson University Press, 1985).
2. See in particular the chapter on "Islam and Other Religions" by Bernard Lewis, *The Jews of Islam* (Princeton, NJ: Princeton University Press, 1984), 3–66.
3. Kedourie: "The Ottoman system was far from perfect. It was narrow and hidebound. It knew nothing of the richness, the flexibility and the opportunities existing in the western tradition. But its conventions were well established and its modalities well understood." While the West now urged Middle Eastern states to allow Muslims, Jews, and Christians to live in harmony, "the Ottoman state was organized in such a way as to fulfill precisely this requirement." Elie Kedoure, *The Chatham House Version and other Middle-Eastern Studies* (London: Weidenfeld and Nicolson, 1970), 315–16.
4. "'I would use the term despotism,' An Interview with Elie Kedourie," *Middle Eastern Lectures* 1 (1995): 80, 82.

15

Syria in the Fertile Crescent

When the revolution (or uprising, or insurgency) started in Syria in 2011, many people saw it as the obvious continuation of the so-called Arab Spring. There had been revolutions in Tunisia, then Egypt and Libya—countries with Mediterranean shorelines. When conflict broke out in Syria, analysts initially read it as an extension of the same process.

In retrospect, it was not. The countries of North Africa are fairly homogeneous and overwhelmingly Sunni Muslim. There are regional and tribal differences in Libya, and Egypt has an important Coptic Christian minority. But revolutions in these countries did not involve the transfer of power from one religious or sectarian or ethnic group to another.

In Syria, political transformation threatened to do precisely that. And so what evolved in Syria wasn't an extension of the "Arab Spring," but a continuation of another series of conflicts, far more devastating in their effects. Going back from the present moment, chronologically, its predecessors included the post-2003 Iraqi civil war, the Kurdish insurgency in Turkey, the Lebanese civil war from 1975 through 1989, and, still more remotely, the Armenian genocide of 1915. These might conveniently be called the wars of the Fertile Crescent.

Inventing the Fertile Crescent

What is the "Fertile Crescent"? What the Arabs somewhat laboriously call "Iraq and Sham" or "Iraq and the Levant" (from which derive ISIS and ISIL) has a perfectly serviceable English name. It was invented by James Henry Breasted, an American Egyptologist at the University of Chicago, and popularized in his 1916 book *Ancient Times*. Breasted defined the Fertile Crescent as the expanse of territory set between the desert to the south and the mountains to the north—a place constantly under pressure from invaders, precisely because it is sustaining of life (Breasted called it "the cultivable fringe of the desert"). He marked it as a zone of "age-long struggle . . . which is still going on."[1]

"Fertile Crescent" gained popularity in the West because it seemed fertile in another way, as the site of the earliest biblical narratives and the birthplace of monotheism. It was the presumed locale of the Garden of Eden, which generations of early cartographers sought to place on a map.[2] It was the site of the Tower of Babel, which purported to explain the emergence and diffusion of different languages. It was the stage for the wanderings of the patriarch Abraham, who crossed it from east to west—a migration in the course of which he came into communion with the one God. The Bible, before it linked the Holy Land to Egypt, linked it to Mesopotamia. And while the peoples of the Fertile Crescent may have been many, and of many languages, they were the first to imagine God as one.

The Fertile Crescent thus came to signify diversity amidst unity: a multitude of peoples believing in the existence of one God. This was in contrast to Greece and Egypt, which were cases of single peoples of one ethnic origin and language believing in many gods. It was in the Fertile Crescent that Islam would be tested as a unifying force for diverse populations. Only after passing that test did it expand across the globe. The Fertile Crescent itself then would be folded into the great Islamic empires. In the last of them, the Ottoman, it sometimes flourished and more often languished as a single, borderless expanse.

Sykes-Picot

But in 1916, the same year that Breasted popularized the phrase Fertile Crescent, Britain and France concluded the Sykes-Picot agreement for the partition of the Ottoman Empire, dividing this zone into states and drawing straight borders through the desert. Within those borders, Britain and France imposed one faction over all others in political orders that depended to some degree or another on coercion. Power in Iraq and Syria coalesced around minorities. In Iraq, a Sunni minority was imposed over a Shi'ite majority; in Syria, a Shi'ite-like minority, the Alawis, over a Sunni majority. (The Kurds, minorities in both countries, were at the bottom of the heap.)

In Mesopotamia, Britain imported a Sunni monarchy from Arabia and bound it to the indigenous Sunnis of Baghdad and its surroundings, giving them dominion over a vast territory unified under the name of Iraq. The French initially tried a very different approach in Syria. Whereas the British sought to unify, the French originally intended to divide: for a period in the 1920s and 1930s, what would become Syria was in fact divided into an Alawite state, a Druze state, the states of

Aleppo and Damascus, and Lebanon. In 1937, the French acceded to the demands of Syrian nationalists, and also unified Syria (excluding Lebanon). But at the same time, the French worked to empower minorities, above all the Alawis, by recruiting them into the military, in order to keep Arab nationalism in check. After independence, the Alawis parlayed that advantage into their own dominion.

While the rulers of Syria and Iraq stood, from a sectarian point of view, on opposite ends of the spectrum, they were both cases of postcolonial minority-domination in states engineered from the outside. Still, there was a difference. Syria's ruling minority was much more of a minority. The Alawis in Syria are probably no more than twelve percent of the population whereas the Sunnis in Iraq are probably about twice that percentage. And while the ruling Sunni minority in Iraq had an integral connection with the wider Sunni majority in the region, the ruling Alawis in Syria had no such backstop, and ended up relying on distant Iran.

Perhaps Breasted would have warned us that this order couldn't last. That it lasted as long as it did was the result of ruling minorities modernizing their repressive machinery in ways the ancients could never have imagined. But this machinery was discredited and dismantled by the United States in Iraq, and it has broken down from within in Syria. Power is now shifting from one religious or sectarian group to one which happens to be larger or more powerful or more connected to sources of outside support. Or it is fragmenting altogether.

From Strength to Weakness

There is much irony in the contraction of Iraq and Syria. Both states, at their twentieth-century high watermarks, were strong enough to project their power beyond their borders, and they even tried to redraw them. Iraqi nationalists believed that Iraq should have been awarded still wider borders, especially along the Persian Gulf littoral. Syrian nationalists likewise claimed that "greater" Syria should have been incorporated within Syria's borders. The 1919 General Syrian Congress passed this resolution: "We ask that there should be no separation of the southern part of Syria, known as Palestine, nor of the littoral Western zone, which includes Lebanon, from the Syrian country. We desire that the unity of the country should be guaranteed against partition under whatever circumstances."[3]

But it wasn't to be. A separate Lebanon and Palestine came into existence. For this reason, Syria refused to reconcile itself to its own borders. Indeed, for three years, from 1958 to 1961, Syrians readily agreed to dismantle their own independent state, and incorporate Syria into a union with Egypt called the United Arab Republic.

Iraqi president Saddam Hussein, when he thought he had the opportunity, attempted to redraw Iraq's borders by force, through his invasion of Iran and his occupation and annexation of Kuwait. Syrian president Hafez Assad likewise occupied Lebanon and gave safe haven to the Kurdish PKK, which was headquartered in Damascus. Iraq and Syria seemed to have become powers in their own right. In the case of Syria, in particular, American secretaries of state and even presidents came to Damascus as supplicants, hoping to win its ruler over to their geopolitical concepts of regional order.

Now all that has been reversed. Not only is Syria no longer capable of projecting its power beyond its borders; others are meddling inside Syria, to advance their own agendas, in alliance with the various domestic factions, while Syrian refugees flee the country in the millions. Syria's elites once regarded the state's external borders as inadequate to Syria's great historical role, but Syria is now incapable of preserving unity even in its "truncated" borders. Syrians were educated to believe that the state of Syria was the nucleus of a greater Syria, itself the nucleus of a greater Arab unity. But in practice, Syria itself could not resist imploding into a de facto partition, driven by deep internal divisions.

Now it is not Syria's power, but Syria's weakness, that threatens the region. Albert Hourani, the historian of the Middle East, once wrote this: "Even were there no Syrian people, a Syrian problem would still exist."[4] That is exactly where the Middle East is now stuck. There is no Syrian people, but there is still a Syrian problem, and it will continue to dominate the region and worry the world, perhaps for years to come.

Since this disorder has no name—certainly none as succinct as "Sykes-Picot"—I propose to call it, for now, the Breasted Fertile Crescent. This would be a Fertile Crescent made up of shifting principalities, subject to occasional intervention by surrounding powers, characterized by variety and diversity, essentially without fixed borders—a place where Shi'ites struggle against Sunnis, Arabs against Kurds, the desert against the sown. The Breasted (dis)order will persist, until some great outside power or group of regional powers proves willing to expend the energy needed to restructure the Fertile Crescent in accord with their interests—something the Ottomans did for four hundred years, Europe did for fifty years, and America has not yet attempted at all.

Notes

1. James Henry Breasted, *Ancient Times: A History of the Early World* (Boston, MA: Ginn, 1916), 100–1.
2. See Alessandro Scafi, *Mapping Paradise: A History of Heaven on Earth* (Chicago, IL: University of Chicago Press, 2006).
3. J. C. Hurewitz, *The Middle East and North Africa in World Politics: A Documentary Record*, vol. 2: *British-French Supremacy, 1914–1945* (New Haven, CT: Yale University Press, 1979), 181.
4. A.H. Hourani, *Syria and Lebanon: A Political Essay* (London: Oxford University Press, 1946), 6.

16

Arab Spring, Arab Crisis

This is an extraordinary time in the Middle East, but just what we have witnessed has eluded consensus. That is reflected in the terminology. Some called it the "Arab Spring," by analogy to the democratic transformations in Eastern Europe a generation ago. When it became clear that the path was not going to be as smooth as in Europe, others backtracked and called it the "Arab Awakening," which sounded like a longer-term proposition. Still others, who saw Islamists initially triumph in elections, took to calling it the "Islamist Winter." The terminological confusion is a reflection of analytical disagreement.

Another source of confusion has been the widespread resort to historical analogies. When it seemed that the transition would be a rough one, or might even be aborted, commentary began to appear comparing the events to Europe in 1848.[1] When optimists wanted to make the point that sometimes successful revolutions take a long time, they pointed to the American revolution of 1776.[2] When pessimists wanted to emphasize that revolutions conceived in idealism could go astray, they pointed to the Russian Revolution of 1917. Finally, some circled back to 1989, but this time not with an emphasis on the "Spring" analogy to Poland, but on the "Balkan Ghosts" analogy to Bosnia.[3] Analogies are a crutch, to which we return when our analysis is thin.

As a historian by training, I have no difficulty predicting that the debate over terminology and the application of analogies will go on for many years to come. If historians still debate the causes of the French Revolution, there is no reason to think the events of the past few years won't be debated far into the future. That is how we historians make our living.

But makers of policy make their living in a different way. They rely on analysis of the moment, and must make judgment calls based on present evidence, in order to predict the future trajectory on which to base policy and strategy. So while it would suit me just fine to say that it is simply too early to tell, let me go out on a limb for those who must decide now, and make some generalizations.

Competing Explanations

Let us agree that what we are witnessing is a very profound crisis. Regimes have fallen, hundreds of thousands have died, millions are refugees. There is even a nominal price tag. In 2015, the Arab Strategic Forum in Dubai estimated that in the economic downturn that followed the "Arab Spring," the affected countries incurred losses of $830 billion, including $460 billion in infrastructure damage, $290 billion in lost GDP, and $49 billion in costs associated with refugees.[4]

This is wealth destruction on a massive scale. And it is not as if these economies had a big buffer to absorb this hit: the already-poor have become desperately poor. As against these mounting costs, the gains have been debatable. Has there been progress toward good governance and the rule of law? Or descent into rule by militias and pervasive insecurity? The situation differs from country to country, and there are supposedly bright spots. (Tunisia is usually cited here.) But overall, it is hard to be optimistic about any of the impacted countries, which are mired in various degrees of turmoil.

But before we can say what sort of crisis this is, let us say what sort of crisis it is not. It isn't just a repudiation of authoritarian rule. It is true that the kind of rule based on personality cult and pervasive fear has lost its grip. The United States contributed to that by removing Saddam Hussein from power in 2003. Saddam was the avatar for a certain kind of regime, and his fall exposed others who ruled in the same way. His removal dissipated the aura of fear that surrounded such regimes, because the praetorian guards entrusted with their defense could be put to flight. The enablers of these regimes were prepared to torture to defend them. What they weren't prepared to do was to fight and die. That proved to be the case from Tunisia to Egypt to Libya.

But if it was a revulsion against authoritarian rule, and a yearning for the dignity conferred by democracy, how does one explain the support of Egyptians for a Muslim Brotherhood regime which was itself authoritarian? Or the counterrevolution in Egypt, which returned a military junta to power by coup? Perhaps this isn't a political crisis of authoritarianism versus democracy, between bad (authoritarian) guys and good (democratic) guys. In the case of Egypt, there isn't even an agreement over who the bad guys and good guys are. And there isn't a consensus over Syria either, where only a handful of the players are committed to democracy in a form we would recognize.

If it wasn't about freedom and democracy, was it a "return to Islam"? It briefly did look just like that. For a moment, it seemed like another analogy, Iran 1979, might be apt. Certainly the status quo has been eroded by the spread of an Islamist social movement among the masses. But Islamists did not lead the uprisings, and they have not been able to consolidate their early victories in elections and secure positions of dominance. Islamists have struggled without success to translate their social base into coherent and effective politics. Perhaps this is because people aren't persuaded they have the answer to the crisis, or even understand it. The Islamic State, or ISIS, has been a beneficiary of the chaos in Syria and Iraq, but it represents an opportunistic exploitation of the disorder, not its cause.

Was it an economic crisis? Much commentary focused on the demographic youth bulge which has surged through the Arab world. This part of the world is in a transition to lower rates of fertility, but it is now paying the price of extraordinarily high fertility rates registered twenty to thirty years ago. Millions of young people have flooded the labor markets, and no economy in the world could keep up. The turmoil is sometimes interpreted as the outburst of frustrated young men venting their rage at their own indolence and impotence.[5]

But if this were primarily an economic crisis, why did it erupt at a time of economic expansion and growth? And why wasn't it anticipated that the resulting instability would actually *worsen* the economic plight of these countries?

Failed Hybrid

Having now questioned various explanations and found them wanting, I proceed to my sweeping generalization. This is a crisis of culture. That is to say, it is more than a political or social or economic crisis. Of course it has elements of all of these things, but at its most fundamental, it is a crisis of culture—to be precise, the implosion of the hybrid civilization that dominated the twentieth century in the Arab world.

That hybrid was the defensive, selective adaptation of Islamic traditions to the ways of the West. The idea was that the tradition could be preserved, that its essence could be defended, while making adjustments to modernity as needed. The timeless character of the political, religious, and social traditions of the region could be upheld, even as upgrades were made to accommodate modernity. In Turkey,

Atatürk's cultural revolution had thrown all of tradition overboard and embraced the ways of Europe without reservation. The Arabs resisted the notion, and their leaders promised them a different path, a hybrid of the Arab-Islamic tradition with Western-style modernity.

This hybrid civilization pretended to be revolutionary, but it permitted the survival of those premodern traditions that block progress, from authoritarianism and patriarchy to sectarianism and tribalism. This hybrid civilization has now failed, and what we have seen is a collapse, not of a political system, but of a moral universe left behind by time.

That failure was long concealed by a mixture of regime maneuvering and the prop of oil. It has been cushioned in those places in the Arab Gulf where rulers have given up on the better part of Arab-Islamic civilization, inviting the Louvre and the Guggenheim and American universities to build branches, and allowing expatriates to outnumber the Arabs. These are the places that have become refuges from chaos elsewhere, and that have even profited from it. But in the great centers of Arab-Islamic civilization, from Cairo to Damascus to Baghdad, the crisis of the political order is primarily a symptom of the collapse of their own hybrid of tradition and modernity.

The failure of the hybrid is most dramatically evidenced by the rise of sectarianism. The Sunni-Shi'ite divide has many layers, including a disparity of power, often the legacy of colonialism. But the mindset of sectarianism is thoroughly premodern. Modern nationalism was devised at least in part to blunt sectarianism among Muslims.

But because the tradition had to be respected, the hybrid civilization of the region tolerated the exclusion of Jews and the marginalization of Christians. It was only one step from there to the defamation by Shi'ite of Sunni, by Sunni of Alawi, and on and on. The jihad of Muslim against Muslim, whether waged by Lebanon's Hezbollah in Syria, or by ISIS in parts of Iraq and northern Syria, is a huge reversal. It is like a page taken straight out of eighth- or ninth-century Islamic history. Here we are in a Middle East where the major divide is not over the form of government, or the nature of the economic system, or the extent of individual liberty. It is over a dispute dating from the seventh century of Islam—the sort of thing Europe left behind when it secularized during the Enlightenment.

There are some who would actually reify this by inscribing it on the map. There is a certain line of reasoning, that what the Middle East really needs is a new map, drawn along sectarian lines. The 1916 Sykes-Picot map is coming apart at the seams, so the argument goes.

The lines on the political map are losing their meaning, the lines that aren't yet on the map are becoming realities. An alternative map is needed, and most of the alternatives have a standard feature: divvying up the Fertile Crescent along sectarian and ethnic lines.

There is no question that the present crisis is weakening some states, and that they are losing their ability to project central power up to their borders. Sectarian and ethnic separatism has tremendous purchase. But even if new lines could be drawn, how would this solve the crisis? How would it make the region better suited to embrace modernity? The fact is that sectarian statelets, predicated on premodern identities, could well go the other way. Think about the Sunni Islamist quasi-states centered around Raqqa in northern Syria and Gaza on the Mediterranean. These aren't going to become the next Dubai or Qatar, and not just because they don't have oil. If the map does come undone, and new statelets or quasi-states or mini-states are born, that is just as likely to bring about more sectarian and ethnic conflict as ease it.

In summation, there are millions of people who now must reconfigure the way they see themselves and the world, not just through a political revolution, but through a cultural one. There is no way any outside power can deliberately accelerate or channel this transformation. And since we are much closer to the beginning of that process than the end, the region will remain a cauldron for years if not decades to come.

Notes

1. Among many examples: Kurt Weyland, "The Arab Spring: Why the Surprising Similarities with the Revolutionary Wave of 1848?," *Perspectives on Politics* 10, no. 4 (2012): 917–34; and Steven Philip Kramer and Judith S. Yaphe, "The European Spring of 1848 and the Arab Spring of 2011: Lessons to Be Learned?," *Mediterranean Quarterly* 25, no. 4 (2014): 45–63.
2. William Kristol, "Stand for Freedom," *Weekly Standard*, February 14, 2011; Max Boot, "Disorganized Rebellion Doesn't Mean Defeat," *Commentary* blog, April 20, 2011, archived at https://web.archive.org/web/20110504053924/http://www.commentarymagazine.com/2011/04/20/disorganized-rebellion-doesn%E2%80%99t-mean-defeat/.
3. James Stavridis, "Syria Ghosts," *ForeignPolicy.com*, November 6, 2015, archived at https://web.archive.org/web/20160103210509/http://foreignpolicy.com/2015/11/06/lessons-from-the-balkans-for-syria/.
4. Lizzie Dearden, "Arab Spring 'cost affected countries $830 billion', report claims," *Independent*, December 15, 2015.
5. Raggui Assaad, "Demographics of Arab Protests," interview with Council on Foreign Relations, February 14, 2011, archived at https://web.archive.org/web/20110227090809/http://www.cfr.org/egypt/demographics-arab-protests/p24096.

17

Listening to Arabs

"Linkage" might best be described as a domino theory peculiar to the Middle East. It rests on the assumption that the Israeli-Palestinian conflict, more than any other issue, prompts the rise of terrorism, weakens friendly governments, and makes it impossible for the United States—the major supporter of Israel—to win Arabs and Muslims over to the good cause. These people are so preoccupied with the fate of the Palestinians that they cannot see the United States as a friend. The region is rife with conflicts that impact U.S. interests, but peoples and governments won't respond to American efforts to resolve them, unless the United States conjures up a resolution for the Palestinians first.

"Linkage" has had many prominent adherents over the years. The most notable, perhaps, was former U.S. president Jimmy Carter. He was once asked this: "Is the Israel-Palestine conflict still the key to peace in the whole region? Is the linkage policy right?" Carter's answer: "I don't think it's about a linkage policy, but a linkage fact. . . . Without doubt, the path to peace in the Middle East goes through Jerusalem."[1]

Authors Dennis Ross and Alan Makovsky have compiled a long list of similar statements for a book appropriately entitled *Myths, Illusions, and Peace.* They did a thorough job of refuting the "linkage" myth, even before much of the Arab world unraveled into chaos.[2] Today hardly anyone argues that a resolution of the Israeli-Palestinian conflict would make a whit of difference to the civil wars in Syria and Libya, Sunni-Shi'ite sectarianism, the rise of the Islamic State, Iran's imperial interventions, or the challenge of Kurdish nationalism. Occasionally, someone will claim that extremists or terrorists use the Israeli-Palestinian conflict as a "recruiting argument," so resolving it might help in the fight against Al Qaeda or ISIS.[3] But as these terrorists use dozens of "recruiting arguments," the claim is rather less ambitious than the classic "linkage" argument.

But there is a lingering argument made for "linkage" that doesn't rest on what the "extremists" say. This is the claim that Arab leaders friendly to the United States insist upon it. Surely Arab rulers who are America's friends know what moves their subjects, and if they say that the Israeli-Palestinian conflict stands at the summit of Arab grievances, this cannot be dismissed. Even if we think it doesn't deserve such an elevated status, so the argument goes, we would be foolish to ignore the analyses of our best Arab friends. And they consistently tell us that there is nothing that Washington could do that would have more of a positive effect than bringing this one conflict to resolution.

Or do they tell us this? Former Nebraska senator Chuck Hagel certainly said so. After twelve years as a U.S. senator, Hagel served President Obama as secretary of defense for two years, from 2013 to 2015. While a senator, Hagel repeatedly and publicly expressed his belief in "linkage." He claimed to have reached this conclusion by talking with leaders of the Middle East: I'm just repeating what they've told me, he would say. So it is interesting to go back and see just what they did tell him—an exercise made feasible thanks to WikiLeaks. This is valuable not because Hagel remains important (as of this writing, he isn't), but because his case perfectly demonstrates a more widespread pathology that feeds the "linkage" thesis. It might best be described as selective hearing while listening to Arabs.

The Core Conflict

But first, let us consider how Senator Hagel thought the Middle East works. In 2002, he put it this way:

> The Arab-Israeli conflict cannot be separated from America's foreign policy. Actions in the Middle East have immense consequences for our other policies and interests in the world. We are limited in dealing with other conflicts until this conflict is on a path to resolution. America's policy and role in the Middle East, and the perception of our policies and role across the globe, affects our policies and interests in Afghanistan, South Asia, Indonesia, and all parts of the world.[4]

In 2006, Hagel put it this way:

> The core of all challenges in the Middle East remains the underlying Arab-Israeli conflict. The failure to address this root cause will allow Hezbollah, Hamas, and other terrorists to continue to sustain popular Muslim and Arab support—a dynamic that continues to undermine America's standing in the region and the Governments of Egypt, Jordan, Saudi Arabia, and others, whose support is critical for any Middle East resolution.[5]

The vocabulary here—"core," "root cause," "underlying"—is taken from the standard "linkage" lexicon, which elevates the Arab-Israeli or Palestinian-Israeli conflict to a preeminent status. That same year, he again described the "underlying" Arab-Israeli conflict as the "core" of the region's maladies:

> In the Middle East, the core of instability and conflict is the underlying Arab-Israeli problem. Progress on Middle East peace does not ensure stability in Iraq. But, for the Arab world, the issue of Middle East peace is inextricably, emotionally and psychologically linked with all other issues. Until the United States helps lead a renewed Israeli-Palestinian peace process, there will be no prospect for broader Middle East peace and stability.[6]

In 2008, Hagel developed this into a full-blown "ripple" theory, in a passage in his book, *America: Our Next Chapter*. There he wrote that the Israeli-Palestinian conflict

> cannot be looked at in isolation. Like a stone dropped into a placid lake, its ripples extend out farther and farther. Egypt, Syria, Jordan, and Lebanon feel the effects most noticeably. Farther still, Afghanistan and Pakistan; anything that impacts their political stability also affects the two emerging economic superpowers, India and China.[7]

The notion that the greater Middle East would be a "placid lake" were it not for the Israeli-Palestinian conflict can only be regarded as extreme, even for someone in the grip of "linkage" fever. But Hagel, doubling down, extended the conflict's baleful influence even beyond the world of the Arabs and South Asian Islam, suggesting that it "affects" India and China in a detrimental way, although he didn't explain how.

That same year, Hagel made the most far-reaching claim for "linkage." By this time, Americans knew considerably more about the complexities of the Middle East than they had known in 2002. Wars in Afghanistan and Iraq had demonstrated the salience of deep conflicts that defined the politics of the region, and that went back in time before there was an Israel. The great Sunni-Shi'ite divide, the region-wide Kurdish question, the rivalries of tribes, the chasm between rulers and ruled—all were sources of conflict and instability with long and autonomous histories. That was what made Hagel's 2008 statement so striking: he was clearly aware that the "linkage" thesis looked shakier than ever, but he dug in his heels anyway:

> The strategic epicenter of the Middle East [is] the Israeli-Palestinian issue. Why do I say that more than any other reason? It is the one issue, the one issue alone, the Israeli-Palestinian issue alone. Fixing that alone is not going to fix every problem in the Middle East. We understand that. We have religious hatred. We have centuries of it. We have regional, tribal issues. Yes, all complicated. But that one issue, the Israeli-Palestinian issue shapes almost every other issue, not just the optics of it, but the reality of it. It is allowed to—as it plays itself out to dominate relationships, to dominate the people who would like a different kind of world. I know that there is a lot made on the issue of—well it's important, but it certainly doesn't affect everything. It does.[8]

In this convoluted remark, Hagel was clearly struggling to force all of the new and "complicated" American knowledge about the Middle East into his old template. He knew that his "linkage" thesis looked less plausible than it once did. How exactly could the Israeli-Palestinian issue "affect everything" and "shape almost every other issue," not just the "optics" but the "reality"? Hagel couldn't say how, except to assert that "it does."

But Hagel, knowing his bald assertion might seem dubious, did something new. He invoked the authority of Middle Eastern leaders:

> I don't know any other way to gauge this, than you go out and listen to the leaders. You listen to Jewish leaders, and you listen to Arab leaders. You sit down with all the leaders with all those countries, and I have many times, different leaders, and they will take you right back to the same issue. Right back to this issue. Now I am not an expert on anything, and I'm certainly not an expert on the Middle East. Most of the people in this room, especially those that were on the panels tonight know a lot more about this issue than I do. But I do listen. I do observe. I am somewhat informed. That informs me that when the people of the Middle East themselves tell me that this issue has to be dealt with or there will not be a resolution to any other issue in the Middle East.[9]

No other issue in the entire Middle East can be resolved until Israel and the Palestinians deal with theirs: this was Hagel's long-standing belief, now placed in the mouths of authoritative interlocutors, those Middle Eastern leaders he met on his travels, and who always took him "right back to this issue."

Meeting Arabs and Jews

On the face of it, this is a plausible assertion. It is often said that Arab leaders never miss an opportunity to browbeat American officials over U.S. neglect of the Palestinians. A senior American diplomat once made this complaint: "Every American ambassador in the region knows that official meetings with Arab leaders start with the obligatory half-hour lecture on the Palestinian question. If we could dispense with that half-hour and get down to our other business, we might actually be able to get something done."[10]

But are these the sorts of discussions that Hagel had with Arab leaders? We do not have a record of all his meetings with them, but we have several accounts, via WikiLeaks. These seem to contradict Hagel's own assertion that his Arab interlocutors always came "right back to this issue." In fact, it was usually the third or fourth item on the agenda, sometimes raised not by Arab leaders but by visiting Americans. Arab leaders who met Hagel expressed a very wide range of concerns, usually focused on Iran and Iraq. (There is one important exception, to which we will return presently.) Here are the publicly documented instances, from his trips to the region between 2004 and 2008:

- On December 1, 2004, King Abdullah of Jordan had lunch in Amman with Hagel (as well as Senators Joe Biden, Dianne Feinstein, and Lincoln Chafee). The account may not be complete, but the discussion as reported focused only on Iraq and the "negative role" of Iran. King Abdullah, looking ahead to Iraqi elections in January, "worried that elections held without credible Sunni participation could lead to cantonization or civil war," and opined that Iraqi Shi'ites were loyal to Iran, not Iraq. "The King painted a picture of a monolithic Shia Arab/Iranian threat to Jordan and Israel if they 'take over' southern Iraq."[11] (A few days later, King Abdullah said much the same in an interview with the *Washington Post*, coining the phrase "Shi'ite crescent" to describe the menace.)[12]
- On December 4, 2004, the Crown Prince of Bahrain, Sheikh Salman bin Hamad Al Khalifa, received Hagel, Feinstein, and Chafee. The conversation also focused on impending elections in Iraq, which the Bahrainis feared might be captured by "radical elements." Later, Feinstein raised the Israeli-Palestinian issue, urging Bahrain and Gulf governments to "speak out on the need for a two-state solution in Palestine in order to ostracize extremists on both sides and bring the Arab media on board." Sheikh Salman gently deflected this, suggesting that the United States, "even if politically difficult, must engage in a public discourse that demonstrates that the goal of promoting democracy in the Middle East includes Palestinians as well."[13] So it wasn't the Arab ruler who "came

back to the issue," but a peace-process-fixated American senator—an
effort artfully foiled by Sheikh Salman.

- A meeting in Amman with Jordan's King Abdullah on November 29,
2005 was dominated again by Iran and Iraq. (Attending: Hagel, Senator
Tom Carper and Representative Ellen Tauscher.) The monarch, still in
his "Shi'ite crescent" mode, expressed his fear that Iran would establish
its dominance over Iraq: "If this influence was not checked, he warned,
it could lead to effective Iranian rule of southern Iraq, and to an even
more active and dangerous Hizballah in Lebanon." King Abdullah's
second concern: Syria, where he speculated that too much pressure
on the Assad regime could lead to a "possible takeover of the country
by the Muslim Brotherhood"—which, "the king warned, would be very
negative for both Syria and the region." Israel and the Palestinians? This
figured as the third item on the agenda. In this case, Abdullah didn't
"warn" about anything, but simply highlighted Jordan's commitment to
train and reform Palestinian security forces, Jordan's interest in more
economic cooperation with the Palestinian Authority, and a vague hope
that there might be an "increased dynamism" in Israel, as a result of
changes in the Labor Party.[14]

- Hagel (and Carper and Tauscher) met with Saudi King Abdullah,
Crown Prince Sultan, and Foreign Minister Sa'ud al-Faisal, in Riyadh on
November 30, 2005. Again, the top agenda issues were Iraq followed by
Iran. Hagel would later go on the record as opposing the 2007 "surge"
in Iraq ("the most dangerous foreign policy blunder in this country
since Vietnam").[15] But in 2005, when Hagel asked the Saudis about a
U.S. troop withdrawal, King Abdullah "urged the U.S. not to withdraw
forces or lose focus until Iraq was stabilized." The Saudi foreign minister
added that "the U.S. should consider increasing troop levels in the short
term to ensure the political process concludes successfully." Only after
a lengthy discussion of Iran did they get to Israel and the Palestinians.
Prince Sultan explained the various Saudi peace proposals, and praised
Israel's then-prime minister Ariel Sharon as "a clever and courageous
man" who might "move in a direction which serves Israel and the Israeli
people." (This section of the dispatch carried the headline: "Sharon as
Peacemaker: Saudis Surprisingly Pragmatic.")[16] Hagel later would claim
that lack of a resolution of the Israeli-Palestinian conflict "undermines"
the Saudi (and other pro-American) governments. But he didn't hear
that from the Saudis, who in their 2005 meeting with him treated the
issue as a midlevel priority.

- On December 4, 2005, Hagel (accompanied by the U.S. ambassador to
Egypt) met with Egyptian President Mubarak in Cairo. At the top of
the agenda: the threat posed by the prospect of Shi'ite ascendency in
Iraq. "In Mubarak's view, the Shi'a were extremely difficult to deal with
and given to deception," and they represented a potential Iranian fifth
column in Saudi Arabia, Bahrain, and other Gulf states. Second: Syria,
where he advised the United States to "avoid stating publicly that it
sought 'regime change.'" It was Hagel who raised the Palestinian-Israeli

issue, thanking Egypt for supporting the peace process. Mubarak responded by calling Ariel Sharon, "a strong leader, the strongest since Begin," and he went on to blame Syria's late leader, Hafez Assad, for failing to reach a peace deal with Yitzhak Rabin. Mubarak then circled back to "the untrustworthiness and duplicity of the regime in Tehran," with illustrative examples. In this conversation, it was Hagel, not Mubarak, who had "come right back" to the Israeli-Palestinian issue.[17]

- On May 31, 2007, Lebanese Prime Minister Fouad Siniora received Hagel (as well as Senators Patrick Leahy, Thad Cochran, Ken Salazar, Ben Cardin, and Representative Peter Welch). The prime minister dwelt at length on the UN resolution establishing the Hariri tribunal (it "meant the end of an era of impunity for assassins and Lebanon would now never turn back"). He then gave a detailed preview of the army's plan to crush the terrorist group Fatah al-Islam, holed up in the Palestinian refugee camp of Nahr al-Barid near Tripoli. Siniora did urge the United States to persuade Israel to open talks based on the Saudi peace initiative. If the opportunity were missed, "it would give considerable momentum to extremists in the region and all that entailed."[18]
- On July 20, 2008, the Emir of Kuwait, Sheikh Sabah Al Sabah, received Hagel (as well as Senator Barack Obama). The conversation focused on Iraq, oil prices, and Aljazeera. Israel and the Palestinians weren't discussed.[19]

So in none of these meetings was there a preliminary half-hour lecture on Palestine. In most of them, the threat posed by Iran loomed larger than any anxiety over the absence of an Israeli-Palestinian agreement. Looking back at these meetings in 2008, Hagel claimed that "the people of the Middle East themselves tell me that this issue has to be dealt with or there will not be a resolution to any other issue in the Middle East." In none of these meetings did any Arab leader tell Hagel any such thing.

Hagel didn't just claim to get the linkage message from Arab leaders. "You listen to Jewish leaders, and you listen to Arab leaders." (By "Jewish," he must have meant Israeli.) Hagel met many Israelis, and only he and they know what they told him. But on at least one occasion, he heard one of them brusquely dismiss the "linkage" argument. Hagel (and Senator Biden) met with then-prime minister Ariel Sharon in December 2004, and one of the Americans in the delegation (unnamed in the dispatch) had the temerity to suggest that "progress towards Israeli-Palestinian peace would have a dramatic impact on ending regional and international terrorism. Sharon quickly stated that Israel should not be held responsible for terrorism, asserting that it was the target of terror even prior to June 1967. It was not correct to believe that terror would disappear if the Israeli-Palestinian dispute were solved. The only thing that Israel was 'responsible' for, he maintained, was defending its people."[20] If "Jewish leaders" told Hagel anything that reinforced his thesis, Ariel Sharon definitely was not among them.

Neither was his successor, Ehud Olmert, who told Hagel (and several other senators) in May 2007 that Arab fear of Iran had created a situation where, "for the first time, we are not enemy number one."[21] On that same visit, then-foreign minister Tzipi Livni told the senatorial delegation that "there was a new understanding in the region that the Iranian threat is an 'existential' one and has become more significant than the Israeli-Palestinian conflict."[22]

Abdullah of Jordan: Linkage Man

In Hagel's meetings (as revealed in the WikiLeaks sample), there was one exception—one meeting in which an Arab leader said something approximating what Hagel claimed they all told him. In Hagel's meetings with King Abdullah in 2004 and 2005, he heard little about the Palestinians, and a lot about the "Shi'ite crescent" and a possible Iranian takeover of southern Iraq. But in a meeting in Amman in May 2007 with Hagel (plus Leahy, Cochran, Salazar, Cardin, and Welch), the Jordanian monarch did a turnaround. King Abdullah "highlighted his view that the Palestinian-Israeli conflict is the key issue facing Jordan and the region." He claimed that "within as little as one and a half years the opportunity for a two-state solution may be lost." Jordanian then-foreign minister Abdelelah al-Khatib told the visiting senators that "lack of progress on peace was undermining efforts on other issues such as stabilizing Iraq, Lebanon, and isolating Syria and Iran."[23]

Why did King Abdullah change his tune? Thanks to the U.S. "surge" in Iraq, he had come to believe that Iran had been checked. In June 2008, Lally Weymouth interviewed him for the *Washington Post*. "I remember a couple of years ago, you warned against the danger posed by Iran to moderate Arab regimes," she told him. "Do you view Iran as the number one threat in this region?"

> *King Abdullah:* I think the lack of peace [between Israel and the Palestinians] is the major threat. I don't see the ability of creating a two-state solution beyond 2008, 2009. I think this is really the last chance. If this fails, I think this is going to be the major threat for the Middle East.
>
> *Weymouth:* But aren't you concerned that Iran is a threat both to your country and to other countries in the region?

King Abdullah: Iran poses issues to certain countries, although I have noticed over the past month or so that the dynamics have changed quite dramatically, and for the first time I think maybe I can say that Iran is less of a threat. But if the peace process doesn't move forward, then I think that extremism will continue to advance over the moderate stands that a lot of countries take.[24]

So Jordan's King Abdullah became the "linkage" lead man, and it is not difficult to see why. Jordan is the Arab state that sits astride the West Bank, that has a Palestinian majority, and that shares the longest border with Israel. Were things to go very wrong between Israelis and Palestinians on the West Bank, Jordan would be the first to feel it. So it is Jordan's national interest to elevate Israeli-Palestinian peace to preeminence. In particular circumstances, such as the Iraq war and the Syrian civil war, it will strike other chords. But its default position is to declare, always with urgency, that the sky is about to fall on Israelis and Palestinians, that the world must act now to prevent that, and that a Palestinian state will help solve every problem, everywhere. In that respect, Jordan is unique in the Arab world.

King Abdullah of Jordan seems to have been the only Arab leader whose message strictly conformed to Hagel's *idée fixe* about "linkage." This would become significant in July 2008, when candidate Barack Obama set off for the Middle East, accompanied by Hagel (and Senator Jack Reed). This visit would be described as "an intense bonding experience" between Hagel and Obama, in which they "delved deeply into policy discussions—'wonkfests,' as one former aide called them."[25] The swing included a stop in Amman. (King Abdullah returned from Aspen to be there, and at the end of the visit, he personally drove Obama to the airport.) We do not have a leaked record of the king's meeting with the delegation. But the press statement issued by the royal palace reported that the king stressed to Obama "that ending the Israeli occupation of Palestinian land and achieving a just settlement to the Arab-Israeli conflict tops the priorities of the people of the Middle East."[26]

The king's view of how linkage actually operated came through in Obama's own account, in a press interview:

I think King Abdullah is as savvy an analyst of the region and player in the region as, as there is, one of the points that he made and I think a lot of people made, is that we've got to have an overarching strategy recognizing that all these issues are connected. If we can solve the Israeli-Palestinian process, then that will make it easier for

Arab states and the Gulf states to support us when it comes to issues like Iraq and Afghanistan.

It will also weaken Iran, which has been using Hamas and Hezbollah as a way to stir up mischief in the region. If we've gotten an Israeli-Palestinian peace deal, maybe at the same time peeling Syria out of the Iranian orbit, that makes it easier to isolate Iran so that they have a tougher time developing a nuclear weapon.[27]

So Obama, under the combined influence of Hagel and Abdullah, became a convert to "linkage." It was this notion that propelled the Obama administration, from its very first day, into a flurry of efforts to restart Israeli-Palestinian negotiations. The very urgency with which this campaign was launched may have been its undoing, producing the self-defeating U.S. demand for an Israeli settlement freeze. Hagel wasn't implicated in that decision. The "linkage" mindset was.

The Wrong Conflict

As secretary of defense, Hagel later watched haplessly as disaster unfolded in Syria—the horrific reprisals by the regime and its use of chemical weapons, the gruesome theatrics of ISIS, the flood of millions of refugees across Syria's borders into neighboring countries and Europe, the intervention of regional and outside powers, the bombing by the Russians, and the fecklessness of President Obama. Consider this quote from Hagel:

I think it is so serious now, I think we are at the most dangerous time maybe we have seen ever in the Middle East with all the combustible elements . . . The president needs to get seriously engaged now. If we do not do that now at this moment, and I mean this moment, then the possibility of this escalating into a Middle East catastrophe, which would drag in all nations of the world, if for no other reason than just the energy dynamic here. The ramifications, the significance of all of this is astounding once you start to chart it out.[28]

This would have been an exact assessment of the Syrian war that occurred on President Obama's watch. But Hagel didn't make it about Syria. He made it during the Israel-Hezbollah mini-war in the summer of 2006. That conflict, lasting a little over a month, quickly de-escalated when Israel used its military might to enforce its redlines against Hezbollah. The war did not "drag in" any other party, and the endgame assured stability on Israel's northern border for years to come. But in Syria, where the Obama administration failed to enforce U.S.

redlines, a conflict escalated into a full-blown political and humanitarian catastrophe that indeed threatened to drag in "all nations of the world."

It is not the Israeli-Palestinian conflict that is "linked" to everything in the region. To the contrary: the conflict is containable, because a powerful Israel deters regional adversaries from actively intervening on behalf of the Palestinians. It is the Syrian conflict that is "linked" to almost every other conflict, because it involves the most durable fissure in the region, the Sunni-Shi'ite cleavage, and because no player is strong enough to impose order.

If Hagel had listened closely to his Arab interlocutors, he would have understood this. Nearly all of them harped on the Shi'ite and Iranian threat. At least two of them warned of the dangers of regime instability in Syria—this, several years before the "Arab Spring." Arab leaders weren't telling Americans that the Palestinian question eclipsed all others. They were insisting to Hagel, and to anyone who would listen, that the ascent of Iran and the war in Iraq were throwing the entire region out of balance.

But no one listened; instead, like Hagel, people heard what they wished to hear. That was the tragedy of "linkage." It proved to be a huge diversion from a necessary focus on far more dangerous and destabilizing conflicts in the Middle East. While Western diplomats, led by the Americans, fiddled obsessively with the Rubick's Cube of the "peace process," a large part of the Arab world came undone, and no one had the presence of mind to develop a strategy to prevent it. The "linkage" purveyors bear much of the responsibility for the grim consequences of this neglect.

Needless to say, they will never admit it.

Notes

1. Jimmy Carter interviewed by Nathan Gardels, *Huffington Post*, December 12, 2006, archived at http://web.archive.org/web/20061219120347/http://www.huffingtonpost.com/nathan-gardels/jimmy-carter-takes-on-isr_b_36134.html.
2. Dennis Ross and David Makovsky, *Myths, Illusions, and Peace: Finding a New Direction for America in the Middle East* (New York: Viking, 2009), 12–90.
3. Robert Malley, a "peace processor" recycled by the Obama administration as a coordinator of the campaign against ISIS, provided a perfect example in a 2015 conference: "It stands to reason that resolving this conflict would at least help. It wouldn't resolve, but it would be a major contribution to stemming the rise of extremism and to allow the kind of cooperation that

is needed [to take on] what should be a common challenge, which is the challenge of [ISIS] and of other extremist organizations." Robert Malley's remarks at *Ha'aretz*-New Israel Fund conference, New York City, December 13, 2015, posted at https://www.youtube.com/watch?v=o8iV-a8fLgY, accessed February 24, 2016.

4. Senate, Senator Hagel of Nebraska, "Peace in the Middle East," *Congressional Record*, 107th Cong., 2d sess. (June 14, 2002), 148, pt. 8:S5578.

5. Senate, Senator Hagel of Nebraska, "The Middle East—A Region in Crisis," 109th Cong., 2d sess. (July 31, 2006), 152, pt. 12:S8421.

6. Speech by Senator Chuck Hagel, "A 21st-Century Frame of Reference," Johns Hopkins University School of Advanced International Studies, Washington, DC, December 7, 2006, archived at http://web.archive.org/web/20130130153511/http://votesmart.org/public-statement/227433/hagel-speech-on-iraqmiddle-east.

7. Chuck Hagel, *America: Our Next Chapter: Tough Questions, Straight Answers* (New York: Ecco, 2008), 82.

8. Speech by Senator Chuck Hagel, Israel Policy Forum Annual Event, December 4, 2008, New York, archived at http://web.archive.org/web/20160224220731/http://www.israelpolicyforum.org/news/his-own-words-sen-chuck-hagel-middle-east/.

9. Ibid.

10. Quoted by Ethan Bronner, "Why America Chases an Israeli-Palestinian Peace," *New York Times*, November 20, 2010.

11. David Hale, charge d'affaires (Amman), dispatch of December 5, 2004, archived at http://web.archive.org/web/20160224221530/https://wikileaks.org/plusd/cables/04AMMAN9593_a.html.

12. King Abdullah interviewed by Robin Wright and Peter Baker, *Washington Post*, December 8, 2004.

13. William T. Monroe, ambassador (Manama), dispatch of December 7, 2004, archived at http://web.archive.org/web/20160224222212/https://wikileaks.org/plusd/cables/04MANAMA1823_a.html.

14. David Hale, ambassador (Amman), dispatch of December 6, 2005, archived at http://web.archive.org/web/20160224225433/https://wikileaks.org/plusd/cables/05AMMAN9393_a.html.

15. Ted Barnett, "GOP Senator: Bush Plan Could Match Vietnam Blunder," CNN.com, January 11, 2007, archived at http://web.archive.org/web/20070115055257/http://edition.cnn.com/2007/POLITICS/01/11/iraq.congress/.

16. Michael Gfoeller, deputy chief of mission (Riyadh), dispatch of December 18, 2005, http://web.archive.org/web/20160224230424/https://wikileaks.org/plusd/cables/05RIYADH9342_a.html.

17. Francis J. Ricciardone, ambassador (Cairo), dispatch of December 6, 2005, archived at http://web.archive.org/web/20160224231048/https://www.wikileaks.org/plusd/cables/05CAIRO9055_a.html.

18. Jeffrey D. Feltman, ambassador (Beirut), dispatch of May 31, 2007, archived at http://web.archive.org/web/20160224231453/http://wikileaks.cabledrum.net/cable/2007/05/07BEIRUT773.html.

19. Deborah K. Jones, ambassador (Kuwait), dispatch of July 24, 2008, archived at http://web.archive.org/web/20160224231843/http://wikileaks.cabledrum.net/cable/2008/07/08KUWAIT835.html.

20. Daniel Kurtzer, ambassador (Tel Aviv), dispatch of December 16, 2004, archived at http://web.archive.org/web/20160224232059/https://wikileaks.org/plusd/cables/04TELAVIV6387_a.html.
21. Richard H. Jones, ambassador (Tel Aviv), dispatch of June 11, 2007, archived at http://web.archive.org/web/20160224232440/https://wikileaks.org/plusd/cables/07TELAVIV1691_a.html.
22. Richard H. Jones, ambassador (Tel Aviv), dispatch of June 11, 2007, http://web.archive.org/web/20160224232720/http://wikileaks.cabledrum.org/cable/2007/06/07TELAVIV1684.html.
23. David Hale, ambassador (Amman), dispatch of June 10, 2007, archived at http://web.archive.org/web/20160224232926/https://wikileaks.org/plusd/cables/07AMMAN2464_a.html.
24. Lally Waymouth, "A Conversation with King Abdullah of Jordan," *Washington Post*, June 22, 2008.
25. Daniel Klaidman, "The Origins of Obama's Relationship with Chuck Hagel," *Newsweek/The Daily Beast*, January 14, 2013, archived at https://web.archive.org/web/20130112105032/http://www.thedailybeast.com/newsweek/2013/01/13/the-logic-of-hagel.html.
26. Quoted by Natalie Gewargis, "Obama Hitches a Royal Ride," *ABC News*, July 22, 2008, archived at http://web.archive.org/web/20120801195252/http://abcnews.go.com/blogs/politics/2008/07/obama-hitches-a/.
27. Barack Obama interviewed by Tom Brokaw, "Meet the Press," *NBC News*, July 27, 2008, archived at http://web.archive.org/web/20130315065947/http://www.nbcnews.com/id/25872804/ns/meet_the_press/t/meet-press-transcript-july/.
28. Chuck Hagel interviewed by Larry King, "Larry King Live," CNN, July 13, 2006, archived at http://web.archive.org/web/20070623091144/http://edition.cnn.com/TRANSCRIPTS/0607/13/lkl.01.html.

Part IV

Inventing Israel's History

18

What Happened at Lydda

(With responses by Benny Morris)

In thirty minutes, at high noon, more than two hundred civilians are killed. Zionism carries out a massacre in the city of Lydda.
—Ari Shavit, *My Promised Land*[1]

Perhaps no book by an Israeli has ever been promoted as massively in America as *My Promised Land: The Triumph and Tragedy of Israel*, by the *Ha'aretz* columnist and editorial-board member Ari Shavit. The prepublication blitz began in May 2013, when the author received the first-ever Natan Fund book award, which included an earmark of $35,000 to promote and publicize the book. The prize committee was co-chaired by the columnist Jeffrey Goldberg and Franklin Foer, editor of the *New Republic*; among its members was the *New York Times* columnist David Brooks. Not only was the choice of Shavit "unanimous and enthusiastic," but Goldberg and Foer also supplied florid blurbs for the book jacket. Goldberg: "a beautiful, mesmerizing, morally serious, and vexing book," for which "I've been waiting most of my adult life."[2] Foer: "epic history... beautifully written, dramatically rendered, full of moral complexity... mind-blowing, trustworthy insights."[3]

Upon publication in November 2013, the book proceeded to receive no fewer than three glowing encomia in the *Times*—from the columnist Thomas Friedman ("must-read"), the paper's literary critic Dwight Garner ("reads like a love story and thriller at once"), and the *New Republic*'s literary editor Leon Wieseltier ("important and powerful... the least tendentious book about Israel I have ever read").[4] From there it jumped to the *Times*'s "100 Notable Books of 2013" and to the non-fiction bestseller list, where it spent a total of six weeks.

The *Times* was hardly alone. The editor of the *New Yorker*, David Remnick, who is credited by Shavit with inspiring the book and curating its journey into print, hosted a launch party at his home and appeared with Shavit in promotional events at New York's 92nd Street Y, the Council on Foreign Relations, the Jewish Community Center of San Francisco, and the *Charlie Rose Show*. Jeffrey Goldberg likewise surfaced alongside Shavit both on *Charlie Rose* and at campus whistle stops.

"What happened during the first week of my book's publication went beyond anyone's expectation, beyond my dreams," marveled Shavit in an interview.[5] In January 2014, he collected a National Jewish Book Award. In short order, he became a must-have speaker for national Jewish organizations from AIPAC to Hadassah, and a feted guest at the Beverly Hills homes of media mogul Haim Saban and the producer-director Tony Krantz. "If you want to see what prophecy looks like among Jews in the early part of the twenty-first century," wrote an attendee at one of these soirées, "follow Ari Shavit around Los Angeles."[6]

Beyond Shavit's powerful writing style and engaging personal manner, what inspired this outpouring? "My book," he said, "is a painful love story," the love in question being his professed "total commitment to Israel, and my admiration for the Zionist project,"[7] tempered by his conspicuously agonized conscience over the misdeeds of that state and that project. It was, undoubtedly, this dual theme that gave the book its poignant appeal to many American Jewish readers eager to revive a passion for Israel at a time when Israel is defined by much of liberal opinion as an "occupier." To achieve his artfully mixed effect, Shavit adopted a particular strategy: confessing Israel's sins *in order* to demonstrate the tragic profundity of his love.

And the sins in question? The obvious one in the book is the sin of post-1967 "occupation." But many readers were especially taken aback to learn of an earlier and even more hauntingly painful sin. This one, detailed in a thirty-page chapter titled "Lydda, 1948," concerns an alleged massacre of Palestinian Arabs that preceded an act of forcible expulsion. Shavit's revelation: Lydda is "our black box." In its story lies the dark secret not only of the birth of Israel but indeed of the entire Jewish national movement—of Zionism.

The Lydda chapter gained resonance early on because Shavit's friends at the *New Yorker* decided to abridge and publish it in the magazine. There, it ran under an expanded title: "Lydda, 1948: A City, a Massacre, and the Middle East Today."[8] The meaningful addition is obviously the word "massacre." An informed reader might have heard of another 1948 "massacre," the one in April at the Arab village of Deir Yassin. But at

Lydda? Who did it? Under what circumstances? How many died? Was it covered up?

"Massacre" is Shavit's chosen word, but he doesn't define it. Instead, he proposes a narrative of the events that occurred around midday on July 12, 1948, in the midst of Israel's war of independence, when Israeli soldiers in Lydda faced an incipient uprising. This narrative he claims to have constructed from interviews he conducted twenty years ago, "in the early 1990s." He spoke then with Shmarya Gutman, the Israeli military governor of Lydda who negotiated the departure of its Arab inhabitants; the commander (his name was Mula Cohen) of the Yiftah brigade, which quelled the uprising; and someone identified only by his nickname, "Bulldozer," who fired an antitank shell into a small mosque, supposedly killing seventy persons at one blow. Shavit's dramatic culmination comes in the assertion that leads this article: "In thirty minutes, at high noon, more than two hundred civilians are killed. Zionism carries out a massacre in the city of Lydda."[9]

So explosive is this claim that Shavit seems to have realized it could play into the hands of those eager to delegitimate Israel's very existence. "I really take issue with people who pick out Lydda and ignore the rest of the book," he has lamented (a complaint perhaps best directed to the *New Yorker*).[10] In interviews and appearances, he has gone farther, insisting that Israel's deeds in Lydda must be seen in the context of a brutal war in a brutal decade; that the Arabs would have done worse to the Jews; and that Western democracies did do worse to their own "Others," from Native Americans to Aboriginal Australians, so who are they to preach moral rectitude to Israel?

This sort of damage control, whatever its short-term effect, is unlikely to negate the one probable long-term impact of Shavit's book: its validation of the charge of a massacre at Lydda, carried out by Zionism itself and thereby epitomizing the ongoing historical scandal that is the state of Israel.

So whether Shavit "takes issue" or not, his narrative of Lydda invites an inevitable question: is it true?

Others have found Shavit's account of Lydda "riveting" (Avi Shlaim),[11] "a sickening tour de force" (Leon Wieseltier),[12] and "brutally honest" (Thomas Friedman).[13] As I read through it, however, the alleged actions and attitudes of Shavit's Israeli protagonists struck me as implausible. To me they seemed to personify much too readily Shavit's broader thesis: that "Zionism" had been preprogrammed to depopulate the country of its Arabs, and that this preprogramming filtered down even to the last soldier. In Lydda, soldiers licensed by "Zionism" then became wanton killers of innocents, smoothing the work of expulsion.

Perhaps my suspicion was stoked by the fact that, time and again over the decades, Israeli soldiers have stood accused of just such wanton killing when in fact they were doing what every soldier is trained to do: fire on an armed enemy, especially when that enemy is firing at him. That such accusations might even be accompanied by professions of "love" for Israel is likewise no novelty. (See under: Richard Goldstone.) When such charges are made today, they tend to be subjected to rigorous investigation. Could Shavit's narrative withstand a comparable level of scrutiny?

Shavit relies largely on his interviews, conducted those many years ago. Since he doesn't cite documents in a public archive, I have no way of knowing whether he fairly represents his subjects. But it did occur to me that these same protagonists may have told their stories to others. And, with a bit of research, I discovered that they had.

Shmarya Gutman, Mula Cohen, "Bulldozer," and others who fought in Lydda in July 1948 not only were interviewed by others but were even interviewed on film at the very places where they had fought. The evidence reposes in the archives of the museum of the Palmah (the Haganah's strike force) in Ramat Aviv, where I found it and where it may be consulted by anyone.[14] Especially valuable is the uncut footage filmed by Uri Goldstein in preparing a 1989 documentary on the Yiftah brigade: the Israeli army unit, comprising fighters from the prestate Palmah, that conquered Lydda.[15] The same museum also holds transcripts of relevant interviews archived in the Yigal Allon Museum at Kibbutz Ginosar.

Some of the testimony in the archives echoes the account given by Shavit. But there are major inconsistencies; not only are these numerous, but they form a pattern. In what follows, I invite you, the reader, to detect that pattern on your own. Remember that the evidence derives largely from testimony given by the same people whom Shavit interviewed only a few years later. I have supplemented it with additional oral testimony by Israeli soldiers whom Shavit should have interviewed, if he had wanted to be thorough.

A caution: "Zionism carries out a massacre" is a lapel-grabbing phrase, meant to excite and provoke. In comparing accounts of a battle, however, sober details make all the difference. As it happens, many of Shavit's readers have praised his book for adding complexity to Israel's story, thus replacing old "myths" with a more nuanced understanding. Shavit himself has proclaimed that Israel is "all about complexity. If you don't see that, you don't get it."[16] For anyone with a taste for complexity, what follows should constitute indispensable reading alongside the rather simpler tale entitled "Lydda, 1948."

Lydda, July 11–13, 1948

First, recall the overarching framework. By the summer of 1948, Israel's war of independence had entered a new phase. Now Israel battled not only local Arab irregulars but also Arab armies, first and foremost the Transjordanian Arab Legion, deployed in Jerusalem and just east of Jewish towns and settlements on the coastal plain. On July 4, 1948, Prime Minister David Ben-Gurion approved a military plan called "Larlar," an acronym for Lydda-Ramleh-Latrun-Ramallah. The operation was meant to open a broad corridor to Jerusalem, which was in danger of being severed from the Jewish state.

Lydda, along the route from Tel Aviv to Jerusalem, was an Arab city of some twenty thousand, swollen by July to about twice that size by an influx of refugees from Jaffa and neighboring villages already occupied by Israeli forces. The 5th Infantry Company of the Transjordanian Arab Legion (approximately 125 soldiers) was deployed in the city, supported by many more local irregulars who had been making months-long preparations for battle.

On July 11, Israeli troops under the command of Moshe Dayan put Lydda (and Ramleh) in a state of shock with a guns-ablaze dash skirting both towns. But the city was not yet subdued. That evening, the 3rd Battalion of the Yiftah brigade moved into southern approaches to the city, took the two landmarks of the Great Mosque and the Church of St. George, and ordered the population to report there. Soon both places of worship, but especially the Great Mosque, were crammed full of men, women, and children. After a brief while, the women and children were sent home.

Still, this left most of the city to be taken, and there were only about three hundred Israeli soldiers to take and hold it. It was full of local armed irregulars, while the remnants of the Arab Legion had barricaded themselves in the city's police station.

By the next day, July 12, as Israeli forces were strengthening their hold on the city, two or three armored vehicles of the Arab Legion appeared on the northern edge and began firing in all directions. This encouraged an eruption of sniping and grenade-throwing at Israeli troops from upper stories and rooftops within the town, and from a second, small mosque only a few hundred meters from the armored-vehicle incursion. Israeli commanders feared a counterattack by the Legion in coordination with the armed irregulars still at large in the city. The order came down to suppress the incipient uprising with withering fire. The Great Mosque and the church were unaffected, but Israeli forces struck the small mosque with an antitank missile.

After a half-hour of intense fire, the battle died down. Overnight, the Arab Legion withdrew from the police station, ending any prospect of an Arab counterattack. The next day, the Israeli military governor reached an agreement with local notables that the civilian population would depart from Lydda and move eastward. Israeli soldiers, acting under orders, also encouraged their departure. Within a few hours, a stream of refugees made its way to the east, emptying the city.

Shavit's claim of a massacre is conveyed in passages relating to the "small mosque" (named the Dahmash mosque), in and around which the massacre supposedly took place. These passages lead the reader in a single direction: in Lydda, unarmed civilians were murdered wholesale by revenge-seeking soldiers, whose commanders then covered up the crime.

Because Shavit breaks up his telling of events with flashbacks, his narrative is choppy. Below, I have reassembled its key passages to tell his story in chronological order and in his own words, italicizing some passages for emphasis. In each instance, I then state the main "takeaway" point and explore why Shavit's narrative poses problems—not only because some other sources contradict it (contradictions in historical sources are inevitable) but because among those sources are the very same people whose oral testimony forms the bedrock of Shavit's reconstruction of events.

In what follows, all translations from Hebrew are my own.

A City Resists

Here is how Shavit's reconstruction begins:

> In the early evening [of July 11], the two 3rd Regiment [should be: Battalion] platoons [of the Yiftah brigade] are able to penetrate Lydda. Within hours, their soldiers hold key positions in city center and confine thousands of civilians in the Great Mosque, *the small mosque,* and St. George's cathedral. *By evening,* Zionism has taken the city of Lydda.[17]

Takeaway: The small mosque came under Israeli control on the first day, and it was among the places in which Israeli soldiers detained

174

Arab civilians. There they would have been disarmed and placed under guard.

Problem: As long ago as November 1948, only months after Lydda's conquest, the military governor Shmarya Gutman, in a published account, stated unequivocally that the city center wasn't taken by evening: "We went to bed while only that part of the city around the Great Mosque and the church was held by the Israeli army. In the city itself, they had not yet penetrated."[18] Those Arab men who reported to the Great Mosque and the Church of St. George (parts of a single complex on the southern edge of the city) arrived unarmed, and Israeli soldiers put them under guard. But the small mosque, according to Gutman, was not a place where Israeli soldiers concentrated local inhabitants. Gutman emphasized the point in his 1988 film interview by the documentarian Uri Goldstein. The interviewer, trying to set the scene for later events at the small mosque, wanted first to establish its status.

> *Goldstein:* This firing into the [small] mosque was after grenades were thrown from there?
>
> *Gutman:* After the grenades were thrown. That's the small mosque.
>
> *Goldstein:* But people were detained there.
>
> *Gutman:* There wasn't a concentration of many people there. There they didn't detain. That wasn't a mosque where they detained. And from there they threw on the guys—who moved in formation of twos and threes—began to throw grenades on them.
>
> *Goldstein:* It doesn't add up. They detained people there, so how did they have grenades and all that?
>
> *Gutman:* They didn't detain people in that mosque. There were two mosques. In the small mosque, which was off on the side, from inside the courtyard they began to throw [grenades]. . . . It wasn't a place of detention.[19]

In this film interview, then, Gutman repeats four times that those in the small mosque weren't detained there by Israeli forces, and that it wasn't a place of detention. On the first night, the small mosque lay beyond the limited zone of Israeli control, which didn't extend into the city proper. If Gutman's recollection is accurate, it means that Israeli forces had no idea who might be in the small mosque, why they had assembled there, or what weapons they might have.

In the second key passage, Shavit explains what caused things to go wrong the next day, July 12:

> Two Jordanian armored vehicles enter the conquered city in error, setting off a new wave of violence. *The Jordanian army is miles to the east,* and the two vehicles have no military significance, but . . . some of the [Israeli] soldiers of the 3rd Regiment mistakenly believe them to mean that they face the imminent danger of Jordanian assault.[20]

Takeaway: Since the conventional enemy army had retreated and now lay "miles to the east," the Israeli forces were never under military threat.

Problem: Shavit makes no mention whatsoever of the Transjordanian Arab Legion's continued presence not "miles to the east" but in Lydda itself, in the former British police station, just over a half-kilometer (roughly 0.3 miles) south of the Great Mosque. This structure—which today houses the national headquarters of Israel's border police—is a British-built Tegart fort, designed to withstand attack. When Israeli forces entered Lydda, it is where the remaining Arab Legion contingent, reinforced by local police and foreign volunteers, barricaded itself.

Gutman, in his 1988 film interview, repeatedly refers to the Arab Legion forces in the police station as a looming threat. "From the police station," he says, "heavy fire was directed at our men, and they couldn't reach the streets approaching the place. That is, there was a feeling that there was a serious force there."[21] Even as the civilians streamed to the Great Mosque and the church, "all the time there was firing from the police station. They laid down heavy fire and there was a feeling of war."[22]

This was precisely the context in which the Israeli commanders interpreted the sudden appearance of the Transjordanian armored vehicles. As Gutman wrote a few months after the events:

> It was clear to us that the city wasn't conquered, and that at any moment the enemy's armored cars could enter and put an end to our conquest. And above all, the police station was in the hands of the enemy. This was a great fortress, overlooking all of Lydda, from which it was possible to break into the city.[23]

It was "in the midst of the firing from the police station," says Gutman in his film interview, that "there appeared two armored vehicles from the olive groves, and they began to fire on our troops everywhere. It was something awful. We didn't have any means against armored vehicles."[24]

The armored vehicles thus fit into a larger military context. In that context, the Arab Legion force in the police station remained a major concern. Even after the armored vehicles were repelled, Gutman did not believe the battle was over: "We didn't know that the war was dying down. We were sure it would reignite, because they hadn't left the police station, and the police station was a fortress."[25] Indeed, when the Israelis sent a delegation of Lydda notables to plead with the Legionnaires to surrender, the garrison fired on them, killing one leading notable and wounding a judge.

Only on the night of July 12 did the Arab Legion forces retreat from Lydda. Gutman:

> The sturdy police building held by the enemy fighting force encouraged the city. This was a serious military force with great firepower. We hesitated to confront it. We didn't have a large enough force to outflank it or attack it. So we decided to rain fire on it all night, to break the morale of the besieged. During the night, an offensive was launched, but without attempting to storm and take the station. The entire city shook from the booms of the shooting, and it sometimes seemed that it was being destroyed to its foundation.[26]

Finally, the Arab Legionnaires ran out of ammunition and food and lost radio contact with their HQ. So they slipped away. "We must admit it," concluded Gutman at the time: "They fought courageously, their command was serious, and they refused to surrender. We could have defeated them only with heavy weapons, but in those hours, such weapons were only in units fighting on the eastern front."[27]

In retrospect, the threat posed by the Arab Legion forces might seem insubstantial; but only in retrospect. Moreover, as Gutman emphasizes, it was the Legion's *abandonment* of the police station that finally broke the spirit of Lydda's inhabitants and persuaded its notables to embrace flight from the city. Here is Gutman's contemporary report of his dialogue with the city's notables:

> I told them: "I have come now from the police station. There is no sign of the Arab Legion."

> They were dumbstruck and despairing. I learned from this that the city, and they, too, had still pinned their hopes on the police station. They were sure that with its help, they would still strike at the Jewish army.

> They sank into deliberations. They still didn't believe me.

> I added for emphasis: "I've come just now from there. There isn't a soul from the Legion. If you don't believe me, open the window and see for yourselves!"

And they believed. They couldn't but believe.

Depression was etched on their faces. As though their wings had been clipped. They said not a word; they sat dumbstruck, and hung their heads.[28]

Amazingly, both in his book and in the version published in the *New Yorker,* Shavit makes not a single mention of the police station or of the battle surrounding it. It is entirely absent from his own account of Gutman's dialogue with Lydda's notables. In Shavit's conversations with Gutman, over "long days on [Gutman's] kibbutz," did the latter omit all reference to the police station? It seems improbable, but only Shavit knows the answer.

The Small Mosque

In a third passage, Shavit sets the scene for the mosque massacre as a revenge killing, done outside the chain of command and exceeding any calculation of military necessity:

An agitated young soldier arrives [at the church], saying that grenades are being thrown at his comrades from the small mosque. . . . [Gutman] realizes that if he does not act quickly and firmly, things will get out of hand. He suggests shooting at any *house* from which shots are fired, shooting into every *window*, shooting at *anyone suspected* of being part of the mutiny.[29]

Takeaway: Gutman, despite his "firmness," didn't authorize specific action against the small mosque itself, presumably because it couldn't be deemed a military target.

Problem: According to Gutman's film interview, he didn't just "suggest" returning fire against houses, windows, and suspect persons. Instead, he gave authorization specifically to strike the small mosque, which had now become a military target:

From a small mosque, they began to throw bombs at soldiers. Two of our guys were killed. They asked me: "What should we do?" I answered: "It is permissible to fire into the mosque." And they did it.[30]

Gutman also answered the primary objection to doing so, raised by the soldiers themselves:

They asked me: "It's forbidden to harm the mosque, it's a holy place." I said: "A place from which they throw bombs must be taken out." And they took it out, and it's true that there were a few local casualties there.[31]

So a counterattack on the small mosque, according to this interview of Gutman, was a military necessity, sanctioned by Gutman's own authority as military governor. It was part of the improvised plan to suppress the uprising.

Next, in the fourth passage, Shavit zeroes in on his villain, "Bulldozer," the operator of a bazooka-like PIAT (Projector Infantry Anti-Tank weapon) whom he has already portrayed at length as someone "traumatized" by war and who took a "delight in killing." Shavit doesn't give the name of Bulldozer, but he is plainly identifiable on the Palmah veterans' website as Shmuel (Shmulik) Ben-David.[32] Shavit:

> When Bulldozer approaches the small mosque, he sees that there is indeed shooting. From somewhere, somehow, grenades are thrown.... One of the training-group leaders is wounded when a hand grenade, apparently thrown from the small mosque, explodes and takes his hand clear off. *This incident provokes* Bulldozer to shoot the antitank PIAT into the mosque.[33]

Takeaway: Bulldozer wasn't acting under orders, but instead allowed an "incident" to "provoke" him.

Problem: According to many sources, the counterattack against the mosque and the resort to the PIAT were done on orders from commanders who (naturally) viewed the enemy use of grenades not as "provocation" but as warfare. As we have just seen, the highest order came from the military governor, Gutman. ("They asked me: 'What should we do?' I answered: 'It is permissible to fire into the mosque.'") Moshe Kelman, the 3rd Battalion commander, told the author Daniel Kurzman that it was his own idea to use a PIAT:

> "We've got to pierce those walls" [said Kelman].
>
> "But they're a yard or a yard and a half thick," an officer pointed out. "And we haven't got any artillery."
>
> "We've got a PIAT."[34]

Kelman's direct subordinate, Daniel Neuman, commanded the squad that moved toward the small mosque. In his 1988 film interview with Goldstein, with Bulldozer standing right beside him at the very spot in Lydda where the action unfolded, he explains how he ordered the PIAT strike:

> We somehow dashed forward in formation. . . until we got to this place, where a grenade was thrown at us. Now we were in a double

bind. There was the grenade, and we're in a narrow alley, with no room to maneuver, and snipers continue to fire on us. So I looked around, I looked and surmised that from the building next to me, they threw the grenade. I pointed, I indicated to the PIATnik to fire a shell in there. He fired a shell.[35]

Ezra Greenboim, a squad commander who preceded Bulldozer down the alley by the small mosque, would likewise recall summoning the PIAT operator:

From inside the mosque, grenades were thrown at us. I remember the shout: "Grenade!" We hit the dirt, because there wasn't time to take cover. . . . Because we were certain—I say "certain," maybe it wasn't so—but at that moment because we were certain that grenades were thrown from the window of the mosque, we called the PIATist.

And from Greenboim's testimony in the same interview by Goldstein: "Everyone hit the dirt. There were wounded from the grenade itself, and then the order came to fire the PIAT."[36]

Finally, Bulldozer himself also says, in the same 1988 interview, that he was expressly dispatched to the mosque with his PIAT:

I received an instruction to run immediately with the PIAT to the small mosque. We came running, under fire from both sides of the street, down this alley, where we're standing now. Fire came from the houses, and especially from the second stories. Just as we were running, a grenade was thrown at us from the mosque—not from inside the building, but from its roof. Three people took shrapnel. I was lightly wounded by a fragment, which didn't keep me from functioning.

Bulldozer adds that the appearance of the training-group leader (his name was Yisrael Goralnik) with a hand missing from the battle against the armored vehicles "certainly didn't give us joy, so we decided to take out the mosque from which the shooting originated."[37] But even here, he doesn't ascribe the decision to himself alone.

Indeed, in none of these accounts, including his own, did Bulldozer fire his weapon on his own initiative. Every soldier, in every account, recalls facing deadly grenades and receiving orders to take out their source. Only in Shavit's account does the counterattack on the mosque become one "traumatized" killer's on-the-spot reaction to a mere "provocation."

In the fifth passage, Shavit essentially accuses Bulldozer of aiming at a civilian as opposed to a military target:

> *He does not aim at the minaret* from which the grenades were apparently thrown *but at the mosque wall behind which he can hear human voices.*[38]

Takeaway: Bulldozer passed over the minaret, a clear and perhaps legitimate target, preferring to zero in on the "human voices" of supposed detainees in the small mosque.

Problem: Bulldozer himself says in his interview with Goldstein that the grenade thrown at him came from the roof of the mosque—not the minaret—therefore presenting no target visible to the soldiers in the alley below.[39] Greenboim, for his part, says they were certain the grenades came from a window, that is, from inside the mosque itself, and it was at that window that the PIAT was aimed.[40] There is no mention of the minaret in any of the testimony.

In researching this essay, I visited the small mosque to gain a sense of the site. That someone would have thrown grenades from so exposed a position as the mosque's stout minaret, or would have remained there for even a moment if he had, beggars belief.

Sixth passage:

> He [Bulldozer] shoots his PIAT at the mosque wall from a distance of six meters, *killing seventy.* . . . And when the PIAT operator is himself wounded, *the desire for revenge grows even stronger.* Some 3rd Regiment soldiers *spray the wounded* in the mosque with gunfire. . . . They told [Bulldozer afterward] that *because of the rage they felt* at seeing him bleed, they had *walked into the small mosque and sprayed the surviving wounded with automatic fire.*[41]

Takeaway: Palmah soldiers wantonly massacred wounded Arabs in a state of vengeful rage, and took pride in it.

Problem: Shavit's account rests on what Bulldozer remembered being told by some of his buddies while he was hospitalized. Bulldozer himself didn't enter the small mosque; he had sustained a gash to an artery in his neck from the recoil of the PIAT, and was evacuated immediately. Shavit seems not to have spoken to any Israelis who actually entered the small mosque.

In fact, at least three Israelis were eyewitnesses to the scene inside the mosque: Daniel Neuman, who commanded the counterattack; Ezra

Greenboim, who was right alongside Bulldozer when he fired the PIAT and who afterward entered the small mosque; and Uri Gefen, who arrived after the counterattack and also entered the mosque. In 1988, Uri Goldstein interviewed Neuman and Greenboim on camera outside the small mosque; two years earlier, Gefen and Greenboim shared their recollections in a long conversation, of which there is a transcript.

Daniel Neuman, the squad commander, gives this account of what happened after the PIAT attack:

> Two doors or the gate—there was a large wooden gate—flew wide open. I rushed in with the unit, using grenades and submachine guns. And then it was quiet. Inside there were a number of people, I don't know how many, some of them hit by our action, because what the PIAT left undone, the grenades did. We looked, we searched, we found weapons there. It wasn't almost certain, it was absolutely certain, that they operated against us from there.[42]

So it was standard combat procedure to follow up a PIAT attack with grenades and gunfire. During his interview of Greenboim, Uri Goldstein returns to the storming of the mosque, and veterans' voices off-camera chime in: "After the PIAT, they went in with grenades. You don't just walk in after a PIAT. You go in with grenades and fire."[43] To these soldiers, it was obvious that you didn't just walk into a place where a surviving enemy might be waiting to kill you.

When Gefen and Greenboim finally did surveil the mosque, they were taken aback by what they saw. Gefen: "The people inside were hurt, hurt badly, some of them killed, some wounded, and it was a difficult scene."[44] Ezra Greenboim was also shocked by the sight. He couldn't believe that a PIAT had done the damage he saw:

> After the shot, I went into the mosque. And what I saw, very soon after it occurred, since nothing had changed in the meantime, was indeed a group of people, children, men, the elderly, in a condition I couldn't define, and I couldn't understand what had happened. I'd feared that the PIAT shell hadn't even penetrated the building, because it hit a window bar, but possibly it did penetrate. . . . To this day, I don't know what happened in the mosque. I can speculate. Maybe the PIAT hit some explosives on the site. Maybe it struck a pile of grenades that was in the mosque. I don't think there was anyone there before us. I don't think if they had been wounded in the [initial] conquest of Lydda, the same wounded people would have remained there. . . . The matter of the mosque dogs me; as I said, I don't know what happened, but we didn't do it.[45]

Greenboim does relate a story that would have been worth including in Shavit's account, both because of its poignancy and because of its relevance to the claim that Israeli soldiers sprayed the wounded in a spasm of vengeance:

> In the passageway, I remember a wounded Arab on the ground, so badly wounded that I thought it would be an act of mercy to finish him off, because he was torn apart, and I said, this will be a last act of kindness that I can do for this Arab, who was unarmed. And just as I raised my Tommy gun and told the guys around me to move away, so they won't witness the sight—and I, all agitated that I am going to do this, which is the most awful thing I'm capable of doing—the Arab looks at me and says in Yiddish: *hob rahmones*, that is, have mercy on me, but in Yiddish. These words in Yiddish stopped me in my tracks, I froze. Because at that very moment, I heard the *hob rahmones* of many, many Jews who came from over there [in Europe]. This use of Yiddish, which was the language of our people, from over there. . . . I didn't [shoot], I couldn't do it.[46]

Greenboim, it should once again be emphasized, had been right there when Bulldozer was gashed by the recoil of the PIAT: "It was like [Bulldozer] had been slaughtered, he was wounded in the neck. A stream of blood flowed out of him, like a fountain."[47] And the same Greenboim then *nearly* shot an unarmed, wounded Arab with automatic weapon fire—exactly the scenario alleged by Shavit. But the situation was utterly different, the motive was anything but rage and revenge, and he didn't shoot him.

There are, of course, discrepancies in the soldiers' accounts. Gefen says some in the mosque were killed, some were wounded. Greenboim, by contrast, says most were unharmed but were pressed back against the walls in a state of shock. (This seems to contradict his report of his own shock at the extent of the carnage.) These must have been fleeting impressions: Greenboim also recalls that, before encountering the wounded Arab in the passageway, "I saw the sight inside [the small mosque], and I bolted out." How many died from the PIAT attack versus the grenades and gunfire is beyond conjecture.

The soldier Uri Gefen shared with his comrade-in-arms Greenboim the lasting impression left by what they saw in the small mosque: "How many years does a man live? So all our days we will remember it, no helping it, whether we want to or not, we can't escape from it—the small mosque."[48] But in the course of their long and frank conversation, there is no hint that anyone was killed in that place except in the course of combat.

As the small mosque is so central to Shavit's narrative, it is hard to fathom why he didn't make use of such eyewitness testimony, even if he didn't collect it himself. At the very least, it adds layers of complexity that are so obviously (one is tempted to say "painfully") missing from "Lydda, 1948."

As a side note, it is also worth considering how the toll of seventy dead in the mosque may have entered Shavit's account, where it is repeated five times. Shavit doesn't give a source for this number, but it seems to have originated in his visit to Lydda in 2002, when he wrote an article about the present-day politics in the city. On that occasion he met an elderly Arab school principal, who would have been about twenty in 1948. Shavit, paraphrasing him: "Seventy were massacred there, they say. [The principal] doesn't know himself, he didn't see it with his own eyes, but that's what they say. Seventy."[49]

In 1948, the military governor, Gutman, gave a different estimate: "The Arabs who threw bombs were struck with a PIAT, and thirty fell straightaway."[50] This is the casualty count often given in Israeli sources. Some Arab sources, in contrast, claim casualties in the hundreds. It's not clear why Shavit prefers one account to another, why he doesn't give a range of possible numbers, or, most importantly, why he repeats the figure of seventy dead five times over, firmly imprinting it on the mind of the reader as though it were a well-attested fact.

A Battle with Two Sides

Moving on directly from what happened inside the small mosque, we come to Shavit's seventh passage:

> Others toss grenades into neighboring houses. Still others mount machine guns in the streets and *shoot at anything that moves*. . . . After *half an hour of revenge*, there are scores of corpses in the streets, seventy corpses in the mosque. . . . *In thirty minutes*, at high noon, *more than two hundred civilians are killed*. [In the *New Yorker* version: "In thirty minutes, two hundred and fifty Palestinians were killed."] Zionism carries out a massacre in the city of Lydda.[51]

Takeaway: Palmah troops sank into a Zionism-inspired orgy of revenge killings of civilians, in numbers exceeding the most reliable estimates of those killed two months earlier at Deir Yassin.

Problem: In the book, Shavit writes of more than 200 dead, and in the *New Yorker* of 250. In the latter version, Shavit adds that the more specific figure is "according to *1948* by [the historian] Benny Morris."

Morris's own source is a contemporary Israeli military summary of the conquest of Lydda, later published (in 1953) in the official history of the Palmah. More than any eyewitness testimony, it is this figure—especially when contrasted with the small number of Israeli casualties (four dead and twelve wounded)—that has given rise to the claim that what occurred must have been a massacre and not a battle. In Morris's words, "The ratio of Arab to Israeli casualties was hardly consistent with the descriptions of what had happened as an 'uprising' or battle."[52]

But not all historians believe this body count to be reliable. The Hebrew University historian Alon Kadish, who has looked at the conquest of Lydda in depth, believes the estimate may be of Arab casualties for the entirety of the fighting over several days, and that "it is doubtful that the number of Arabs killed on July 12 reached 250 or even half that number."[53] Moreover, the official report does not label the dead as civilians—as Shavit does in the book—instead describing those killed as "enemy losses."[54] Even Morris (in his book on Glubb Pasha, the British trainer and commander of the Arab Legion) describes those killed more comprehensively as both "townspeople and irregulars."[55]

As for the most explosive element of Shavit's claim—namely, that the action in the streets, like that at the small mosque, also had no basis in military necessity but was carried out in "revenge"—here he simply contradicts himself. He cites Gutman and Mula Cohen as *ordering* a harsh response, and the interviews I consulted confirm it. The decision to lay down intensive fire was made by commanders who estimated that they faced an emergency situation.

The brigade commander, Mula Cohen, used just that term in an interview during which he recalled issuing his orders. Told that the city had erupted in sniping, Cohen announced: "This is an emergency, fire in all directions; tell the men to enter the houses of the locals; anyone who walks about with a weapon is an enemy."[56] Nor does the revenge motif line up with similar orders given by the military governor, Gutman (in this case, as told by him to Goldstein): "We have to lay down fire on all the houses, and put an end to this business."[57]

In short, as in the case of the small mosque, so in the instance of the battle around it, soldiers were operating under orders to lay down heavy fire, even as they themselves came under fire. "There are still exchanges of fire in the town," reported the Yiftah brigade to the overall HQ of the front. "We have taken many wounded."[58] The fight to repulse the Arab Legion's armored vehicles, just 200 meters (approximately 220 yards) from the small mosque, was so chaotic that one Israeli private went missing and was never found.[59] Brigade commander Mula Cohen thought the response had been proportionate:

> We didn't want to kill Arabs. In my opinion, and to this very day, I am sure we did what we needed to do, and no more than that. Of course, in such a situation, there are all sorts of deviations and sorts of things. But in no way was there mass killing.[60]

Mula Cohen's claim was that a few "deviations" didn't constitute a "massacre" of 250, and this has been at the core of a very lively debate among leading Israeli historians of the 1948 war. Shavit gives no hint that such a debate exists. Benny Morris, citing the disparity of casualties, persists in calling the events a "massacre," so Shavit invokes him. But there is another view, championed by Alon Kadish and Avraham Sela (in a book devoted to the conquest of Lydda), that the events of that day were a straightforward battle.[61] Mordechai Bar-On has weighed the contesting views, finding merit in both sides of the argument but coming down largely on the side of Kadish and Sela.[62] In short, Shavit, far from representing the consensus of scholarship, has taken one side in an Israeli debate and formulated it in the most extreme way—although his American readers would never know it.

After the fighting died down, the Israelis faced the issue of disposing of the dead. Shavit's eighth and final passage:

> News comes of what has happened in the small mosque. The military governor orders his men to bury the dead, *get rid of the incriminating evidence.* . . . At night, when they were ordered to clean the small mosque and carry out the seventy corpses and bury them, *they took eight other Arabs to do the digging of the burial site and afterward shot them, too,* and buried the eight with the seventy.[63]

Takeaway: Gutman, the military governor, knew that what happened at the small mosque was a crime, and sought to "get rid" of the evidence. So dehumanized by now were the Israeli soldiers that they could shoot anyone simply in order to cover up their crimes.

Problem: Shavit doesn't explain why burying the dead would constitute a cover-up. He himself writes of the "heavy heat" and the "scorching heat" of July, which punished the fleeing refugees from Lydda the next day and which would have rapidly affected the corpses and heightened the urgent need to inter them. Nor does Shavit cite any eyewitness source for this tale of the murder of an Arab burial detail, with its obvious evocation of the Holocaust.

Apparently, Shavit failed to interview an Arab inhabitant of Lydda, aged twenty in 1948, who claimed to have participated, along with his brother and cousin, in a ten-man detail ordered to remove the bodies from the mosque—this, after a delay of several days. This Arab townsman, Fayeq Abu Mana (Abu Wadi'), who was still living in Lydda decades later, described the task in a 2003 interview:

> They said to go to the mosque and take the corpses out from there. How to take them out? The hands of the dead were very swollen. We couldn't lift the corpses by hand, we brought bags and put the corpses on the bags and we lifted them onto a truck. We gathered everyone in the cemetery. Among them was one woman and two children. They said burn. We burned everyone.[64]

Abu Mana, who passed away in 2011, obviously survived this grim task unharmed. There is even a photograph of him in the Lydda cemetery, pointing out where the bodies, according to him, were not buried but burned to ash.[65] He numbered them at seventy, all but three of them men, and he may have been the local source for that number. In his frequent retelling of the story (a more detailed version exists in Arabic),[66] he makes no mention of the murder of anyone assigned to the detail. If his wife is to be believed, all were taken prisoner after finishing the job.[67]

New Myths for Old?

Even after revisiting Shavit's sources, we can't be certain about what happened in and around the small mosque in Lydda on July 12, 1948. I don't pretend to such certainty, nor do I pretend to have resolved the contradictions in the accounts I have examined. I am a historian, but I haven't made a study of the 1948 war, and I haven't tracked down every source. There are no documents for this episode, only oral testimonies, with all their attendant hazards. Officers and soldiers contradict themselves, they contradict their comrades, and Israelis and Palestinians obviously contradict one another. But what I uncovered in just a few days of archival research was more than enough to reinforce my initial doubts about Shavit's account, and should be enough to plant at least a seed of doubt in the mind of every reader of *My Promised Land*.

That seed may have sprouted even earlier in the editorial offices of the *New Yorker*, or at least in its fact-checking department. In the magazine's abridgment, tellingly, we learn that Israeli soldiers "confined thousands of Palestinian civilians at the Great Mosque," but the small mosque is omitted as a place of civilian detention. It is then mentioned in only three sentences: "Some Palestinians fired at Israeli soldiers near a small mosque." "One [Israeli soldier] fired an anti-tank shell into the small mosque." And finally: "But then news came of what had happened in the small mosque. The military governor ordered his men to bury the dead."

But what supposedly *did* happen in the small mosque? About that, the *New Yorker* reader is left completely in the dark. Nor is there any mention there of Bulldozer, of seventy dead, or of the Arab burial detail and its alleged liquidation. These are strange omissions in an article whose very headline touts the Lydda "massacre" as a scoop. Do the omissions reflect a judgment that parts of Shavit's story, and his numbers, weren't sufficiently documented? David Remnick, the editor of the *New Yorker*, owes an explanation to his readers.

Beyond such disparities, highly suggestive in themselves, the fact is that not only are some of Shavit's assertions impossible to verify, but by relying on the same eyewitnesses interviewed by Shavit (and on a few he should have interviewed), one can quite easily construct an entirely different story from his. That is the story not of a vengeful "massacre" committed by "Zionism," but of collateral damage in a city turned into a battlefield. This is Lydda not as a "black box" but as a gray zone—a familiar one, since many hundreds of Israeli military operations in built-up areas have fallen into it.

It is in this gray zone, not in Shavit's "black box," that real complexity resides. But nowhere does Shavit give his readers a clue that anything in his dramatic narrative of Lydda is contested. To the contrary, at the end of his source notes is this assurance:

> I read hundreds of books and thousands of documents. . . . To make sure all details are correct, oral histories were checked and double-checked against Israel's written history. The exciting process of interviewing significant individuals was interwoven with a meticulous process of data-gathering and fact-checking.[68]

The details are correct, then; the facts have been checked. The historian Simon Schama, in a gushing review, affirms that the book is "without the slightest trace of fiction."[69] And many of Shavit's readers are understandably treating his book and this chapter as history. The book received the National Jewish Book Award in *History*, and the *New Yorker* ran the abridged chapter under the rubric of "Dept. of History."

Yet Shavit, while claiming that he has followed a rigorous method, also tries to have it both ways: "*My Promised Land*," he writes in those same source notes, "is not an academic work of history. Rather, it is a personal journey." That inspires rather less confidence: one cannot make a "personal journey" to a day in 1948. Immediately after insisting that all the details and facts have been vetted, Shavit then adds still another caveat: "And yet, at the end of the day, *My Promised Land* is about people. The book I have written is the story of Israel as it is seen by individual Israelis, of whom I am one."[70] At day's end, are we reading oral history after all? Or something still stranger—what Simon Schama, in his review, classifies as "imaginative reenactment"?

It is this confusion that leaves *My Promised Land* even more vulnerable than the 1958 novel *Exodus* by Leon Uris, the last "epic" account of 1948 to seize the imagination of its Jewish and non-Jewish readers. If *Exodus* was misleading, at least its readers were forewarned that it was *fiction*. Shavit's readers can't be sure just what they are reading: "imaginative reenactment," the "story of Israel," oral history, "epic history," or "Dept. of History" history. Yet how it was written bears on how it should be read, and how many grains of salt the reader needs to add.

At the end of "Lydda, 1948," Shavit suddenly entertains the thought that "Zionism" may not have committed the massacre after all: "The small-mosque massacre could have been a misunderstanding brought about by a tragic chain of accidental events." What, then, *was* "Zionism" responsible for? It was, he writes, "the conquest of Lydda and the expulsion of Lydda." These were "no accident. They were an inevitable phase of the Zionist revolution."[71]

It is a debate worth having, but this statement follows by only a few pages the assertion that in Lydda, the massacre was what facilitated the expulsion. Putting a thought into the head of the military governor, Shmarya Gutman, as Lydda's notables resign themselves to departing the city, Shavit writes: "Gutman feels he has achieved his goal. Occupation, massacre, and mental pressure have had the desired effect."[72] So perhaps the massacre was desired after all, perhaps even planned? There are those, among Palestinians and their supporters, who already claim that massacres invariably preceded expulsions, and so must have been willed no less than were the expulsions themselves.[73]

Shavit seems to think he can deflect this reading of his Lydda chapter. "Let's remember Lydda, let's acknowledge Lydda," he protests, "yet let no one use Lydda in order to doubt Israel's legitimacy." But of course that is precisely what many are already doing and will continue to do, citing and echoing the confessedly tormented Ari Shavit as they point accusingly not just at the actions of Israel's soldiers but at the murderous intentions of Zionism itself, with Lydda as a prime exhibit in the ever-expanding criminal indictment against the Jewish state.

If Shavit is sincere in expressing alarm at the misuse of his account, he can take action. He can deposit his interviews in a public archive so that researchers may compare them with other interviews given by the very same persons—and with Shavit's own account in his book. And he can conduct his own comparison. It isn't too late to revisit the Lydda "massacre" and honestly flag the points of contention in the forthcoming paperback edition and in the anticipated translations into German, French, Spanish, Italian, Polish, Hungarian, and Chinese. (He needn't bother about the Hebrew edition; its reviewers will do the job for him.)

As for the grandees of American Jewish journalism who rushed to praise Shavit's Lydda treatment, they have a special obligation to help launch the debate by sending readers to this essay. They know who they are.

First Response by Benny Morris

To begin with, here are the generally undisputed facts of, to borrow Martin Kramer's title, "What Happened at Lydda":

On July 11, 1948, as part of the Israel Defense Forces' "Operation Dani," designed to take control of the road between Tel Aviv and (Jewish) west Jerusalem, armored vehicles and jeeps of the 89th Battalion, 8th Brigade, commanded by Lt. Col. Moshe Dayan, dashed down from Ben-Shemen through the Arab town of Lydda to the outskirts of its sister town of Ramleh and then back to Ben-Shemen, machine guns blazing. In the foray, which lasted about three-quarters of an hour, dozens of Arabs were killed.

Minutes later, four companies of the 3rd and 1st Battalions of the Palmah's Yiftah Brigade, 300–400 soldiers in all, pushed into Lydda and took up positions in the center of town. In the following hours, Arab men, and some women, were herded or made their way to the town's medieval Church of St. George and the Great Mosque next door. Among the town's 20,000–30,000 inhabitants and refugees were several hundred militiamen, some of whom had not been disarmed. There was no formal surrender, but the Israelis thought the battle was over. The night passed quietly.

Just before noon on the following day, July 12, two or three Jordanian armored cars drove into town and a firefight broke out; the Yiftah men suffered a number of casualties. The sound of the battle triggered sniping by local militiamen from windows and rooftops. The Israelis felt hard-pressed, confused, perhaps even panicky. Moshe Kelman, commander of Yiftah's 3rd Battalion, ordered his men summarily to suppress what they would later call a "rebellion," and to shoot anyone "seen on the street" or, alternatively, at "any clear target." The troops also fired into houses. One of the targets, where dozens apparently died, was the town's small Dahmash Mosque.

Later that afternoon and during the following day, the Israelis expelled the population of Lydda—and of neighboring Ramleh, whose notables had formally surrendered—eastward toward the Jordanian-held West Bank. Today, the descendants of the refugees from these two towns fill the camps around Ramallah and Amman.

And now we have another story, a story of two cherry pickers, each of whom distorts history in his own way.

In his best-selling book *My Promised Land*, the journalist Ari Shavit distorts in the grand manner, by turning Lydda into the story of the 1948 war and indeed of Zionism itself. Insisting that, at Lydda, "Zionism commit[ed] a massacre," he writes: "Lydda is our black box. In it lies the dark secret of Zionism." (As an aside, I would suggest here a much more telling "black box" or key to understanding both Zionism and the conflict. It is Kibbutz Yad Mordekhai, where for four to five days in May 1948 a handful of Holocaust survivors held off the invading mass of the Egyptian army, giving the Haganah/IDF time to organize against the pan-Arab assault on the newborn state of Israel.)

As for Martin Kramer, he distorts by whitewashing and/or ignoring the expulsion and by effectively denying that it was preceded by a massacre. Instead, he writes, Lydda was a story of "collateral damage in a city turned into a battlefield": not a black box but a "gray zone."

Both Shavit and Kramer present us with a methodological problem: neither of them uses or refers to contemporary documentary evidence—which, in my view, is the necessary basis of sound historiography. Documents may lie or mislead, but to a far lesser degree than do veterans remembering (or "remembering") politically and morally problematic events decades after they have occurred. In *My Promised Land*, Shavit offers neither footnotes nor bibliography; concerning 1948, he refers only to interviews (about which he provides no details) that he himself conducted decades ago. Kramer, a Middle East expert, relies on interviews done by others, also decades ago.

As it happens, the problematic events at the Dahmash Mosque are not mentioned at all in contemporary IDF documents. One can assume that something very nasty did occur there, since both Jewish and Arab oral testimonies agree on this. But the circumstances surrounding the incident—were the people in the mosque armed or were they disarmed detainees; did they or did they not provoke the Israelis by throwing grenades at them?—remain unclear. I'll return to this incident below.

Now to our two authors.

In *My Promised Land,* Ari Shavit does something unusual, perhaps even unique, which (apart from his abilities as a writer) may help to account for the book's American success. He simultaneously satisfies three different audiences. Mainly through his moving portraits of Holocaust survivors, he presents a persuasive justification of Zionism, thus catering to supporters of Israel. But as a bleeding-heart liberal he also caters to the many Jews and non-Jews—call them agnostics—who now find fault with Zionist behavior over the decades. And finally he caters to forthright Israel-bashers: those for whom every new or rehashed or invented detail of Jewish atrocity is grist for the anti-Israel mill.

His chapter on Lydda is the cameo performance. Following the book's publication, in appearances before largely Jewish audiences, Shavit heatedly argued that he had been misunderstood, enjoined readers to view "Lydda" in context, and denied that he had posited it as the defining narrative of Zionism/Israel. The columnist doth protest too much, methinks. After all, Shavit engineered advance publication of the chapter as a stand-alone piece in the *New Yorker,* and it was he who defined "Lydda" as the key to Zionism.

Well, it isn't and it wasn't. Yes, Lydda was simultaneously the biggest massacre and biggest expulsion of the 1948 war. But no scoop there; decades ago, Israeli historians described what happened in great detail. Lydda wasn't, however, representative of Zionist behavior. Before 1948, the Zionist enterprise expanded by buying, not conquering, Arab land, and it was the Arabs who periodically massacred Jews—as, for example, in Hebron and Safed in 1929. In the 1948 war, the first major atrocity was committed by Arabs: the slaughter of thirty-nine Jewish coworkers in the Haifa Oil Refinery on December 30, 1947.

True, the Jews went on to commit more than their fair share of atrocities; prolonged civil wars tend to brutalize combatants and trigger vengefulness. But this happened because they conquered four hundred Arab towns and villages. The Palestinians failed to conquer even a single Jewish settlement—at least on their own. The one exception was Kfar Etzion, which was conquered on May 13, 1948 with the aid of the Jordanian Arab Legion, and there they committed a large-scale massacre.

In any event, given the length of the war, the abundant quantity of Jewish casualties—5,800 killed out of a population of 630,000—and the fact that the Arabs were the aggressors, the conflict was relatively atrocity-free. By my estimate, all told, Jews deliberately killed 800–900 civilians and POWs between November 1947 and January 1949. Arabs killed approximately two hundred Jews in similar circumstances. Compare this, for example, with the eight thousand Bosnians murdered in Srebrenica, in civilized Europe, over three days in July 1995 by an aggressor people, the Serbs, who were never seriously in peril.

As for expulsions: in most places in 1948, Arabs simply fled in the face of actual or approaching hostilities, while some, as in Haifa in April, were advised or instructed by their own leaders to evacuate. Most were not expelled, although Israel subsequently decided, quite reasonably in my judgment, to bar the refugees from returning.

Shavit, while checking off the relevant boxes, effectively fails to put "Lydda" in context: the context, that is, of a war initiated by the Arabs after the Jews had accepted a partition compromise and in which the Jews, three years after the Holocaust, felt they faced mass murder at Arab hands. Yes, Shavit does allow in passing that the Arabs rejected the UN partition plan of November 1947. But he writes: "[Immediately afterward] violence flares throughout the country"—as if it were unclear who started the shooting and as if the Palestinians were not responsible for a war that resulted in occasional massacres and masses of refugees.

Martin Kramer's cherry picking is of a different order. Declining to look at or judge Shavit's book as a whole, he zooms in on what happened in Lydda on July 11–13, 1948 and especially on the events at the Dahmash Mosque at around 1:00 PM on July 12. Describing and quoting Shavit's account and comparing it with the testimony of various Palmah soldiers thirty or forty years later, he shows how Shavit has manipulated and tilted the evidence to blacken Israel's image. He is particularly critical of Shavit's contention, for which Shavit cites no source, that the Israelis also murdered the eight-man detail assigned to dispose of the Arabs' bodies. In all, Kramer questions Shavit's integrity.

Fair enough. But Kramer clearly has an agenda. He more or less justifies the soldiers' behavior by citing the veterans' testimony that grenades were thrown at them from the mosque, prompting them to fire a rocket (or rockets) at the building. But they would say that, wouldn't they, after the bodies of dozens of men, women, and children were subsequently peeled off the walls? The mosque stood—and stands—as one of several contiguous buildings in an alley. In the dust and heat and noise and terror of the moment, who could have seen and said with certainty from which building or rooftop a grenade, or grenades, were thrown (if any, indeed, were thrown)?

Dozens of documents were produced in July 1948 by Yiftah Brigade headquarters, the 3rd Battalion, and the IDF general staff about what happened in Lydda during those days, and they are preserved in Israeli archives. As I noted above, none of them mentions the mosque incident. Perhaps those who wrote them knew why.

But the existing documents are crystal clear on two points, both of which Kramer obfuscates or elides: that there was mass killing of townspeople by Dayan's July 11 column and, subsequently, even apart from the mosque incident, in the suppression of the sniping; and that the slaughter was followed by an expulsion. About the latter, all that Kramer tells us is that on the morning of July 13, the Israeli intelligence officer Shmaryahu Gutman negotiated with town notables the release of the detained Arab young men, with the notables agreeing to a mass evacuation as a quid pro quo.

There is no contemporary IDF documentary reference to this negotiation or "deal"; the story rests solely on Gutman's say-so. If there really was such a deal, it apparently lacked authorization from Gutman's superiors, since at 6:15 PM on July 13, Dani HQ cabled Yiftah HQ as follows: "Tell me immediately, have the Lydda prisoners been released and who authorized this?" Kramer adds, as a sort of cover, that Israeli troops "encouraged" the evacuation. Nothing more.

But the documents tell us a straightforward and radically different story. At a cabinet meeting on June 16, 1948, Prime Minister and Defense Minister David Ben-Gurion defined Lydda and Ramleh as "two thorns" in the side of the Jews; in his diary for May and June he repeatedly jotted down that the towns had to be "destroyed." When news of the shooting in Lydda reached IDF HQ at Yazur after noon on July 12, Yigal Allon, the commander of Operation Dani, pressed Ben-Gurion for authorization to expel the inhabitants. According to Yitzhak Rabin, then serving as Allon's deputy, Ben-Gurion gave the green light. At 1:30, Rabin issued the following order to the Yiftah brigade: "(1) The inhabitants of Lydda must be expelled quickly, without attention to age. . . . (2) Implement immediately."

A similar order went out from Dani HQ to the Kiryati Brigade, whose 42nd Battalion had occupied Ramleh. In both towns, the troops began expelling the inhabitants. At 11:35 AM on July 13, Dani HQ informed the operations office of the IDF general staff that the troops "are busy expelling the inhabitants." At 6:15 PM, Dani HQ queried Yiftah HQ: "Has the removal of the population of Lydda been completed?" By evening, the two towns had been cleared.[74]

It is also abundantly plain from the documents that (although the Hebrew term *tevah*, slaughter, was studiously avoided) the expulsion was preceded by a massacre, albeit a provoked one. Dozens if not hundreds of Arab civilians were shot in the streets and in their houses. Yiftah Brigade intelligence, summarizing the events a few days later, wrote that in Lydda on July 12, the 3rd Battalion had killed "about 250 [Arabs] and wounded a great many." (The figure appears in the July 1948 documents, not only in the 1950s "official history of the Palmah" cited by Kramer.) For their part, Yiftah's soldiers had suffered two-to-four killed, two of them apparently as a result of fire from troops of the Jordanian Arab Legion.

This disproportion speaks massacre, not "battle." Yet Kramer calls what happened "A Battle with Two Sides" and quotes the Israeli historian Alon Kadish, who suggests that the Yiftah body count was wrong or, alternatively, that 250 was the number of Arab dead during all of the fighting in and around Lydda between July 9 and July 12. In her biography of Yigal Allon, the historian Anita Shapira dismisses Kadish's arguments as "implausible." I would say the same, basically, about Kramer's description of what happened.

First Rejoinder by Martin Kramer

The entry of historians into the debate over Ari Shavit's Lydda chapter, in his bestselling book *My Promised Land*, constitutes progress. Efraim Karsh and Benny Morris, who for decades have been in almost continuous dispute over the events of 1948, seem to have converged in opposition to Shavit's turning the July 1948 events in Lydda into the "black box" of the 1948 war and of Zionism. In response to my essay, Karsh writes: "Lydda was one of the very few exceptions that proved the rule, not—as Shavit argues—the rule itself."[75] And Morris concurs: Shavit "defined 'Lydda' as the key to Zionism. Well, it isn't and it wasn't. . . . Lydda wasn't representative of Zionist behavior."

But that's where the convergence over Lydda ends. Karsh congratulates me for "putting to rest the canard of an Israeli massacre of Palestinian Arab civilians in that city in July 1948." Morris condemns me for "effectively denying" that the expulsion of the city's inhabitants "was preceded by a massacre, albeit a provoked one."

It would have been quite an accomplishment to put to rest the "massacre" claim or "effectively" disprove it. My purpose was more modest. I sought to plant a seed of doubt regarding Shavit's baroque narrative of it, using the same range of oral sources he used. This I believe I have done, and as long as Shavit remains silent, that seed of doubt should grow.

In the *New Yorker* abridgment of his Lydda chapter, Shavit invokes Benny Morris as his source. (Morris isn't mentioned in the book, but the magazine's fact-checkers apparently demanded a published source for the "massacre" claim.) And indeed, Shavit's account ultimately rests on the foundation laid by Morris. Morris's narrative of the "massacre" is austere in comparison to Shavit's, because Morris claims he never resorts to oral testimony to establish a fact, only to add "color."[76] But his own paternity of the "massacre" trope can't be denied, even if he is repelled by the way Shavit has framed Lydda as a litmus test of Zionism. That being the case, in my remarks here I'll focus on Morris in lieu of Shavit, who has not deigned to respond to my essay.

As Morris himself admits, not a single contemporary Israeli document makes any mention whatsoever of the events of July 12, 1948 at the Dahmash mosque: the "small mosque" that was supposedly the scene of one Israeli massacre. What Morris calls the "crystal clear" documentary proof of a wider "massacre" on the same day is an Israeli military summary of the fighting that lists "enemy casualties" at 250 versus four Israeli dead. According to Morris, "this disproportion speaks massacre, not 'battle.'" And that's it. On this slim reed rests Morris's claim not only that there was a "massacre" at Lydda but that it was the "biggest massacre" of the 1948 war.

The claim is particularly audacious, given that Morris has made mistake after mistake over the years in assembling his narrative. In the first edition (1987) of his book on the 1948 Palestinian refugees, he claimed that "dozens of unarmed detainees in the mosque and church compounds in the center of the town were shot and killed."[77] In fact, none of the unarmed detainees in the Great Mosque and the Church of St. George was harmed during the fighting. Morris seemed not to know that there was another mosque, the Dahmash or "small" mosque, which was the locus of fighting—something any Palmah veteran of the battle could have told him, or that he could have learned by carefully rereading the account by Lydda's military governor, Shmarya Gutman, published way back in November 1948.[78]

Later, after learning of his error, Morris shifted the locus of the "massacre" to the small mosque (whose name he couldn't pronounce properly, to judge from his spelling of it: Dahaimash).[79] But he began referring to those inside it as "POWs,"[80] in which case they all would have been men, under stiff armed guard. In his response to me, he now allows that they included some women and children, and admits that it's "unclear" whether they were even detainees.

Given this patchy record, it's hard to regard Morris as a meticulous investigator of the Lydda "massacre." His interest in Lydda has centered instead upon the flight of its inhabitants—and, specifically, who ordered that flight—and it's therefore not surprising that he steers his response back to that well-worn subject. It wasn't my focus, but I'll touch upon it later.

First, to the matter of the small mosque. Morris writes that I "more or less justify the soldiers' behavior [in striking the small mosque] by citing the veterans' testimony that grenades were thrown at them from the mosque." He then effectively accuses the soldiers either of returning fire recklessly or of altogether imagining the grenade attack. Morris seems to think that not a single soldier is credible. After all, he writes, "they would say that [grenades were thrown], wouldn't they, after the bodies of dozens of men, women, and children were subsequently peeled off the walls?" (Thus, by borrowing from the stock of presumably unreliable oral testimony, does Morris add dark red "color.")

So let me adduce still more testimony for the grenade attack, this time from an entirely different direction. As it happens, the Palestinian narrative of Lydda also has a grenade thrown at the Israelis from inside or nearby the small mosque. Indeed, Palestinians even preserve the name of the supposed grenade-thrower: Jamil Haroun. Here is Reja-e Busailah, a refugee from Lydda and blind poet who became a professor of English in Indiana: "It is said that Jamil Haroun threw a grenade at a group of Jewish soldiers, killing several, and then ran for shelter into the mosque."[81] The wife of the Lydda resident who claimed to have been forced to remove the bodies from the small mosque told a similar story: "There was a young man named Jamil Haroun, who threw a grenade on an army vehicle when it was parked in what is now Palmah Square," where the small mosque stands. And Jamil Haroun is also named, by the Palestinian chronicler Aref al-Aref in his list of 1948 war casualties, as having been "killed with those killed in the mosque" on July 12.[82]

Morris now writes the following about what happened *inside* the small mosque: "One can assume that something very nasty did occur there, since both Jewish and Arab oral testimonies agree on this." Well, it seems that both Jewish and Arab oral testimonies agree that something nasty happened *outside* the mosque: a grenade attack on Israeli soldiers. If the convergence of oral testimonies is your standard for making assumptions, then you should at least be consistent.

As I showed in my essay, there's plenty of testimony from Israeli soldiers who entered the small mosque—evidence used neither by Shavit (which is inexcusable) nor by Morris (which is no more than one would expect). And as I showed, the soldiers were shocked by what they saw inside the building. Here is another witness, Hanan Sever, who reached the mosque after the events: "When I entered, a grim scene unfolded before my eyes. The mosque was full of bodies. There were old people and children, men and women, all of them cast about dead in a jumble, in groups or singly, one atop another. There were thirty bodies there. Maybe more."[83]

No one disputes that the result was tragic, and the Israeli eyewitnesses say so themselves. But the accidental killing of civilians in war doesn't constitute "massacre." Nor can Morris produce evidence of a deliberate targeting of innocents in the small mosque. "In my long study of the Israeli-Arab conflict," he has written, "and, specifically, the 1948 war, my experience has been that wherever there was smoke, there was fire: almost invariably, a document surfaces corroborating oral traditions of massacre."[84] Yet here we are, sixty-six years later, and there's not a single document regarding the small mosque.

Why? Morris's answer is conspiracy. He insinuates that Israeli officers made sure to omit the small mosque "massacre" from their reports. "None of [the documents] mentions the mosque incident," acknowledges Morris, who then hisses: "Perhaps those who wrote them knew why." Thus does Morris's argument become absurdly circular: a document would prove a negligent or deliberate "massacre," but to all intents and purposes, so does the absence of a document. In fact, however, all we have is the testimony of the Israeli soldiers, who claim to have returned fire at enemy fire. Anything else is speculation.

As for a wider "massacre" on July 12, Morris finds his sole documentary evidence in a military report of the day's fighting, which lists 250 enemy casualties against four Israelis. According to Morris, "this disproportion speaks massacre, not 'battle.'"

If that were true, then a whole range of recent Israeli (and American) military actions would qualify as massacres. Consider, for example, "Cast Lead," Israel's 2008 operation against Hamas in Gaza. What should one call the deaths of 1,166 Palestinians (the official Israeli estimate) in that operation, weighed against thirteen Israeli dead (four from friendly fire)? Indeed, how should one describe Israel's 2014 military operation in Gaza, "Protective Edge?" Or, for an American example, should the Battle of Mogadishu (of "Black Hawk Down" fame) be renamed a massacre? There, about five hundred Somalis died; the American toll: eighteen.

Even this cursory list highlights the absurdity of claiming that "disproportion speaks massacre." Disproportion poses a question, but it doesn't answer it. That's the role of the historian, who then looks beyond the disproportion at circumstances and context.

Then there is the figure of 250 itself: the prime piece of evidence on which the "massacre" edifice rests. In the first edition of his book on the 1948 refugees (p. 345), Morris claimed that this figure, "while a general estimate, was given in contemporary military dispatches and had no political or propagandistic intent or purpose." The naïveté of this statement is stunning. The late Israeli general Yehoshafat Harkabi, a battalion commander in 1948 who became a university professor, wrote this about the 1948 war:

> Neither the Arabs nor we had numbers and estimates regarding Arab losses that had any reasonable approximation of certainty. True, we had estimates based on commanders' assessments of the results of battles. But these were unreliable: at times, the fighters were liable to exaggerate enemy losses.[85]

The historian Itamar Radai, in his just-published history of the 3rd Battalion, writes that the basis for the Lydda estimate is unclear, and adds: "During the War of Independence, the number '250' sometimes was a symbolic figure, representing a large number of killed. The best-known case was Deir Yassin, in which all sides, each for its own purpose, adopted the number of 254 killed. . . . It later became clear that the number of killed at Deir Yassin was about 100."[86]

As the Tel Aviv University historian Anita Shapira has noted, the figure of 250 enemy killed at Lydda was "a very high number of fatalities compared to previous battles."[87] This has rendered it suspect. The Hebrew University scholars Avraham Sela and Alon Kadish have concluded that "any attempt to calculate 'actual' numbers of casualties in Lydda would be futile."[88] Unfortunately for Morris, his entire argument for a broader "massacre" rests on this one "statistic," the accuracy of which it is impossible to ascertain.

Unlike the "massacre," at any rate, the battle between Israeli troops and local fighters *is* attested by a contemporary document, which Morris himself added to the revised version (2004) of his book on the refugees. It is a message from the Yiftah brigade to overall HQ of the operation, on the afternoon of July 12: "Battles have erupted in Lydda. We have hit an armored car with a two-pounder [gun] and killed many Arabs. There are still exchanges of fire in the town. We have many wounded."[89] That perfectly evokes what I call "a battle with two sides." Yet while Morris added the Yiftah brigade message in the revised edition, he didn't alter his interpretation of the events by one iota.

Lydda was no fishing village or mountain hamlet. It was a market city with an important church, immediately adjacent to the country's railway hub and airport, and its conquest made headlines in Israel, the Arab countries, and the West. There were plenty of eyes and ears in Lydda. Two "embedded" journalists, Keith Wheeler of the *Chicago Sun-Times* and Kenneth Bilby of the *New York Herald Tribune*, entered the city on July 12, accompanied by Yigal Allon's aide Yeruham Cohen, and had to take cover on Lydda's main street when gunfire broke out. (Cohen remembered "small, uncoordinated battles in various corners of the city.")[90] The professional photographer Boris Carmi took a portrait of a smiling Yiftah-brigade soldier right outside the Dahmash mosque.[91] Yitzhak Sadeh, then commander of the 8th brigade, invited two poets, Natan Alterman and Yaakov Orland, to tour Lydda while there were still bodies in the streets. (Alterman declined.) Aside from the hundreds of officers and soldiers of the Yiftah brigade who captured the city, hundreds more from the Kiryati brigade replaced them a day after the fighting.

That the "largest massacre" of the 1948 war could have occurred in this place and in these circumstances, and not generate a single document, contemporary press report, or photograph, defies belief. Were some innocents killed, either in the crossfire or by jittery or undisciplined or even rampaging soldiers? Mula Cohen, commander of the Yiftah brigade, said (in a quote that I included in my essay) that there were "deviations" that day but no "mass killing." No one has yet proved otherwise.

Scattered atrocities don't add up to a massacre (a distinction drawn by Morris himself in his analysis of an alleged "massacre" at Tantura),[92] and neither do the unintended deaths of bystanders in the midst of fire-fights. Documents may surface one day casting the episode in another light; so far, they haven't.

Morris also claims that I "obfuscated or elided" the July 11 shock-and-awe sprint along the fringes of Lydda and Ramleh by Moshe Dayan's 89th Battalion. (A strong case has been made that this column didn't enter Lydda, but only skirted it.)[93] The contemporary account of who died was given by the "embedded" reporter Kenneth Bilby: "The corpses of Arab men, women, and even children were strewn about in the wake of this ruthlessly brilliant charge."[94] In *My Promised Land,* Shavit cuts out the men (that is, those who could be fighters), and writes this: "More than a hundred Arab civilians are shot dead—women, children, old people." Apparently, the *New Yorker'*s fact-checkers doubted the accuracy of this sentence, including the fatality count (Morris in his book *1948* and in response to me writes "dozens"), so the magazine version of Shavit's chapter reads thus: "Dozens of Arabs were shot dead, including women, children, and old people."

Notice how this event gets bargained down on the way from book to magazine: "more than a hundred" becomes "dozens," and the shooting of women, children, and old people now just "includes" women, children, and old people. A "massacre"? Even Shavit doesn't call it that, saving the word for the events of the following day, July 12. At one time, Morris too wasn't so certain about how to describe this episode. In his original book on the refugees, he provided not a single detail about the raid except to say that it "dented" Arab civilian morale and the will to resist.[95] In the revised edition, he wrote that Dayan's maneuver "combined elements of a battle and a massacre."[96] In his response to me, Morris now calls it "a mass killing of townspeople." A massacre is born.

But there is a reason this famous raid hasn't gone down in Israeli history as a "massacre" or "mass killing." It is largely because Dayan's column, operating in hostile enemy territory, charged through a rain of enemy fire and lost nine men and many vehicles along the way. There is also doubt as to how many people the column killed. The late Elhanan Orren, who wrote the detailed military history of this front, concluded that the enemy casualty figures of between 100 and 150 given in Dayan's own report were "very exaggerated," and that the raid "did not cause heavy losses to the enemy."[97]

The toll of Arab dead from Dayan's raid isn't even mentioned in more recent scholarship like Mordechai Bar-On's biography of Dayan and Anita Shapira's study of Yigal Allon.[98] So Morris's accusation of obfuscation and elision must apply to those two historians as well. If they concede that Dayan committed a massacre at Lydda, I'll reconsider.

One thing seems certain, however. Contrary to Morris (in his revised refugee book),[99] the famed poet Natan Alterman did not compose his poem *Al Zot,* condemning the killing of innocent Arabs as war crimes, in reaction to Dayan's raid. The foremost authorities on Alterman, and most recently his biographer Dan Laor, insist that the poem was inspired by the wanton killing of Arab civilians in the village of Al-Dawayima, west of Hebron, in October 1948.[100] *Al Zot* has sometimes been adduced (by Morris but not by Shavit) as indirect evidence for brutal conduct at Lydda. It shouldn't be.

Finally, Morris accuses me of "whitewashing and/or ignoring the expulsion" of Lydda's inhabitants. I don't know why: the subject of my essay was the "massacre," not the "expulsion." I suppose this is a maneuver so that Morris can repeat here, yet again, his much-contested claim that an order to expel came from David Ben-Gurion himself. Shavit, in his book, echoes that claim: "Yigal Allon asks Ben-Gurion what to do with the Arabs. Ben-Gurion waves his hand: Deport them."

As usual, things are never as simple as Shavit portrays them. One leading Israeli historian has argued that Ben-Gurion never "waved" orders, and might just as well "have waved his hand to get rid of a fly."[101] The entire question has been hotly debated among Israeli historians for decades. I'll simply refer readers to the contrary view, most thoroughly elaborated by Ben-Gurion's biographer Shabtai Teveth.[102]

In reading through the oral testimony, I was impressed by an aspect of the Lydda flight that that both Morris and Shavit seem to have elided or ignored. A large portion of the Arab population in Lydda in July 1948 wasn't from Lydda, but consisted of refugees from Jaffa and villages to the west. "There were masses of refugees there," recalled the military governor, Shmarya Gutman, in a 1988 film interview. "I could determine the names of all the villages from the region that had fled to Lydda. It was possible to estimate the number. The impression was that in the city, where there should have been 12,000 people, there were about 35,000."[103]

Reja-e Busailah, in his memoir of the events, reports numbers almost twice as large, but in the same rough proportion of residents to refugees: "Originally we had numbered from 20,000 to 25,000. We grew to from 60,000 to 65,000 by the time the town fell." These outsiders "had settled on the sidewalks and under the olive trees."[104]

Those refugees, having already fled their homes to escape the Jews, didn't need encouragement to flee again. A safe road leading east was enough, and that road opened when the Arab Legion abandoned the Lydda police station. Gutman remembered that when he announced to the inhabitants of Lydda that they could leave, "they were so happy. In any case, there were [already] refugees there. Why be refugees in hell? They would be refugees in a safer place."[105]

As for the residents, there is testimony that many fled believing they would return in victory. Buseilah recalls the reaction of some (perhaps most) to Gutman's announcement that they were free to leave:

> The oldest male among us finally went out and came back shortly. He was joyous, bubbling almost. Salvation had come. They were going to let us go. And we should go, else they would kill us all. . . . We should return very shortly. It will not take the Arab armies long before they drive them out of Lydda and Ramleh, out of Jaffa and beyond. In a matter of weeks, if not days, we should be back. Most believed this, in the face of the new reality.[106]

So the word "expulsion" cannot suffice to describe everything that happened in Lydda. There was also self-propelled flight.

I repeat: I can't construct an absolutely certain narrative of the events in Lydda on July 12, 1948. There are too many gaps and contradictions in the record. But with a little digging, I've had no trouble casting doubt on Shavit's stick-figure dramatization and Morris's smug assertions.

Why does it matter?

"Zionism carries out a massacre in the city of Lydda." Shavit's repellent statement, derided even by Morris, is part of the answer to why it matters. There are those who claim that Israel came into being through massacre, which Zionism facilitated and legitimated. Today it is possible to take a "Nakba" tour of Lydda (now called Lod). There, one will be told by the Arab guide that what transpired in the town, from massacre through expulsion, was part of a "systematic policy," and therefore "an action of Zionism."[107] How systematic? Here is a Palestinian professor whose institute collects oral testimonies:

> There was a brain behind the massacres, call it a master plan, call it an outline, because there is a pattern to the killings, and a logic to this pattern. After working in different archives, my picture is that Palestine in 1948 was a theater of Israeli massacres, a continuous show of Palestinians massacred, of killings and destruction, and of psychological warfare.[108]

In this narrative, the "original sin" of Israel's birth wasn't expulsion. The Palestinians wouldn't have fled their homes had there not been repeated and planned massacres, which have since been sealed up in "black boxes." Lydda stands as the prime example.

"Disproportion speaks massacre, not 'battle.'" This equally repellent statement, by Morris, is just as defamatory of Israel as Shavit's. On Morris's principle, every occasion on which Israel exacts a numerically "disproportionate" cost in the lives of others—as it often must do, if it is to deter and defeat its enemies—constitutes evidence of massacre; to sustain its very existence, Israel must massacre again and again, decade after decade. There are those who busily quantify and tabulate just that allegation. "Since January 2005," we may read in the latest such exercise, "the conflict has killed 23 Palestinians for every one Israeli it claims."[109] Israel thus can never be legitimate; it is a perpetual war crime, on an ever-larger scale. So saith the "disproportion."

Shavit and Morris thus validate the argument for Israel's dismantlement. As anyone familiar with their politics knows, that is not their intent. Israel is precious to both of them, and they call themselves Zionists. But at an earlier point in their lives, they became habituated to ripping events from their context, which was the hallmark of what was once called the "new history." Their treatment of Lydda is a relapse into a past addiction, which consists of simplification, exaggeration, and decontextualization—in short, the very behavior displayed by those now addicted to hatred of Israel.

In the summer of 2014, someone posted a video clip from Lod (Lydda). It shows a demonstration by Arab residents (who comprise about a quarter of the town's population) and possibly some Jews, in Palmah Square, alongside the small mosque. The demonstrators, waving Palestinian flags, are protesting against "Protective Edge," Israel's operation in Gaza. They carry a large banner with this message: "Stop the massacre in Gaza."[110]

At the site of one presumed "massacre," yet another is presumed. This is how myths evolve into a mythology. And that is why it's so important to recognize that even in Lydda, supposed site of the "largest massacre" of 1948, we just can't be certain there was a "massacre" at all.

Second Response by Benny Morris

I have to admit that, prior to reading his essay, "What Happened at Lydda," I had never read anything by Martin Kramer. But I had heard that he was a serious Middle East scholar, albeit of subjects far removed from the 1948 war. His essay, however, is imbued with clear political purpose—"Israel is defined by much of liberal opinion as an 'occupier,'" Kramer writes at one point in an essay that ostensibly deals with July 1948—and thus smacks more of propaganda than of history (even though the minutiae of his criticism of Ari Shavit's manipulation of texts and facts regarding one minor episode in the war—what happened at a mosque in Lydda on July 12, 1948—are illuminating, if not so much about the war as about Shavit).

In my response to Kramer's essay, I argued that "disproportion" speaks "massacre." Kramer has now replied to my argument in a manner disingenuous if not forthrightly mendacious. Yes, in contemporary warfare between advanced technological societies and Third World societies—the United States versus Iraq, for example, or Israel versus Hamas—the application of air power and sophisticated artillery by a Western power can lead to completely disproportionate losses on the part of ill-armed Arab ground forces, and these do not necessarily speak of massacre. But in the Israeli-Arab war of 1948, two or more relatively primitive armies came to grips. When, in a specific battlefield, one side was more powerful than the other, a "disproportion" in losses might arise. That happened, for example, in the successive battles between the Haganah/IDF and Jordan's Arab Legion at Latrun in May–June 1948, where many more Israelis died than Jordanians due to the Legion's efficient use of its mortars and 75-mm artillery batteries and to Israeli paucity in or misuse of heavy weaponry. But when the disproportion is 250:0 or 250:2, as occurred, according to contemporary IDF documents, between the IDF and the Lydda townspeople, some of them armed, on July 12 of the same year, then "battle" is surely not the name of the game; "massacre" is more like it.

To Kramer, this was a "battle with two sides." And now, to mislead his readers, he says in his reply that there was indeed a "battle"— between the Yiftah-brigade soldiers and the two or three Jordanian armored cars that had penetrated Lydda. But that is not at issue. Sure, there was an Israeli-Jordanian battle (or, more accurately, a skirmish, in which there were Israeli casualties) around noon on July 12. But the question is whether what transpired afterward, between the townspeople, some of whom sniped at the Israelis, and the Yiftah troops—an action that ended in 250 dead townspeople—was a battle. Given the vanishingly small number of Israeli losses, "battle" is a tendentious misnomer, Kramer's sophistry and verbal acrobatics notwithstanding.

In his reply, Kramer dredges up new oral testimony about what happened at the small mosque. (I bow to Kramer's expertise in Arabic as to how the name of the mosque should be transliterated.) But this testimony still fails to prove that anyone from within the mosque threw a grenade at the Israeli troops outside, triggering the IDF rocketing of those inside. Anyway, the event at the mosque was merely one (small) part of the Lydda massacre that afternoon ("small" insofar as it accounted, reportedly, for only 30 to 70 of the 250 Arab dead).

Kramer may be right in saying, as he now does, that "250" as recorded in the IDF documents was a rough estimate. I doubt that the IDF soldiers actually counted the bodies as they gathered and buried them, or that they recorded the process. But even if the ratio was 200:0 or 200:2, it would still point to a massacre. Kramer, incidentally, writes of 250 "casualties" when the document actually says "some 250 dead . . . and many wounded." Historians—indeed, English-speakers—should know the difference between "dead" and "casualties."

Kramer says that the figure of 250 and its corollary of "disproportion" are my sole proof that a massacre or massacres occurred in Lydda on the afternoon of July 12, 1948. As he puts it: "On this slim reed rests Morris' claim" of massacre. But that is simply not true. In my books, and in my response to Kramer's essay, I also quoted from contemporary documents—Kramer, for some reason, avoids documents like the plague, preferring interviews by others conducted decades after the event (was he trained as a historian or as an anthropologist?)—showing that Yiftah HQ ordered its troops to shoot "anyone seen on the streets." Finally, Mula Cohen, Yiftah's commanding officer, when recalling these events in *Sefer Hapalmah*, wrote: "The brutality of the war here reached its peak. The conquest of the city. . . awakened instincts of revenge [*yitzrei-nakam*] that sought an outlet."[111] When you couple a desire for revenge, and shooting anyone seen in the streets, with 250 dead townspeople, what do you get?

As for the run on the previous day (July 11) by Moshe Dayan's 89th battalion through the peripheries of Lydda and Ramleh, all the documents agree that dozens of people—maybe 100–150—were hit, men, women, and children. True, the column suffered nine dead and some wounded. But the shooting was hardly a targeted killing of militiamen, and couldn't have been one given the nature of the run (I'm sure even Kramer will agree with this). Granted, it wasn't a deliberate massacre— but without doubt it was a mass killing that included civilians. Did these comprise many of the casualties? Most of the casualties? I don't know. No one does.

Perhaps part of the problem stems from the meaning of the word "massacre." Of course, all would agree that if you line up one hundred civilians or unarmed POWs against a wall and shoot them, you have a massacre. But what occurred in Lydda was more complicated. A firefight with two Jordanian armored cars and sniping by armed townspeople provoked mass killing by a small IDF contingent that felt vulnerable and panicky: 300–400 men in the center of a town that they thought had surrendered (it hadn't) and that contained tens of thousands of locals and refugees. And the Arabs were the ones who had started the war.

But whatever the extenuating circumstances, had IDF troops acted in such a manner today, given current legal and moral norms, they would most likely have been put on trial—by Israel. One can argue that one shouldn't "judge" soldiers' behavior in the past by today's standards. Agreed. But this doesn't change the fact that they committed a massacre.

I shouldn't really waste time on this, but Kramer's assurances to the contrary notwithstanding, Natan Alterman's poem *Al Zot* was indeed probably about Lydda and not, as he says, about Dawayima (a village near Beit Jibrin that was the site of an IDF massacre in October 1948). Why Kramer is so "certain" about this—as he is so certain about almost everything he writes—I don't know. The fact that Dan Laor, Alterman's latest biographer, believes it is neither here nor there; Laor offers no proof either way. Certainly, there is no proof; we don't have anything like, for instance, a diary entry by Alterman saying explicitly that he has composed a poem about Dawayima. But what he describes in *Al Zot* conforms to what happened in Dayan's raid in Lydda—and the poem does speak explicitly of an incident in a town or city (*ir*) and not a village (*kfar*). In any case, there is no doubt in my mind that Alterman published his poem in the daily *Davar*, on November 19, in protest against a series of atrocities committed by IDF during October and early November, of which Dawayima was just one. Those interested in the whole series can find detailed descriptions, insofar as the accessible documents allow, in my 2004 book, *The Birth of the Palestinian Refugee Problem Revisited.* (Of course, Kramer might dismiss these descriptions of mine as anti-Zionist propaganda as they are based on IDF, Israeli government, and Western diplomatic documentation from 1948 rather than on oral testimony by the participants given decades after the event.)

Finally, Kramer continues to elide—in effect, deny—that following the massacre, the IDF expelled Lydda's (and neighboring Ramleh's) inhabitants. He says in his reply that this wasn't the subject of his essay, and that the debate about the expulsion is a "well-worn subject." (I suppose the Second World War is also a "well-worn subject," but I believe historians still write about it.) He denies that he has whitewashed or elided. But that's precisely what he did, clearly and, to my mind, for political reasons. In his reply he continues to ignore the plain, simple, explicit import of the July 12–13 IDF documentation on the subject. The Lydda (and Ramleh) townspeople were expelled, on orders from on high, and the officers expelling them knew that they were carrying out an expulsion and, at its end, knew that they had carried out an expulsion. This may not have sat well with the conscience of Shmarya Gutman, the Israeli military governor of Lydda; indeed, in his famous November 1948 article on Lydda, Gutman compares what happened to the townspeople with the exile of the Jews by the Romans 2,000 years earlier. But that's what happened, whatever justifications or stories he may have concocted afterward.

Gutman—and he is the sole source for this story—writes, as paraphrased by Kramer: "The next day, the Israeli military governor reached an agreement with local notables that the civilian population would depart from Lydda and move eastward. Israeli soldiers, acting under orders, also encouraged their departure. Within a few hours, a stream of refugees made its way to the east, emptying the city." So: there was an Israeli-Arab "agreement" for the Arab exodus and there was some Israeli "encouragement." Now really. I'm sorry, but what can I do? The documents speak clearly, explicitly of *geyrush*: expulsion.

In my 2004 book, I give due credence to other factors in the exodus of the inhabitants of Lydda and Ramleh: they wanted their menfolk released, they didn't look forward to life under Jewish rule, and so forth. But none of this detracts from the fact that the event as a whole was an expulsion. (Kramer's fellow expulsion deniers, Alon Kadish, Avraham Sela, and Arnon Golan, the last of whom is actually a good, serious historian, conclude in their Hebrew book on the conquest of Lydda that there was a "partial expulsion," since some five hundred of Lydda's inhabitants remained in place. Again: now really.)

Kramer's goal, throughout, appears to be to create or enhance a white-as-snow image of Israel. Like me, he is outraged by today's widespread, untrue, and ill-willed misrepresentation of Israel, in the media and on college campuses, as a monstrous state. Well should he be outraged. But unlike Kramer, in countering this image I am unwilling to distort and misrepresent the past.

Second Rejoinder by Martin Kramer

First, a word of thanks to Benny Morris. His work wasn't the subject of my essay, but he accepted an invitation from the editors to wade in as a respondent. Were it not for him, there wouldn't have been any debate in *Mosaic* at all. Ari Shavit, the author of *My Promised Land,* whose account of Lydda was the subject of my essay, remains silent. So do those who boosted Shavit's book while shedding belated tears of contrition over Lydda. They haven't so much as tweeted the existence of the essay or the exchange that followed. What are they waiting for?

Here once again, as in his original response, Morris would distract us from his dubious claim (elaborated by Shavit) that Israeli troops committed a "massacre" in Lydda by reverting to the subsequent expulsion of the town's Arabs. He even calls me an "expulsion denier." So I will state my view more plainly for his benefit. On July 12, after the aborted Palestinian uprising in Lydda, an order came down from on high—just how high is debated—to expel the Arab inhabitants. But there were many thousands of Arabs on the road out of Lydda who didn't wait for an order to leave, and never heard one. As I wrote, "the word 'expulsion' cannot suffice to describe *everything* that happened in Lydda" (emphasis added). Whether that makes me guilty of "expulsion denial" (which, like "Nakba denial," draws an abhorrent analogy to Holocaust denial), I leave to readers to decide.

Now back to the Lydda "massacre." Morris thinks the aim of my essay was to "create or enhance a white-as-snow image of Israel." In a summary of my essay that appeared elsewhere, I wrote this: "My motive hasn't been to protect Israel's honor against the charge of massacre. There are some well-documented instances from 1948. It's just that Lydda isn't one of them."[112] Morris now speculates that I might dismiss those other instances "as anti-Zionist propaganda as they are based on IDF/Israeli government/Western diplomatic documentation from 1948 rather than on oral testimony."

Untrue: documentation dispels doubt. And its absence increases doubt. The Lydda "massacre," according to Morris the "largest" of 1948, is dubious precisely because of the total absence of any IDF, Israeli government, or Western diplomatic documentation—Morris's own catalogue of what it would take to prove it. So he must cling tenaciously to the one shred he has, from a document not kept secret but published almost sixty years ago: the disproportion, in the Yiftah brigade's report of the battle, between 250 enemy killed versus only two Israelis. According to Morris, in a battle between "relatively primitive armies" in which neither side has a clear advantage in firepower, that "speaks massacre."

But the battle in Lydda (after the retreat of the Arab Legion) wasn't between "relatively primitive armies." It was between the Israeli army, outnumbered but equipped with antitank PIATs and heavy machine guns, versus many more locals armed with "sten guns, tommyguns, rifles (French, Italian, and German), and some dating back to the Ottoman period."[113] Morris again: "If, in a specific battlefield, one side was more powerful than the other, a 'disproportion' in losses might arise." Isn't that a precise description of the Lydda battle? What is the story of the small mosque, if not one of superior firepower (a PIAT) exacting a high toll ("dozens," writes Morris) with one shot? The sides to an exchange of fire don't have to be equal for their (mis)match to be a battle, and that battle doesn't become a "massacre" simply because the outcome is lopsided.

But just how "disproportionate" was the killing in Lydda? That still depends largely on whether the figure of 250 deserves to be taken seriously. Even Morris now recognizes that it wasn't the result of a count. "I doubt that the IDF soldiers actually counted the bodies as they gathered and buried them," he concedes. (Indeed, they may have imposed that task on the remaining Arabs: one veteran of the battle said that "we didn't gather the bodies. It wasn't our business.")[114] So even Morris has no idea how the number was reached.

As I mentioned in my essay, the historian Alon Kadish was the first to discount the number, and deeply ("it is doubtful that the number of Arabs killed on July 12 reached 250 or even half that number").[115] And as I noted in my earlier reply to Morris, the historian Itamar Radai has warned that in the 1948 war, 250 was probably a "symbolic" number, simply meaning "a lot"—like the estimate for Deir Yassin, where 254 turned out to be 100 (or like Teddy Katz's discredited claim about a "massacre" at Tantura, which he also put at 250).[116] In his latest reply, even Morris seems willing to bargain to make a point: so what if it was 200? (Perhaps if we go another round, he'll come down some more.)

I empathize with Morris: he needs to find estimates of Arabs killed and expelled to do his work, and the main (sometimes only) source is Israeli battle reports. But from the Bible to Vietnam, enemy body counts are the most inflatable figures in history. I wasn't shocked when

I read Yehoshafat Harkabi's matter-of-fact statement that Israeli commanders often exaggerated enemy losses in 1948. I don't imagine the exaggeration was ever on the scale of Samson killing a thousand with a jawbone, but it would have conveyed the same message: a courageous handful of men, with few means, defeated the many.

While the "disproportion" may speak massacre to Morris today, it seems safe to assume that Mula Cohen, the Yiftah commander who signed the report of the battle, didn't imagine he was confessing to a "massacre." And I doubt that the editors who included it in the heroic *Sefer Hapalmah* in the 1950s regarded it as the smoking gun of a war crime. So just what did such "disproportion" speak at that time? A handful of courageous Palmahniks, with few means, defeated the many—*and conquered Lydda.*

Why does that last phrase need to be emphasized? After his earlier, guns-ablaze race past Lydda and Ramleh, Moshe Dayan met with Mula Cohen, who would remember the encounter this way:

> Dayan said: "I'm going to Tel Aviv to Ben-Gurion, to inform him that I conquered Lydda." And that's the whole big story of "I conquered Lydda," whereas Lydda hadn't been conquered at all. The 3rd Battalion advanced slowly. Night fell, and Dayan's battalion is gone.[117]

So who conquered Lydda? Moshe Dayan's 89th battalion, made up of former Lehi fighters and village boys, in its 47-minute blitzkrieg? Or Cohen's (and Yigal Allon's) Yiftah brigade, led by kibbutzniks, who occupied the town, repelled the Arab Legion's incursion, put down an incipient uprising, and drove the Legion out of Lydda's police station? Dayan's report claimed he killed 100–150 of the enemy ("very exaggerated," wrote the campaign's historian); Cohen's report claimed (counterclaimed?) 250. Are we supposed to take these numbers literally? Or did commanders err on the side of glory? It's a valid question, for which there won't ever be a clear answer. What's certain is that for the persons who reported the figure of 250 enemy killed on July 12, 1948 and published it in *Sefer Hapalmah* a few years later, the number didn't "speak massacre." It shouted that the Palmah, and no one else, conquered Lydda.

As supporting evidence, Morris adduces Cohen's statement that the conquest of Lydda put the soldiers in a vengeful mood. This, says Morris, primed them for massacre. (His quotation isn't from a contemporary document but from a later recollection by Cohen, proving once again that Morris never relies on the flawed memory of soldiers—except when he does.) There are two problems here. First, Morris has torn the quote from its context. Cohen was explaining why the soldiers of the Yiftah brigade descended into *looting*. Stealing and theft, not killing, were the "outlet" that "relieved the tension."[118]

Second, there is testimony by squad commander Hanan Sever, given even earlier than Cohen's, to a very different mood among the conquering soldiers after they took the town:

> In all the coffee houses, soldiers sat sipping fine coffee from demi-tasses. The tension dropped and slacked off entirely. The battle ended in carelessness, as each man turned to amuse himself. We entirely forgot the fact that we were conquerors who numbered only 300, whereas the conquered numbered in the thousands, many of whom were Arab Legion soldiers still with their weapons; in only a few minutes, the conquest could turn into a defeat. Still, for some reason, a deep sense of confidence settled in our hearts, and with the carelessness of youth, we pushed aside the last bit of caution.[119]

(An evocative photograph of Yiftah soldiers in Lydda, by Boris Carmi, perfectly illustrates this passage.)[120] On the morning of the "massacre," Sever said his own soldiers patrolled streets "in apathetic and calm relaxation," and he had to urge them to stay alert.[121] If Morris thinks he can establish the "massacre" by portraying Yiftah's soldiers as prowling Lydda for revenge, he'll have to work harder—and with oral testimony.

Morris finally hits the nail on the head with this sudden observation: "Perhaps part of the problem stems from the meaning of the word 'massacre.'" Morris should know, since he's confused the meaning by expanding it. When he first wrote about Lydda, in the first edition of his book on the refugees (p. 206), he didn't use "massacre" to describe the events there, reserving it for cases such as Deir Yassin and Al-Dawayima. But in the revised edition (p. 428), he inserted the word in a sentence on Lydda without any new evidence or explanation. Lydda thereafter featured prominently on his list of twenty-four wartime massacres.[122] Not only that, but Morris presumed that all 250 enemy supposedly killed in Lydda were massacred.[123]

Still, despite his condemnation of other historians for denying the "massacre," Morris himself now allows that the issue isn't obviously self-evident. In this second response to me, he admits that the Lydda case is "more complicated" than his archetype of massacre allows. In his earlier response, he even created an entirely new subcategory for Lydda, describing it as "a massacre, albeit a provoked one"—the provocation presumably consisting of enemy bullets and grenades flying at soldiers. In fact, nowhere does Morris provide any rigorous definition of "massacre," how it differs from "mass killing" (of which he accuses Moshe Dayan), or how it relates to "atrocities" (which he applies to Tantura). Instead, he substitutes repetition for definition—reiterating the same claim again and again, as if this established it as a fact.

I'm not a historian of 1948, but I am a historian practicing in a much larger and more established field of study, and I know best practices when I see them. I just don't see them in the narrative of a "massacre" at Lydda. Indeed, were it not for the bogus claim of "massacre" at Tantura, the Lydda accusation would constitute the most blatant excess of Israel's "new historians." As the 1948 veterans disappear, such claims have grown ever more extravagant: first, the creeping reclassification of complex battles as "massacres," then the spread of the notion that Israel's leaders "covered up for the officers who did the massacres,"[124] and finally the florid elaboration of freshly discovered "massacres" in popular works ranging from "imaginative reenactments" to theatrical plays.[125]

For the last thirty years, new myths (in the guise of "new history") have replaced old ones (the much-derided "old history"). This process has now peaked in a single decadent sentence, written by Ari Shavit and indebted to Benny Morris: "Zionism commits a massacre in the city of Lydda." That this misplaced and overwrought confession has gone unchallenged by American Jewish thought leaders is proof that they aren't competent to reconstruct an accurate narrative of Israel. Perhaps a few younger readers of this exchange will be inspired to attempt the task.

Notes

1. Ari Shavit, *My Promised Land: The Triumph and Tragedy of Israel* (New York: Random House, 2013), 108.
2. Jeffrey Goldberg's endorsement, Ari Shavit's website archived at http://web.archive.org/web/20131205061027/http://www.arishavit.com/book/.
3. Franklin Foer's endorsement, Ari Shavit's website archived at http://web.archive.org/web/20131205061027/http://www.arishavit.com/book/.
4. Thomas Friedman, "Something for Barack and Bibi to Talk About," *New York Times,* November 16, 2013; Dwight Garner, "Son of Israel, Caught in the Middle," *New York Times,* November 19, 2013; and Leon Wieseltier, "The State of Israel," *New York Times,* November 21, 2013.
5. Stewart Kampel, "A Talk with Ari Shavit," *Hadassah Magazine* (February–March 2014).
6. Rob Eshman, "Ari Shavit: The Promised Man," *Jewish Journal*, February 20, 2014, archived at http://web.archive.org/web/20140307190456/http://www.jewishjournal.com/rob_eshman/article/ari_shavit_the_promised_man.

7. Alan Johnson, "Saving the Promised Land: Interview with Ari Shavit," *Fathom*, June 2, 2014, archived at http://web.archive.org/web/20140609004029/http://www.fathomjournal.org/conversation/saving-the-promised-land/.
8. Ari Shavit, "Lydda, 1948: A City, a Massacre, and the Middle East Today," *New Yorker* (October 21, 2013): 40–46.
9. Shavit, *My Promised Land*, 110.
10. Johnson, "Saving the Promised Land."
11. Avi Shlaim, "The Idea of Israel and My Promised Land," *Guardian*, May 14, 2014.
12. Wieseltier, "The State of Israel."
13. Friedman, "Something for Barack and Bibi to Talk About."
14. I am indebted to Dr. Eldad Harouvi, director of the archives, who expertly guided me through the collection.
15. Uri Goldstein, *Yiftah: Mi-Metulla ad ha-Negev* ([Tel Aviv:] Ohalei Palmah Association, 1989). Quotes cited below are referenced to the transcripts in the Palmah Museum.
16. Quoted by Sally Quinn, "Fear, Creativity and Soul Searching: A Secular Jew's Journey Through 'My Promised Land,'" *Washington Post*, December 5, 2013.
17. Shavit, *My Promised Land*, 109.
18. Avi-Yiftah [Shmarya Gutman], "Lod Yotzet la-Golah," *Mi-Bifnim* 13, no. 3 (November 1948): 452–61.
19. Palmah Museum, transcript of *Yiftah*, part 2, cassette 79.
20. Shavit, *My Promised Land*, 109.
21. Palmah Museum, transcript of *Yiftah*, part 2, cassette 78.
22. Palmah Museum, transcript of *Yiftah*, part 2, cassette 79.
23. [Gutman], "Lod Yotzet la-Golah," 454.
24. Palmah Museum, transcript of *Yiftah*, part 2, cassette 79.
25. Ibid.
26. [Gutman], "Lod Yotzet la-Golah," 457.
27. Ibid.
28. Ibid., 458–9.
29. Shavit, *My Promised Land*, 121.
30. Palmah Museum, transcript of *Yiftah*, part 2, cassette 79.
31. Ibid.
32. See his entry on the Palmah Museum website, archived at http://web.archive.org/web/20140707171210/http://info.palmach.org.il/show_item.asp?levelId=38495&itemId=6316&itemType=0&fighter=74576. Ben-David died in April 2010.
33. Shavit, *My Promised Land*, 114, 117.
34. Quoted by Dan Kurzman, *Genesis 1948: The First Arab-Israel War*, 2nd ed. (New York: Da Capo Press, 1992), 515–16.
35. Palmah Museum, transcript of *Yiftah*, part 2, cassette 82.
36. Beit Yigal Allon Museum, transcript of interview of Uri Gefen by Ezra Greenboim (May 1986), 32.
37. Palmah Museum, transcript of *Yiftah*, part 2, cassette 82.
38. Shavit, *My Promised Land*, 114.
39. Palmah Museum, transcript of *Yiftah*, part 2, cassette 82.
40. Beit Yigal Allon Museum, transcript of interview of Uri Gefen by Ezra Greenboim (May 1986), 32.

41. Shavit, *My Promised Land*, 114, 117, 125.
42. Palmah Museum, transcript of *Yiftah*, part 2, cassette 82.
43. This does not appear in the transcript (previous note), but it is audible in the DVD.
44. Beit Yigal Allon Museum, transcript of interview of Uri Gefen by Ezra Greenboim (May 1986), 32.
45. Ibid., 33.
46. Ibid.
47. Ibid.
48. Ibid., 34.
49. Ari Shavit, "Lod Ke-Mashal," *Ha'aretz*, May 15, 2002.
50. [Gutman], "Lod Yotzet la-Golah," 456.
51. Shavit, *My Promised Land*, 108, 117.
52. Benny Morris, *The Birth of the Palestinian Refugee Problem Revisited*, 2nd ed. (Cambridge: Cambridge University Press, 2004), 428.
53. Alon Kadish, "Ha-'Tevah' ve-ha-Geyrush," in *Kibush Lod, Yuli 1948*, ed. Alon Kadish, Avraham Sela, and Arnon Golan (Tel Aviv: Haganah Archives and the Ministry of Defense, 2000), 46.
54. Zerubavel Gilead, ed. *Sefer Hapalmah*, vol. 2 (Tel Aviv: Hakibbutz Hameuhad, 1953), 571.
55. Benny Morris, *The Road to Jerusalem: Glubb Pasha, Palestine and the Jews* (London: Tauris, 2002), 177.
56. Mula Cohen, *La-Tet u-le-Kabel: Pirkei Zikhronot Ishiim* (Tel Aviv: Hakibbutz Hameuhad, 2000), 141.
57. Palmah Museum, transcript of *Yiftah*, part 2, cassette 79.
58. The original of this report in reproduced by Zeev and Tehilah Ofer, *Yiftah: Hativat Palmah ba-Milhemet ha-Atzmaut* (Tel Aviv: Kvutzat Havrei Hativat Yiftah-Palmah, 2013), 185.
59. His name was Michael Cohen. See his entry at the Israel Defense Forces website devoted to missing soldiers, archived at http://web.archive.org/web/20150505091406/http://www.aka.idf.il/Eitan/pratim/pirteyErua/?docId=33304.
60. Beit Yigal Allon Museum, transcript of interview of Mula Cohen by Ezra Greenboim (1996).
61. Kadish, Sela, and Golan, *Kibush Lod, Yuli 1948*. The argument is also summarized in English in this article: Alon Kadish and Avraham Sela, "Myths and Historiography of the 1948 Palestine War Revisited: The Case of Lydda," *Middle East Journal* 59, no. 4 (Autumn 2005): 617–34.
62. Mordechai Bar-On, "Be-Hazara el Lod ve-Ramleh," *Cathedra* 99 (March 2001): 166–70.
63. Shavit, *My Promised Land*, 121, 125.
64. Testimony of Fayeq Abu Mana, January 11, 2003, Zochrot website, archived at http://web.archive.org/web/20151210144250/http://www.zochrot.org/en/testimony/50254. The best-known Palestinian account available in English also ascribes estimates of the mosque casualties to locals who had removed the bodies and obviously lived to talk about it: "I heard from some colleagues who had helped to remove the dead from the mosque. . . ." Spiro Munayyer, "The Fall of Lydda," *Journal of Palestine Studies* 27, no. 4 (Summer 1998): 94. And this: "According to a doctor, who told me about

six months after the incident—after the Israelis released him—the corpses were removed ten days after the massacre. He said it was a difficult task, what with the stench and decomposition in July." Reja-e Busailah, "The Fall of Lydda, 1948: Impressions and Reminiscences," *Arab Studies Quarterly* 3, no. 2 (Spring 1981): 138.

65. Photograph archived at http://web.archive.org/web/20150509005536/http://www.yaffa48.com/site/online/2011/07/20/1_645057_1_34.jpg.
66. Archived at https://web.archive.org/web/20121001122544/http://www.palestine48.com/default1.asp?flag=qr&report_id=145.
67. Interview with Ra'ifa Abu Mana, September 10, 2012, Zochrot website, archived at https://web.archive.org/web/20140707154554/http://zochrot.org/node/54194.
68. Shavit, *My Promised Land*, 424.
69. Simon Schama, "The Story of Israel," *Financial Times*, February 14, 2014.
70. Shavit, *My Promised Land*, 423–24.
71. Ibid., 131.
72. Ibid., 122.
73. For example, Saleh Abdel Jawad, "Zionist Massacres: The Creation of the Palestinian Refugee Problem in the 1948 War," in *Israel and the Palestinian Refugees*, eds. Eyal Benvenisti, Chaim Gans, and Sari Hanafi (Berlin: Springer, 2007), 59–127
74. For more details and sources, see Morris, *The Birth of the Palestinian Refugee Problem Revisited*, 424–34.
75. Efraim Karsh, "The Uses of Lydda," *Mosaic Magazine*, July 6, 2014, archived at http://web.archive.org/web/20150920060250/http://mosaicmagazine.com/response/2014/07/the-uses-of-lydda/. Karsh's response is not included in the present volume.
76. Morris, *The Birth of the Palestinian Refugee Problem Revisited*, 4.
77. Benny Morris, *The Birth of the Palestinian Refugee Problem, 1947–1949* (Cambridge: Cambridge University Press, 1987), 206.
78. [Gutman], "Lod Yotzet la-Golah," 456 (mention of "a second mosque," from which bombs were thrown).
79. Morris, *The Birth of the Palestinian Refugee Problem Revisited*, 428.
80. Benny Morris, "The New Historiography: Israel Confronts Its Past," in *Making Israel*, ed. Benny Morris (Ann Arbor: University of Michigan Press, 2007), 11.
81. Busailah, "The Fall of Lydda," 137.
82. Interview with Ra'ifa Abu Mana, September 10, 2012, Zochrot website, archived at https://web.archive.org/web/20140707154554/http://zochrot.org/node/54194; Aref al-Aref, *Al-Nakba: Nakbat Bayt al-Maqdis wa'l-Firdaws al-Mafqud*, vol. 6: *Sijill al-Khulud: Asma' al-Shuhada' alladhina Istashhadu fi Ma'arik Filastin* (Sidon: al-Maktaba al-'Asriya, 1962), 26.
83. Hanan Sever, *Agada shel Hesed* (Tel Aviv: Sa'ar, 2010), 148.
84. Benny Morris, "The Tantura 'Massacre' Affair," *The Jerusalem Report*, February 4, 2004.
85. Y. Harkabi, "'Al Avedot ha-'Aravim be-1948," *Ma'arachot* 166 (March 1965): 5.
86. Itamar Radai, *Ha-Gdud Ha-Shlishi* (Mikve Israel: Yehuda Dekel, 2014), 161, n. 82.

87. Anita Shapira, *Yigal Allon, Native Son: A Biography* (Philadelphia: University of Pennsylvania Press, 2008), 226.

88. Kadish and Sela, "Myths and Historiography," 630.

89. Morris, *The Birth of the Palestinian Refugee Problem Revisited*, 427–28.

90. Yeruham Cohen, *Le-Or ha-Yom uva-Mahshakh* (Tel Aviv: Amikam, 1969), 159.

91. Meitar Collection, "Portrait of a Yiftah Solder in Lydda," catalogue no. 14975, archived at http://www.webcitation.org/6dg8y0fMN.

92. Benny Morris, "The Tantura 'Massacre' Affair."

93. Kadish, Sela, and Golan, *Kibush Lod, Yuli 1948*, 33–36.

94. Kenneth W. Bilby, *New Star in the Near East* (New York: Doubleday, 1950), 43.

95. Morris, *The Birth of the Palestinian Refugee Problem*, 205.

96. Morris, *The Birth of the Palestinian Refugee Problem Revisited*, 426.

97. Elhanan Orren, *Ba-Dderekh el Ha'ir: Mivtza Dani, Yuli 1948* (Tel Aviv: Ma'arachot, 1976), 107.

98. Mordechai Bar-On, *Moshe Dayan: Israel's Controversial Hero* (New Haven, CT: Yale University Press, 2012); and Shapira, *Yigal Allon*.

99. Morris, *The Birth of the Palestinian Refugee Problem Revisited*, 489.

100. For the argument that *Al Zot* refers to Al-Dawayima, see Menachem Finkelstein, *"Ha-Tor Ha-Shvi'i" ve-"Tohar Ha-Neshek": Natan Alterman al Bitahon, Musar, u-Mishpat* (Tel Aviv: Hakibbutz Hameuhad, 2011), 151–58; Ziva Shamir, "Masa ha-Tochaha shel Natan Alterman me-Nekudat Taztpito shel Shofet," *Gag* 25 (Winter 2011): 13–22; and Dan Laor, *Alterman: Biografia* (Tel Aviv: Am Oved, 2013), 366–67. Laor originally believed the poem referred to Lydda, but concluded otherwise in this recent biography.

101. Yoav Gelber, *Palestine, 1948: War, Escape and the Emergence of the Palestinian Refugee Problem* (Eastbourne: Sussex Academic Press, 2001), 162.

102. Shabtai Teveth, "Charging Israel with Original Sin," *Commentary* 88, no. 3 (September 1989): 24–33.

103. Palmah Museum, transcript of *Yiftah*, part 2, cassette 79.

104. Busailah, "The Fall of Lydda," 128.

105. Palmah Museum, transcript of *Yiftah*, part 2, cassette 79.

106. Busailah, "The Fall of Lydda," 139.

107. Nakba Day Tour of Lydda, website of Oasis of Peace, archived at http://web.archive.org/web/20140529185531/http://wasns.org/nakba-day-tour-of-lydda-al-lid-lod.

108. Saleh Abdel Jawad quoted by Susan Slyomovics, "The Rape of Qula, a Destroyed Palestinian Village," in *Nakba: Palestine, 1948, and the Claims of Memory*, eds. Ahmad H. Sa'di and Lila Abu-Lughod (New York: Columbia University Press, 2007), 29.

109. Max Fisher, "This Chart Shows Every Person Killed in the Israel-Palestine Conflict since 2000," *Vox* website, archived at http://web.archive.org/web/20150407175927/http://www.vox.com/2014/7/14/5898581/chart-israel-palestine-conflict-deaths.

110. Screen shot of the banner archived at http://web.archive.org/web/20150425060215/http://rotter.net/User_files/forum/53c425153cb1e914.jpg.

111. *Sefer Hapalmah*, 2:885.

112. Martin Kramer, "Massacre at Lydda?," *Commentary* blog, July 1, 2014, archived at http://web.archive.org/web/20140802133424/http://www.commentarymagazine.com/2014/07/01/massacre-at-lydda/.

113. Busailah, "The Fall of Lydda," 127.

114. Interview with Hanan Sever, archived at http://web.archive.org/web/20151119102416/http://gifted.telhai.ac.il/loadedFiles/chanan.pdf.

115. Kadish, "Ha-'Tevah' ve-ha-Geyrush," 46.

116. Radai, *Ha-Gdud Ha-Shlishi*, 161, note 82.

117. Cohen, *La-Tet u-le-Kabel*, 140.

118. *Sefer Hapalmah*, 2:885. Cohen introduces the paragraph on vengefulness with these words by Cohen: "We stood before another test: the impulse of the fighters to loot."

119. Quoted by Radai, *Ha-Gdud Ha-Shlishi*, 157.

120. Meitar Collection, "Soldiers of Yiftah brigade rest in Lydda," catalogue no. 14974, archived at http://www.webcitation.org/6dibUDOm6.

121. Sever, *Agada shel Hesed*, 477.

122. Ari Shavit, "Survival of the Fittest" [interview with Benny Morris], *Ha'aretz*, January 8, 2004.

123. Morris, *The Road to Jerusalem*, 177.

124. Benny Morris quoted by Ari Shavit, "Survival of the Fittest," *Ha'aretz*, January 8, 2004.

125. See Motti Lerner's play *The Admisssion*, which was inspired by the Tantura case.

19

Shabtai Teveth and the Whole Truth

Shabtai Teveth, prolific author and the authorized biographer of David Ben-Gurion, passed away on November 2, 2014 at the age of eighty-nine. He had gone silent twelve years earlier, following a debilitating stroke. It was on the pages of *Commentary*, in 1989, that he launched one of the most thorough broadsides on Israel's "new historians."[1] It repays reading now (as does Hillel Halkin's *Commentary* review of Teveth's *Ben-Gurion and the Holocaust*).[2] It is also a reminder of how desperately Israel still needs truth-tellers like Teveth, who knew the flaws of Israel's founders perfectly well, but never let that overshadow the nobility of their cause.

By the time I met Teveth, in the early 1980s, he was already renowned for his journalistic achievements at *Ha'aretz*, but also for his best-selling books, most famously his up-close account of the heroic armored battles of the June 1967 Six-Day War. (It appeared in English under the title *The Tanks of Tammuz*.)[3] Approaching sixty years of age, he had set aside journalism in order to devote himself to a monumental biography of David Ben-Gurion, a project he had commenced some years earlier, when the Old Man was still alive and willing to talk.

I was new in Israel, and the native-born Teveth became a friend and my guide to the intricacies of the country's history, politics, and journalism. In return, I helped him to prepare an English edition of a spin-off of his biographical project: a book eventually entitled *Ben-Gurion and the Palestinian Arabs*, published by Oxford in 1985.[4] In that work, Teveth argued that Ben-Gurion perfectly understood Arab opposition to Zionism, but also recognized the danger of acknowledging its depth. So B-G conducted a carefully calibrated policy that held out the hope of a peaceful settlement, even while preparing for confrontation. The book covered the 1920s and 1930s, but Ben-Gurion would implement the same approach right up to 1948.

Work on the book became a kind of tutorial course on the history of Israel, taught to me by Teveth. In turn, I taught him some of the odder subtleties of English. For years afterward, he would call me at some ungodly hour of the morning, to ask how he might best render this or that Hebrew phrase into polished English without sacrificing even an iota of its original meaning.

Teveth wrote like a journalist up against a deadline. He would rise very early, go for a swim, head for his office (he didn't work at home, but kept a separate apartment filled to the brim with his research materials), and then would bang out a few thousand words on his typewriter before lunch. I don't think he ever had a day of writer's block.

Over the years, we developed a regular routine. Perhaps once a month, we would meet for lunch in a restaurant somewhere in north Tel Aviv where he kept his office. By lunchtime, Sabi (as his family and friends called him) had finished a full day's work, and he was primed for competitive conversation, usually smoothed by a glass of Scotch, for which he had a refined taste. I couldn't return all of his volleys, and the only real match he had in conversation was the late Zvi Yavetz, the historian of ancient Rome and a master raconteur in his own right. When Sabi and Zvi got rolling, showering the table with sparks of erudition and wit, the spectacle inspired awe and envy.

The Turn to Biography

I once asked Sabi why he had set journalism aside, since his *Ha'aretz* columns had landed on the breakfast tables of the most influential people in Israel. His many books, prior to the Ben-Gurion project, had been contemporary reportage of the highest order, attracting large numbers of readers. (These included a book on the first years of Israel's post-1967 policies in the West Bank, a biography of Moshe Dayan, and an exploration of poverty in Israel.)[5] Sabi answered that he didn't want to spend an entire lifetime breathing heavily over the doings of politicians.

The older I grow, the more I appreciate that decision to move from punditry to history. Teveth came to recognize the ephemeral nature of most journalism. He believed he was fortunate to have witnessed the last chapter in the founding of Israel (as a young soldier in the Palmah and then as an army journalist), and that this was a story that would be told again and again by future generations, each time from a point still more remote from the events. If he wrote that history now, meticulously and honestly, that telling would last beyond him.

The Ben-Gurion project, which ultimately reached four volumes (three thousand pages) in Hebrew, belongs to the genre of the big-canvas biography, of the sort exemplified by Robert Caro's study of Lyndon Johnson or Martin Gilbert's official biography of Winston Churchill.[6] Indeed, it was Teveth's finest hour in 1987 when the 967-page English version of the B-G biography (pre-1948) received a glowing review from Gilbert on the front page of the *New York Times Book Review,* accompanied by a photograph as well as a short profile of Teveth (written by Tom Friedman).[7] This was before the internet, and I remember rushing over to Sabi's home to see the review section, urgently dispatched by his New York publisher.

The Friedman profile includes an odd quote. "Israel has been going through a difficult period during these last thirteen years," Teveth told Friedman. "But all this time I feel as though I have been working in a bunker full of light and hope. In my bunker the Jewish state is yet to be born. The Jewish people have a strong leader and the world is huge." I personally never heard Sabi talk of his historical work as a nostalgic retreat from contemporary Israel. He regretted the diminished quality of Israel's leaders, but this only fortified his determination to remind Israelis of a moment in living memory when they had a leader equal to world history at its most demanding.

There had been a leader who might have risen to that stature: Moshe Dayan, Ben-Gurion's favorite, who seemed poised to succeed the Old Man as the very personification of Israeli grit. Teveth had written a biography of him—admiring but not reverential—that appeared in 1971, while Dayan still basked in the glow of the Six-Day War.[8] Dayan's prospects were dashed by the Yom Kippur War in 1973, when suddenly he became the clay-footed personification of Israeli hubris. Teveth nevertheless remained loyal to Dayan, and it was he who mediated between Dayan's longtime admirers and Tel Aviv University, to bring forth the Moshe Dayan Center for Middle Eastern and African Studies.

The monumental biography of Ben-Gurion secured for Teveth the National Jewish Book Award in 1987 and the Israel Prize, Israel's highest civilian honor, in 2005. But the project remained unfinished, in part because every few years he would suspend it to write a spin-off. He wrote a book on the 1933 murder of Chaim Arlosorov. (Its conclusions so enraged the then-prime minister Menachem Begin that he appointed an official commission of inquiry to refute it.)[9] He wrote another book on Ben-Gurion's response to the Holocaust, and still another on the

1954 Lavon Affair (both also appeared in English).[10] And there was that book on Ben-Gurion and the Palestinian Arabs. These digressions, while important works in their own right, took time from the biography, and when Teveth suffered his stroke, he hadn't yet gotten to the year for which Ben-Gurion's life had been a preparation: 1948.

"New Historians"

We are fortunate, then, that one of those digressions took the form of a direct confrontation with the so-called new historians. Avi Shlaim, one of Teveth's targets, later called him "the most strident and vitriolic" critic of the self-declared iconoclasts who set about smashing the conventional Israeli narrative with reckless abandon.[11] In the spring of 1989, Teveth fired off a barrage of full-page critiques in three consecutive weekend editions of *Ha'aretz*. (These pieces formed the nucleus of his later *Commentary* article.) Teveth pummeled the "new historians" (Shlaim and Benny Morris), whose indictments of Israel's conduct in 1948 he described as a "farrago of distortions, omissions, tendentious readings, and outright falsifications." I recall waking up early each Friday morning and rushing down to my doorstep to grab the newspaper and flip to that week's installment.

A year later, he published a thirty-five-page review of Benny Morris's *Birth of the Palestinian Refugee Problem,* pursuing error and bias into the most remote footnotes. This was Teveth at his forensic best: he had read the same documents in the same archives, and he showed that they did not always say what Morris claimed they said. "Morris's work was received with great expectations," Teveth concluded. "On examination, however, these have been disappointed. This problem [of how the Palestinian Arabs became refugees], therefore, will have to wait still further for a more comprehensive and honest study, that would be worthy of the great human and national tragedy it represents."[12]

The "new historians" retaliated by trying to label Teveth as "old." True, he was a generation older than them, but the "old"-naming could reach absurd proportions. For example, Shlaim once described him, repeatedly, as a "member of the Mapai old guard."[13] Nonsense: Teveth was famously associated with Mapai's *young* guard, and indeed built his journalistic reputation as a muckraker by attacking Mapai's veteran party stalwarts.[14]

Teveth concluded his *Commentary* article by dismissing the "new historians," since "history, thank goodness, is made of sterner and more intractable stuff than even their wholesale efforts of free interpretation can dissimulate." This proved to be overly optimistic. Demolishing Israel's "myths" and creating new ones turned into a popular pastime for younger academics and activists. Benny Morris's book on the Palestinian refugee problem has become the most-read and most-cited book on the 1948 war. One hardly need wonder what Teveth would say about the latest iteration of "free interpretation" (pioneered by Morris in the revised edition of his book), accusing Israel of various massacres that somehow escaped notice until just now.[15] Nothing good, I imagine.

I wish I could announce that Teveth's legacy will be ever-enduring, but a younger generation of readers will have to discover him first, and that hasn't happened yet. He wrote mostly in the era before the internet, so his most important writings aren't accessible at a click. He disappeared from the scene years before he died, so the obituaries were few and perfunctory. And he wrote big books that almost no one has read cover-to-cover. Teveth not only told truths about Israel, he told whole truths, and that required a minute retrieval and examination of all the evidence. There were reviewers who complained that Teveth left his readers "drowning in a sea of detail," and that "intimate descriptions of daily doings" caused them to lose the "overall thread."[16]

Teveth was familiar with the criticism, and he rejected it. At one point, he had recited the list of groceries Ben-Gurion purchased while in London in November 1938. "Trivial," he acknowledged, "yet how well this information helps the biographer in describing the loneliness of Ben-Gurion, who ate in his hotel room and there listened to the radio speeches by Hitler and Chamberlain, speeches that decided the fate of the world and the fate of both Europe's Jews and Zionism."[17] Such level of detail assures that while the general reader may not persevere, every future biographer of Ben-Gurion will keep those four volumes on his or her desk. Perhaps that was Teveth's aim all along.

I missed Sabi very much after he fell ill, and suspect I'll miss him still more with the passage of time. This is not only because he was my friend. It is because I see no one who combines his mix of passion, energy, and encyclopedic knowledge in the pursuit of every recoverable fragment of evidence needed to establish the truth.

Notes

1. Shabtai Teveth, "Charging Israel with Original Sin," *Commentary* 88, no. 3 (September 1989): 24–33.
2. Hillel Halkin, "Ben-Gurion and the Holocaust: Review," *Commentary* 103, no. 1 (January 1997): 64–6.
3. Shabtai Teveth, *The Tanks of Tammuz* (New York: Viking Press, 1969).

4. Shabtai Teveth, *Ben-Gurion and the Palestinian Arabs* (New York: Oxford University Press, 1985).
5. Two of these appeared in English: Shabtai Teveth, *The Cursed Blessing: The Story of Israel's Occupation of the West Bank* (New York: Random House, 1971); and *Moshe Dayan: The Soldier, the Man, the Legend* (Boston, MA: Houghton Mifflin, 1973).
6. English version: Shabtai Teveth, *Ben-Gurion: The Burning Bround, 1886–1948* (Boston, MA: Houghtom-Mifflin, 1987).
7. Martin Gilbert, "Israel Was Everything: Review," *New York Times*, June 21, 1987.
8. The Hebrew appeared in 1971; the English version, in 1973.
9. Shabtai Teveth, *Retzah Arlosorov* (Tel Aviv: Schocken, 1982).
10. Shabtai Teveth, *Ben-Gurion's Spy: The Story of the Political Scandal That Shaped Modern Israel* (New York: Columbia University Press, 1996).
11. Avi Shlaim, "La guerre des historiens israéliens," *Annales* 59, no. 1 (January–February 2004): 161–69; English original, "The War of the Israeli Historians," archived at http://web.archive.org/web/20060526053857/http://users.ox.ac.uk/~ssfc0005/The%20War%20of%20the%20Israeli%20Historians.html.
12. Shabtai Teveth, "The Palestine Arab Refugee Problem and Its Origins: Review Article," *Middle Eastern Studies* 26, no. 2 (April 1990): 248.
13. Shlaim, "The War of the Israeli Historians."
14. The subject of an article by Rafi Mann, "Minapetz u-Miromem," *Ha-Ayin Ha-Shvi'i*, November 14, 2014, archived at http://web.archive.org/web/20141128172622/http://www.the7eye.org.il/133825.
15. See the article "What Happened in Lydda," Chapter 18 in this volume.
16. Dan Giladi, "Indeed, Just a 'Man of Strife'?," *Journal of Israeli History* 26, no. 1 (2007): 91–104.
17. Shabtai Teveth, "History versus Biography," in *Middle Eastern Lives: The Practice of Biography and Self-Narrative*, ed. Martin Kramer (Syracuse: Syracuse University Press, 1991), 111.

20

Who Censored the
Six-Day War?

Shortly after the June 1967 war, a book entitled *Siah Lohamim* ("*Soldiers'
Talk*") appeared in Israel. It consisted of transcripts of tape-recorded
discussions and interviews involving some 140 officers and soldiers,
all kibbutz members. The initiators of these heart-to-hearts were
themselves young kibbutznik intellectuals, most notably the educator
Avraham Shapira and the then-rising young writer Amos Oz.[1]

In the midst of the country's widespread jubilation at its lightning
victory over the combined forces of Egypt, Jordan, and Syria, the tape
recorders had captured the dissenting voices of these fighters. They
spoke of their gut-wrenching fear of combat, the cheapening of life in
war, their revulsion at killing, and their unexpected feelings of identification with the Arab enemy. While most of the kibbutzniks saw the
war as justified, some expressed doubts about the supposed sanctity
of the conquered land, even of Jerusalem, and disgust at the incipient
Israeli occupation. Hovering over it all was the Holocaust—primarily
fear of its reenactment by Arabs against Israel's Jews but also distress
over seeming parallels between some of Israel's actions and those of
the Nazis in the Second World War.

The book struck a chord: *Soldiers' Talk* was a phenomenal success,
selling some 100,000 copies in Israel, and its kibbutznik editors and
participants became minor celebrities, frequently appearing on the
lecture circuit and in the media. Its fame also spread abroad: in the
words of Elie Wiesel, this was "a very great book, very great," thanks
to "its integrity, its candor. No sleights of hand, no masks, no games.
This is the truth, this is how it was."[2] Eventually the book was translated into a half-dozen languages, most notably in an abridged English
version under the title *The Seventh Day: Soldiers' Talk About the Six-
Day War*.[3] The dialogues even provided fodder for a play performed
in New York.

Over the decades, as war followed war, *Soldiers' Talk* was forgotten, or remembered only vaguely as the prototype of a genre mocked by both left and right and known pejoratively as "shooting and crying." Most young Israelis today have never heard of it.

Mor Loushy, an Israeli filmmaker at the start of her career, learned about the book in graduate school. Upon realizing that it drew on recorded conversations, she set out to find the original reel-to-reel tapes. According to a *New York Times* report, she then "cajoled" Avraham Shapira, the "aging kibbutznik and philosophy professor" who had been chief editor of *Soldiers' Talk*, "to share the original audiotaped interviews that he had denied to legions of journalists and historians." Loushy "spent eight months listening to 200 hours of the tapes," identifying the voices and tracking down the former soldiers, now men on the cusp of old age.[4]

In the finished 2015 film, *Censored Voices,* the technique employed by Loushy to bring tapes and veterans together is arresting. The veterans are shown pensively listening to their own voices, recorded nearly a half century ago, but they aren't asked to reflect in retrospect, and there are no experts to fill in gaps. The effect is thus to transport the viewer back in time to 1967, and to create a sensation of eavesdropping on intimate confessions. The play-back of the tapes is overlaid at intervals with footage from 1967, selected to juxtapose the euphoria of victory against the dark side of the war.

The most dramatic moments in the film come when soldiers testify to witnessing or perpetrating acts of brutality tantamount to war crimes. One soldier admits to lining people up and finishing them off: "It's as though we murdered them. Practically, it's war, and every civilian and every person is your enemy." Another: "I knew I had to carry out orders. People were spotted up on the rooftops, I didn't think at all whether they were civilians or not civilians, whether it was necessary to kill them or not. Everyone we see, we kill." Another: "The next day we turned over the last fifty prisoners and at night we killed about fifty guys. The paratroopers let them bury them all and then an officer came up and finished off the rest of the prisoners, quickly, no problems."

Soldiers also tell of expulsions: "We were ordered to carry out what was called evacuation of the inhabitants. You take this Arab, rooted in his village, and turn him into a refugee, just expel him from there, and not just one or two or three. When you see a whole village go, like sheep, wherever they're taken, and there is no sign of resistance, you realize what Holocaust means."

The bottom line, for one reviewer, is that the 1967 war emerges

> not as an Israeli victory against annihilation at the hands of surround-
> ing Arab countries, but as a nation's questionable transformation
> from a defensive David to a Goliath who exiled and murdered Arab
> civilians to the bewilderment of its own troops.[5]

Here, then, is the presumed reality of the 1967 war as experienced by those who fought in it. But did we not already know much if not all of this from *Soldiers' Talk* itself? And if not, why not?

Enter now the promotional claim made by Loushy for her movie— and for her movie's urgent timeliness. "The Israeli army," she writes, "censored the recordings, allowing only a fragment of the conversations to be published" in the book.[6] And because "the Israeli state had censored these conversations, so it also tells the story of fear. We have, as a society, silenced and denied other voices."[7] This being the case, she predicts that "the reemergence of those censored voices in Israeli society will undoubtedly stir a great storm," and declares the special relevance of her film to "the present Israeli reality of our right-wing government still attempting to silence alternative voices."[8]

Loushy even puts a figure on the extent of the alleged suppression. Although the editors had "wanted to publish [these conversations] as a book," she has been quoted as saying, "the Israeli censorship censored 70 percent of what they wanted to publish."[9] In this claim, Shapira himself has backed her up. In a report on Israel's Channel 2, he appears with an open file before him. "Here on my desk is a small portion of 200 hours of transcribed conversations. We made a submission to the censor as was customary and required by law. The material was returned to us with approximately 70 percent of it deleted, completely deleted."[10]

This 70-percent figure has popped up regularly in news items and reviews, duly making an appearance in the American Jewish weeklies *Forward* and *Jewish Journal*: "The Israeli government censored 70 percent of the material. Shapira published the remaining 30 percent in his book."[11] And the figure was picked up by the *Economist*: "70 percent of the interviews were censored at the time by the army, anxious that the soldiers' stories of murdering prisoners, shooting civilians, and deporting Palestinian villagers should not cast a shadow over the glorious victory."[12] The film itself opens with the on-screen assertion that the military allowed only 30 percent of the recordings to be published, the only independent factual claim made in *Censored Voices*.

Is it true? As I watched *Censored Voices* gain momentum in film festivals and the media, something about its back story seemed to me implausible, and on closer examination my suspicions grew. So I followed them. It turns out that the history of *Soldiers' Talk* is far from a simple tale of scandalous state censorship. Rather, there is compelling reason to doubt whether the military censor "brutally" (Loushy's term)[13] censored the conversations, or censored them much at all.

If that is so, as I hope to demonstrate in what follows, then the promotional hype surrounding *Censored Voices* is a deception. And if that is so, it casts into doubt the good faith of the filmmakers. After all, *Censored Voices*, like *Soldiers' Talk*, is itself a product of careful selection. Its director asks us to trust her to have extracted those materials that are both factually sound and broadly representative of the Six-Day War.

Such trust would be sorely misplaced.

Censorship or Self-Censorship?

Any inquiry into the editorial history of *Soldiers' Talk* leads quickly to the work of Alon Gan, a third-generation kibbutznik who today teaches history at the Kibbutzim College of Education. In 2003, Gan completed a Tel Aviv University doctoral thesis on *Soldiers' Talk* with the active assistance of Avraham Shapira himself.[14] According to Gan, Shapira gave him access to the original tapes and transcripts. Here is how a 2005 kibbutz newspaper describes that access:

> [Shapira] opened his private archive to Alon [Gan], his outstanding student, and revealed to him the raw material: tens of audio tapes kept at Yad Tabenkin [the kibbutz movement's archives] and hundreds of pages of transcripts that had turned yellow in his home at [Kibbutz] Yizrael, for preparation of Alon's doctoral thesis.[15]

It was Gan who first discovered and documented the discrepancies between the taped conversations and the first edition of *Soldiers' Talk*. Of course, much of the raw material was bound to be cut anyway. The conversations had produced 200 hours of tape. As one of the project's interviewers would later recall, "most of the shelved tapes didn't make the collection for trivial editorial reasons: narrowness of perspective, space limitations, avoiding endless repetitions. Heart-to-heart conversations took precedence over conversations whose participants had difficulty opening up."[16] "We had a lot of material," said one of the editors, "and just a small part of it went into the book."[17]

Clearly, however, other editorial principles operated as well. Discarded in particular was material that didn't suit the editors' political agenda. Shapira's interviewers, for example, had gone to Merkaz Harav Yeshiva in Jerusalem in the hope of finding religious soldiers troubled by the same doubts that afflicted the secular kibbutzniks. That five-hour conversation included soldiers who would later become some of the leading lights of the settler movement. Amram Hayisraeli, one of the kibbutzniks who participated in this dialogue, would later call it "perhaps the most important conversation" in the project.[18]

But when Amos Oz read the transcript, he broke into a rage: not one of the six religious soldiers "understood the pain, the moral problem, or that there was any problem at all." Oz denounced them as "crude, smug, and arrogant," and "as quite simply, inhuman."[19] Shapira for his part opted to exclude the religious soldiers altogether, and then to dissemble about it: "I decided that the conversations wouldn't be included. . . . I didn't reveal the real reasons to others, and I rationalized it by citing 'technical reasons.'"[20]

But the editors exercised self-censorship on their own side of the political spectrum, too. For instance: some soldiers had expressed either very radical leftist views or mentioned alleged atrocities against Arab civilians and POWs. In the published text, these references had been either eliminated or tucked under a heavy blanket of euphemism. As Gan's dissertation reveals in some detail, the editors specifically tweaked and softened passages alleging actions that could be read as contradictory to the Israeli ideal of "purity of arms" or even as war crimes.

In brief, Shapira and his team carefully massaged the material that would enter the published text. Although Gan speculates that in any case "the external censor would not have permitted the editors to publish" certain materials,

> it can't be denied that the editors [themselves] created a picture that emphasized the positive side and the moral dimension in the soldiers' conduct, and downplayed these descriptions. . . . Different editing of the testimony would have presented the image of some of the soldiers and officers in a different light (or, more precisely, darkness).[21]

"Of course there was censorship," Gan concludes, "most of it by the editors themselves, whether for security reasons, or for societal-public reasons, or out of a sense of responsibility to the interviewees."[22] Above all, in Gan's view, what motivated Shapira and his colleagues to make the cuts was

> a sense of great public responsibility. It was obvious to them that some of the testimony was social dynamite, which should not be published in order not to divert attention from the general atmosphere that the editors wanted to make vivid to the reader.[23]

70 Percent

What happened next? As Gan documents, the "first edit, undertaken by Avraham Shapira [and] done without consideration for external censorship" was printed privately for circulation in kibbutzim. Clearly marked "internal, not for sale," and issued between drab covers in October 1967, it didn't trigger the need for approval by the censor.

But copies soon circulated beyond the kibbutzim, and the editors also sent copies to newsmen and writers. Mentions of the conversations and even excerpts from them began to appear in the press. As interest grew, the editors decided to pursue commercial publication—a step requiring submission of the private edition to the chief military censor, Col. Walter (Avner) Bar-On. There the project became stuck: according to Gan, "the chief censor proposed to delete nearly every politically loaded sentence, every sentence describing moral dilemmas such as looting, treatment of prisoners, refugees, etc."[24]

Had the process ended there, *Soldiers' Talk* would have been gutted. But it didn't end there. In January 1968, the editors contacted the army's chief education officer, Col. Mordechai ("Morele") Bar-On (no relation to Walter/Avner Bar-On), and pleaded for his intervention. Impressed by the project, he took it under his wing, asking the chief of staff, Lt. Gen. Yitzhak Rabin, for permission to assume responsibility for all content that didn't expose military secrets. Rabin agreed, and Mordechai Bar-On became instrumental in seeing the project through censorship.

What deletions did the censor demand? In Shapira's possession, there is a copy of the private edition marked with the many excisions and changes proposed by Walter Bar-On (in green) and the fewer ones suggested by Mordechai Bar-On (in blue). Together these would have made very substantial alterations to an already diluted text, constituting wholesale state censorship. Shapira and Oz rejected the proposed changes in toto; Oz was particularly vehement. A negotiation ensued. "I sat with Mordechai Bar-On," Shapira said in a recent interview, "and together we went over the deletions of the censor, and what we could restore, we restored."[25]

The outcome? Gan saw the copy with the censors' markings, and discovered that almost everything had been restored:

> When one compares the public edition with the proposed changes of the censor [Walter Bar-On] and the proposals of Mordechai Bar-On, with the exception of a few changes, it is apparent that the stubbornness of the initiators of the collection to stick, almost exactly, to the first [private] edition, paid off. Mordechai Bar-On apparently accepted [the editors'] arguments and succeeded in persuading Walter Bar-On to agree to them.[26]

The public edition, released in May 1968, carried the caveat that "minor alterations have been made" upon the editors' judgment; Gan finds the alterations "indeed 'minor.'" His unequivocal conclusion:

> Aside from minor deletions, the public edition was largely if not entirely identical to the private edition. . . . On the basis of this evidence, it is apparent that the role of external censorship was small, in comparison to the censorship imposed by the initiators of the collection before the censor's intervention.[27]

If this is true, it is doubtful that either the chief censor or Mordechai Bar-On ever saw or heard any of the more disturbing allegations made by soldiers in Loushy's film, all of which had been excised in advance by the editors in preparation of the private edition. Gan also quotes remarks to the same effect made in 1968 by the novelist and educator Yariv Ben-Aharon, one of the editors:

> We imposed a severe censorship, we reworked and shortened and cut a lot, and also shelved. The official censorship deleted very little. It's obvious that due to our censorship, there are some flaws in the book, and there are several misses. There are people who speak about killing in general, and the details aren't in the book. This leaves the impression of self-righteousness.[28]

In sum, the claim made by Loushy (and belatedly by Shapira) about massive state censorship of *Soldiers' Talk* is directly contradicted by Gan's in-depth study of the editorial history of the book. It is also directly contradicted by Yariv Ben-Aharon. And the accusation of "brutal" state censorship is similarly contradicted by Mordechai Bar-On, who was intimately involved in steering the text past the censor.

Bar-On, later one of the founders of Peace Now, is still active at eighty-six, and takes some pride in the fact that he managed to get *Soldiers' Talk* through military censorship with few changes. "I became the spokesperson for the book [in the army]," he recently recalled. "Here and there I softened some sentence, but overall, not much."[29] "I don't remember today what we weeded from the text," he has written in his recent autobiography, *Child of the Previous Century:* "not much, and anyway, they were things that the editors understood should be downplayed or softened."[30] When I asked him about the claim that the censor had nixed 70 percent of the material, he scoffed: "Maybe two or three percent."

Mor Loushy never consulted Bar-On, who hadn't even heard of *Censored Voices* when I asked him about it a few weeks after it premiered in Israel.

Making Headlines

The scandal of official censorship, especially by the state of Israel, is headline-making; stringent self-censorship by a kibbutznik editor isn't. That Loushy's film benefits from her narrative of "brutal" censorship goes without saying, and that narrative has been deployed relentlessly in the promotion of *Censored Voices*.

But why has Shapira himself contributed to it? Some context is provided by earlier charges and countercharges in the wake of Gan's research.

Gan's revelations, appearing as they did in an unpublished PhD dissertation, didn't draw attention in 2003. But that changed two years later when the Israeli journalist and historian Tom Segev devoted several pages to *Soldiers' Talk* in his book *1967: Israel, the War, and the Year that Transformed the Middle East.* Segev, relying entirely on Gan's dissertation, accused Shapira and his team of deliberate doctoring. "Parts of the transcripts were altered," he wrote, "in a few cases to the point of distortion, before the book went to press, in order to suit the words to the image of innocent young soldiers, humanists in distress. . . . The editors were careful to avoid distancing the speakers from the national consensus—rather, they did just the opposite, placing them at its forefront and center."[31]

In a subsequent interview, Segev went further: "It's amazing how thoroughly this thing was edited, censored, inauthentic. There was a confluence of interests between society, which needed an image like this, and the kibbutz, which needed an image like this. They invented this thing."[32] Benny Morris echoed the charge in a review of Segev's book: "The original transcripts were altered and censored by the editors. . . [who] managed to create a 'candid,' moving, liberal antiwar text that bore only a partial resemblance to what was actually said in the original conversations."[33]

Suddenly the *editors*, and above all Avraham Shapira, stood publicly accused of tampering with the soldiers' words in order to keep them within acceptable bounds. Shapira, who had been celebrated for initiating *Soldiers' Talk*, now found himself in the dock for bowdlerizing it. "What Tom Segev attributes to me in his book and interview," he replied, "is very hurtful, not only to the credibility of a central area of my work since 1960, but to my own human character."[34] For his part, Gan, on whose dissertation Segev had relied, recoiled at this use of his work: "To attribute to [Shapira] manipulation, distortion, and deliberate myth-making is unfair and incorrect. . . . Segev made claims, in my name, that I didn't intend."[35]

Whether Shapira's editing robbed *Soldiers' Talk* of its integrity is debatable. But one thing is certain: faced with this criticism, he didn't offer the excuse of military censorship. To the contrary, he insisted: "I take upon myself full and total responsibility for the editing of *Soldiers' Talk* in its book form—internal responsibility toward all of the participants, and public responsibility."[36]

Shapira nonetheless learned his lesson. By allowing Gan to compare the book with the original transcripts, he had exposed himself to withering criticism, mostly from Israel's revisionist school of "new historians." In that light, it isn't hard to understand why he later cold-shouldered other journalists and historians anxious to see the original transcripts. As reported by Loushy, "A lot of major news outlets from Israel tried to take [the material] from [Shapira] and so did foreign journalists. He never agreed to give it to anyone."[37] And no wonder: their aim would have been to expose still more gaps between what was said and what was published.

Why, then, did he give that access to Loushy, a recent film graduate with only one earlier production to her name, and a person no less eager to uncover still more gaps? Loushy attributes it to personal chemistry:

> I started chasing after him and at first he didn't answer my calls. Finally I went to a lecture that he gave. Immediately he told me, "OK, come to my kibbutz." From the first moment we met, there was something there. I don't know how but he believed in me and we started this amazing journey together.[38]

This is all very cinematic: the wizened old guru impulsively yields to the importunities of an eager young acolyte, and grants her unconditional access to his locked treasure chest of secrets. Perhaps it's true. Yet Loushy, who desperately needed Shapira's cooperation to make her movie, was evidently prepared to do something today that Alon Gan, in a supervised and refereed PhD dissertation, could never have done in 2003: absolve Shapira of any blame for self-censoring the book.

Did Shapira suggest this to her? Was it her idea? Whatever the precise origins of the claim of a "brutal" 70-percent official censorship, it conveniently lifted the stigma from Shapira. ("Yes, there was censorship," he has said in a new interview, "and it wasn't by us.")[39] It also conferred on Loushy's "scoop" the strong whiff of scandal that attends to official cover-ups. Israel's soldiers not only committed crimes, but Israel's military censor then tried to conceal them. State censorship of atrocity stories can be read as a de facto admission of their veracity.

The Trouble with War Stories

What, then, of the stories told by the soldiers? It would be naive to assume that Israeli soldiers were incapable of committing any of the acts they describe in the film. Expulsions and killings of civilians and even prisoners had precedents in 1948 and 1956. But it would be just as naive to assume that the events unfolded as the soldiers described them.

This is due to the usual trouble with war stories—they mutate and grow in the telling. That isn't a cliché. A body of research, mostly in relation to veterans' claims of post-traumatic stress disorder, has analyzed and quantified the problem. One influential study established that nearly 40 percent of Vietnam veterans who claimed to have experienced combat-related stress hadn't had combat exposure in the first place. They were also the ones who more commonly described having witnessed or committed battlefield atrocities.[40] Sir Simon Wessely, the prominent psychiatrist, has summarized the conclusion this way: "War stories change according to who is doing the telling, who is doing the listening, and why the story is being told now."[41] If one's view is that Israeli soldiers are no more virtuous than other soldiers, one must accept that their testimonies are no more reliable, either.

The historian's solution is to take soldiers' accounts as a point of departure, and then cross-reference them with other sources. The problem with the concept of *Soldiers' Talk* is that it wasn't meant to assemble the evidence that would make this possible. Amos Oz, himself a writer of fiction, set the tone for the project from the beginning: talk not about what you did during the war, he instructed participants, but about what you experienced. "The key word here," Oz recently reminisced, "is what you felt."[42] *Soldiers' Talk* wasn't a project to uncover and document war crimes. It was about eliciting the emotions of the soldiers, in a way more consistent with internal group therapy than with investigation. As a result, the organizers made no effort to collect and corroborate details about specific events, and soldiers gave no names, places, or dates.

Not only does *Censored Voices* make no attempt to fill in the missing details. It further obfuscates the picture. Footage is shown to illustrate some of the claims—bodies of enemy soldiers strewn along the road, refugees trudging with their possessions on their backs—but it isn't actual footage of the scenes described by the speaking soldiers, and it bears no identifying captions.[43] We hear voices making confessions or allegations, but we don't know who is speaking, and the soldiers are identified by name only at the end. ("For the most part," notes one American reviewer, "the men are treated as interchangeable.")[44] In these circumstances, the veracity of any individual allegation is difficult if not impossible to establish.

But let us assume for argument's sake that the actions described in *Censored Voices* took place as described. Let us even assume that the instances Loushy did not include—she claims there are dozens more—have some grain of truth in them. Would this warrant a revision of the way Israel and the world see the 1967 war? Hardly.

Expulsions of Palestinian Arabs? A few instances (above all, villages in the Latrun salient) are well-attested, but no expulsion affected more than a few thousand people, and some of those expelled were allowed to return (most notably, to Qalqiliya). A much larger number, two hundred thousand, left the West Bank of Jordan for the East Bank. A UN special representative who visited in July 1967 said in a report that he had "received no specific reports indicating that persons had been physically forced to cross to the East Bank." After mentioning Israel's claims that it had not "encouraged" their departure, and Arab allegations of brutality and intimidation, the report singled out "the inevitable impact upon a frightened civilian population of hostilities and military occupation as such, particularly when no measures of reassurance are taken."[45] In short, they fled.

When all was said and done, the 1967 war did not result in the massive displacement of Palestinian Arabs that characterized the war of 1948. That earlier war had emptied entire Arab cities: Jaffa, Lydda,

Ramleh. The 1967 war emptied none. Instead, it ended with Israel in occupation of solidly Palestinian Arab territories. *Censored Voices* conveys the impression that 1967 had an impact on the Palestinians similar to 1948, when in fact its character and consequences could not have been more different.

Killings of prisoners and surrendering or fleeing enemy soldiers? These happened, and we can infer it from Yeshayahu Gavish, who was head of Israel's Southern Command in 1967. In a debriefing after the war, he referred to the confusion regarding Egyptian prisoners:

> The blame falls on me, not on the staff. It is true that we didn't know what to do with the prisoners. . . . Our conflict in this war was to destroy the enemy—that was the order, and it is pretty stupid to put in the same sentence, "destroy the enemy" and "take prisoners." It wasn't resolved. It began in the first stage, and later we had to deal with the prisoners, and it became clear that destroying the enemy had a certain meaning, with a huge percentage of them wandering around in the field.[46]

But the confusion didn't last. Israel ultimately took six thousand Egyptian prisoners, and thousands more were sent on their way to the Suez Canal (where, according to some Israeli witnesses, Egyptian forces initially fired on them for retreating). After the war, Israel collected Egyptian stragglers from all over Sinai and sent them home. The International Committee of the Red Cross (ICRC) reported this operation in July 1967:

> A large number of Egyptian soldiers were in dire straits in the Sinai Desert after the cease-fire. The ICRC delegates were active in the rescue operations, responsibility for which was assumed first and foremost by the Israeli authorities. These operations were made difficult by the fact that the territory was enormous and that many of the soldiers were widely dispersed. They had often to be sought by helicopter, sometimes one by one, and supplies had to be taken to them by tank-lorries. Some 12,000 troops were enabled to return to their home country. The conveyance of isolated troops towards the eastern bank of the Suez Canal and then to the other side was continued until, by the end of June, the operation was nearing completion.[47]

"I am not saying there were no aberrations," allowed then-Prime Minister Yitzhak Rabin in 1995, during an earlier round of claims about prisoners killed in the 1967 war. But "these events were real exceptions."[48] Prominent Israeli chroniclers of the war have likewise referred to these as "isolated incidents of Israeli abuses" (Michael Oren) and "isolated acts of abuse" (Yossi Klein Halevi).[49] If this is true, then the high-resolution focus on such cases in *Censored Voices* is wildly disproportionate. "There were ugly things," said one of the original interviewees upon viewing the film, "but to turn them into such a severe situation, it's exaggerated. . . . Suddenly, in the eyes of my grandson, I will seem like someone who kills prisoners and expels people. It's not true."[50]

Do such instances, however many they may be, negate or detract from the Israeli narrative of the necessity and justice of the war? Or are they simply evidence that even necessary and just wars aren't ever waged entirely within the rules? The answer of *Censored Voices* to this question is not all that different from the answer given by Breaking the Silence, an Israeli NGO that collects and disseminates testimony of unnamed Israeli soldiers who claim to have witnessed war crimes. Both seize upon events that may be isolated occurrences and isolate them still further, ripping them from their broader context and waving them like bloodied sheets. If Israel cannot wage perfect war, the premise goes, it must not wage war at all, even in its own defense.

The methodology of *Censored Voices* is even more selective than that of Israel-bashing NGOs. Loushy chose events based on the additional criterion of entertainment value. Danny Sivan, the film's producer (and Loushy's partner) has admitted that they didn't want "stories that just transmit information, but that do something to you in the gut, in order to create an emotional cinematic experience and not just an informative document."[51]

Admittedly, a movie theater isn't the ideal setting for forensic analysis of something so complex as a fast-moving, three-front war that changed Israel and the Middle East. A film is not a book or a PhD dissertation. The problem is that, for many of its viewers, *Censored Voices* is likely to be their only encounter with the 1967 war. How many of them are even capable of setting what they have watched in context? For that matter, how many reviewers are so capable? Given the widespread ignorance of Israel's history, even among Israelis, the number is distressingly small.

Of course, this perfectly suits Israel's critics at home and abroad. After almost fifty years of "occupation," they are so embittered that they will automatically retail the worst about Israel's conduct in 1967 without so much as a caveat. If the occupation is an ongoing sin, then it must have been conceived in original sin. Not only does *Censored Voices* benefit from this suspension of critical judgment. It depends on it.

Whither Public Responsibility?

An Israeli columnist, reacting to the film, has written that Loushy's "naiveté exceeds that of a flower child from the 1960s."[52]

Far from it. Every Israeli who hopes to earn fame by making documentaries knows there is a persistent demand for films exposing Israel's misdeeds, especially if they are attested by Israelis themselves. And nothing is so marketable as a story exposing crimes covered up by the state itself. The formula is irresistible to film-festival directors, high-brow European television channels, and the *New York Times*. Loushy, a graduate of Israel's best-known film school, aimed her film with manipulative precision. Her savvy grasp of the market explains her single-minded selection of content and, more importantly, her steady propagation of the "brutal" censorship meme, seemingly made more credible by giving it a number.

In fact, as I have shown, the claim detracts from the credibility of the film. The voices in *Censored Voices* weren't censored, they were heavily redacted, and by the very man, Avraham Shapira, whom Mor Loushy warmly embraced on the stage at the Tel Aviv premiere. "If those voices had been published in 1967," Loushy told the *New York Times*, "maybe our reality here would be different."[53] That's an open question. But she has deliberately deflected her complaint onto the wrong party.

Behind this deception lurks the really interesting back story of *Soldiers' Talk*. Muki Tzur, another of the book's editors, has recalled that in 1967, "the country still had the aspect of an underground society that kept its secrets, believing in the value of self-censorship."[54] Once upon a time, Israel's intellectual elites, even on the left, still felt enough public responsibility to restrain themselves. Now their successors are busy elves in a cottage industry catering to the world's critics of Israel—doubters, defamers, delegitimizers.

It's not only that they broadcast unsubstantiated claims and strip away all context. They also go on to spew bogus accusations of "silencing" and "censoring"—to create the impression that the state of Israel is engaged in the massive cover-up of crimes. The agonized soldiers, the forgotten tapes, and the memorable numbers are all vehicles to deliver this message: Israel is guilty. It is too late for individuals to be tried for these crimes, but there must be atonement. For Loushy, that atonement is self-evident: Israel must end the "occupation." Only thus can it cleanse itself of sins.

The ascendence of this argument in the Israeli mainstream left isn't accidental. The Second Intifada, the debacle of Gaza, Palestinian refusal to talk—all of these have undercut the rationale for peace as a transaction between Israelis and Palestinians. How can Israelis and Jews be persuaded that a Palestinian state is still an urgent necessity—so much so that it might even justify unilateral withdrawal? Some invoke demography, but others instill guilt. Yes, a Palestinian state is a huge risk. Yes, there is no partner. Yes, the rockets may fall. Yes, the blood may flow. But if we end the "occupation," we will cleanse ourselves of guilt. If this is the aim of such revelations, then the desired effect is only enhanced by exaggerating the "crimes," ripping them out of context, and claiming they were somehow covered up.

This is the present-day purpose of such historical exposés. (Ari Shavit's treatment of Lydda in 1948 is another example.) But that isn't necessarily their present-day effect. Israel's critics adduce the claims of Loushy as evidence that Israel repeatedly commits and covers up the same crimes. A reviewer of Loushy's film insists that "year after year since 1967, including in recent weeks, Palestinians, with faces and names, are still expelled, imprisoned without trial and killed."[55] Incredibly, Loushy is oblivious to this use of her work: "I find it difficult to believe that someone would attack Israel because of the film."[56] She grossly underestimates the resourcefulness of Israel's enemies, who will mine any vein for historical evidence of Israeli misdeeds and then deploy it to condemn Israel in the present.

This isn't a reason to avoid research critical of Israel's history. It is a reason to establish facts scrupulously, from a full range of sources, and put them in broader context. That is primarily the work of historians, but famed novelists and beginning directors don't get a pass.

Notes

1. Avraham Shapira, *Siah Lohamin: Pirke Hakshavah ve-Hitbonenut* ([Tel Aviv]: Kevutsat Haverim Tze'irim meha-Tenu'ah ha-Kibbutzit, 1968).
2. Interview with Elie Wiesel, *Ha'aretz*, March 28, 1969 (Friday supplement).
3. English abridged version: Avraham Shapira, *The Seventh Day: Soldiers' Talk about the Six Day War* (New York: Scribner, 1971).
4. Jodi Rudoren, "Disillusioned by War, Israeli Soldiers Muted in 1967 Are Given Fuller Voice," *New York Times*, January 25, 2015.
5. Chandra Johnson, "With New Eyes: Sundance Films Look Back at Age-Old Conflicts," *Deseret News National*, February 2, 2015.
6. *Censored Voices* website, archived at http://web.archive.org/web/20150101024126/http://www.censoredvoices.com/about.

7. Mor Loushy interviewed by Jena Keahon, *Indiewire*, January 29, 2015, archived at http://web.archive.org/web/20150429030231/http://www. indiewire.com/article/meet-the-2015-sundance-filmmakers-50-mor- loushy-assembled-censored-voices-out-of-secret-radical-conversa- tions-20150129.

8. Mor Loushy interview, *Filmmaker*, January 24, 2015, archived at http://web. archive.org/web/20150202083215/http://filmmakermagazine.com/92669- the-israeli-public-will-find-it-hard-to-confront-our-misconduct-censored- voices-director-mor-loushy/.

9. Michael Roddy, "Israeli Film Gives Voice to Soldiers' Self-Doubts After '67 War," Reuters, February 11, 2015.

10. Tzion Nanus, television report, Israel Channel 2, broadcast May 30, 2015.

11. This was via the report from Sundance by Anthony Weiss for the Jewish Telegraphic Agency, which ran in the *Forward* and the *Journal*, as well as the *Times of Israel* and *Ha'aretz*. See Anthony Weiss, "'Censored Voices' of '67 War Speak Out at Sundance," *Forward*, February 2, 2015, archived at http://web.archive.org/web/20150520222242/http://forward.com/the-as- similator/213913/censored-voices-of-67-war-speak-out-at-sundance/.

12. "War, Then and Now," *Economist*, May 18, 2015.

13. Loushy quoted on the film PR website *Noise*, archived at http://web. archive.org/web/20151218104509/http://noisefilmpr.com/portfolio/cen- sored-voices.

14. Alon Gan, "Ha-Siah she-Gava? 'Tarbut ha-Sihim' ke-Nisayon le-Gibush Zehut Meyahedet la-Dor ha-Sheni ba-Kibbutzim" (PhD diss., Tel Aviv University, 2002).

15. Arnon Lapid, "Siah ha-Emet ve-ha-Sheker," Kibbutz Movement website, June 30, 2005, archived at http://web.archive.org/web/20151218110020/ http://www.kibbutz.org.il/itonut/2005/shonot/050630_segev.htm.

16. Comment by Shulamit Tana in a thread on *Censored Voices*, forum of *The Marker*, April 30, 2015, archived at http://web.archive.org/ web/20151218110428/http://cafe.themarker.com/post/3218838/.

17. Amram Hayisraeli, remarks at a conference on the Six-Day War held by the Israeli Galili Center for Defense Studies, February 3, 1987, transcript in Yad Tabenkin Archives, Ramat Efal, item no. 182725.

18. Televised news report by Avital Livne-Levi, "Siah Lohamim 2007," *Mabat Sheni*, Israel Channel 1, June 5, 2007, posted at https://www.youtube.com/ watch?v=jXhsTaA-t3U, accessed December 18, 2015.

19. Amos Oz, *In the Land of Israel* (rev. ed; Orlando: Harcourt, 1993), 133. See also Amnon Barzilai, "Kach Nignaz 'Siah Lohamim' shel Merkaz Harav," *Ha'aretz*, June 16, 2002.

20. Gan, "Ha-Siah," 111.

21. Ibid., 123.

22. Lapid, "Siah Ha-Emet."

23. Gan, "Ha-Siah," 115.

24. Ibid., 113.

25. Abraham Shapira interviewed by Yaakov Bar-On, *Ma'ariv*, June 4, 2015.

26. Gan, "Ha-Siah," 113.

27. Ibid., 115.

28. Yariv Ben-Aharon interviewed by Bashan Rafael, *Ma'ariv*, July 12, 1968.

29. Mordechai Bar-On interviewed by Yair Sheleg, *Makor Rishon,* December 26, 2014 (weekend supplement).
30. Mordechai Bar-On, *Ben ha-Me'ah she-Avra: Autobiografia* (Jerusalem: Carmel, 2011), 341.
31. Tom Segev, *1967: Israel, the War, and the Year that Transformed the Middle East* (New York: Metropolitan Books, 2007), 444, 447. The Hebrew original first appeared in 2005.
32. *Yedi'ot Aharonot,* June 3, 2005.
33. Benny Morris, "Provocations," *The New Republic,* July 23, 2007.
34. Lapid, "Siah Ha-Emet."
35. Ibid.
36. Ibid.
37. Mor Loushy interviewed by Kevin Ritchie, *Realscreen,* February 12, 2015, archived at http://web.archive.org/web/20150216203751/http://realscreen. com/2015/02/12/berlinale-15-mor-loushy-unearths-censored-voices/.
38. Ibid.
39. Abraham Shapira interviewed by Yaakov Bar-On, *Ma'ariv,* June 4, 2015.
40. B. C. Frueh et al., "Documented Combat Exposure of US Veterans Seeking Treatment for Combat-Related Post-Traumatic Stress," *British Journal of Psychiatry* 186 (June 2005): 467–72.
41. Simon Wessely, "War Stories," *British Journal of Psychiatry* 186 (June 2005): 473.
42. Amos Oz interview by Gili Izikovich, *Ha'aretz,* June 6, 2015.
43. A disclaimer at the end of the film explains that the archival film is illustrative and does not depict the specific events described by the soldiers.
44. Ben Keningsberg, review of *Censored Voices, Variety,* January 29, 2015, archived at http://web.archive.org/web/20150426110051/http:// variety.com/2015/film/reviews/sundance-film-review-censored- voices-1201417616.
45. *Report of the Secretary-General under General Assembly resolution 2252 (ES-V) and Security Council resolution 237 (1967),* October 2, 1967, at stable url http://hdl.handle.net/11176/77081.
46. Document quoted by Yossi Mdrisovic, "Aluf Pikud ha-Darom Hizhir be-Sikum Milhemet Sheshet Ha-Yamim: 'Tzarich La'asot Yoter,'" *Yedi'ot Aharonot,* June 4, 2015.
47. "The ICRC and the War in the Near East," *International Review of the Red Cross* (Geneva) 7, no. 76 (July 1967): 349.
48. "Rabin Rejects Any Probe of Alleged Israeli War Crimes," *Los Angeles Times,* August 21, 1995.
49. Michael B. Oren, "Unfriendly Fire," *The New Republic,* July 23, 2001; Halevi quoted by Rudoren, "Disillusioned by War."
50. Tzion Nanus, television report, Israel Channel 2, broadcast May 30, 2015.
51. Daniel Sivan interviewed by Avner Shavit, *Walla News,* June 7, 2015, archived at http://web.archive.org/web/20150609230454/http://e.walla. co.il/item/2860608.
52. Gabi Avital, "War Stories Seized by Moral Purists," *Israel Hayom,* June 1, 2005, archived at http://web.archive.org/web/20150719012311/http://www. israelhayom.com/site/newsletter_opinion.php?id=12737.
53. Rudoren, "Disillusioned by War."

54. Muki Tzur, "Otzar ha-Ruah shel Pachi," Muki Tzur personal website, October 14, 2014, archived at http://web.archive.org/web/20151218184044/ http://mukitsur.co.il/%D7%90%D7%95%D7%A6%D7%A8-%D7%94%D7%A8%D7%95%D7%97-%D7%A4%D7%A6%D7%99.

55. Ilan Pappe, "New Evidence from 1967 War Reveals Israeli Atrocities," *Electronic Intifada*, June 23, 2015, archived at http://web.archive.org/ web/20150726213806/https://electronicintifada.net/content/new-evidence-1967-war-reveals-israeli-atrocities/14635.

56. Mor Loushy interviewed by Ely Zuzovsky, *Bamahane*, June 18, 2015.

Part V

Elders of Zion

21

The *Exodus* Conspiracy

Exodus by Leon Uris must rank high on any list of the most influential books about the Middle East. The novel, published in 1958, popularized the story of Israel's birth among millions of American readers. The 1960 film, based on the book and starring Paul Newman as Ari Ben Canaan, reached many more millions. *Exodus* is still of interest, not for what it says about the creation of Israel (the commander of the ship Exodus said Uris "wrote a very good novel, but it had nothing to do with reality. *Exodus*, shmexodus"),[1] but for what it reveals about mid-twentieth-century America. So more inquiry into the American context of *Exodus* is welcome—provided you get the facts right.

In September 2010, Rashid Khalidi, the Edward Said Professor of Arab Studies at Columbia University,[2] offered his audiences an account of how Leon Uris came to write the book. In a speech at Brooklyn Law School, Khalidi made this claim:

> This carefully crafted propaganda was the work of seasoned professionals. People like someone you probably never heard of, a man named Edward Gottlieb, for example. He's one of the founders of the modern public relations industry. There are books about him as a great advertiser.
>
> In order to sell the great Israeli state to the American public many, many decades ago, Gottlieb commissioned a successful, young novelist. A man who was a committed Zionist, a fellow with the name of Leon Uris. He funded him and sent him off to Israel to write a book. This book was *Exodus: A Novel of Israel*. Gottlieb's gambit succeeded brilliantly. *Exodus* sold as many copies as *Gone With the Wind*, which up to that point was the greatest best-seller in U.S. history. *Exodus* was as good a melodrama and sold just as many copies.[3]

Khalidi made a similar assertion in another speech a few weeks later, this time at the Palestine Center in Washington:

> Now, I think it's worth noting that this book was not the unaided fruit of the loins as it were, the intellectual loins of Leon Uris. He wrote

245

it, of course, but the book was commissioned by a renowned public relations professional, a man who was in fact considered by many to be the founder of public relations in the United States, a fellow by the name of Edward Gottlieb, who desired to improve Israel's image, and who chose Uris to write the novel after his successful first novel on World War II, and who secured the funding which paid for Uris's research and trip to Israel. Given that many of the basic ideas about Palestine and Israel held by generations of Americans find their origin either in this trite novel or the equally clichéd movie, Gottlieb's inspiration to send Leon Uris to Israel may have constituted one of the greatest advertising triumphs of the twentieth century. The man deserves his place in the public relations pantheon.[4]

A Myth Unravels

Khalidi warned his Brooklyn audience that Gottlieb would be "someone you probably never heard of." Quite right: I regard myself as reasonably informed about the history of American Zionism, and I had never heard of Edward Gottlieb. Khalidi claimed there were "books about him as a great advertiser," so I did a search, but I couldn't find one. When Gottlieb died in 1998, at the age of eighty-eight, no major newspaper ran an obituary. That seemed to me a rather scant trail for "the father of the American iteration of Zionism" and "the founder of public relations in the United States."

One reason for the thin record, I discovered, is that Edward Gottlieb wasn't the founder or even one of the founders of American public relations. He had been a journalist in the 1930s, and in 1940 joined the long-established public relations firm of a true founder, Carl Byoir.[5] After Pearl Harbor, Gottlieb did radio and informational work for the war effort in the European theater of operations. In 1948 he opened his own shop, Edward Gottlieb and Associates, which grew into a respected mid-size firm, focused primarily on products. Most notably, Gottlieb popularized French champagne and cognac in the United States. When he sold his company in 1976 to a bigger competitor, it ranked sixteenth in size among PR firms in America. He seems to have been well-regarded, but he was not dominant in the business. If the *Encyclopedia of Public Relations* constitutes "the public relations pantheon," then Gottlieb is noticeable only by his absence.[6]

Gottlieb is likewise completely absent from works on American Zionism—there isn't a single reference. Moreover, his name does not appear in the two scholarly studies of Leon Uris: Matt Silver's *Our Exodus: Leon Uris and the Americanization of Israel's Founding Story,*[7] and Ira Nadel's *Leon Uris: Life of a Best Seller*.[8] I wrote to both authors, asking them whether they had encountered the name of Edward Gottlieb in Uris's personal papers, housed at the University of Texas and cited extensively in both studies. Silver wrote back that "I didn't see anything about Edward Gottlieb,"[9] and Nadel answered that "I never came across G[ottlieb]'s name."[10]

Both biographers are in agreement that the idea for a novel on Israel originated with Uris (encouraged by Dore Schary, a Jewishly-active Hollywood executive); that Uris's agent Malcolm Stuart pushed him to realize his plan; that Uris successfully shopped the idea in Hollywood studios and New York publishing houses; and that his research trip to Israel in 1956 was financed by advances on the film rights and book from MGM and Random House. (United Artists and Doubleday subsequently acquired the rights.) The contracts and correspondence are preserved in Uris's papers. And the Gottlieb "commission"? Silver wrote to me that "my feeling is that this reference could be a complete canard."[11] Nadel wrote to me that "the story is a complete fabrication."[12]

Khalidi was trained as a historian, so I figured he would not have concocted the Gottlieb story out of whole cloth. He must have had a source. As it happens, the Gottlieb claim figures in three books that are classics in the Israel-bashing canon. In *Deliberate Deceptions* (1993), Paul Findley wrote that *Exodus* "was actually commissioned by the New York public relations firm of Edward Gottlieb."[13] In *Fifty Years of Israel* (1998), Donald Neff wrote that Gottlieb "hit upon the idea of hiring a writer to go to Israel and write an heroic novel about the new country. The writer was Leon Uris."[14] And in *Perceptions of Palestine* (1999), Kathleen Christison wrote that Gottlieb "selected Uris, and sent him to Israel" in an "astute public-relations scheme."[15]

And on what source did Findley, Neff, and Christison rely? All of them referenced a 1985 how-to book on public relations, *The Persuasion Explosion: Your Guide to the Power and Influence of Contemporary Public Relations* by Arthur Stevens, a public relations professional. This is a breezy advice book full of PR do's and don't's, which no one would mistake for a history of the business. (A typical chapter title: "Success DOES Smell Sweet.") Stevens in his book relates the Gottlieb story to illustrate a point:

> The cleverest public relations in the world cannot successfully promote, for any length of time, a poor cause or a poor product. By contrast, skillful public relations can speed up the acceptance of a concept

whose time has come. A striking example of this involved eminent public relations consultant Edward Gottlieb. In the early 1950s, when the newly formed State of Israel was struggling for recognition in the court of world opinion, America was largely apathetic. Gottlieb, who at the time headed his own public relations firm, suddenly had a hunch about how to create a more sympathetic attitude toward Israel. He chose a writer and sent him to Israel with instructions to soak in the atmosphere of the country and create a novel about it. The book turned out to be *Exodus*, by Leon Uris.[16]

So this is the origin of the Gottlieb story: an example in a how-to book. Even so, I wondered how Stevens came to write this paragraph. Did he have a published source or documentary evidence? Was this part of the folklore of the business? So I tracked Stevens down and asked him. In an e-mailed reply, he told me that he had interviewed Gottlieb, "whom I knew well at the time," around 1984:

> The comments he made to me during my interview of him were those that went into the book. It wasn't hearsay I made use of or the reporting of prevailing folklore floating through the public relations world at the time. What I reported is what he actually told me during my interview. Obviously, I cannot vouch for the accuracy or reliability of what he said.[17]

So this was not a claim based on any document or even part of PR lore. It was Gottlieb himself who told Stevens the story of how he supposedly chose Uris and sent him to Israel. "I didn't get that information from any other source," Stevens wrote me, "but directly from the horse's mouth."[18] Ultimately, Gottlieb is the sole source of the Gottlieb story—told by him twenty-eight years after Uris set off for Israel.

Gottlieb and Israel

But this still left a question. Since Gottlieb doesn't appear in any account of American Zionism, why would he expect such a claim to be credible? "Only Edward Gottlieb would know if what he told me was true," Stevens wrote me. But that wasn't so, because there was a living witness to Gottlieb's own operations: Charlotte Klein, one of the first women to reach the top rungs of a public relations firm. Klein worked for Edward Gottlieb and Associates from 1951 to 1962, making vice president in 1955.

Klein had been the subject of a short academic study, and there I finally found evidence for some connection between Gottlieb and Israel. The Government of Israel became a Gottlieb client in 1955;

Charlotte Klein managed the account, and even traveled to Israel that year.[19] This was about the time Uris began to take his book and film proposal around New York and Hollywood. Could the Gottlieb story still contain a grain of truth?

The study of Klein noted that she was still active at the age of eighty-eight and living in Manhattan. So I wrote to Klein informing her of Khalidi's claim that Gottlieb had commissioned Uris to write *Exodus*. I received this reply:

> I was in charge of the Israel account at Edward Gottlieb and Associates and if Ed had ever talked to Uris about Israel I would have known it. As a matter of fact, Ed sought the Israel account because of me. I was one of his top employees and I told him that I was going to leave because I wanted to do work that was socially significant and would seek a job at the United Nations. He didn't want me to leave and called me from outside the office soon after and said "Is the Government of Israel socially significant enough?" I stayed with him and handled the account which we kept for several years. There was never a discussion about Uris or regarding a possible book about Israel.[20]

When I told her that Stevens said he had heard the story from Gottlieb, she added this:

> 1984, of course, is a long time from 1955 and Ed may have met Uris and felt he influenced him. However, there never was money enough on the account for Ed to "commission" anyone to write a book. I am also pretty sure that Ed would have bragged about meeting and talking to Uris if this happened. He would have asked me to come up with some ideas of what Uris ought to cover. I would have had a meeting of my staff on the Israel account and would have drawn up a plan to include people in Israel for Uris to contact. As part of our work for Israel we did suggest mainly to media people to go to Israel to write about any special events going on there or to cover specific news that was happening there.[21]

So Charlotte Klein, who handled the Israel account for Gottlieb, was unequivocal: Gottlieb did not commission *Exodus*, and the name of Leon Uris never came up in the Israel work of the firm.

I could have stopped my pursuit here, but I decided to go one more lap. Perhaps there was some record of the Gottlieb-Israel relationship in official Israeli records? So I paid a visit to the Israel State Archives in Jerusalem, and found the Israeli foreign ministry files related to Gottlieb. These include contracts, reports, budgets, invoices, and press clippings, all awaiting a future historian.[22]

The documents explain the relationship in detail. Gottlieb's firm had a subentity, Intercontinental Public Relations, Inc. (ICPR), with offices in Washington and New York. The subentity did work that required foreign agent registration. Israel's contracts with ICPR ran for two years (an initial year and one renewal), from February 1, 1955 through January 31, 1957. The relationship was handled on Israel's end by Harry (Yehuda) Levin, counselor at the Israeli embassy in Washington. The PR firm's biggest coups involved *Life* magazine. This included arranging a meeting between visiting Prime Minister Moshe Sharett and the top executives of *Life*, resulting in a *Life* editorial strongly critical of the Arab refusal to accept Israel.[23] This was the firm's biggest score, but Klein also worked to place Israel-related stories in magazines, newspapers, and trade journals.

The record shows that Israeli officials saw such outsourcing of PR as a (pricey) stopgap, until these tasks could be assumed by professionally-trained Israelis (and soon enough they were). The files make fascinating reading for anyone interested in the early history of Israeli public relations in America—but they do not contain a single mention of Leon Uris.

The Purpose of Myth

In sum, the Gottlieb "commission" never happened. Uris's biographers dismiss it, Gottlieb's most knowledgeable associate denies it, and no documents in Uris's papers or Israeli archives testify to it. It originated as a boast by Gottlieb to another PR man, made almost thirty years after the (non-)fact. And given its origin, it is precisely the sort of story a serious professional historian would never repeat as fact without first vetting it (as I did).

Yet it persists in the echo chamber of anti-Israel literature, where it has been copied over and over. In Kathleen Christison's book, it finally appeared under the imprimatur of a university press (California). In Khalidi's lectures, it acquired a baroque elaboration, in which Edward Gottlieb emerges as "the father of the American iteration of Zionism" and architect of "one of the greatest advertising triumphs of the twentieth century."

What is the myth's appeal? Why is the truth about the genesis of *Exodus* so difficult to grasp? Why should Khalidi think the Gottlieb story is, in his coy phrase, "worth noting"?

Because if you believe in Zionist mind-control, you must always assume the existence of a secret mover who (as Khalidi said) "you probably never heard of" and who must be a professional expert in deception. This "seasoned" salesman conceives of *Exodus* as a "gambit" (Khalidi) or a "scheme" (Christison). There is no studio or publisher's advance, only a "commission," which qualifies the book as "propaganda"—an "advertising triumph." In Khalidi's Brooklyn Law School talk, he added that "the process of selling Israel didn't stop with Gottlieb. . . . It has continued unabated since then." It was Khalidi's purpose to cast *Exodus*, like the case for Israel itself, as a "carefully crafted" sales job by Madison Avenue "madmen." Through their mediation, Israel has hoodwinked America.

In fact, the deception lies elsewhere. *Exodus*, novel and book, was universally understood to be a work of fiction. In contrast, Rashid Khalidi claimed to speak in the name of history—that is, carefully validated truth. "I'm a historian," he once said. "What I can do best for the reader or audience is provide a background for which to see the present, not tell them about the present."[24] Again: "I'm a historian and I try not to speculate about the future."[25] And this: "I'm a historian, and I look at the way idealism has tended to operate, and it's not a pretty picture."[26] Once again: "I'm a historian, it's not my job to attack or defend anybody."[27]

Khalidi insistently claimed the status of an objective historian—someone whose opinions rest on facts subjected to professional investigation. In the Gottlieb case, however, Khalidi showed himself as someone eager to repeat and embellish a story simply because of its political utility, without even a cursory check of its historical veracity. That is standard operating procedure for a PLO spokesman (Khalidi's earlier vocation).[28] It is literary license in a novelist. It is malpractice in a historian.

Notes

1. Ruthie Blum Leibowitz, "Leon Uris 'Exodus' Novel Had Nothing to Do with Reality, Skipper Said," *Jerusalem Post*, December 26, 2009.
2. See the favorable profile by Chris Hedges, "Casting Mideast Violence in Another Light," *New York Times*, April 20, 2004.
3. Transcript of a lecture, by Rashid Khalidi, Brooklyn Law School, September 22, 2010, by Sherry Wolf, "Madmen for Israel: Selling Zionism," *Sherry Talks Back* blog, archived at http://web.archive.org/web/20101030060202/http://sherrytalksback.wordpress.com/2010/09/24/madmen-for-israel-selling-zionism/.
4. Transcript of the 2010 Edward Said Memorial Lecture by Rashid Khalidi, October 7, 2010, archived at https://web.archive.org/web/20101011123144/http://thejerusalemfund.org/ht/display/ContentDetails/i/16422.
5. "Carl R. Byoir: A Retrospective," The Museum of Public Relations website, archived at https://web.archive.org/web/20150226085307/http://prvisionaries.com/byoir/cbintro.html.

6. *Encyclopedia of Public Relations*, ed. Robert L. Heath (Thousand Oaks, CA: Sage, 2004). This encyclopedia has fifty-five entries devoted to individual "practitioners." Gottlieb is not among them.

7. Matt Silver, *Our Exodus: Leon Uris and the Americanization of Israel's Founding Story* (Detroit: Wayne State University Press, 2010).

8. Ira Nadel, *Leon Uris: Life of a Best Seller* (Austin: University of Texas Press, 2010).

9. Email from Matt Silver to the author, November 11, 2010.

10. Email from Ira Nadel to the author, November 13, 2010.

11. Email from Matt Silver to the author, November 11, 2010.

12. Email from Ira Nadel to the author, November 13, 2010.

13. Paul Findley, *Deliberate Deceptions: Facing the Facts about the U.S.-Israeli Relationship* (Chicago: Lawrence Hill Books, 1993), xxv.

14. Donald Neff, *Fifty Years of Israel* (Washington, DC: American Educational Trust, 1998), 19.

15. Kathleen Christison, *Perceptions of Palestine: Their Influence on U.S. Middle East Policy* (Berkeley: University of California Press, 1999), 103.

16. Arthur Stevens, *The Persuasion Explosion: Your Guide to the Power and Influence of Contemporary Public Relations* (Washington, DC: Acropolis Books, 1985), 105.

17. Email from Arthur Stevens to the author, November 27, 2010.

18. Ibid.

19. Diana Martinelli and Elizabeth Toth, "Lessons on the Big Idea and Public Relations: Reflections on the 50-Year Career of Charlotte Klein," *Public Relations Journal* 4, no. 1 (Winter 2010): 334–50.

20. Email from Charlotte Klein to the author, November 25, 2010.

21. Email from Charlotte Klein to the author, November 29, 2010.

22. The following four files in the Israel State Archives: ISA/RG93.8/MFA/397/2, ISA/RG93.8/MFA/397/3, ISA/RG93.8/MFA/397/4, and ISA/RG93.8/MFA/397/5.

23. "Israel Is Here to Stay: Unless the Arabs Accept This, There Can Be No Peace," *Life Magazine*, March 19, 1956.

24. Quoted by Dana Al-Qadi, "Expert on Middle East Urges Change in U.S. Mindset," *The Online Gargoyle*, April 8, 2007, archived at https://web.archive.org/web/20111016093633/http://www.uni.illinois.edu/og/2007/04/rashid_khalidi_speaks_at_illin.htm.

25. Quoted by Jonathan Shainin, "Nation building," *Salon.com*, December 18, 2006, archived at http://web.archive.org/web/20121021122359/http://www.salon.com/2006/12/18/khalidi/.

26. Quoted by Eyal Press, "The Left Gets Real," *The Nation*, August 14, 2006.

27. Quoted by Joshua Steinman, "University Professors Labeled anti-Israeli by Campus Watch site," *Chicago Maroon*, October 29, 2002.

28. Martin Kramer, "Khalidi of the PLO," *Sandbox* blog, October 30, 2008, archived at http://web.archive.org/web/20150922001709/http://martinkramer.org/sandbox/2008/10/khalidi-of-the-plo/.

22

In the Words of
Martin Luther King

As the veneration of Martin Luther King, Jr. has deepened in America, he has been recruited posthumously to more causes. This is encouraged by his memorial in Washington. Inscribed on the pedestal of King's statue, and on the walls of the surrounding enclosure, are quotations attributed to King. Although he spoke all of these words in specific contexts, they are assembled as though they convey eternal verities, much like the biblical passages which King himself quoted. What would King think about this or that matter in the present? Just conjure up a quote from King in the past.

Both Israelis and Palestinians (and their supporters) are avid recruiters of King, presuming that something he once said more than half a century ago justifies this claim or that policy today. This appropriation is done piecemeal, perhaps because there is no comprehensive study of King's views on the Middle East. As a result, not a few errors and omissions of fact mar most efforts to press King's ghost into service.

Many of these surround the events of 1967, the year before King's assassination. The Six-Day War fully mobilized many of the American Jews who had embraced the civil rights struggle and who marched with King. They now looked to King in the expectation that he would show his support for the cause of Israel. At the same time, the war broke out at a time when King's leadership was being challenged by the militant Student Nonviolent Coordinating Committee (SNCC). SNCC strongly sympathized with the Arabs, and took a stand against Israel in the war's aftermath. King, a Nobel Peace Prize laureate and a pacifist, found himself caught between these antagonistic forces, and torn by the war and its consequences.[1]

King supported Israel's right to exist, and said so repeatedly. "Israel's right to exist as a state in security is incontestable," he once wrote. And this: "The whole world must see that Israel must exist and has the right to exist, and is one of the great outposts of democracy in the world."[2]

But did he support Israel in the war? Why didn't he visit Israel? And did he really say that anti-Zionism was tantamount to antisemitism? These three questions have given rise to discussion, much of it marred by factual errors. The questions cannot possibly be answered, unless and until the errors are corrected.

The Six-Day War

Did King support Israel in the 1967 war? The belief that he did rests in part upon his signing a statement by prominent Christian theologians that began to circulate on May 28, 1967, and that eventually appeared as an advertisement in the *New York Times* on June 4, the day before Israel went to war. At the time the statement was formulated, the Johnson administration seemed to have left Israel to face its enemies alone.

Entitled "The Moral Responsibility in the Middle East," the statement found the Middle East to be "on the brink of war."

> President Nasser of Egypt has initiated a blockade of an international waterway, the Straits of Tiran, Israel's sea lane to Africa and Asia. This blockade may lead to a major conflagration.
>
> The Middle East has been an area of tension due to the threat of continuing terrorist attacks, as well as the recent Arab military mobilization along Israel's borders. Let us recall that Israel is a new nation whose people are still recovering from the horror and decimation of the European holocaust.

The statement went on to "call on the United States government steadfastly to honor its commitments to the freedom of international waterways. We call on our fellow Americans of all persuasions and groupings and on the administration to support the independence, integrity, and freedom of Israel. Men of conscience all over the world bear a moral responsibility to support Israel's right of passage through the Straits of Tiran."

Among the endorsers of this statement were the renowned theologian and ethicist Reinhold Niebuhr (a steadfast supporter of Israel), and John C. Bennett, theologian and president of the Union Theological Seminary (who initiated the statement).[3] Distinguished they may have been, but in an article about the statement in the *New York Times,* there was only one subheading: "Dr. King Among Signers."[4]

By any objective reading, this statement was a call—perhaps even a call to arms—to the United States to stand by Israel. The reaction was swift in coming. "What is saddening," wrote one critic in a letter to the *New York Times* on June 2, "is that respected public leaders like Martin Luther King who have courageously opposed American actions in Vietnam should now associate themselves with vague calls for American intervention on behalf of Israel."[5] Not only did King stand accused of abandoning his antiwar pacifism. He was thought to have ignored the claims of the Arabs, a perception that has persisted. For example, as recently as 2010, Ussama Makdisi, a prominent Arab-American historian, criticized King's signing of the "Moral Responsibility" statement:

> That a man like Martin Luther King could stand so openly with Israel, despite his own private qualms and criticism by younger, more radical, black Americans who had discovered the plight of the Palestinians, indicated the degree to which Zionism was embraced by the American mainstream. . . . One of the ways [King] reciprocated Jewish American support for desegregation in the United States was by turning a blind eye to the plight of the Palestinians.[6]

Makdisi thus spread the notion that at a crucial moment in 1967, King suspended his conscience to cut a deal with the Jews.

But did the "Moral Responsibility" statement accurately reflect King's position? King claimed in private that he never saw the text as published, and would not have signed it if he had. This is documented by the FBI wiretaps of Stanley Levison, one of King's advisers, whose communist past made him a target of government surveillance. The declassified transcripts contain the verbatim record of conference calls conducted among King, Levison, and two other confidants, activist Andrew Young and legal counsel Harry Wachtel.

On June 6, 1967, the day after the war began, King said this to his associates:

> Did you see the ad in the *New York Times* Sunday [June 4]? This was the ad they got me to sign with [John C.] Bennett, etc. I really hadn't seen the statement. I felt after seeing it, it was a little unbalanced and it is pro-Israel. It put us in the position almost of setting the turning-hawks on the Middle East while being doves in Vietnam and I wouldn't have given a statement like that at all.

None of King's advisers asked him how his name wound up on a statement he "really hadn't seen," but they instead looked ahead. Levison urged him to stay away from details ("they are not being discussed rationally"). The aim was "to keep the Arab friendship and the Israeli friendship at the same time." If King called for negotiations while asserting Israel's "incontestable" right to a homeland and its territorial integrity, it would be enough for Israel's supporters.[7]

Two days later, on June 8, King told his advisers he had come under growing pressure to make his own statement on the Middle East.

> The statement I signed in the *N.Y. Times* as you know was agreed with by a lot of people in the Jewish community. But there was those in the negro community [who] have been disappointed. SNCC for one has been very critical. The problem was that the *N.Y. Times* played it up as a total endorsement of Israel. What they printed up wasn't the complete text, even the introduction wasn't the text. I can't back up on the statement now, my problem is whether I should make another statement, or maybe I could just avoid making a statement. I don't want to make a statement that backs up on me[;] that wouldn't be good. Well, what do you think?

King's confidants went back and forth, suggesting that he say as little as possible, that he urge an end to the fighting and refer to the role of the United Nations. "I don't think you have to worry too much about losing the support of the Jewish community at this time," advised Wachtel. "They're very happy at this point, with their apparent victory. I think you should just stride very lightly and stress the end of violence."[8] So over the next days, King worked to avoid the subject and keep attention focused on Vietnam.

But Wachtel was wrong: supporters of Israel, who followed his words closely, noticed the silence. An internal memo of the American Jewish Committee reported that he spoke twice in Washington during the week of the war, and made no reference to it. "The fact that King twice in the week failed to discuss the war has a variety of implications, which I think the recipients of this memo can infer on their own."[9]

It was only on June 18, when King appeared on the ABC Sunday interview program "Issues and Answers," that he finally answered direct questions on the subject. After giving boilerplate replies about the importance of Israeli security and the need for Arab economic development, one of the interviewers cut to the quick: "Should Israel in your opinion give back the land she has taken in conflict without certain guarantees, such as security?" King gave this answer:

> Well, I think these guarantees should all be worked out by the United Nations. I would hope that all of the nations, and particularly the Soviet Union and the United States, and I would say France and Great

Britain, these four powers can really determine how that situation is going. I think the Israelis will have to have access to the Gulf of Aqaba. I mean the very survival of Israel may well depend on access to not only the Suez Canal, but the Gulf and the Strait of Tiran. These things are very important. But I think for the ultimate peace and security of the situation it will probably be necessary for Israel to give up this conquered territory because to hold on to it will only exacerbate the tensions and deepen the bitterness of the Arabs.[10]

It is remarkable that this last sentence does not figure in the latter-day polemics over King and Israel, even though King spoke it on national television. It goes far to clarify King's position on the consequences of the Six-Day War: King supported Israeli actions to assure its "survival," but did not favor Israel's continued hold on the territories it had conquered.

King also passed over an opportunity to make an exception of Jerusalem. He perfectly understood the Jerusalem issue, having visited the Jordanian side of the city in 1959. (In a sermon following that visit, he explained to his congregants that "the holy city has been divided and split up and partitioned.")[11] Israel annexed East Jerusalem on June 28, 1967, reuniting the city and setting off debates within and among churches.

On July 12, a statement by sixteen leading Protestant theologians appeared in the *New York Times*; the signatories once more included Reinhold Niebuhr. "During the past twenty years the City of David has experienced an artificial division," the statement announced. "We see no justification in proposals which seek once again to destroy the unity which has been restored to Jerusalem." The statement went on to praise Israel, "whose record over the last twenty years in providing free access to Christian shrines within its jurisdiction inspires confidence that the interests of all religions will be faithfully honored."[12] This time, King did not appear among the signatories.

The day after the cease-fire, King had told his advisers that Israel "now faces the danger of being smug and unyielding."[13] As his concerns grew, he now faced a practical question: whether to carry through on a planned trip to an Israel flush with victory.

The Visit That Wasn't

Why didn't King visit Israel? This was the question posed by Yaacov Lozowick, director of the Israel State Archives, on Martin Luther King, Jr. Day, 2013. On that occasion, the Israel State Archives published a batch of Israeli documents from before the Six-Day War, about a possible visit by King to Israel.[14] The correspondence made for fascinating reading, but left a question hanging, as explained by Lozowick:

> In a nutshell, the Israelis thought it would be a fine idea to host MLK in Israel, and the more important he grew, the more convinced they were that it was something they should make happen. King, from his side, kept on saying all the right words, but kept on not coming. Those are the facts. What do they mean? Hard to say.[15]

In fact, it is not hard to say. But the answer lies far from the Israeli archives, in the FBI wiretaps.

In 1966, King entered an agreement to lead a Holy Land pilgrimage, in partnership with Sandy Ray, pastor of a Baptist church in Brooklyn, who took up the promotion of the trip. King's assistant, Andrew Young, visited Israel and Jordan in late 1966 to do advance planning with Jordanian and Israeli authorities. The pilgrimage was rumored to be in the works from that time, and King received letters of encouragement and invitations from the prime ministers of Israel and Jordan, and from the Israeli and Jordanian mayors of divided Jerusalem. On May 16, 1967, King publicly announced the plan at a news conference, reported by the *New York Times* the following day.[16]

The pilgrimage would take place in November, and King insisted that it would have no political significance whatsoever. The organizers hoped to attract five thousand participants, with the aim of generating revenue for King's Southern Christian Leadership Council (SCLC). King was slated to preach on the Mount of Olives in Jordanian East Jerusalem (November 14), and at a specially constructed amphitheater near Capernaum on the Sea of Galilee in Israel (November 16). The pilgrims would pass from Jordan to Israel through the Mandelbaum Gate in Jerusalem. King, who knew the situation on the ground, thought he could strike just the right balance between Israel and Jordan.[17]

The Six-Day War threw a wrench into the plan. Ray was still keen on going forward, and he immediately sent his own tour agent to Jerusalem to get a read on the situation. She came back enthusiastic: "I firmly believe that Dr. King's visit will prove to be a much more historic event then we ever dreamed possible. Everyone, from the Governments down to the people on the streets were asking me about Dr. King. . . . We desperately need a new Press Release from Dr. King reaffirming the Pilgrimage plans."[18]

So what happened? King got cold feet, and this isn't a guess. We have it straight from King himself, again in the FBI wiretaps. In a conference call among King and his advisers, on July 24, 1967, King noted that the responses to the pilgrimage promotion had been "fairly good." (Andrew Young said about six hundred people had sent in deposits.) But if King went to the Middle East, "I'd run into the situation where I'm damned if I say this and I'm damned if I say that no matter what I'd say, and I've already faced enough criticism including pro-Arab." He had met a Lebanese journalist who told him that the Arabs now had the impression he was pro-Israel, and that "you don't understand our problem or something like that. And I expect I would run into a continuation of this." King asked for advice, but set this tone:

> I just think that if I go, the Arab world, and of course Africa and Asia for that matter, would interpret this as endorsing everything that Israel has done, and I do have questions of doubt.[19]

King added that "most of it [the pilgrimage] would be Jerusalem and they [the Israelis] have annexed Jerusalem, and any way you say it they don't plan to give it up." After some to-and-fro among his advisers, in which it was suggested that he balance an Israel trip with a visit to King Hussein in Amman or Nasser in Cairo, King announced that "I frankly have to admit that my instincts, and when I follow my instincts so to speak I'm usually right. . . . I just think that this would be a great mistake. I don't think I could come out unscathed."[20]

King procrastinated out of deference to Ray, who had laid out money on promotion of the pilgrimage. But on September 22, 1967, he wrote the following to Mordechai Ben-Ami, the president of the Israeli airline El Al, which was to have handled part of the flight package:

> It is with the deepest regret that I cancel my proposed pilgrimage to the Holy Land for this year, but the constant turmoil in the Middle East makes it extremely difficult to conduct a religious pilgrimage free of both political overtones and the fear of danger to the participants.
>
> Actually, I am aware that the danger is almost non-existent, but to the ordinary citizen who seldom goes abroad, the daily headlines of border clashes and propaganda statements produces a fear of danger which is insurmountable on the American scene.[21]

He ended by promising to revisit the plan the following year, but he never did.

The Quote

"When people criticize Zionists, they mean Jews. You're talking anti-Semitism!" These words, reportedly spoken by King in the aftermath of the war, are often quoted by supporters of Israel. Israeli Prime Minister Benjamin Netanyahu quoted them in his address to the Knesset on International Holocaust Remembrance Day in 2011.[22] The quote also appeared in a State Department report on antisemitism.[23]

But some Palestinians and their sympathizers, who resent the stigmatizing of anti-Zionism as a form of antisemitism, have tried to discredit the quote. Just what sort of anti-Zionism crosses that fine line is a question beyond my scope here. But what of the quote itself? How was it first circulated? What is the evidence against it? And might some additional evidence resolve the question of its authenticity?

King's words were reported by Seymour Martin Lipset, at that time the George D. Markham Professor of Government and Sociology at Harvard, in an article he published in the magazine *Encounter* in December 1969—that is, in the year after King's April 1968 assassination. Lipset:

> Shortly before he was assassinated, Martin Luther King, Jr. was in Boston on a fund-raising mission, and I had the good fortune to attend a dinner which was given for him in Cambridge. This was an experience which was at once fascinating and moving: one witnessed Dr. King in action in a way one never got to see in public. He wanted to find what the Negro students at Harvard and other parts of the Boston area were thinking about various issues, and he very subtly cross-examined them for well over an hour and a half. He asked questions, and said very little himself. One of the young men present happened to make some remark against the Zionists. Dr. King snapped at him and said, "Don't talk like that! When people criticize Zionists, they mean Jews. You're talking anti-Semitism!"[24]

For the next three-plus decades, no one challenged the credibility of this account. No wonder: Lipset, author of the classic *Political Man* (1960), was an eminent authority on American politics and society, who later became the only scholar ever to preside over both the American Sociological Association and the American Political Science Association. Who if not Lipset could be counted upon to report an event accurately? Nor was he quoting something said in confidence only to him or far back in time. Others were present at the same dinner, and Lipset wrote about it not that long after the fact. He also told the anecdote in a magazine that must have had many subscribers in Cambridge, some of whom might have shared his "fascinating and moving" experience. The idea that he would have fabricated or falsified any aspect of this account would have seemed preposterous.

That is, until almost four decades later, when two Palestinian-American activists suggested just that. Lipset's account, they wrote, "seems on its face . . . credible."

> There are still, however, a few reasons for casting doubt on the authenticity of this statement. According to the *Harvard Crimson*, "The Rev. Martin Luther King was last in Cambridge almost exactly a year ago—April 23, 1967" ("While You Were Away" 4/8/68). If this is true, Dr. King could not have been in Cambridge in 1968. Lipset stated he was in the area for a "fund-raising mission," which would seem to imply a high profile visit. Also, an intensive inventory of publications by Stanford University's Martin Luther King Jr. Papers Project accounts for numerous speeches in 1968. None of them are for talks in Cambridge or Boston.[25]

When Lipset's integrity was called into question, in 2004, he was probably unaware of it and certainly unable to respond to it. He had suffered a debilitating stroke in 2001, which left him immobile and speech-impaired. (He died of another stroke in 2006, at the age of 84.) Since then, others have reinforced the doubt, noting that Lipset gave "what seemed to be a lot of information on the background to the King quote, but without providing a single concrete, verifiable detail."[26]

To all intents and purposes, this constituted an assertion that Lipset might have fabricated both the occasion and the quote. Such an extraordinary claim raised this question: could Lipset's account be substantiated with "concrete, verifiable detail"?

Bear in mind Lipset's precise testimony: King rebuked the student at a dinner in Cambridge "shortly before" King's assassination, during a fundraising mission to Boston. Note that Lipset didn't place the dinner in 1968. King was assassinated on April 4, 1968, so "shortly before" could just as well have referred to the last months of 1967.

In fact, King did come to Boston for the purposes of fundraising in late 1967—specifically, on Friday, October 27. Boston was the last stop in a week-long series of benefit concerts given by Harry Belafonte for King's SCLC. In the archives of NBC, there is a clip of King greeting the audience at the Boston concert.[27] The *Boston Globe* also reported King's remarks and the benefit concert on its front page the next morning.[28]

Greetings by Martin Luther King, Jr., sandwiched between an introduction by Sidney Poitier and an act by Harry Belafonte, before nine thousand people in Boston Garden—it would be difficult to imagine any appearance more "high profile" than that.

And the dinner in Cambridge? When King was assassinated, the *Crimson*, Harvard's student newspaper, did write that he "was last in Cambridge almost exactly a year ago—April 23, 1967."[29] That had been a very public visit, during which King and Dr. Benjamin Spock held a press conference to announce plans for a "Vietnam Summer." War supporters picketed King.[30]

But in actual fact, that was not King's last visit to Cambridge. In early October 1967, when news spread that King would be coming to Boston for the Belafonte concert, a junior member of Harvard's faculty wrote to King from Cambridge, to extend an invitation from the instructor and his wife:

> We would be anxious to be able to sit down and have a somewhat leisured meal with you, and perhaps with some other few people from this area whom you might like to meet. So much has happened in recent months that we are both quite without bearings, and are in need of some honest and tough and friendly dialogue. . . . So if you can find some time for dinner on Friday or lunch on Saturday, we are delighted to extend an invitation. If, however, your schedules do not permit, we of course will understand that. In any case, we look forward to seeing you at the Belafonte Concert and the party afterwards.[31]

Who was this member of the Harvard faculty? Martin Peretz.

In October 1967, Peretz was a twenty-nine-year-old instructor of Social Studies at Harvard and an antiwar New Leftist. Four months earlier, he had married Anne Farnsworth, heiress to a sewing machine fortune. Even before their marriage, the couple had made the civil rights movement one of their causes, and Farnsworth had become a top-tier donor to the SCLC. A year earlier, Peretz had informed King that a luncheon with him was "one of the high points of my life"—and that "arrangements for the transfer of securities are now being made."[32] As Peretz later wrote, "I knew Martin Luther King, Jr. decently well, at least as much as one can know a person who had already become both prophet and hero. I fundraised for his Southern Christian Leadership Conference."[33] Much of that charity began in the Peretz home.

But as Peretz noted in his invitation, "much has happened in recent months," necessitating "some honest and tough and friendly dialogue."

Peretz was then (and subsequently remained) an ardent supporter of Israel, and he was alarmed at the manner in which black militants denounced Israel following the June war. In August, the radical SNNC issued a newsletter claiming that "Zionist terror gangs" had "deliberately slaughtered and mutilated women, children and men, thereby causing the unarmed Arabs to panic, flee and leave their homes in the hands of the Zionist-Israeli forces." The newsletter also denounced "the Rothschilds, who have long controlled the wealth of many European nations, [who] were involved in the original conspiracy with the British to create the 'State of Israel' and [who] are still among Israel's chief supporters." Peretz, who a few years earlier had been a supporter of SNCC, condemned the newsletter as vicious antisemitism, and Jewish supporters of the civil rights movement looked to King and the SCLC to do the same.[34]

King's secretary, Dora McDonald, replied to the Peretz invitation on King's behalf: "Dr. King asked me to say that he would be happy to have dinner with you." King would be arriving in Boston at 2:43 in the afternoon. "Accompanying Dr. King will be Rev. Andrew Young, Rev. Bernard Lee and I." And so it was that King came to dinner at the Peretz home at 20 Larchwood Drive, Cambridge, in the early evening of October 27, 1967.

The dinner was attended by Peretz's senior Harvard colleague, Seymour Martin Lipset, and it was then and there that Lipset heard King rebuke a student who echoed the SNCC line on "Zionists": "When people criticize Zionists, they mean Jews. You're talking anti-Semitism!" Peretz would later assert that King "grasped the identity between anti-Israel politics and antisemitic ranting."[35] Lipset preserved King's words to that effect, by publishing them as a personal recollection. (Just to run the contemporary record against memory, I wrote to Peretz, to ask whether the much-quoted exchange did take place at his Cambridge home on that evening. His answer: "Absolutely.")

A few days later, King's aide, Andrew Young, thanked Peretz and his wife

> for the delightful evening last Friday. It is almost too bad we had to go to the concert, but I think you will agree that the concert, too, proved enjoyable but I am also sure a couple of hours conversing with the group gathered in your home would have been more productive.[36]

(I wrote twice to Andrew Young to ask whether he had any recollection of King's words. I received no response.)

Little more than five months after the Cambridge dinner, King lay dead, felled by an assassin in Memphis. (Peretz delivered a eulogy at the remembrance service in Harvard's Memorial Church.)[37] There is plenty of room to debate the precise meaning of King's off-the-record words at the Cambridge dinner. Was he only referring to the clearly antisemitic meaning of "Zionists" in the rhetoric of SNCC militants? Or was he making a general statement? We will never know. And just how much weight should be accorded to words spoken privately and never repeated publicly? (Had Lipset not written an article more than a year after the event, King's words would have been lost forever.) My own view is that this dinner table remark can't always bear the oversized burden imposed on it.

But the assertion that King couldn't possibly have spoken it, because he wasn't in or near Cambridge when he was supposed to have said it, is baseless. Lipset: "Shortly before he was assassinated, Martin Luther King, Jr. was in Boston on a fund-raising mission, and I had the good fortune to attend a dinner which was given for him in Cambridge." Every particular of this statement is corroborated by a wealth of detail. There is a date, an approximate time of day, and a street address for the Cambridge dinner, all attested by contemporary correspondence in King's papers.

The Balancing Act

King's careful maneuvering before, during, and after the Six-Day War demonstrated a much deeper understanding of the Arab-Israeli conflict than critics credit him with possessing. The two Palestinian-Americans who sought to dismiss the Cambridge quote suggested that the conflict "was probably not a subject he was well-versed on," and that his public statements in praise of Israel "surely do not sound like the words of someone familiar with both sides of the story."[38] Not so. King had been to the Arab world, had a full grasp of the positions of the sides, and was wary of the possible pitfalls of favoring one over the other. He struck a delicate balance, speaking out or staying silent after careful assessments made in consultation with advisers who had their ears to the ground—Levison and Wachtel (both non-Zionists) in the Jewish community, and Andrew Young, whom King dispatched to the Middle East as his emissary.

For this reason, it is an offense to history, if not to King's memory, whenever someone today summons King's ghost to offer unqualified support to Israel or the Palestinians. King understood moral complexity, he knew that millions waited upon his words, and he sought to resolve conflict, not accentuate it. The pursuit of an elusive balance marked his approach to the Arab-Israeli conflict while he lived. There is no obvious reason to presume he would have acted differently, had he lived longer.

Notes

1. Some of the episodes discussed in this article were treated in brief by Murray Friedman, *What Went Wrong? The Creation and Collapse of the Black-Jewish Alliance* (New York: Free Press, 1995), 250–53; and Taylor Branch, *At Canaan's Edge: America in the King Years, 1965–68* (New York: Simon & Schuster, 2006), 556–57, 620–21, 624, 632.

2. Jewish Telegraphic Agency, "Dr. King Repudiates Anti-Semitic, Anti-Israel Black Power Stand," October 10, 1967, archived at http://web.archive.org/web/20160229154145/http://www.jta.org/1967/10/11/archive/dr-king-repudiates-anti-semitic-anti-israel-black-power-stand; "Martin Luther King Jr: 'Israel . . . is one of the great outpost of democracy in the world'" (video excerpt from interview), posted at https://www.youtube.com/watch?v=kvr2Cxuh2Wk, accessed February 29, 2016.

3. "Dr. King, Other Prominent U.S. Christian Clergymen Urge Support for Israel," Jewish Telegraphic Agency, May 29, 1967, archived at http://web.archive.org/web/20160109103941/http://www.jta.org/1967/05/29/archive/dr-king-other-prominent-u-s-christian-clergymen-urge-support-for-israel; *New York Times,* May 28, 1967.

4. "8 Church Leaders Ask Aid to Israel," *New York Times,* May 28, 1967.

5. Letter by David Lelyveld, *New York Times,* June 2, 1967. Lelyveld was the son of prominent Reform rabbi and civil rights activist Arthur Lelyveld, at that time president of the American Jewish Congress.

6. Ussama Makdisi, *Faith Misplaced: The Broken Promise of U.S.-Arab Relations, 1820–2001* (New York: Public Affairs, 2010), 268–69.

7. Transcript of conference call, June 6, 1967, in *The Martin Luther King, Jr., FBI File, Part II: The King-Levison File* (microfilm), ed. David J. Garrow (Frederick, MD: University Publications of America, 1987), reel 8 (hereafter: *King-Levison File*).

8. Transcript of conference call, June 8, 1967, *King-Levison File.*

9. Brant Coopersmith, "War in the Middle East," memo to Harry Fleischman, American Jewish Committee, June 12, 1967, American Jewish Committee archives, quoted by Marc Schneier, *Shared Dreams: Martin Luther King, Jr. and the Jewish Community* (Woodstock, VT: Jewish Lights, 1999), 164. As of January 2016, the archives of the American Jewish Committee cannot locate this memo. I am grateful to Arthur Perler for attempting (unsuccessfully) to locate this memo in Fleischman's papers at New York University.

10. King interviewed by Tom Jerriel and John Casserly, ABC "Issues and Answers," June 18, 1967, The King Center Digital Archive, transcript archived at http://web.archive.org/web/20150304113151/http://www.thekingcenter.org/archive/document/abcs-issues-and-answers-mlk-interview.

11. King's Easter Sunday sermon, "A Walk through the Holy Land," delivered at the Dexter Avenue Baptist Church, Montgomery, Alabama, on March 29, 1959, in *The Papers of Martin Luther King, Jr.,* vol. 5, *Threshold of a New*

Decade, January 1959–December 1960, eds. Clayborne Carson et al. (Berkeley: University of California Press, 2005), 164.

12. "Jerusalem Should Remain Unified" (advertisement), *New York Times,* July 12, 1967.

13. Transcript of conference call, June 11, 1967, *King-Levison File.*

14. Shlomo Mark and Hagai Zoref, "Dr. Martin Luther King and Israel: Documents on his Relations with the State of Israel and Efforts to Arrange his Visit to Israel," Israel State Archives website, archived at http://web.archive.org/web/20150602221743/http://www.archives.gov.il/ArchiveGov_Eng/Publications/ElectronicPirsum/MartinLutherKing/.

15. Yaacov Lozowick, "What was Martin Luther King Thinking," *Israel's Documented Story* [blog of the Israel State Archives], January 17, 2013, archived at http://web.archive.org/web/20130126073039/http://israelsdocuments.blogspot.co.il/2013/01/what-was-martin-luther-king-thinking.html.

16. "Dr. King to Lead Fall Pilgrimage to the Holy Land," *New York Times,* May 16, 1967.

17. A brochure outlining this itinerary is preserved in the Andrew Young Papers, Auburn Avenue Research Library, Atlanta, Ga., Box 21, Folder 5: "Pilgrimage to the Holy Land with Martin Luther King, Jr., 1967." I am grateful to Düden Yeğenoğlu for scanning the brochure for me.

18. Letter from Emily Ann Fortson, *Records of the Southern Christian Leadership Conference, 1954–1970, Part 1: Records of the President's Office* (microfilm), ed. Randolph Boehm (Bethesda, MD: University Publications of America, 1995), reel 3.

19. Transcript of conference call, July 24, 1967, *King-Levison File.*

20. Ibid.

21. King to M. Ben Ari (Tel Aviv), September 22, 1967, The King Center Digital Archive, archived at http://web.archive.org/web/20160109135316/http://thekingcenter.org/archive/document/letter-mlk-ben-ari.

22. Benjamin Netanyahu, address to the Knesset on International Holocaust Remembrance Day, January 26, 2011, Israeli Foreign Ministry website, archived at http://web.archive.org/web/20130621165247/http://www.mfa.gov.il/mfa/pressroom/2011/pages/pm_netanyahu_knesset_international_holocaust_remembrance_day_26-jan-2011.aspx.

23. U.S. Department of State, Office of the Special Envoy to Monitor and Combat Anti-Semitism, *Contemporary Global Anti-Semitism: A Report Provided to the United States Congress* (Washington, DC: United States Department of State, 2008), 53.

24. Seymour Martin Lipset, "The Socialism of Fools: The Left, the Jews, and Israel," *Encounter* 33, no. 6 (December 1969): 24.

25. Fadi Kiblawi and Will Youmans, "Israel's Apologists and the Martin Luther King, Jr. Hoax," *Electronic Intifada* website, January 18, 2004, archived at http://web.archive.org/web/20110608073134/http://electronicintifada.net/content/israels-apologists-and-martin-luther-king-jr-hoax/4955.

26. Ibrahim ibn Yusuf, "My Father Once Heard MLK Denounce Israel," *The Hasbara Buster* blog, January 21, 2009, archived at https://web.archive.org/web/20100805042356/http://thehasbarabuster.blogspot.com/2009/01/my-father-once-heard-mlk-denounce.html.

27. "Martin Luther King Addresses Civil Rights Concert Audience at Boston Garden," NBCUniversal Archives, archived at http://web.archive.org/web/20120315140806/http://www.nbcuniversalarchives.com/nbcuni/clip/5112496815_s01.do.
28. William J. Fripp, "King Attacks Vietnam War Cost At Hub Concert to Aid 'Exodus,'" *Boston Globe*, October 28, 1967.
29. "While You Were Away: King Began Peace Drive Here" (editorial), *Harvard Crimson*, April 8, 1968.
30. "Rev. Martin Luther King, Jr. is flanked by policeman as he is picketed by group of Harvard students," photograph, April 23, 1967, archived at http://web.archive.org/web/20120316172519/http://www.corbisimages.com/stock-photo/rights-managed/U1553138/rev-martin-luther-king-and-dr-benjamin.
31. Martin Peretz (Cambridge) to Dr. and Mrs. King (Atlanta), October 9, 1967, The King Center Digital Archive, archived at http://web.archive.org/web/20120316143636/http://www.thekingcenter.org/archive/document/letter-martin-peretz-mlk.
32. Martin Peretz (Cambridge) to King (Atlanta), November 8, 1966, The King Center Digital Archive, archived at http://web.archive.org/web/20120316143443/http://www.thekingcenter.org/archive/document/letter-martin-peretz-mlk-0.
33. Martin Peretz, "Dr. King's Children Cash Out," *The Spine* (Peretz's blog), April 18, 2009, archived at https://web.archive.org/web/20160109152559/https://newrepublic.com/article/49108/dr-kings-children-cash-out.
34. Kathleen Teltsch, "S.N.C.C. Criticized for Israel Stand," *New York Times*, August 16, 1967. The relationship of Peretz to the civil rights movement and Israel is discussed at length by Jonathan Kaufman, *Broken Alliance: The Turbulent Times between Blacks and Jews in America* (New York: Scribner, 1988), 197–236.
35. Peretz, "Dr. King's Children."
36. Andrew J. Young to Dr. and Mrs. Martin Peretz (Cambridge), November 1, 1967, The King Center Digital Archive, archived at http://web.archive.org/web/20120316143413/http://www.thekingcenter.org/archive/document/letter-andrew-young-dr-and-mrs-peretz. The letter went on to solicit a contribution.
37. "Peretz on King at Memorial Church," *Harvard Crimson*, April 13, 1968.
38. Kiblawi and Youmans, "Israel's Apologists."

23

Israel and the Iraq War

It is generally agreed that the Iran nuclear deal in 2015 was a defeat for the American Israel Public Affairs Committee (AIPAC) and other groups that promote the pro-Israel perspective in Washington. "Pro-Israel Group Went 'All In,'" announced a *New York Times* headline, "but Suffered a Stinging Defeat."[1] "These kinds of defeats aren't supposed to happen to AIPAC," wrote two prominent Washington journalists.[2]

In response, others pointed out that AIPAC had lost battles with presidents before, citing examples from the administrations of Ronald Reagan (in 1981, over the AWACs sale to Saudi Arabia), and George H. W. Bush (in 1991, over loan guarantees). "Win some, lose some" seemed to be the message in these catalogues of defeats. But the cataloguers thought they had to go back almost twenty-five years to find the last rout.[3]

This was an error. Israel and its lobby were defeated in 2002, during the George W. Bush administration, and over the very same issue of Iran. In that year, as the Bush administration turned its post-9/11 wrath on Saddam Hussein's Iraq, Israel urged its American ally to focus instead on the threat posed by Iran's nuclear ambitions. The United States chose to embark on regime change and nation-building in Iraq, which ultimately not only undermined U.S. resolve in the Middle East, but also enhanced Iran's geopolitical leverage. The Israeli failure in 2002 thus set the stage for the debacle of 2015.

The 2002 failure has gone largely unrecognized, and the most recent comprehensive history of U.S.-Israel relations omits it altogether.[4] The reason is simple: it didn't happen in the public spotlight, and Israel chose to downplay it. When the Bush administration decided to strike Iraq, Israel clambered onto the bandwagon, further obscuring the defeat. Indeed, so thoroughly was it obscured, that critics of Israel and antisemitic conspiracy theorists could dare to claim that *Israel* led America into the Iraq war.

Topping the list of these critics were two influential professors of international relations, John Mearsheimer of the University of Chicago and Stephen Walt of Harvard. In a paper that made headlines in 2006, they claimed it was Israel and the "Israel Lobby" that had sent the United States on a fool's errand in Iraq, prodding the Bush administration into an "unnecessary" war. One version of their study appeared in the *London Review of Books;*[5] a longer, footnoted version was posted on the website of the Kennedy School of Government at Harvard.[6] An expanded version later appeared as a book, entitled *The Israel Lobby.*[7]

In a section of their initial paper entitled "Israel and the Iraq War," they sought to establish that Israel's leaders, intelligence agencies, and public opinion enthusiastically supported a war to remove Saddam. Israel exerted "pressure" on the United States, fed Washington "alarming reports" on Iraq's WMD capabilities, and beat the war drums in the media. Israelis were "so gung-ho for war that their allies in America told them to damp down their hawkish rhetoric, lest it look like the war was for Israel." "Pressure from Israel and the Lobby was not the only factor behind the decision to attack Iraq in March 2003," they wrote, "but it was critical."[8] Bottom line: Israel was more of a liability than anyone had imagined.

Why Iraq?

It is worth pausing to consider why this claim was critical to Walt and Mearsheimer. Their main argument wasn't that the Palestinians were paying a terrible price for U.S. support for Israel. In most quarters, that would draw a simple shrug. Instead, the duo insisted that *Americans* were paying that price. They paid it on 9/11; the killers of 9/11 set out on their mission because of their rage against unconditional U.S. backing for Israel. And they were paying it in Iraq because Israel sent America there, to avoid doing what Israel should have done years ago: give the Palestinians their state. Because Americans were dying, from Manhattan to Baghdad, America shouldn't indulge Israel any longer.

Of the two blame-claims, 9/11 and Iraq, the former got less traction. Very early on, Americans decided that Osama bin Laden, a Saudi, and the fifteen of the nineteen 9/11 hijackers who were Saudis, hadn't set out to kill Americans over Israeli settlements on the West Bank. They believed that Al Qaeda hated America for everything it is and does, a view confirmed by the *9/11 Commission Report.* The report's narrative showed how the 9/11 plot developed precisely during the years when the Clinton White House coddled Yasser Arafat.[9] The report became a bestseller, and it had a profound impact.

For this reason, the Iraq claim became more crucial to the Mearsheimer-Walt thesis, and it meant more to them too. They had both opposed the war before it started, describing it as "unnecessary" and arguing that Saddam could be deterred and contained, even if he acquired nuclear weapons.[10] Much to their chagrin, their argument had no effect in Washington. To the two professors, the United States had become an anomaly, a baffling place where the national interest (as they saw it) no longer drove foreign policy. Their explanation? They settled on the distorting influence of the "powerful Israel lobby."[11]

In their original paper, Walt and Mearsheimer had a straightforward chain of causation for the Iraq war: Israel pushed the "Israel Lobby" (with a capital "L"), which pushed the neocons, which pushed the Bush administration into war. But to reach this conclusion, the two authors overlooked, omitted, or concealed a veritable mountain of contrary evidence about Israeli policy.

Iran First

"If you told Israeli leaders and analysts two years ago that the U.S. would be on the verge of attacking Iraq today, they would have been astonished and confused. The dominant perception across the political spectrum was that Iraq was not a serious threat." So wrote the analyst Barry Rubin in the *Jerusalem Post* in October 2002, five months before the U.S. attack. Rubin pointed out that sanctions had debilitated Iraq's military, leaving the country impoverished and without allies. "If anyone was a danger from that part of the world, Israeli politicians and intelligence experts believed, it was Iran, a country facing none of Saddam's problems."[12]

This late-1990s Israeli view of Saddam Hussein as weakened wasn't kept secret, and it annoyed those Americans who were busily compiling the dossier against Saddam. Laurie Mylroie, an analyst known for arguing that Saddam sponsored every act of terror and possessed every kind of WMD, made little headway in Israel, and it frustrated her to no end:

> Many Israelis [wrote Mylroie in 1998] refuse to accept and incorporate, even now, the information that suggests the U.S. did not win the [1991 Gulf] war and Saddam remains very dangerous. A few do—like Ehud Ya'ari/Ze'ev Schiff/Gerald Steinberg, Bar Ilan University/the editors of the *Jerusalem Post*. But most do not and their work is so systematically distorted that it is fit for little more than wrapping fish.[13]

Mylroie called Israel's refusal to recognize Iraq's guiding role in Islamist terrorism (including the 9/11 attack) "a strategic intelligence failure . . . not less than the strategic intelligence failure that preceded the Yom Kippur War."[14]

Israel's Iran focus continued into the new millennium. In November 2001, journalist Seymour Hersh reported Israel's concern that the post-9/11 "war on terror" had diverted U.S. attention from Iran, even as Iran accelerated its nuclear program with Russian help. Hersh wrote that "even Israel's most skeptical critics in the American intelligence community—and there are many—now acknowledge that there is a serious problem." But the Bush administration put Israel off with assurances that it would get to Iran later. Hersh:

> The Bush Administration continues to concentrate on the threat posed by Saddam Hussein's Iraq. "It's more important to deal with Iraq than with Iran, because there's nothing going on in Iraq that's going to get better," a senior Administration strategist told me. "In Iran, the people are openly defying the government. There's some hope that Iran will get better. But there's nothing in Iraq that gives you any hope, because Saddam rules so ruthlessly. What will we do if he provides anthrax to four guys in Al Qaeda?" He said, "If Iraq is out of the picture, we will concentrate on Iran in an entirely different way."[15]

In late 2001, Israeli prime minister Ariel Sharon sent a delegation to Washington headed by Dan Meridor, who had informal responsibility for intelligence affairs. Meridor made the trip because (according to a U.S. official) it was "the only way they're going to get anybody's attention in the Bush Administration" on the Iran issue. According to Hersh, "the Israelis found Washington preoccupied with Iraq."[16] In January 2002, Natan Sharansky, then deputy prime minister in the Sharon government, revealed the disagreement to an Israeli journalist in words that summarized the issue in a nutshell: "We and the Americans have different priorities. For us, Iran comes first and then Iraq. The Americans see Iraq, then a long pause, and only then Iran."[17]

The following month, ahead of a visit by Israeli prime minister Ariel Sharon to Washington, the *Washington Post* carried a story under the headline: "Israel Emphasizes Iranian Threat."

> As Prime Minister Ariel Sharon arrives today for a White House visit, Israeli officials are redoubling efforts to warn the Bush administration that Iran poses a greater threat than the Iraqi regime of Saddam Hussein.

A series of Israeli leaders have carried that message to Washington recently in the hope of influencing a debate that has centered not on Iran but on whether to pursue the overthrow of the Iraqi government.[18]

The article went on to quote Israeli defense minister Fouad Ben-Eliezer: "Today, everybody is busy with Iraq. Iraq is a problem. . . . But you should understand, if you ask me, today Iran is more dangerous than Iraq." The article added: "Though Israeli officials have few kind words for Saddam Hussein, they see him posing less of a threat than Iran after more than a decade of U.N. sanctions and international isolation."[19]

But the Bush administration had made its decision, and throughout spring and summer, the allies of the United States jumped on board. Even so, rumblings of dissent could still be heard from Israel. On October 6, 2002, the *New York Times* ran a story from Jerusalem under the headline: "Sharon Tells Cabinet to Keep Quiet on U.S. Plans" for Iraq. The paper reported that Sharon had instructed his ministers to stop talking about Iraq, and then summarized the opinions of the military echelon:

> Even as Mr. Bush has sought in recent days to play up the imminence and potency of the Iraqi threat, some of Israel's top security officials have played both down.
>
> Lt. Gen. Moshe Yaalon, Israel's chief of staff, was quoted in the newspaper *Ma'ariv* today as telling a trade group in a speech over the weekend, "I'm not losing any sleep over the Iraqi threat." The reason, he said, was that the military strength of Israel and Iraq had diverged so sharply in the last decade.
>
> Israel's chief of military intelligence, Maj. Gen. Aharon Farkash, disputed contentions that Iraq was eighteen months away from nuclear capability. In an interview on Saturday with Israeli television, he said army intelligence had concluded that Iraq's time frame was more like four years, and he said Iran's nuclear threat was as great as Iraq's.
>
> General Farkash also said Iraq had grown militarily weaker since the Persian Gulf war in 1991 and had not deployed any missiles that could strike Israel.[20]

On October 16, 2002, the *Los Angeles Times* ran a front-page story by its Israel correspondent under this headline: "Not All Israelis Welcome Prospect of War With Iraq."

A muted debate is underway here over whether a U.S.-led war against Israel's archenemy Saddam Hussein is, in fact, a good idea.

While it is widely assumed that Israelis are gloating over the prospect of Hussein getting his comeuppance after the Persian Gulf War, when 39 Iraqi Scud missiles rained down on Israel, the reality is far more complex and the reactions more ambivalent.

No doubt Israelis more than almost anyone would prefer a Middle East without Hussein, but some question whether the status quo of a weakened and contained Iraq isn't better than a war that could further inflame anti-Israel sentiments in the Arab world.[21]

The report also quoted Generals Yaalon and Farkash, adding that "Israeli military specialists have been debating for several years whether Iraq or Iran poses more of a threat. Most specialists believe it is Iran, because it is richer and has been more directly implicated in international terrorism." And the reporter also had an explanation for the muted tone of the debate: "Those most enthusiastic about Washington's campaign dread any suggestion that Israel is egging on the U.S. And those with misgivings are loath to say anything that might embarrass Israel's most steadfast ally."[22]

Incredibly, Mearsheimer and Walt, in their section on "Israel and the Iraq War," didn't cite the articles in the *New York Times*, or the *Los Angeles Times*, or the statement by Sharansky, or the testimony of Rubin and Mylroie. (The *Washington Post* piece was cited later, but in the wrong context. Mearsheimer and Walt chronologically misplaced Ben-Eliezer's remark, about Iran being more dangerous than Iraq. They dated it to "one month before the Iraq war"—in other words, in the context of the debate over what should be done after Iraq. In fact, Ben-Eliezer made the statement *one year and one month* before the Iraq war, in the context of the debate about whether to do Iraq at all.)

In their analysis of Israeli public opinion, Mearsheimer and Walt also missed crucial evidence. They quoted a September 2002 *Wall Street Journal* op-ed by Benjamin Netanyahu (then on the political sidelines) in which he made this assertion: "I believe I speak for the overwhelming majority of Israelis in supporting a pre-emptive strike against Saddam's regime."[23] Mearsheimer and Walt:

As Netanyahu suggests, the desire for war was not confined to Israel's leaders. Apart from Kuwait, which Saddam conquered in 1990, Israel was the only country in the world where both the politicians and the public enthusiastically favored war.[24]

They then supported this claim in a footnote, citing a February 2003 poll done by the Steinmatz Center at Tel Aviv University. It showed that 77.5 percent of Israeli Jews favored a U.S. campaign against Iraq.[25]

But that wasn't the only poll taken at the time. Mearsheimer and Walt failed to mention a more Iraq-specific poll cited by Gideon Levy, the far-left *Ha'aretz* columnist who opposed the war, and whom they quoted as an authority on the hawkish mood of Israel's leaders. Levy held that while Israel's leaders favored a war, Israel's public was divided. To support that claim, he cited an opinion poll done by the Dialogue Institute for *Ha'aretz* and published in the paper on February 13, 2003:

> It tuns out that nearly half of Israelis are against an immediate war—20.4 percent think the U.S. should refrain completely from attacking, and another 23.4 percent are in favor of an attack only if all the inspection and mediation efforts fail. Figures in America are amazingly similar.[26]

This hardly conformed to Mearsheimer and Walt's assertion that "the [Israeli] public enthusiastically favored war." Yet they somehow over-looked a major public opinion poll on the subject of their research, conducted for *Ha'aretz*—a newspaper cited almost *ninety* times in their footnotes.

The Thesis Revised

"A number of Israel's defenders—most notably Martin Kramer—have challenged our claim that Israel and the lobby encouraged the United States to attack Iraq." Thus did Walt and Mearsheimer begin their December 2006 rejoinder to my catalogue of evidence omitted from their original paper. "Although Iran was seen as the greater threat," they conceded, "Israel and the lobby still pushed the United States to attack Iraq." But beneath the reassertions, one could sense an impend-ing retreat. Israelis, they wrote, "were not sorry that the United States decided to topple Saddam and they never tried to halt the march to war."[27] Both were arguably true, but this fell far short of their earlier assertion that Israel bore primary responsibility for "pressuring" the United States to go to war.

In the course of 2007, more testimony surfaced about Israeli reser-vations in the lead-up to the Iraq war. In January 2007, former Israeli ambassador to Washington Danny Ayalon revealed that Sharon had cautioned Bush against invading Iraq, in their Washington meeting of February 7, 2002. According to Ayalon, Sharon had urged Bush to formulate an exit strategy if he did go forward—one not based on the chimera of democratizing Iraq.[28] Then in August 2007 came further testimony, this time from an American. "The Israelis were telling us Iraq is not the enemy—Iran is the enemy," revealed Lawrence Wilkerson, who had been chief of staff to Secretary of State Colin Powell. He described the messaging from Israel as "pervasive," and summarized it thus: "If you are going to destabilize the balance of power, do it against the main enemy," that is, Iran.[29]

Mearsheimer and Walt proceeded to turn their paper into a book, which appeared in August 2007. The book version included a number of tactical retreats. "Israel did not initiate the campaign for war against Iraq," they wrote, a statement at odds with the thrust of their original paper. They also admitted that Israel had pushed for Iran over Iraq, and that Israel only joined the Iraq bandwagon when the Bush administration seemed set on Iraq. But they did not dismantle their thesis. Instead, they refined it: the Iraq war must still be blamed on Israel, because in the lead-up to the war, Israel and its lobby worked overtime to ensure that Bush didn't get "cold feet": "Israeli leaders worried constantly in the months before the war that President Bush might decide not to go to war after all, and they did what they could to ensure Bush did not get cold feet."[30] And this: "Top Israeli officials were doing everything in their power to make sure that the United States went after Saddam and did not get cold feet at the last moment."[31]

Mearsheimer and Walt brought not a single footnote, in their copiously footnoted book, to substantiate this new and bizarre claim, predicated on the notion that Bush, Vice President Dick Cheney, and defense secretary Donald Rumsfeld might waver "at the last moment" when they had Saddam squarely in their sights. Nor did they provide any evidence of Israeli worries that the Bush administration would waver on Iraq.

And once again, Walt and Mearsheimer missed evidence—this time, an item pointing to Israel's real worry in the lead-up to the war. It wasn't that Bush would get "cold feet," but that the "long pause" (Sharansky's phrase) would last indefinitely—that is, that the United States would fail to translate an Iraq triumph into a move against Iran. They had good reason to fret.

This surfaced in a dramatic exchange four months before the war, when Ariel Sharon told the London *Times* (November 5, 2002) that Iran should be put under pressure "the day after" action against Iraq. Mearsheimer and Walt brought the quote.[32] But they completely omitted what followed on the very same day: British foreign secretary Jack Straw rebuked Sharon on the BBC. "I profoundly disagree with him," Straw said, "and I think it would be the gravest possible error to think in that way." The London *Times* reported the spat the next day ("Straw and Sharon 'Deeply Disagree'"), adding that both British and U.S. senior diplomats were "dismissive of Sharon's call." The paper went on to quote "a senior American" who spoke these words: "The President understands the nuances. You can't paint Iran as totally black in the same way as you do Iraq. . . . I would have a hard time buying the idea that after victory in Iraq, the U.S. is going to turn its sights on Iran."[33]

So the Israelis had good cause to worry. Walt and Mearsheimer in their book wrote that the Israelis "were convinced that Bush would deal with Iran after he finished with Iraq."[34] No they weren't, because they knew Britain would oppose it, along with plenty of "senior Americans." Precisely because they weren't convinced, they kept coming back to it.

And they were right to worry, because in the end, the United States accommodated the British. There would be no Iran follow-up by the Bush administration. Why? Because British prime minister Tony Blair did Bush an immense favor in Europe by supporting him over Iraq, and the British sent thousands of troops to fight there. Bush's feet were snug and warm—nailing Saddam had 80 percent public support in America— but Blair felt the chill at home. To keep him on board, Bush gave him to understand that there wouldn't be an Iran sequel, at least not on Blair's watch. And Bush even indulged Blair's very different view of "the day after," consisting of U.S. pressure on Israel to restart the "peace process" with the Palestinians.[35]

It's Complicated

What does the full evidence suggest? That the Israeli posture on the Iraq war was much more complex than Mearsheimer and Walt allowed or even imagined. Did two former Israeli prime ministers, Ehud Barak and Benjamin Netanyahu, write tough-guy op-eds in favor of striking Iraq (both, while private citizens)? They did.[36] Did Efraim Halevy, Sharon's national security adviser, give a starry-eyed speech on the new Middle East that would emerge after Saddam fell? He did.[37] Did Israeli intelligence generate some overwrought assessments of Iraq? It did.[38] But Israel also had a debate, one that went missing in the Mearsheimer-Walt version.

Daniel Levy, an Israeli promoter of the so-called Geneva Initiative, grabbed some attention by welcoming the Mearsheimer-Walt paper.[39]

He was hardly hostile to their enterprise. But in a radio interview, he said this:

> I'll give you an Israeli angle on this which may surprise some peo-
> ple and be interesting. . . . Many Israelis felt that engaging in a war
> with Iraq was the right thing to do and was good for Israeli security.
> However, there was a debate, it didn't surface greatly but it was very
> much taking place within the Israeli security establishment and it said
> the following: the strategic threat is Iran, not Iraq. We may limit and
> actually undermine what we can do in Iran if we go for what some
> people have called the wrong war. Now those voices may not have
> been heard very publicly but they were heard inside the security
> establishment.[40]

In a postwar analysis, Israeli analyst (and former general) Shlomo Brom described the disagreement, and what ended it (emphasis mine):

> The ongoing dialogues between various levels of the Israeli and
> American governments over the last decade revealed disagreements
> between the two countries concerning the relative weight of the
> various threats in the Middle East. The United States was wont to
> emphasize the Iraqi threat, while Israel tended to express its under-
> standing that the Iraqi threat was contained and under control, and
> it was the Iranian threat that loomed as far more serious. *Once the
> Bush administration decided to take action against Iraq,* it was more
> difficult for Israel to maintain its position that dealing with Iraq was
> not the highest priority, especially when it was obvious that the war
> would serve Israel's interests. Considering the circumstances, it would
> therefore be difficult to expect the Israeli government to express its
> doubts—if any—about Iraq's capabilities.[41]

In fact, some doubts did leak into statements by Israel's top generals, as we have seen. But once Israel's leaders realized that the Bush adminis-tration was dead serious about ousting Saddam, they jumped onto the bandwagon (as did America's other allies). Israeli politicians joined the chorus, and the Israeli security establishment fell in line. Key Israelis and the pro-Israel lobby ended up helping the Bush administration market the war to Congressional Democrats, in the hope that the administration would reward the favor in the war's aftermath.

Mearsheimer and Walt thus would seem to have had it exactly wrong. It wasn't Israel that persuaded the Bush administration of the war's necessity, but vice versa: the administration persuaded and then enlisted Israel. It did so, in considerable measure, by hinting that the United States would be better positioned to deal with Iran once it had disposed of Saddam. In the end, Israel acquiesced in the U.S. threat perception, which didn't align with its own. Influential Israelis also publicly helped to bolster the arguments made by the Bush administration. As in 1991, Israel again prepared to do something totally foreign to it: absorb an Iraqi strike, perhaps with non-conventional weapons, while forgoing retaliation. Once the die was cast in Washington, Israel had only one overriding desideratum: that the United States move quickly against Iraq, to spare the Israeli public a prolonged period of uncertainty, and to accelerate Act Two, the humbling of Iran.

Ultimately, Israel collected no reward, because the "long pause" never ended. Too many more powerful interests aligned against an Iranian "day after." In particular, the "special relationship" with Britain trumped the "special relationship" with Israel. In Iraq, Iran, and the Gulf, it was Britain, not Israel, that served as America's traditional guide and partner. Sharon could stonewall Tony Blair's efforts on behalf of the Palestinians. But he could not tilt the balance against the British prime minister in any debate over strategy in the Persian Gulf.

The "long pause" continued into the Obama administration, which pushed through an Iran deal that gave rise to deep misgivings across the Israeli political spectrum and a very public crisis in U.S.-Israeli relations. The Iraq war and its aftermath thus proved exactly the *opposite* of what Mearsheimer and Walt claimed they proved. They were evidence not of Israel's irresistible influence, but of the limits of Israel's leverage whenever it came up against other major U.S. interests and alliances.

For the Record

Why has this episode not gone down in history as a defeat of the storied "lobby"? Both Israel and its friends kept the difference of opinion under wraps, and Sharon made sure it never bubbled up by imposing silence. On the American side, no one had an interest in admitting that Americans had spurned good advice. This extended to the neoconservatives in the Bush administration, who had reassured Israel about "the day after," but then failed to deliver on it.

In retrospect, some thought Sharon's silence over the matter was a mistake: "When Bush ignored his advice about Iraq," analyst Yossi Alpher wrote in 2007, "Sharon should have found a respectful and friendly way to make his reservations public."[42] But he didn't, and (as Alpher also noted) that silence allowed Walt and Mearsheimer to turn reality on its head. Their work widely disseminated the false notion that Israel bore special if not unique responsibility for the Iraq war.

It is a canard that still hangs over Israel, suggesting that Israel either profoundly misread the Middle East or profoundly misled the United States. And it continues to resonate wherever stab-in-the-back theories about Iraq fester.

The time has come to write this failure into the history of U.S.-Israel relations. First and foremost, accuracy and comprehensiveness demand it. There is no legitimate reason to bowdlerize the historical record, even if the truth reveals yet another vulnerability in the "special relationship." Restoring the episode to its proper place may also have some practical value, in demonstrating why open disagreements may be preferable to quiet ones. Had Israel's assessment of the Iraqi threat in 2002 been better known, perhaps its assessment of the Iranian threat in 2015 would have been more credible.

In 2015, Israel's disagreement with the U.S. administration over Iran was very public, and some believe that it damaged Israeli credibility and the standing of the pro-Israel lobby. It is far too early to tell, since the ultimate outcome of the Iran deal is unknown. But because the lines were drawn so sharply in 2015, we will know who got it right in a decade. One must hope that as that time passes, it is Israel that will be proven wrong.

Notes

1. Julie Hirschfeld David, "Pro-Israel Group Went 'All In,' but Suffered a Stinging Defeat," *New York Times*, September 11, 2015.
2. Eli Lake and Josh Rogin, "How Obama Out-Muscled Aipac," *Bloomberg Businessweek*, September 17, 2015.
3. "Not since George H. W. Bush was president has the American Israel Public Affairs Committee sustained such a public defeat on an issue it deemed an existential threat to Israel's security." Karoun Demirjian and Carol Morello, "How AIPAC Lost the Iran Deal Fight," *Washington Post*, September 3, 2015.
4. Dennis Ross, *Doomed to Succeed: The U.S.-Israel Relationship from Truman to Obama* (New York: Farrar, Straus and Giroux, 2015).
5. John Mearsheimer and Stephen Walt, "The Israel Lobby," *London Review of Books* 28, no. 6 (March 23, 2006): 3–12.
6. John J. Mearsheimer and Stephen M. Walt, "The Israel Lobby and U.S. Foreign Policy," *KSG Faculty Research Working Paper Series* RWP06-011, March 2006 (hereafter: *Working Paper*).
7. John J. Mearsheimer and Stephen M. Walt, *The Israel Lobby and U.S. Foreign Policy* (New York: Farrar, Straus and Giroux, 2007).
8. *Working Paper*, 30–31.
9. Hence the disappointment with *9/11 Commission Report* among severe critics of Israel, such as University of Michigan professor Juan Cole, who complained that "the 9/11 commission report stupidly denie[d]" that

Israeli "predations" against the Palestinians were a "key source of Muslim rage." Juan Cole, "200,000 Israeli Fascists Demand Colonization of Gaza," *Informed Comment* blog, July 26, 2004, archived at http://web.archive.org/web/20050212160100/http://www.juancole.com/2004/07/200000-israeli-fascists-demand.html.

10. John J. Mearsheimer and Stephen M. Walt, "An Unnecessary War," *Foreign Policy* 137 (January–February 2003): 51–59.

11. Much speculation surrounded the deeper motives of the two authors. For a sample, see Eliot A. Cohen, "Yes, It's Anti-Semitic," *Washington Post*, April 5, 2006; and Richard Cohen, "No, It's Not Anti-Semitic," *Washington Post*, April 25, 2006.

12. Barry Rubin, "U.S. Attack on Iraq: Good for the Jews?," *Jerusalem Post*, October 7, 2002.

13. Laurie Mylroie, *Iraq News*, September 14, 1998, archived at http://web.archive.org/web/20030114175748/http://www.globalsecurity.org/wmd/library/news/iraq/1998/980914-in2.htm.

14. Laurie Myrolie interviewed by Mordechai Twersky, *Jerusalem Post Radio*, October 30, 2001, archived at http://web.archive.org/web/20020105002816/http://www.spiritoftruth.org/post_008.htm.

15. Seymour M. Hersh, "The Iran Game," *The New Yorker*, December 3, 2001.

16. Ibid.

17. Aluf Benn, "Israel Turns Up the Heat on Iran," *Salon.com*, January 28, 2002, archived at http://web.archive.org/web/20140416110440/http://www.salon.com/2002/01/28/mullahs_2/.

18. Alan Sipress, "Israel Emphasizes Iranian Threat," *Washington Post*, February 7, 2002.

19. Ibid.

20. James Bennet, "Sharon Tells Cabinet to Keep Quiet on U.S. Plans," *New York Times*, October 7, 2002.

21. Barbara Demick, "Not All Israelis Welcome Prospect of War With Iraq," *Los Angeles Times*, October 16, 2002.

22. Ibid.

23. Benjamin Netanyahu, "The Case for Toppling Saddam," *Wall Street Journal*, September 20, 2002.

24. *Working Paper*, 31.

25. Ibid, 67, n. 147.

26. Gideon Levy, "A Great Silence Over the Land," *Ha'aretz*, February 16, 2003.

27. John J. Mearsheimer and Stephen M. Walt, *Setting the Record Straight: A Response to Critics of "The Israel Lobby,"* December 12, 2006, archived at http://web.archive.org/web/20110815005740/http://mearsheimer.uchicago.edu/pdfs/A0043.pdf.

28. Yossi Alpher, "Sharon Warned Bush," *The Forward*, January 12, 2007.

29. Gareth Porter, "Israel Warned US Not to Invade Iraq after 9/11," *Inter Press Service*, August 28, 2007, archived at http://web.archive.org/web/20140404201913/http://www.ipsnews.net/2007/08/politics-israel-warned-us-not-to-invade-iraq-after-9-11/.

30. Mearsheimer and Walt, *The Israel Lobby* (book), 234.

31. Ibid., 261.

32. Ibid., 292.

33. Michael Binyon and Miranda Eeles, "Straw and Sharon 'Deeply Disagree,'" *The Times* (London), November 6, 2002.
34. Mearsheimer and Walt, *The Israel Lobby* (book), 261.
35. "To me," wrote Blair in his memoirs, the Israel-Palestine peace process "was the indispensable soft-power component to give equilibrium to the hard power that was necessary if Saddam were to be removed." Tony Blair, *A Journey: My Political Life* (New York: Knopf, 2010), 400.
36. Ehud Barak, "Taking Apart Iraq's Nuclear Threat," *New York Times*, September 4, 2002; Netanyahu, "The Case for Toppling Saddam."
37. Ephraim Halevy, "Future Developments in the Middle East and the Persian Gulf," speech to the Munich Conference on Security Policy, February 9, 2003, archived at http://web.archive.org/web/20151231161256/http://www.webcitation.org/5wW1nxAip.
38. Greg Myre, "Lawmakers Rebuke Israeli Intelligence Services Over Iraq," *New York Times*, March 29, 2004.
39. Daniel Levy, "So Pro-Israel That It Hurts," *International Herald Tribune*, April 4, 2006.
40. Daniel Levy interviewed by Christopher Lydon, *Radio Open Source*, April 4, 2006, at http://www.radioopensource.org/the-israel-lobby/, accessed January 1, 2016.
41. Shlomo Brom, "The War in Iraq: An Intelligence Failure?," *Strategic Assessment* 6, no. 3 (November 2003): 15–16.
42. Alpher, "Sharon Warned Bush."

24

Fouad Ajami Goes to Israel

In a curious way, my exposure to Israel was essential to my coming to terms with Arab political life and its material.
—Fouad Ajami[1]

The scholar and public intellectual Fouad Ajami, who was born in Lebanon and died in 2014 at the age of sixty-eight, specialized in explaining to Westerners the complex and traumatic encounter of the Arab peoples with modernity. He did not write much about Israel per se, or claim any unique insights into its complexities. And yet, at a certain point in his life, he decided he would discover Israel for himself—not only by reading and meeting Israelis abroad, but by visiting the place.

As it happens, I witnessed several of the stages of this discovery, first as his student and later as his friend. Here I want to mark those stages, and then offer some observations on the crucial insight I believe he derived from his quest.

I start with a passage written in 1991:

> At night, a searchlight from the Jewish village of Metullah could be seen from the high ridge on which my village lay. The searchlight was a subject of childhood fascination. The searchlight was from the land of the Jews, my grandfather said. . . . In the open, barren country, by the border, that land of the Jews could be seen and the chatter of its people heard across the barbed wire.[2]

Fouad's native village, Arnoun in southern Lebanon, stands less than five miles from Metullah, the northernmost point in Israel. The story of his discovery of Israel surely begins with this searchlight, beaming and beckoning across an impenetrable border. From childhood, he would later recall, "I retained within me an unrelenting sense of curiosity" about the Jewish state.[3]

Princeton and Palestine

But the actual discovery began only much later, after Fouad passed through Beirut and came to America. In the fall of 1974, I was a Princeton University senior in Fouad's class, Politics 320, "Modernization in the Middle East and North Africa." I was twenty, with two years of study in Israel under my belt; Fouad, recently arrived as an assistant professor of politics, was twenty-nine. Richard Falk, who taught international law at Princeton and would later become notorious as an anti-Israel agitator, played some role in bringing him onto the faculty; he remembered Fouad as one who "shared a critical outlook on the follies of the American imperial role and felt a deep sympathy for the Palestinian struggles for their place in the sun." Falk also claimed that he introduced Fouad to Edward Said, with whom there was a "rapid bonding."[4]

Although I place little faith in Richard Falk's word on anything, I imagine this to be true. Still, I have no personal recollection, from the fall of 1974, of Fouad as a firebrand. In that class there was an Israeli freshman, a twenty-four-year-old artillery captain who had distinguished himself in the October 1973 war and who was the first Israeli officer to go abroad on undergraduate study leave. He later rose to the rank of brigadier general. This young Israeli came right out of central casting—a confident soldier-scholar, not only a sabra but a graduate of Phillips Exeter, the elite New Hampshire boarding school. My vague recollection is that Fouad was fascinated by him, and the class often turned into a back-and-forth between the two of them. When this Israeli was profiled in Princeton's alumni magazine, he said of Fouad that "we get along well. Relationships at Princeton are very intellectual."[5]

After my graduation and a year in New York, I returned to Princeton as a graduate student in 1976. Fouad was still there. He had become a star lecturer, with a huge course in international politics enrolling more than three hundred students. In those years, he still wore his Palestinian sympathies on his sleeve. Many will have seen a YouTube clip from 1978 of an exchange between one Ben Nitay, a twenty-nine-year-old economic consultant known today as Benjamin Netanyahu, and a thirty-three-year-old Fouad in a jet-black beard. In this encounter, which took place a scant two years after the IDF's dramatic rescue of Jewish hostages held by Palestinian terrorists at Entebbe (an operation in which Jonathan Netanyahu lost his life), Fouad is very much the angry Arab, peppering an unflappable Bibi with aggressive questions about Israel's policies toward the Palestinians.[6]

In the archives of the *Daily Princetonian,* I find an April 1979 report under this headline: "Politics Professor Informs Precept of PLO Invitation to Visit Lebanon." According to a student cited in the report, Ajami "told us that Yasser Arafat had invited him and six students to come visit him." According to another student, Ajami "said jokingly the reason he had received the invitation was because he had spoken out for the PLO in the past, and they hoped he would do so again."[7]

That Fouad might have thought to visit Beirut, where he himself grew to manhood, on an invitation from the PLO, speaks of another time and a different Fouad. It is usually said that he broke with the Palestinians over the PLO's abuse of the Shi'ites of his native Lebanon, especially in the lead-up to Israel's 1982 invasion. But the shift was probably expedited by his move from Princeton to the School of Advanced International Studies at Johns Hopkins, and his engagement with *The New Republic,* especially its owner Martin Peretz and its literary editor Leon Wieseltier, and subsequently with Mortimer Zuckerman, publisher of *The Atlantic* and *U.S. News & World Report.*

Among American Jews, Fouad found the kind of free-wheeling, serious intellectual camaraderie that the Arab-American community, then and now, simply couldn't sustain. Israel would not have been the cause of his being drawn into this world, but there he would have been challenged to test his second-hand notions of Israel against the reality.

Crossing the Jordan

And so he did test them. Fouad paid his first visit in 1980, crossing from Jordan over the Allenby Bridge. "It would have been too brave, too forthright to fly into Israel," he later wrote. "I covered up my first passage by pretending that I had come to the West Bank. . . . Venturing there (even with an American passport) still had the feel of something illicit about it."[8]

From then on, he began to pay fairly regular visits, and to fly directly. Because I had been his student, and we could pick each other out in a crowd, I volunteered for the pleasant task of meeting him when he landed at Ben-Gurion airport. Although an American citizen, he had been born in an enemy country, and his Israeli friends wanted to spare him any indignity or delay at the airport. So I would greet him before he entered passport control. Then we would take a seat while border officials scrutinized his papers. Once he had been cleared, we would claim his bags, and I would drive him to his hotel. By the end of this ritual, we would have caught each other up on our news, and I would know what he was hoping to do on his trip.

Here is Fouad's 1991 description of these visits:

> I knew a good many of the country's academics and journalists. I had
> met them in America, and they were eager to tutor me about their
> country. Gradually the country opened to me. I didn't know Hebrew;
> there was only so much of Israeli life that was accessible to me. But
> the culture of its universities, the intensity of its intellectual debates
> would soon strip me of the nervousness with which I had initially
> approached the place. The Palestinian story was not mine. I could
> thus see Israel on its own terms. I was free to take in the world that
> the Zionist project had brought forth. Above all, I think I had wanted
> to understand and interpret Arab society without the great alibi that
> Israel had become for every Arab failing under the sun. In a curious
> way, my exposure to Israel was essential to my coming to terms with
> Arab political life and its material.[9]

The visits were personal, and Fouad usually came alone. He didn't
participate in conferences, deliver lectures, or grant interviews. He did
want to meet public figures; my colleague Itamar Rabinovich arranged
most of those meetings. I have a clear memory of a Sabbath lunch
hosted by Rabinovich at his apartment so that Fouad could meet Yitzhak
Rabin, then out of government; I'm sure Rabinovich made many more
such introductions. On another occasion, in the mid-1990s, I went
through a former student to set up a meeting for Fouad with Benjamin
Netanyahu, then in his first term as prime minister.

I never heard Fouad boast of these meetings, and of course we would
never spread word of them. He wasn't collecting trophies. He wanted
to learn what made the country's leaders tick. But he valued no less
highly his meetings with intellectuals. He felt an especially deep affinity
with the political analyst Meron Benvenisti, a former deputy mayor of
Jerusalem and vocal advocate of binationalism, whose almost tragic
complexity fascinated him.

On weekends, he was sometimes free. I remember Fouad coming to
my home for a Sabbath lunch, and a walk we took to a nearby *moshav*,
a kind of collective farm. He loved the rustic houses, the idling trac-
tors, the scent of freshly turned earth, the dogs lazing in the road—all
reminded him powerfully of his native village, and he shared some
stories of a distant childhood. On the way back we entered a military
cemetery, and I read him some of the tombstones, explaining how each
war came to have its official name. He was thoughtfully silent.

Back in America, Fouad generally steered clear of appearances before
the bevy of organizations that support Israel. He had made an exception

in 1992, when he allowed friends to "draft" him (his word) to speak at a New York fundraiser for the Jerusalem Foundation, alongside Dan Rather and Henry Kissinger.[10] The Arabic press was all over him, and friends learned not to ask this sort of favor again. But in 2012, when the American Friends of Tel Aviv University put on a gala dinner in New York to honor his (and my) mentor Bernard Lewis, Fouad did speak, with humor and emotion.[11] For Lewis, Fouad would do anything—another large story. But he also nodded toward Tel Aviv University, and his statement of friendship is very much worth having in these days of academic-boycott resolutions by bigoted people whose knowledge of Israel and Israeli universities is as nothing compared to his.

Fouad also welcomed publication of his books in Hebrew. Four appeared, in a curious order. First was *The Vanished Imam*, on the political awakening of Lebanon's Shi'ites, rushed to translation in 1988 when Israel was facing a Shi'ite insurgency in Lebanon's south. Then came *The Dream Palace of the Arabs;* only after that, its predecessor *The Arab Predicament,* a full two decades after its original publication; and finally, in 2012, *The Syrian Rebellion.*

The Arabs Could Have Learned

What did Fouad take away from his forays of discovery? Much of what is said on this subject misses the point—a failure exemplified by the absurd claim, made in an old hit piece in *The Nation,* that he "became an ardent Zionist" and even underwent a "Likudnik conversion."[12] Far from it. Fouad was one of those—and I would include among them the late, great Jewish scholar Elie Kedourie—who began as naysayers but reconciled themselves to Israel because it had become, in Kedourie's words, a "going concern." Or, as Fouad put it, "the state that had fought its way into the world in 1948 is there to stay."[13] Fouad wasn't an "ardent Zionist"—and believe me, I know us when I see us. He was a hard-bitten realist who believed that the dreamy denial of Israel's permanence was crippling the Arabs.

Fouad accused Arab elites, and especially Arab intellectuals, of failing in their most critical responsibility: to grasp the power of Zionism and later Israel, and so pursue an urgent accommodation with the new reality. Instead they had done the opposite, feeding Palestinian refugees and Arab publics with the cruel illusion that history could be undone.

Again and again, Fouad would return to the phrases "history's verdict" and "harsh truths." "It would have been the humane thing," he wrote, "to tell the [Palestinian] refugees that huge historical verdicts are never overturned. But it was safer to offer a steady diet of evasion and escapism."[14] And this: "Ever since the Palestinians had taken to the road after 1948, that population had never been given the gift of political truth. Zionism had built a whole, new world west of the Jordan River, but Palestinian nationalism had insisted that all this could be undone."[15] And this: "Arafat refrained from telling the Palestinians the harsh truths they needed to hear about the urgency of practicality and compromise. . . . He peddled the dream that history's verdict could be overturned, that the 'right of return' was theirs."[16] In short, Arab rejection of Israel had been predicated on either willful ignorance or a lie.

Fouad taught himself more about Israel than any Arab intellectual of his generation. He knew its flaws and faults, but he also understood its virtues and strengths. "On a barren, small piece of land," he wrote,

> the Zionists built a durable state. It was military but not militaristic. It took in waves of refugees and refashioned them into citizens. It had room for faith but remained a secular enterprise. Under conditions of a long siege, it maintained a deep and abiding democratic ethos. The Arabs could have learned from this experiment, but they drew back in horror.[17]

"The Arabs could have learned from this experiment"—in that sentence, Fouad suggested the ultimate purpose of his quest. It wasn't to ingratiate himself with the American Jewish establishment, as his critics charged. It was to break down the wall the Arabs thought they had erected around Israel, but in truth had erected around themselves.

By a circuitous route, Fouad traced that beam of light he first glimpsed shining across the night sky from the far northern edge of Israel back to its very source. Yes, he told truths about the Arabs to America. But perhaps his greater legacy will prove to be the truths he told about Israel to the Arabs.

Notes

1. Fouad Ajami, "The End of Arab Nationalism," *The New Republic*, July 12, 1991.
2. Ibid.
3. Ibid.
4. Richard Falk, "Remembering Fouad Ajami," *Global Justice in the 21st Century* blog, July 9, 2014, archived at http://web.archive.org/web/20140928112744/ http://richardfalk.wordpress.com/2014/07/09/1628/
5. Perry Israel, "Princeton Portrait: Veteran of Two Wars, John Shimsoni '78," *Princeton Alumni Weekly*, October 22, 1974. That same semester, incidentally, some of my Jewish classmates decided to invite Fouad to dinner at the

kosher dining facility on campus. I'm sure it was his earliest kosher culinary experience—the first, and quite possibly the worst, of many to come.

6. David Ania, "28 years old Benjamin Netanyahu" [video file], August 3, 2014, https://www.youtube.com/watch?v=YQx3XMkiVbg, accessed on March 4, 2016.

7. Christopher Glocke, "Politics Professor Informs Precept of PLO Invitation to Visit Lebanon," *Daily Princetonian*, April 19, 1979.

8. Fouad Ajami, "The End of Arab Nationalism," *The New Republic*, July 12, 1991.

9. Ibid.

10. Sam Husseini, "Can You Believe What CBS Says About Arabs?," *FAIR* website, October 1, 1992, archived at http://web.archive.org/web/20150117152015/http://fair.org/extra-online-articles/can-you-believe-what-cbs-says-about-arabs/.

11. Ajami speech, Tel Aviv University American Friends, "Bernard Lewis Dinner" [video file], September 25, 2012, from min. 51:25, https://www.youtube.com/watch?v=tv9Xof6CS4c, accessed on March 4, 2016.

12. Adam Shatz, "The Native Informant: Fouad Ajami is the Pentagon's Favorite Arab," *The Nation*, April 28, 2003.

13. Fouad Ajami, "Israel's Triumph," *U.S. News & World Report*, July 10, 2007.

14. Fouad Ajami, "A Reality Check as Israel Turns 60," *U.S. News & World Report*, May 7, 2008.

15. Fouad Ajami, "The Promise of Liberty," *Wall Street Journal*, February 7, 2006.

16. Fouad Ajami, "The U.N. Can't Deliver a Palestinian State," *Wall Street Journal*, June 1, 2011.

17. Ajami, "A Reality Check as Israel Turns 60."

25

"Gaza Is Auschwitz"

Holocaust inversion is the claim that Israel acts toward the Palestinians as the Nazis acted toward the Jews. Just what purpose does the claim serve? That it flourishes on crackpot websites or the alleyways of Karachi is of scant interest. More interesting are situations where it gains traction among people whom we assume to be sophisticated about history and politics, in Western academe and journalism. After all, it is highly unlikely that anyone in these settings really believes that Israel conducts itself as Nazi Germany did. That goes for intellectuals who make or allude to the analogy, as well as their elite audiences. And yet Holocaust inversion continues to surface in these circles, and is even gaining wider dissemination. What actual function do these claims fill?

But before I attempt to answer that question, it is useful to sketch a brief history of Holocaust inversion. It evolved in three stages. In the first stage, it was invented by British sympathizers of the Arabs, even as ashes still filled the crematoria. In the second stage, it was adopted by the Soviet Union, with particular fervor after 1967. Its latest and present iterations are on the left in the West, including the academy, and in the Muslim world—and wherever they overlap.

Let me illustrate with a few examples. We are indebted to the historian Rory Miller, who has shown that the analogy between Zionism and Nazism even predates the creation of Israel.[1] Amazingly, it was a staple of anti-Zionist rhetoric in Britain as early as the mid-1940s, when Europe teemed with Jewish refugees, and before even one Palestinian Arab took to flight. The disseminators of this notion were some British Arabists and the so-called Arab Office, the pro-Arab propaganda outfit set up to make the Palestinian Arab case in London. Their champion, Sir Edward Spears, wrote as long ago as 1945 that

> political Zionism as it is manifested in Palestine today preaches very much the same doctrines as Hitler. . . . Zionist policy in Palestine has many features similar to Nazi philosophy. . . . the politics of

Herrenvolk. . . . the Nazi idea of Lebensraum, is also very in evidence
in the Zionist philosophy. . . . the training of youth is very similar under
both organizations that have designed this one and the Nazi one.[2]

If this claim is even worth mentioning at all, it is to demonstrate that
the attempt to assimilate Zionism to Nazism began even as the collaborationist Mufti of Jerusalem was on the run, even before the word
"Holocaust" became current, and even before the Israeli army fired its
first shot. The approach of anti-Zionists was always to associate Zionism
with the most threatening and ominous evil of the day. (Accordingly, at
the very moment that British Arabists were warning that a Jewish state
would behave in a Nazi manner, anti-Zionist Americans were warning
that it would behave in a communist one.)[3]

Perhaps the most famous case of a British supporter of the Arab
cause propounding the equivalence of Nazism and Zionism was the big-
think historian Arnold Toynbee, a cult figure in the English-speaking
world, known for his penchant for far-fetched analogies. In his *Study
of History,* Toynbee called the contemporary Israeli "a Janus figure, part
American farmer technician, part Nazi *sicarius.*" He also accused Israel
of "inflicting on an innocent weaker neighbour the very sufferings that
the original victim had experienced at his stronger neighbour's hands."[4]
Toynbee finally outdid even himself when he wrote this sentence: "On
the Day of Judgment the gravest crime standing to the German National
Socialists' account might be, not that they had exterminated a majority
of the Western Jews, but that they had caused the surviving remnant
of Jewry to stumble."[5] That stumble, of course, being Zionism and the
creation of Israel, here cast as a more criminal venture even than the
Nazi extermination.

Holocaust Inversion on the Left

The tremendous boost to the equation of Zionism with Nazism came
from the Soviet Union, beginning in the 1950s. It was Soviet propaganda that first began to equate the Star of David with the swastika in
cartoons. It was in the Soviet Union that books were published alleging
Zionist-Nazi collaboration. And after 1967, it was the Soviets who
turned up the volume on the Zionist-equals-Nazi amplifier.

For example, the Soviet Premier Alexei Kosygin said this at the United
Nations in June 1967, when the Israeli occupation was only days old:

> What is going on in the Sinai Peninsula and in the Gaza Strip, in
> the western part of Jordan and on Syrian soil occupied by the Israeli

troops, brings to mind the heinous crimes perpetrated by the Fascists during World War II. . . . In the same way as Hitler Germany used to appoint Gauleiters in the occupied regions, the Israeli government is establishing an occupation administration in the territories seized and is appointing its military governors there.[6]

(In his reply, Israeli foreign minister Abba Eban called the comparison "a flagrant breach of international morality and human decency," and added: "Our nation never compromised with Hitler Germany. It never signed a pact with it as did the USSR in 1939.")[7]

It would be the Soviet example that the Arab propagandists would emulate. They did so at first hesitantly, since Nazism did not have the same depth of negative associations in the Arab world as Zionism itself. But the more Arabs became aware of the Holocaust and the extent of Nazi crimes, the more eager they became to equate Zionism with Nazism. This would spread still further into the Muslim world at large.

A prime example dates from 2001, in the lead-up to the Durban conference, when Shimon Peres was Israel's foreign minister. A cartoon of Peres in a Nazi uniform appeared on the cover of an Egyptian weekly. When this drew criticism, a bevy of Egyptian "intellectuals" wrote to defend it. "Peres committed and commits more ugly acts against the Arabs than the Nazis did against the Jews," wrote one of them. Another wrote that Hitler "is the one who is unjustly treated" in the comparison with Peres.[8]

The preeminent disseminator of Holocaust inversion in the Muslim world today is Turkish president Recep Tayyip Erdoğan, who returns to the theme repeatedly. Here is a prime example, from the summer of 2014:

> What is the difference between Israeli actions and those of the Nazis and Hitler? How can you explain what the Israeli state has been doing in Gaza, Palestine, if not genocide? This is racism. This is fascism. This is keeping Hitler's spirit alive.[9]

In the Western academy, all of these threads have come together: the Arabist tradition, leftist agitprop, and Arab-Muslim nationalism have combined to create hothouse conditions for the spread of Holocaust inversion into the writings and classroom pronouncements of professors. Let me end this short history with two examples drawn from the faculty of Columbia University in New York.

The first one is from Joseph Massad, professor of Arab studies. Massad once had been accused by some students of Holocaust inversion in class, and in his defense, he had insisted that the "lie . . . claiming that I would equate Israel with Nazi Germany is abhorrent. I have never made such a reprehensible equation."[10] So Massad was fully aware of the "abhorrent" and "reprehensible" nature of Holocaust inversion.

But only four years later, after a 2009 flare-up of conflict in Gaza, he published an article entitled "The Gaza Ghetto Uprising." Illustrated by the famous image of a surrendering child in the Warsaw ghetto, the article cited an alleged Israeli plan to "make Israel a purely Jewish state that is *Palästinener-rein.*" Massad characterized the Palestinian Authority—or, rather, "the Israeli-created Palestinian Collaborationist Authority"—as "the *judenrat*, the Nazi equivalent."[11]

Another Columbia professor, Hamid Dabashi, also known for his inflammatory rhetoric, wrote this under the influence of the Hamas-Israel war in the summer of 2014:

> After Gaza, not a single living Israeli can utter the word "Auschwitz" without it sounding like "Gaza." Auschwitz as a historical fact is now archival. Auschwitz as a metaphor is now Palestinian. From now on, every time any Israeli, every time any Jew, anywhere in the world, utters the word "Auschwitz," or the word "Holocaust," the world will hear "Gaza."[12]

Notice how this species of academic Holocaust inversion has evolved. It is more elusive and allusive, and also more theoretical. We are in the world of metaphors. But whatever its form, the claim of Holocaust inversion remains steady: Israel acts toward the Palestinians as the Nazis acted toward the Jews, albeit on a different scale.

Now some will argue that Holocaust inversion is somehow legitimate because it has surfaced from time to time on the Israeli left. An often-cited example is the late philosopher Yeshaiyahu Leibovitz, who called those Israeli judges who authorized moderate physical pressure on Palestinian detainees "Judeo-Nazis."[13] The N-word in Israel does occasionally figure on the Israeli left, although usually in a refined version. An example is the author Amos Oz, who once called violent settlers on West Bank hilltops "Hebrew neo-Nazis." (I say "refined" because, as Oz himself clarified, neo-Nazis aren't Nazis.)[14] To this we can now add a former Shin Bet head, the late Avraham Shalom, and his statement about the Israeli army in the documentary *The Gatekeepers:* it has become "a brutal occupying army that's similar to the Germans in World War II. Similar, but not identical."[15]

While these statements sound like Toynbee's echo, Leibovitz, Oz, and Shalom nonetheless come from within a Zionist frame of reference, and their comparisons are laden with caveats. Nevertheless, the effect of such statements outside Israel is often to validate Holocaust inversion. Former Israeli ambassador Michael Oren, alluding to Shalom, described the result: "I appear on a campus and a student gets up and says to me, 'you are speaking of your desire for peace, but your former FBI head is comparing you to a Nazi state. What are your comments on that?'"[16]

Flawed Tactic?

There is no doubt that Holocaust inversion today fulfills some of the same functions it always did: a tactic to delegitimize Israel, while perhaps simultaneously diminishing the Holocaust. Historian Deborah Lipstadt has said of Holocaust inversion that it "elevates by a factor of a zillion any wrongdoings Israel might have done, and lessens by a factor of a zillion what the Germans did."[17] The fact that Israel sometimes invokes the Holocaust to justify its existence, as well as its actions, creates a powerful incentive among its enemies or critics either to diminish the Holocaust or, when that seems either impossible or immoral, to claim that Israel is replicating it on some scale in its treatment of the Palestinians.

But does this tactic actually work? On the face of it, Holocaust inversion is a trap. It is, as even Joseph Massad once allowed, so "abhorrent" and "reprehensible" that its effect would seem to be to discredit whoever deploys it. And there are supporters of the Palestinian cause, especially Jewish ones, who from time to time urge that it not be used, because it is so patently preposterous.

For example, Norman Finkelstein, whose project has been to delink the Holocaust from Israel, has been known to discourage such comparisons. Finkelstein said that an Arab once told him that even if the Holocaust did happen, "what about the Palestinian holocaust? I said, you know, why do you have to drag in the Palestinian holocaust? What's happening to Palestinians is awful enough, that you don't have to compare it to the Nazi holocaust."[18]

In 2009, Mark LeVine, an American Jewish historian and vituperative critic of Israel, published a piece entitled "Gaza is no Warsaw Ghetto."

After enumerating Israel's crimes, but also describing the scale of what happened in Warsaw, LeVine warned that

> the use of highly charged historical comparisons that do not hold up to scrutiny unnecessarily weakens the Palestinian case against the occupation. In a propaganda war in which Palestinians have always struggled to compete, handing Israel's supporters the gift of inaccurate or exaggerated comparisons does not help this struggle, particularly not in Israel and the United States, the two most important battlegrounds in this conflict.[19]

So if Holocaust inversion is such a "gift" to Israel's supporters, why do people continue to give it—in particular, people who should know better, like professors at Columbia University, who are surrounded by Israel's supporters, and live in one of the world's most Jewishly saturated environments? It is one thing when Holocaust inversion is deployed in Turkey or Palestine—there is makes perfect sense as a tactic. But on the Upper West Side of Manhattan?

I propose two explanations for why Holocaust inversion appears in such settings. The first is that Jews are particularly susceptible to it. That may sound paradoxical: after all, how could Jews, especially in America where Holocaust awareness is very high, be susceptible to equating Nazi extermination of the Jews with Israel's treatment of the Palestinians? The vulnerability emerges from that interpretation of the Holocaust, according to which this unique event burdens the Jews with a unique responsibility. Unsurprisingly, it was two Palestinians who identified this as a point of vulnerability, when they wrote the following:

> The Holocaust does not free the Jewish state or the Jews of accountability. On the contrary, the Nazi crime compounds their moral responsibility and exposes them to greater answerability. They are the ones who have escaped the ugliest crime in history, and now they are perpetrating reprehensible deeds against another people.[20]

The idea that the Holocaust compounds the Jews' moral responsibility wasn't invented by antisemites. It was invented by Jews who concluded that the Holocaust, itself a unique event, obligates Jews uniquely to stand in the first line against injustice anywhere, particularly any injustice that in any way resembles the Holocaust in *any* of its many phases.

It is this concept—one might go so far as to call it a conceit, in presuming that Jews are gifted with some higher moral sensibility—that makes some Jews especially vulnerable to the claims of Holocaust inverters. And it is why Holocaust inversion is often directed precisely at them. (It is also why it can take on the character of Jew-baiting—a tactic directed not at the widest possible audience, but specifically at Jews, in order to provoke a response from Jews.)

Consider two examples of the vulnerability of two fervently Zionist Jews to Holocaust inversion. The first is the case of Jacobo Timerman, the Argentine Jewish dissident in the dark days of the so-called Dirty War, who was finally extricated and brought to Israel. In 1982, he reported on the Israeli invasion of Lebanon, and wrote a book highly critical of it. Needless to say, Holocaust inverters made much of Ariel Sharon's march to Beirut, and Timerman seemed to see through them.

> The Harvard, Princeton, and Columbia professors who went along with [the PLO] for years, were they allies or accomplices?. . . . To speak of a Palestinian genocide, of a Palestinian Holocaust, to compare Beirut with Stalingrad or with the Warsaw Ghetto, will move no one and will only serve to feed their egos and settle accounts with other academics in whom these images can arouse guilt feelings. Jews know what genocide is, a Holocaust, a Nazi.[21]

That was a straightforward repudiation of the Holocaust inverters in American academe: Jews know genocide and Nazism when they see it, and they won't be fooled or cajoled. Yet elsewhere, Timerman showed his own vulnerability precisely to the tactic used by Holocaust inverters when they pinpoint some supposed similarity between Israeli and Nazi conduct, in order to neutralize the Holocaust as a point of Israeli reference:

> From now on our tragedy will be inseparable from that of the Palestinian. Perhaps some of us will try to sidestep the Israeli moral collapse by resorting to statistics and comparing Auschwitz to Beirut. It will be in vain. The victims of Auschwitz would never have bombed Beirut. Our moral collapse cannot be diluted by statistics.[22]

This dismissive reference to "statistics" deeply discounts one of the core characteristics of the Holocaust, which is its scale and scope. Once this is done, the door is wide open precisely to the kind of Holocaust inversion that Timerman so abhors. For then any Palestinian suffering, regardless of its degree, becomes a "similarity" that places Israel in the dock with Nazism.

Another example, perfectly demonstrating the knowledge that Holocaust inversion is perverse, yet opening the door to it, appears in Ari Shavit's book *My Promised Land*—more particularly, in a chapter that is a recycled article from 1991, in which Shavit tells of his reserve duty as a guard at a detention camp in Gaza. There he manages to conjure up an analogy between this detention camp—probably no worse than Guantanamo and undoubtedly better than Abu Ghraib—and a Nazi extermination camp.

> Although unjust and unfounded, the haunting analogy is pervasive.... And I, who have always abhorred the analogy, who have always argued bitterly with anyone who so much as hinted at it, can no longer stop myself. The associations are too strong. Like a believer whose faith is wavering I go over the long list of counterarguments, all the well-known differences. Most obvious, there are no crematoria here. And in the Europe of the 1930s there was no existential conflict between two peoples. Germany, with its racist doctrine, was organized evil. The Germans were in no real danger whatsoever. But then I realize that the problem is not in the similarity—no one can seriously think there is any real similarity. The problem is that there isn't enough lack of similarity. The lack of similarity is not strong enough to silence once and for all the evil echoes.[23]

"There isn't enough lack of similarity. . ." This is exactly the opening that Holocaust inverters seek to enter.

Moral Categories

And that brings me to my key point: the Holocaust inverter in Western academe doesn't believe that there is an actual equivalence between Israel and the Nazis. The Holocaust inverter knows perfectly well the history and scale of the Holocaust—as well as Ari Shavit does. The Holocaust inverter even knows that the analogy is, in some sense, "abhorrent" and "reprehensible." But he or she knows that by making the analogy, the defendant—the supporter of Israel—will be compelled to enumerate all the dissimilarities, and in so doing, leave exposed some superficial similarities that prompt the Timerman response. That is, Auschwitz and Beirut, or Auschwitz and Gaza, are obviously not equivalents, but they belong to the same moral category.

This is precisely the objective of Holocaust inversion, and Jews are the perfect target for it—because who, if not the Jews, have the duty to sound the alarm when any form of injustice or cruelty has the potential to culminate in a holocaust? In the same way, Palestinian propagandists who speak of a Palestinian "holocaust" don't claim that the "Nakba" of 1948 approximates the Holocaust in any historical sense. Their project is to find or allege small-scale similarities—a massacre in Lydda, a forced labor camp at Ijlin, a hidden mass grave in Jaffa—all with the purpose of establishing the Palestinians as victims on an equal plane.

The second reason Holocaust inversion persists, despite its supposedly self-defeating excess, is that it makes lesser but still preposterous analogies sound more reasonable. So Israel is not Nazi, but it is fascist. So it isn't guilty of genocide, but it commits massacres and mass killings. Gaza isn't a concentration camp or the Warsaw ghetto, but it is the world's largest outdoor prison camp. And Israel isn't Nazi Germany, but it is apartheid South Africa.

Having exhausted your outrage against the Nazi analogy, you will be a tad less vociferous in expressing your outrage against these other analogies, which are also specious, but which now appear "reasonable" and worthy of debate. In other words, Holocaust inversion is a rhetorical softening up. Those who use it don't seek to make the Israel-Nazi analogy credible—an impossible task—but to make other analogies seem like debatable propositions.

And that is why the urgings of people like Mark LeVine are pointless. Of course Gaza isn't Auschwitz; LeVine isn't telling the Holocaust inverters something they don't know. But if his argument is that it is a flawed tactic, Holocaust inverters think otherwise, and that it works on the two planes I have outlined.

The counter to LeVine is provided by Jerome Slater, an American Jewish academic critic of Israel. He acknowledges that the Nazi analogy is "much too strong," but it has one merit: it "results in a productive shock of recognition in Israel and among its friends." He then adds:

> Even the most severe criticism of Israel can hardly be counterproductive, in light of the fact that nothing else has proven to be productive. That is not to deny that even limited or hypothetical analogies to Nazi Germany are risky. Nonetheless, because Israel has gone so far down the road to fascism (not Nazism), the risks must be run—desperate times require desperate measures.[24]

So even though Slater knows and admits the analogy to be specious, he still thinks deploying it can be productive in "shocking" Jews, and that it is a risk worth taking. Nothing more thoroughly demonstrates the instrumental use of Holocaust inversion: those who use it don't believe it, but they use to it bait Jews into a reaction—a reaction that will usually be one of outrage, but in some small percentage of instances will provoke someone to hear "evil echoes," in the phrase of Ari Shavit. After all, desperate times require desperate measures. This has been the rationale of dissimulation and deception since time immemorial.

I now come to the question: is it antisemitic? The (now officially discarded) Working Definition of Anti-Semitism of the European Monitoring Center on Racism and Xenophobia makes this statement:

> Examples of the ways in which antisemitism manifests itself with regard to the State of Israel taking into account the overall context could include: Drawing comparisons of contemporary Israeli policy to that of the Nazis.[25]

The crucial caveat here is the "overall context," which I presume means that there must be other less equivocal evidence of antisemitism in the rhetorical package in which the comparisons appear. This is certainly the usual case when Holocaust inversion surfaces in the Arab-Muslim world, in a setting saturated with antisemitic tropes. But Holocaust inversion is usually deployed, sometimes even by Jews and Israelis, as a tactic. It is a despicable tactic, because it plays on the vulnerabilities of the Jews, on their unresolved ambivalence about having power in the world, on their propensity for moral self-flagellation. But that doesn't make Holocaust inversion antisemitic *ipso facto*. It just makes it exploitative.

If Holocaust inversion is a form of exploitation, then how should it be combatted? I have been descriptive so far, not prescriptive. If it is true that people of basic intelligence and honesty simply won't believe it, and that it is usually put forward by people who don't believe it, refuting it by demonstrating that Israel isn't Nazi Germany would be unnecessary and self-abasing. In these instances, Holocaust inversion is probably best ignored, since its purpose is precisely to provoke a discussion around an absurd premise.

The other prescription might be to remove Nazi analogies altogether from currency in regard to Israel. The late Elie Wiesel called comparisons of Nazi Germany with Iran "unacceptable." "Iran is a danger," he once said, "but to claim that it is creating a second Auschwitz? I compare nothing to the Holocaust."[26] If the Holocaust is indeed a unique event in human history, and if Nazi Germany is unparalleled as a nexus of absolute evil, then promiscuously invoking them to make some political point in the present should be rejected across the board.

What are the prospects for such a rhetorical truce? I leave that to you to calculate.

Notes

1. Rory Miller, *Divided Against Zion: Anti-Zionist Opposition in Britain to a Jewish State in Palestine, 1945–1948* (London: Frank Cass, 2000).
2. Ibid., 147–48.
3. In the May 1948 debate before Harry Truman on whether the United States should recognize Israel, Robert Lovett, then Under Secretary of State, said: "How do we know what kind of Jewish state will be set up? We have many reports from British and American intelligence agents that Soviets are sending Jews and communist agents into Palestine from the Black Sea area." Clark Clifford with Richard Holbrooke, *Counsel to the President: A Memoir* (New York: Random House, 1991), 12.
4. Arnold Toynbee, *A Study of History*, vol. 8 (London: Oxford University Press, 1954), 291, 311.
5. Ibid., 291.
6. Text in *Keesing's Record of World Events* 13 (July 1967): 22153ff. For a comprehensive survey of Holocaust inversion in Soviet propaganda and leftist thought, see Robert S. Wistrich, *From Ambivalence to Betrayal: The Left, the Jews, and Israel* (Lincoln: University of Nebraska Press, 2012), 448–78.
7. *Israel's Foreign Relations: Selected Documents, 1947–1974*, ed. Meron Medzini (Jerusalem: Ministry of Foreign Affairs, 1976).
8. Quoted by Götz Nordbruch, "Reinterpreting History: Perceptions of Nazism in Egyptian Media," in *The Middle East and Palestine: Global Politics and Regional Conflict*, ed. Dietrich Jung (New York: Palgrave, 2004), 91.
9. "Turkey PM slams Israel for 'Hitler-like fascism,'" RT.com, August 1, 2014, archived at http://web.archive.org/web/20140804052300/http://rt.com/news/177164-erdogan-israel-gaza-fascism/.
10. "Joseph Massad Responds to the Intimidation of Columbia University," *Electronic Intifada*, November 3, 2004, archived at http://web.archive.org/web/20110609164358/http://electronicintifada.net/content/joseph-massad-responds-intimidation-columbia-university/5289.
11. Joseph Massad, "The Gaza Ghetto Uprising," *Electronic Intifada*, January 4, 2009, archived at http://web.archive.org/web/20110608193956/http://electronicintifada.net/content/gaza-ghetto-uprising/7919.
12. Hamid Dabashi, "Gaza: Poetry after Auschwitz," *Aljazeera* website, August 8, 2014, archived at http://web.archive.org/web/20140809023814/http://www.aljazeera.com/indepth/opinion/2014/08/gaza-poetry-after-auschwitz-201487153418967371.html.
13. Joel Greenberg, "Yeshayahu Leibowitz, 91, Iconoclastic Israeli Thinker," *New York Times,* August 19, 1994.
14. "I object to comparisons to the Nazis. The comparison I made on Friday wasn't to the Nazis but to the neo-Nazis. Nazis erect ovens and gas chambers; neo-Nazis desecrate places of worship, desecrate cemeteries, beat

up innocent people, and scribble racist slogans. That is what they do in Europe, and that is what they do here." For a critique of Oz's statement, see Liel Leibovitz, "No, Rowdy Settlers Aren't Hebrew Neo-Nazis," *Tablet*, May 12, 2014, archived at http://web.archive.org/web/20140515032355/ http://www.tabletmag.com/scroll/172564/rowdy-settlers-arent-hebrew-neo-nazis.

15. Dror Moreh, *The Gatekeepers: Inside Israel's Internal Security Agency* (New York: Skyhorse, 2015), 386. Shalom qualified this: "I'm not talking about their behavior toward the Jews, which is an unusual thing with its own unique aspects. I'm talking about the way they treated the Poles and the Belgians and the Dutch and the Czech and all of them." This comparison is almost as outlandish; for example, nearly three million Poles perished during the German occupation.

16. Yitzhak Benhorin, "Israel's US Envoy: 'Gatekeepers' Hindering PR Efforts," *Ynet*, March 17, 2013, archived at http://web.archive.org/web/20130317214520/ http://www.ynetnews.com/articles/0,7340,L-4357190,00.html. For the history of the Israeli left's penchant for Holocaust inversion, see Edward Alexander, *The Jewish Wars: Reflections by One of the Belligerents* (Carbondale: Southern Illinois University Press, 1996), 33–44.

17. Deborah Lipstadt interviewed by Amy Klein, Jewish Telegraphic Agency, April 19, 2009, archived at http://web.archive.org/web/20150110044610/ http://www.jta.org/2009/04/19/life-religion/denying-the-deniers-q-a-with-deborah-lipstadt.

18. Norman Finkelstein interviewed by Lena Meari and Tanzeen Doha, *Chintaa* website, October 13, 2010, archived at http://web.archive.org/web/20130807235323/http://www.chintaa.com/index.php/chinta/showAerticle/72/english/.

19. Mark LeVine, "Gaza is no Warsaw Ghetto," *Aljazeera* website, February 2, 2009, archived at http://web.archive.org/web/20121008112411/http://www.aljazeera.com/focus/crisisingaza/2009/02/20092191518941246.html.

20. Hazem Saghiyeh and Saleh Bashir, "Universalizing the Holocaust," *Palestine-Israel Journal* 5, nos. 3–4 (1998): 90–97.

21. Jacobo Timerman, *The Longest War: Israel in Lebanon* (New York: Knopf, 1982), 40.

22. Ibid., 157.

23. Ari Shavit, *My Promised Land: The Triumph and Tragedy of Israel* (New York: Random House, 2013), 231.

24. Jerome Slater, "On the Use of Provocative Analogies (Nazism, Fascism)," *Mondoweiss* website, September 13, 2014, archived at http://web.archive.org/web/20140915050611/http://mondoweiss.net/2014/09/provocative-analogies-fascism.

25. Kenneth L. Marcus, *The Definition of Anti-Semitism* (Oxford: Oxford University Press, 2015), 163.

26. Elie Wiesel interviewed by Yaniv Magal, *Globes*, April 19, 2012, archived at http://web.archive.org/web/20151219234156/http://www.globes.co.il/en/article-1000742410.

Epilogue

The chapters in this volume range widely, but readers will have discerned a unifying thread. Most of the pieces revolve around errors, the confusion they sow, and my own attempts to discover and assemble evidence to correct them. In many cases, I have also probed the source of an error, to determine whether it originated in a lack of information, bias, or plain deception.

When an error arises from a lack of information, it is usually enough to provide the missing piece. It may be buried in an archive, an obscure doctoral dissertation, or a corner of the internet. Resorting to sources as varied as FBI wiretaps and WikiLeaks documents, personal testimony and official documents, it is possible to set the record straight and dispel doubt, as I have done in many of these chapters. As for straightforward deception, a kind of intentional error, it can be contested by the same method, accompanied by the exposure of the deception itself—that is, demonstrating that the purveyor of falsehood knows it to be false.

But the most persistent source of error is bias. Errors that arise from bias are not intentional. They are fed by unconscious prejudices. Bias causes us to filter information in a way that leads to conclusions that validate or reinforce the bias. And I deliberately use the word "us," for no one is immune to bias. Just as there is no end to error, so there is no end to bias—the temptation to see, hear, and believe only that which confirms a preconceived idea.

In an earlier time, such ideas were usually religious. In modern times, they have become ideological and political. Once we recognize that bias is ubiquitous, it is possible to construct mechanisms for neutralizing it, opening the way for the growth of knowledge. Logical reasoning, the scientific method, peer review—these are all designed with the explicit aim of neutralizing bias. On the individual level, the mechanism is the deliberate cultivation of objectivity—the willingness at least to try to see contentious issues from the perspective of others.

A major problem in advancing the understanding of the Middle East is that many of its interpreters have made a virtue of bias and a vice of objectivity.

"Objectivity" in Quotes

Edward Said championed the view that bias isn't a problem at all, and that displaying it is a mark of intellectual probity. Said identified the "threat to the intellectual today" as "professionalism,"

> that is, thinking of your work as an intellectual as something you do for a living, between the hours of nine and five with one eye on the clock, and another cocked at what is considered to be proper, professional behavior—not rocking the boat, not straying outside the accepted paradigms or limits, making yourself marketable and above all presentable, hence uncontroversial and unpolitical and "objective."[1]

For Said, "objectivity" is little more than a diversion, deployed by the powerful to silence dissent. The Orientalists were a case in point. Their relationship to their subject was "based finally on power and not really on disinterested objectivity."[2]

This is the credo of advocacy scholarship. "Objectivity" is placed in quotation marks because it is an illusion. Professionalism is ridiculed as a sell-out to the market. Seeing things as others see them is a betrayal of the self. It is a duty to engage in political controversy, and to do so around the clock.

Contrast this with the view of Bernard Lewis, Said's target. Lewis thought that a scholar

> owes it to himself and to his readers to try, to the best of his ability, to be objective or at least to be fair—to be conscious of his own commitments and concerns and make due allowance and, where necessary, correct for them, to try to present the different aspects of a problem and the different sides to a dispute in such a way as to allow the reader to form an independent judgment. Above all, he should not prejudge issues and predetermine results by the arbitrary selection of evidence and the use of emotionally charged or biased language. As a famous economist once remarked, "Complete asepsis is impossible, but one does not for that reason perform surgery in a sewer."[3]

For Lewis, bias is a vice to be checked, not celebrated; evidence needs to be weighed, not doctored; and part of judgment must be deferred to the reader, not dictated by the author(ity). Lewis concedes that absolute objectivity is unattainable, but that does not mean it is unapproachable. As such, it should be free of quotation marks. A version of this view was also championed by Elie Kedourie, as I explained in "Policy and the Academy" (chapter 4).

Which of these two broad approaches is more likely to temper bias, the source of so much error? We can discern the answer in the state of Middle Eastern studies (and much of academe), where "objectivity" has been derided and devalued. The range of views there is narrow, tolerance for dissent is low, and post facto analysis of error is rare. Of course it is crucial that scholars and analysts venture "outside the accepted paradigms or limits," in Said's words. But flagrant politicization polarizes real people who inhabit real institutions, until one in-group succeeds in driving out all others.

In theory it should not be so, but in practice it is. Just as Communism failed to eliminate inequality, so Saidianism (to coin a term) failed to eliminate "accepted paradigms." It simply created new ones, and then enforced them even more zealously than the cautious "professionals" ever did. The result is an entire academic field plagued by self-righteous hubris, in which errors are never admitted, let alone analyzed. And the same narrowing of perspectives is evident in journalism and filmmaking about the Middle East.

The virtue of Lewis's liberal approach is its humility in the face of uncertainty. Self-criticism, hedged language, deference to evidence—these are what allow people holding different views to differ and debate, and even to admit error to one another and probe its causes. If there is any hope that knowledge of the Middle East will advance, it is in institutions and intellectual ecosystems where the Lewisian view prevails. This includes a few fortunate corners of the academy, and the rather larger universe of research institutes, think tanks, and independent publications where diversity of views and disciplined debate are still regarded as essential to arriving at truth.

The "war on error" over the Middle East will make progress to the extent that scholars, analysts, journalists, and filmmakers internalize the idea of continuous self-criticism, and embrace the self-aware struggle against their own biases. This is precisely what the Orientalists achieved when they courageously abandoned medieval prejudice and polemic, and launched the scholarly study of Islam. That was a revolution. A comparable one is long overdue.

Notes

1. Edward Said, *Representations of the Intellectual: The 1993 Reith Lectures* (New York: Pantheon, 1994), 74.
2. Edward Said, *Orientalism* (New York: Pantheon, 1978), 148.
3. Bernard Lewis, *The Shaping of the Modern Middle East* (New York: Oxford University Press, 1994), vii. The economist was Robert Solow.

Index

Abdullah, King (of Saudi Arabia), 158
Abdullah I, King (of Jordan), 120
Abdullah II, King (of Jordan), 157–58, 160–62
Abraham (patriarch), 142
Abu Ghraib, 298
Abu Mana, Fayeq, 187
academe, 9–17; policy and, 39–50. *See also* Kedourie; Middle Eastern studies
Adventures in the East (Scholl-Latour), 100
al-Afghani, Sayyid Jamal al-Din, 87–95
Afghanistan, Afghans, xi, 15, 66, 155, 162. *See also* al-Afghani
AIPAC. *See* American Israel Public Affairs Committee
A'isha (Muhammad's wife), 84
Ajami, Fouad, xxi–xxii, 283–89
Alawis, in Syria, 135–36, 142, 143
Al-Azhar University, 99
Alexandria (Egypt), 135
Algeria, Algerians, 64
Allon, Yigal, 194, 195, 200–2, 211
Alpher, Yossi, 279
Al Qaeda, xvi, 66, 114, 114–15, 137, 153, 270, 272
Alterman, Natan, 200, 202, 207, 217n.100
Al Zot. See Alterman
American Academy of Arts and Sciences, 58
American Israel Public Affairs Committee (AIPAC), 170, 269
American Jewish Committee, 256
American Jewish Congress, 265n5
American Revolution (1776), 147
American University of Beirut, 119
America: Our Next Chapter (Hagel), 155

Amin Osman Pasha, 126
Ancient Times (Breasted), 141
Anderson, Lisa, 13
antisemitism, xxi, 300; Martin Luther King on, 260, 263. *See also* Holocaust inversion; Jews
apartheid, 133, 299
Arabic-English Lexicon (Lane), 3
Arab-Israeli conflict, xix, 120–22, 125, 198, 264–65; Islamist view of, 106, 108, 113–16; linkage and, 153–63; in Middle Eastern studies, 9–10, 16n1, 47. *See also specific wars*
Arab-Israeli war (1948), xix, 120, 128, 288, 299. *See also* Lydda
Arab-Israeli war (1967). *See* Six-Day War
Arab-Israeli war (1973), 128–29, 221, 272, 284
Arab nationalism, 135–36. *See also* pan-Arabism
Arab Predicament, The (Ajami), 287
Arabs: crisis of, xviii–xix, xxi–xxii, 147–51; democracy and, xviii; and Holocaust, 293; memory of Six-Day War, xvii–xviii, 119–23; minority rule among, xviii, 133–39; United States and, 153–63. *See also* Ajami; Arab-Israeli conflict; pan-Arabism; *specific countries and wars*
Arab Spring, xiv, 141, 147–51
Arab Strategic Forum, Dubai, 148
Arafat, Yasser, 105, 107, 271, 285, 288
al-Aref, Aref, 197
Arjomand, Said Amir, 73–74
Arlosorov, Chaim, 221
Armenians, 135, 141
Assad, Hafez, 120, 144, 159

307